Volume One
Foundations of Violence

The pursuit of death and the love of death has characterized Western culture from Homeric times through centuries of Christianity, taking particular deadly shapes in Western postmodernity. This necrophilia shows itself in destruction and violence, in a focus on other worlds and degradation of this one, and in hatred of the body, sense and sexuality. In her major new book project **Death and the Displacement of Beauty**, Grace M. Jantzen seeks to disrupt this wish for death, opening a new acceptance of beauty and desire that makes it possible to choose life.

Foundations of Violence enters the ancient world of Homer, Sophocles, Plato and Aristotle to explore the genealogy of violence in western thought through its emergence in Greece and Rome. It uncovers origins of ideas of death from the 'beautiful death' of Homeric heroes to the gendered misery of war, showing the tensions between those who tried to eliminate fear of death by denying its significance, and those like Plotinus who looked to another world, seeking life and beauty in another realm.

Grace M. Jantzen is Research Professor of Religion, Culture and Gender at the University of Manchester. Her books include *Becoming Divine* (1998), *Julian of Norwich* (2000) and *Power, Gender and Christian Mysticism* (1995).

Death and the Displacement of Beauty

Volume One
Foundations of Violence

Grace M. Jantzen

 Routledge
Taylor & Francis Group

LONDON AND NEW YORK

To Tina Macrae

I would rather see her lovely step
and the radiant sparkle of her face
than all the war-chariots . . . and soldiers . . .
(Sappho)

First published 2004
by Routledge
11 New Fetter Lane, London EC4P 4EE

Simultaneously published in the USA and Canada
by Taylor & Francis Inc
29 West 35th Street, New York, NY 10001

Routledge is an imprint of the Taylor & Francis Group

© 2004 Grace M. Jantzen

Typeset in Goudy by
Keystroke, Jacaranda Lodge, Wolverhampton
Printed and bound in Great Britain by
Antony Rowe Ltd, Chippenham, Wiltshire

British Library Cataloguing in Publication Data
A catalogue record for this book is available from the British Library

Library of Congress Cataloging in Publication Data
A catalog record for this book has been requested

ISBN 0–415–29032–5 (hbk)
ISBN 0–415–29033–3 (pbk)

Contents

PART III
Eternal Rome?   247

Preface

One of the many pleasures of the Lake District is the luminous green of the grass, setting off the beauty of the trees and fells, the becks and tarns, the harsh and gentle landscape. It has been my good fortune to live for the past six years in an ancient cottage in South Lakeland, to wake up daily to the ever-changing beauty of sea and sky, tree and hill, and to walk the fells and valleys letting their beauty soak into my soul. In these years, too, it has been my great privilege to learn to play the cello, and thus to be opened to still another kind of beauty with its multiple demands and rewards.

During this time, the world has spiralled into increasing violence. While I have been practicing Bach or Dvořák, the music has been shattered by training flights of jet aircraft screaming overhead. While I have been sitting on a rocky outcrop or walking among bluebells, children in Afghanistan and in Iraq have been killed and maimed, their water supplies polluted and even the sands of their deserts contaminated. While I have had the peace to read and contemplate, refugee camps in Palestine have burst open with young people whose education and life prospects are disrupted until their only way forward is a trajectory of desperation. In a multitude of ways the western world projects its violence outwards. The world is an increasingly dangerous place. Violence is ugly.

The dissonance between beauty and violence has prompted this project. In my previous work, I began to explore the concepts of necrophilia and natality, the love of death and the love of new life. Here, I wish to take these concepts further, to look at the roots of the preoccupation with death and violence in the western world, and to show how beauty can be a creative response to destructiveness. I offer here the first volume of a multi-volume project, *Death and the Displacement of Beauty*. The fundamental thesis of the project is that the choice of death, the love of death and of that which makes for death, has been characteristic of the west from Homeric and Platonic writings, through centuries of christendom, and takes particularly deadly shapes in western postmodernity. This preoccupation with death shows itself in destruction and violence, in a focus on other worlds and in the degradation and refusal of beauty in this one, in fear and hatred of bodiliness, sensory experience, and sexuality. It is a gendered necrophilia, which calls upon the 'Name of the Father' (whether in theological or psychoanalytical terms) to assert its dominance. It is deeply interwoven with the discourse of 'race' and postcolonialism. I shall show how violence and the love of death has been sedimented in layer upon layer in western history, so that we now live in a material and discursive situation in which our habitus is deadly.

Although diagnosis and analysis is crucial, however, it is not enough. What I wish to show, also, is how the attraction of beauty can inspire resistance and creative response, and can draw forward desire that is premised not upon lack or death but upon potential for new beginning. Preoccupation with death requires a refusal of beauty, or its displacement into some less threatening sphere. Conversely, response to beauty reconfigures consciousness towards creativity and new life. Beauty, creativity, seeks to bring newness into the world, a newness that is at odds with violence. All of these terms – death, beauty, violence, creativity – have long and complicated histories and cannot be used as though they have unambiguous meaning. What I propose to do, therefore, is to consider how their understanding and practice has shaped western culture, and thereby help to effect a shift in the consciousness and praxis of western post/modernity, disrupting the symbolic of violence and beginning to open out a new imaginary of beauty which makes it possible to choose life.

In order to develop this theme, my project runs across some academic currents and conventions. I am telling a long story, a story that will take several books to complete, at a time when grand narratives are suspect; even then I am leaving out many things which could well have been included. I am crossing all sorts of disciplinary boundaries, transgressing in fields outside of my expertise, and inviting readers to go with me in that transgression. Nobody can be expert in all fields, and inevitably different readers will find different parts to their taste. Inevitably, too, I will make mistakes; I hope that readers will point them out for correction in subsequent editions. The important thing, though, is that the issues are raised in such a way that they become part of collective discussion; that we do not turn our eyes away from either beauty or violence; that we begin to hear what each says to the other; that there may be healing and hope.

I have worked mostly from primary classical sources; but in order to be accessible to as wide a readership as possible, I have chosen wherever possible to cite easily available translations, often Penguin, in the hope that many readers will refer back to them. They are not always the most scholarly translations; anyone wishing to explore further should turn to the Loeb Classical Library, which offers the text in Greek or Latin with a careful English translation on the facing page. The exception is Plotinus, where I have used Loeb throughout, since the Penguin translation is inaccurate to the point of distortion. I have indicated in a footnote at the beginning of appropriate chapters the method of reference for the major figures in that chapter: for Plato and Aristotle this is by standard book and line numbers; in most other cases it is to page (not line) numbers in Penguin editions. In citations, I have silently changed punctuation and spelling for consistency; but unless otherwise indicated, all italics are in the original.

Acknowledgements

My debts grow daily; I have more people to thank than I can possibly remember. My first thanks go to Roger Thorp, formerly commissioning editor at Routledge, for his enthusiasm and encouragement of the project at an early stage, and for seeing it through to contract before he left Routledge. He was ably followed by Clare Johnson, who has been helpful throughout the process. It is a fortunate author indeed who has such editorial back-up.

I owe a great debt to the University of Manchester: I am very mindful of the huge privilege and responsibility which a permanent research appointment confers. I am especially grateful to my colleagues in the Department of Religions and Theology and the Centre for Religion, Culture and Gender for many discussions, some of which have taken place within the weekly Departmental Research Seminar: thank you to all staff and postgraduates who have participated. For help with specific points, suggestions of books, and discussion of the project in whole and in part, I wish to thank George Brooke, Philip Alexander, Bernard Jackson, Adrian Curtis, Todd Klutz, Jeremy Gregory, Elaine Graham and especially Graham Ward, among staff; and my current and former postgraduate students, especially Barbara Underwood, Paulo Goncalves, Jeremy Carrette, Steve Nolan, Helen Poade, Karyn Erlenbusch and Nanci Hogan, each of whom has influenced this project more than they might realize. I also wish to thank the librarian and staff of the John Rylands Library, for whom no detail was too small, and who worked with unfailing efficiency to obtain any materials I requested.

Friends and colleagues from elsewhere have also had a great part in the development of the project as a whole and this volume in particular: thanks in particular to Phyllis Mack, Morny Joy, Simeon Underwood, Chris Gibbs, Yvonne Sherwood, Tina Beattie, Pamela Anderson and Beverley Clack. Anna Gibbs helped with some of the typing at an early stage. Sue Rhodes offered her eyes and ears on more than one occasion when they were most helpful. The late Doreen Padfield is remembered daily with gratitude and grief. My nephew, Kevin Block, has been the best of readers: perceptive, encouraging, and challenging. I wish to thank also the Religious Society of Friends (Quakers), especially those of the Kendal Meeting, for their quiet and down to earth peace testimony, looking always for creative alternatives to violence. Jutta purred companionably through many hours of reading and writing.

The members of the Westmorland Orchestra and the Ambleside Cello Club might be surprised to know how much they have contributed to my thoughts about beauty as we make music together: I would like to thank all of them, and in particular Mabel Leech, Olive Dewhurst-Maddox, Margaret Lees, Joan Pollock, Paul Patchett, Rosemary Handley, Mark Carson, Elizabeth Oxborrow and Ann Armer. Above all others I thank Tina Macrae, brilliant cellist and teacher *extraordinnaire*: I have learned more about beauty from her than from many books. Besides all this, Tina has also given much practical help, including a great deal of typing, checking and domestic backup; and has always been ready with crucial moral support and encouragement. I dedicate this book to her, with great respect.

I wish to acknowledge permission to quote extracts from copyright material as follows: Reproduced by permission of Penguin Books Ltd. (UK): from *Electra and Other Plays* by Sophocles, translated by E.F. Watling (Penguin Books, 1953), Copyright (c) E.F. Watling, 1953: pp. 76, 63, 93, 104, 86, 116, 179, 178, 119, 161; from *Medea and Other Plays* by Euripides, translated by Philip Vellacott (Penguin Books, 1963), Copyright (c) Philip Vellacott, 1963: pp. 109, 125, 142, 130, 146; from *The Bacchae and Other Plays* by Euripides, translated by Philip Vellacott (Penguin Books, 1954, 1973), Copyright (c) Philip Vellacott, 1954, 1973: pp. 99, 106, 110, 125, 92, 111, 107, 122, 171; from *On the Nature of the Universe* by Lucretius, translated by R.E. Latham (Penguin Books, 1951). Revised with introduction by John Goodwin, Translation (c) R.E. Latham, 1951, Revisions, introduction and notes (c) John Goodwin, 1994: pp. 91, 94, 79, 77, 109, 113, 121, 124, 97, 122, 98, 29; from *Prometheus Bound and Other Plays* by Aeschylus, translated by Philip Vellacott (Penguin Books, 1961). Copyright (c) Philip Vellacott, 1961: pp. 124, 125, 131, 147, 145, 98, 42; from *Alcestis/Hippolytus/ Iphigenia in Tauris* by Euripides, translated by Philip Vellacott (Penguin Books, 1953), Copyright (c) Philip Vellacott, 1953: p. 127; from *Orestes and Other Plays* by Euripides, translated by Philip Vellacott (Penguin Books, 1972), Copyright (c) Philip Vellacott, 1972: pp. 178, 239, 248, 251, 253, 254, 255, 284, 415, 148, 120, 121, 123, 381, 419.

Used by permission of Penguin Books (UK) Ltd. and Viking Penguin, a division of Penguin Group (USA) Inc. from *The Oresteia* by Aeschylus, translated by Robert Fagles (Penguin Ancient Classics, 1977), Copyright (c) Robert Fagles, 1977. p. 131, 133, 164, 192, 222, 226, 233, 259, 260, 261, 264, 269, 164.

Used by permission of Viking Penguin, a division of Penguin Group (USA) Inc. from *The Iliad* by Homer, translated by Robert Fagles, Copyright (c) Robert Fagles: pp. 77, 83, 87, 89, 265, 210, 589, 604, 609, 547, 552, 553; from *The Odyssey* by Homer, translated by Robert Fagles, Copyright (c) Robert Fagles: pp. 169, 77, 85, 213, 156, 474, 265, 256, 272, 165, 155, 237, 240, 273, 274, 122, 460, 125, 159, 96, 463.

Beauty, gender and death

Chapter 1

Redeeming the present
The therapy of philosophy

At the height of the bombardment of Sarajevo, so the story goes,[1] a string quartet visited that city. One morning, as bombs were falling, the cellist took his instrument out into a square and began to play. Soldiers, hearing him, rushed to order him to take shelter. 'You are mad,' they said; 'get inside. Look! Can't you see what's happening?' 'Yes,' he said. 'Look. Can't *you* see what's happening? And you say that *I* am mad?'

Who is mad and who is sane in a world in which beauty confronts death, and violence silences creativity? How can we learn to name what is happening, and find resources for transformation? Where are the springs of hope, that could bring newness and flourishing into a death-dealing world? Not all sources of hope are intellectual, of course; but my concern here is with what intellectuals can offer. It is my belief that what the world sorely needs from intellectuals is an analysis of how the thought patterns of the west[2] have shaped and mis-shaped the world, and how they might be changed to enable human flourishing. There is a widespread 'demand for a transformative practice of philosophy . . . that would be capable of addressing, criticizing, and ultimately redeeming the present' (Critchley 1998: 10). How can newness enter the world? Where may we look to find the resources for redeeming the present?

There can be little doubt that the world is in sore need of redemption. Whatever their many differences, contemporary thinkers from many disciplines tend to be sharply critical of the trajectories that have shaped the west from classical antiquity and christendom to its turn to 'modernity' from about the seventeenth century onwards. My project as a whole will require detailed investigation of those trajectories and how they have formed the contours of the present: I begin in this volume with its foundations in Greece and Rome, which formed the basis of western education for millennia and without which modernity cannot be understood. But from the outset, the general features of modernity are easily rehearsed. It is founded on the rise of science and the exaltation of empiricism as the foundation of knowledge; the tentacles of this science in militarism and technology; capitalism, commodification and utilitarianism; colonialism, slavery, the free market economy, the hegemony of the west and the exploitation of the rest; the reconfiguration of what counts as knowledge through digital technology;

the destabilization of traditional social structures and the rise of individualism within increasingly faceless urban conurbations; and, more recently, the rhetoric of 'terrorism' as a justification for military aggression and economic exploitation.

Of course much nuancing is necessary; of course there are welcome aspects to many features of modernity, especially in the privileged west. But one would need to be singularly unmindful of the effects of western modernity on the rest of the world's peoples, on the earth itself, and on the narrowing of the human spirit in the west to think that the primary response to modernity should be celebration. Moreover one would need to be singularly optimistic to suppose that these effects will somehow spontaneously right themselves without effort and without cost in a newly arrived era of postmodernity: it would be like hoping that a deep-seated neurosis would melt away of itself and cause no further harm.

'The point, however, is to change it': to change the world of post/modernity, and to change the thought patterns which have rigidified into its death-dealing discursive and material structures. The world, to be sure, is changing, and with great rapidity. As the twenty-first century proceeds, the pace of violence increases. The ground shifts under our feet as smart military hardware and digital technologies enable 'precision violence'; and genetically modified species raise new questions of what constitutes the human. But these changes, arguably, are continuations of trajectories that already cut deep ruts through modernity. They can be seen as manifestations of a compulsion to repeat, in ever new and magnified ways, the patterns practiced in western thought since its infancy. As in any such compulsion, the repetitions are the unproductive repetition of the same, continually escalating and gaining increasing momentum.

What is necessary is to find some way of thinking – and living – otherwise, some path to the healing of the western psyche so that instead of its death-dealing structures the present may be redeemed and the earth and its peoples may flourish. If I am right in characterizing the west as in the grip of a cultural neurosis of which its death-dealing structures are symptoms, as I shall argue later, then the task of the intellectual can be likened to that of a therapist who seeks by patient listening to bring the repressed dimensions of history to the fore and to release the springs of wellbeing.

I am not suggesting that the psychoanalytic model of neurosis and therapy is in every respect applicable to the social order, and certainly not that it is the only model. The analogy must be modified, for example, by attention to ideologies and their function; and also by the dynamics of resistance within any power structure. Nevertheless, although the analogy must be qualified and supplemented, these volumes will demonstrate that it is a useful one for probing the psychic structures of the west, its cultural symbolic. I shall explore how that symbolic has come to be formed by a triangulation of death, gender, and religion, and is threatened by beauty and birth, even though (or in part because) it is from these that a redemption of the present could come. I suggest in particular that using the therapeutic analogy brings to mind a series of related questions, questions that will be heightened as we develop a critical genealogy. What is it exactly that is being repressed in the violent, death-obsessed symbolic of the west? What deep fears underlie the repression? How are those fears related to longings and desires? What are these desires, and how could they be released for human flourishing? How can attention to beauty and natality release the springs of creativity by which newness can enter the world?

Necrophilia, necrophobia and natality

A central thesis of these volumes is that a constitutive feature of the western symbolic is a preoccupation with death and, with it, a longing for other worlds: I shall discuss some of the current symptoms of this preoccupation in chapter 2. My argument is that it is this obsession with death, largely suppressed, which is acted out in the violent and death-dealing structures of modernity, structures of violence which have been well-learned from our classical past. From militarization, death camps and genocide to exploitation, commodification and the accumulation of wealth, from the construction of pleasure and desire to the development of terminator genes, from the violence on the streets to the heaven-obsessed hymnody of evangelical churches, preoccupation with death and the means of death and the combat with death is ubiquitous. It is a necrophilia so deeply a part of the western symbolic that it emerges at every turn: as I shall show more fully in chapter 2, our language is full of metaphors of war, weaponry, violence and death.

'Necrophilia' means, literally, love of death or of dead bodies. In the literature of psychoanalysis and criminology it refers to a pathological erotic attraction to corpses or things associated with dead bodies, or to a desire to touch or handle or dismember them. It has been broadened by writers such as Erich Fromm to refer to a major personality disorder characterized by malignant aggression: Fromm uses these categories in an extensive analysis of Hitler's character (1977: chs 12 and 13). In what follows, I am using the term as rooted in this psychoanalytical literature, but widening it still further, to signify a cultural fascination and obsession with death and violence, a preoccupation with death which is both dreaded and desired. It is this obsession with death which, I shall show, characterizes the habitus of western modernity, with devastating consequences for humankind and the earth.

But if death is dreaded, as it surely is, would it not be more accurate to think in terms of necrophobia rather than necrophilia? As we shall see in a moment, great efforts are often made to evade the realities of death: hospital personnel, undertakers and funeral directors, clergy, and journalists collude with the public to keep death out of sight or at least disguise its character. Such behaviour bespeaks fear, surely, rather than desire. And yet once again it is important to look deeper. It is a commonplace of psychoanalytic theory that deep dread and denial such as we often find manifested in relation to death is closely related to unacknowledged desire: the anxiety indicates preoccupation. Although the preoccupation with death presents itself as a dread or fear, literally a phobia, Freud has shown how such phobias, as obsessions, are simultaneously a love or desire for the very thing so dreaded. In fact, Freud believed that *Thanatos*, a death drive, was as strong as *Eros*, and closely linked with it. Whereas he held that it was a universal of human nature, I shall show that it is a gendered construction of western modernity, with precursors in christendom and classical antiquity. If this is correct, then necrophilia, in the widened sense that I am using it, is the underside of necrophobia. The dread and the desire are two sides of the same obsession.

It is this obsession, the evidence for which will unfold throughout this project, and above all its resolution that is my concern. Sometimes, when dread is to the fore, it will seem more accurate to use the terminology of necrophobia; at other times when, as in Plato or some medieval Christian writings on mortification, death is presented as a focus of longing, necrophilia will be more appropriate. Both terms are used as short-hand for the ways in which obsession with death has manifested itself in the west. It is this obsession and its resolution that is of literally life and death importance, not the terms themselves. Only by resolving the obsession with death can there be hope for life.

That hope for life I am labelling 'natality'. I shall explore its meaning more fully in chapter 4; but as a beginning of the discussion, it is useful simply to place natality – the fact that we were born, that we are all 'natals' – against the fact that we shall all die, that we are all 'mortals'. I suggest that in the west's obsession with death and mortality, our natality has been largely ignored. Yet it is in birth, in natality, that newness enters into the world; and it is in the fact of new life that every other form of freedom and creativity is grounded, a creativity that is contrary to violence and destruction. If natality is ignored in an obsession with death and violence, it is small wonder that the world hovers on the brink of destruction. My intention is not to set up binaries: mortality/natality; destruction/creativity. Instead, I shall be suggesting that the fundamental imbalance of attention and emphasis is part of the violent pattern of the west, and that this imbalance is in urgent need of attention if we are to redeem the present.

The habitus

A useful hermeneutical tool for understanding how psychic structures manifest themselves in a 'logic of practice' has been developed by Pierre Bourdieu (1990; 1998) with his concept of 'habitus'. The habitus is the 'common sense world' as it appears to, and is inhabited by, its participants. As human beings learn the language of their society and are socialized into it, they acquire a sense of how to behave in all sorts of practical situations: what things are good to eat, and when, and how (muesli for breakfast and roast chicken for dinner: most English folk would have considerable difficulty reversing the order). We learn how to behave to different sorts of people; what to wear in different contexts. A whole range of attitudes, tastes, and values acquired through upbringing and training develop within us a sense of 'how things are done' in the multiple situations, trivial and complex, which make up our daily life. It is this complex of tastes, preferences, learned behaviour patterns, and so on that make up the habitus, which then serves as the disposition to behave in ways congruent with it when confronted with practical choices.

> 'Subjects' are active and knowing agents endowed with a *practical sense* . . . which orient the perception of the situation and the appropriate response. The habitus is this kind of practical sense for what is to be done in a given situation – what is called in sport a 'feel' for the game, that is, the art of *anticipating* the future of the game, which is inscribed in the present state of play.
>
> (Bourdieu 1998: 25)

In most situations in daily life we spontaneously know what to do; we have a sense of what is needed or appropriate and how to do it. This spontaneous 'common sense' is not arbitrary; it derives from our whole socialization and the internalization of the objective structures of language and social rules and patterns, from what is often referred to as the 'symbolic', the psychic structures developed in individuals within their societies. But while 'common sense' is not arbitrary, neither is it mechanical. The habitus, rather, is the disposition from and by which choices are made, 'a spontaneity without consciousness or will' which generates 'reasonable' or 'common sense' response and behaviour (Bourdieu 1990: 55–6).

The symbolic involves the system of language and, more generally, the patterns of thought, including the system of values of a society. The habitus incorporates these structures, internalizes them so that they become the disposition or, as we might say, the personality structure, from which actions and attitudes are generated in a unified rather than a chaotic manner. It is this that makes social life possible: within a fairly limited range of possibilities, we know what sort of behaviour is expected in various social roles and contexts even as we put our own distinctive personal style on the ways in which we fill these roles. The habitus thus integrates the social and the individual, internalizing the objective structures of the symbolic and incorporating them in dispositions for action.

> Habitus are generative principles of distinct and distinctive practices. . . . But habitus are also classificatory schemes, principles of classification, principles of vision and division, different tastes. They make distinctions between what is good and what is bad, between what is right and what is wrong, between what is distinguished and what is vulgar, and so forth. . . . [T]hese principles . . . become symbolic differences and constitute a veritable *language*.
>
> (Bourdieu 1998: 8)

One of the useful aspects of the notion of habitus is the way in which it enables us to make sense of the fact that people in a single society can behave in quite different ways, depending on their position within that society. If 'common sense' were a matter of a shared symbolic only in the formal sense of a shared language and society, then it would be difficult to understand how there could be such variations of what would be taken as common sense within a society. However, if common sense is a question of habitus, then differences *within* a society can come into play. Different members and groups of society will be socialized differently, in such a way that the dispositions to behave which seem natural and obvious to one may not appear so to another. Thus in any society there is on the one hand a 'common code', a general concordance of habitus; yet there is also variation according to class and gender conditioning; and within this there is further variation of personal style. But these variations are not random or arbitrary; rather, they relate back to the common style not only in their conformities but even in their differences (Bourdieu 1990: 59–60).

Habitus, moreover, is not inborn, but is socially constructed. It is a product of history: the individual's personal history, but also the history of her class, and more widely, of the society which is composed of these classes. Because habitus is the formation of disposition of action and attitude, it will tend to remain stable. It will seem like 'common sense' to do things as they have always been done. Continuing along the same line will seem natural; challenging it will require effort. Habitus is thus self-perpetuating. People are resistant to the disruption of their settled habitus, and find ways of not getting into situations where it might be challenged. In this way individual and class habitus can flow along without disruption and people can feel secure and unthreatened, knowing what to expect day by day, and knowing how to cope with their life-world. It also means, however, that 'common sense' and 'ordinary situations' can remain unchallenged. Thus if, as I shall argue, necrophilia has come to be our habitus in the western world, it has grown as familiar and even comfortable as an old slipper, and we have difficulty noticing it or recognizing that there could be any problem with it.

Yet this is to oversimplify. It is true that each class or sub-culture has to a certain extent its distinctive habitus and avoids situations which would challenge it while providing itself with plenty of occasions that reinforce it. However, the classes and groups in society vary in power, including the power which they can exert over one another. Bourdieu sees this variation as difference of symbolic capital, with different classes possessing unequal shares. Those who have more symbolic capital can exert pressure or domination ('symbolic violence') on those who have less. Moreover, those who are in the more powerful position do not have to take account of the perspective or habitus of those whom they are dominating. In terms of social structure, the dominated internalize and cooperate with the perspective of the dominant, even though this may be to their own hurt.

> Symbolic violence rests on the adjustment between the structures constitutive of the habitus of the dominated and the structure of the relation of domination to which they apply: the dominated perceive the dominant through the categories that the relation of domination has produced and which are thus identical to the interests of the dominant.
>
> (Bourdieu 1998: 121)

Thus domination is not simple coercion; it usually proceeds with the cooperation of the dominated. They have to such an extent internalized the attitudes of class, race, or gender difference that cooperation may seem the only possible, natural, or morally right thing to do.

We will revisit issues of power frequently in these volumes, taking into account Foucault's discussion of resistance and counter-power. For present purposes, what I wish to emphasize is the naturalization which seems to attend on habitus, since it is this naturalization which has a direct bearing on my account of the preoccupations of western modernity. Because the habitus is the disposition formed by the internalization of past experience and training, the actions and attitudes that spring from this disposition feel entirely natural. They are spontaneous responses, not perceived as unusual or against the grain. Thus for example if a husband and wife live in a society where women are deemed to be inferior to men and exist to serve them, then it may feel natural to both of them for the wife to do her husband's bidding, and unnatural for her to object.

> The *habitus* – embodied history, internalized as a second nature and so forgotten as history – is the active presence of the whole past of which it is the product. As such, it . . . produces history on the basis of history.
>
> (Bourdieu 1990: 56)

and the social norms that are thus reproduced and perpetuated 'tend to appear as necessary, even natural' (53). 'Natural', here, should be taken in its strong sense, that is, part of the laws of nature. There are of course a multitude of illustrations of this in the west: women have been seen as 'naturally' the ones who should look after the young, the sick, and the old; boys are 'naturally' better at maths and woodwork while girls take 'naturally' to sewing and cooking; homosexual behaviour is 'unnatural' or 'contrary to nature'; Blacks are 'naturally' better at sports and dance than are white people but also have an unfortunate 'natural' propensity to crime, and so on and on. Socially constructed stereotypes are part of the habitus, and as such do not seem like social constructions but rather as built into the order of nature. And since, as I have already said, people avoid situations in which the habitus would be challenged, and repress or deny evidence that would call it into question, this 'naturalization' is self-perpetuating and resistant to change. In this way socially constructed categories of dominance can ground oppression which seems natural to oppressor and oppressed alike.

Such a notion of 'natural' rests on a theory of meaning derived from Aristotle, which has been disrupted by Saussure's theory of language and his post-structuralist followers (Lévi-Strauss 1963; Saussure 1983; Harris 1988). It relies on a representational idea of language which has been largely discredited, complete with the notion that there are 'real', 'natural' things outside the sign system to which we can have direct access. 'Naturalization' can thus be recognized as a failure (or refusal) to understand the ways in which subjects are constructed through the discursive and material patterns of their lives; its prevalence bears out Bourdieu's account of the habitus as 'producing history on the basis of history' and seeing that production as natural.

It can further be observed that what is taken as natural does not need to be theorized for the participants. In fact, theory can get in the way. Someone who is constantly and self-consciously theorizing about what to say or do at a party will get on much less well than someone who can relax and behave 'naturally'. But of course it is obvious that this 'natural' behaviour is in fact a product of long socialization and training. Most English women would be at a loss to know what 'behaving naturally' would mean if they found themselves in a Native American sweat lodge or in the courtyard of a peasant farm on the Yellow River. Social skills, like skills of a game or artistic skills, are examples of learned practical behaviour, acquired sometimes through long training and effort; and are a product of having grown up in a particular society.

Now this means that it is possible for a society to be in the grip of a dominant symbolic system, and for its habitus to be shaped by the internalization of that symbolic, without paying attention to it as such or bringing it to scrutiny. If this is the case, then not only will individuals 'naturally' act in accordance with it; social policies and social structures also will reflect and reinforce it. Culture will be filled with symptoms of this symbolic; its master discourses will be framed by it; the everyday functioning of systems and individuals will be in accordance with it – and yet it may never be thought about, never brought to consciousness. Indeed there may be a strong resistance to doing so, since bringing it to consciousness would open it to scrutiny and possible challenge. History will be produced on the basis of history, patterns will repeat themselves, the symbolic structures of the habitus will be enacted ever and again.

I believe, and shall show in this volume and the ones that follow it, that such reenactment of the habitus is precisely a description of western post/modernity. The symbolic is saturated with an obsession with (gendered) violence and death, which seems natural, sometimes even profound. Even though it is often unconscious or unrecognized, the social order reveals symptoms of it at every turn, in language, sports, music, and every form of cultural production as well as in social policy formation. The habitus of western society is a disposition towards the enactment of death and its concomitants, especially anxiety and a drive to control, to exert mastery over anything perceived as threatening. Natality, creativity and beauty have been displaced, despised or ignored; at best seen as an unnecessary if pleasant extra to the real business of living. While there is an insatiable desire for novelty, there is little attention to the springs of creativity, the resources of newness that can redeem the present. The joyless habitus of western modernity is acting out a long history of gendered violence and death; and the cultural symbolic has been so shaped that it is hard even to imagine non-superficial alternatives, to think what an emphasis on natality might come to. The urgency of the study derives from the fact that a necrophilic habitus reproduces itself; left unchecked, it will continue to bring about violence, death and destruction, on a larger and larger scale. Unless some way can be found to change the symbolic and develop a habitus freed from the obsession with death and open to the springs of newness and beauty, necrophilia will become a self-fulfilling prophecy.

This project is a search for that way.

Chapter 2

Symptoms of a deathly symbolic

The hour of our death

One of the most obvious indications of the contemporary habitus of necrophilia/phobia is to consider what actually happens in our culture when somebody dies: how is death and its aftermath handled? There are wide variations, of course. But Philippe Ariès, in his now classic genealogy of death in the west, has shown the lengths that are taken to ensure that death in modernity is removed as far as possible from the realities of people's lives, so that death has been made increasingly invisible. Except for accidental or sudden deaths, it is normal for people to die in a hospital or perhaps a hospice rather than in their own homes. Death has become medicalized; and since the function of medicine is often characterized as keeping people alive and curing them of illness, death can be perceived as failure.

> Death has ceased to be accepted as a natural, necessary phenomenon. . . . When death arrives, it is regarded as an accident, a sign of helplessness or clumsiness that must be put out of mind. It must not interrupt the hospital routine, which is more delicate than that of any other professional milieu. It must therefore be discreet.
>
> (1987: 586)

It is now some time since Ariès conducted his investigations, and in many places, especially through the work of the hospice movement, there is greater openness about death and less denial of it as a natural termination of life rather than a failure. Nevertheless, there is also, often, heroic effort to prolong life, by increasingly sophisticated medical technology. One of the great fascinations of genetic engineering is its potential to increase longevity: the media is full of intense debates about how long it will become possible to live, what will be normal life-expectancy. The efforts to prolong life often arise, of course, out of a love for life; but the lengths to which medical intervention is sometimes taken, or the shrill tones of the debates about longevity raise the question whether the real issue is extending life or whether it is not rather postponing death (Overall 2003). Dread of death is not the same as love of life.

Moreover, although in some contexts (like hospices) there is more willingness to acknowledge the reality of death, it nevertheless remains true that death is usually treated as a private occasion. As far as possible anyone not intimately involved with the dying person is kept away. Children are wherever possible shielded from death lest they be distressed. Whereas in times past death was a public event, with family and friends present, and a person would normally die at home and the body be prepared at home for funeral and burial, death has now become much more private and far removed from the routines of life and the household. It is frequently the case that death is surrounded by silence and even hypocrisy. Many doctors still do not tell patients that they are dying, and patients, friends and relatives may find it hard to be honest with one another about what is happening: 'the dying person must pretend not to be dying, and loved ones must participate in the deception. The person is deprived of death, society of mourning' (Vincent 1991: 260). Sedatives keep pain, but also full consciousness, at bay. Indeed Ariès is surely accurate when he observes that in modern society the good death is just the opposite of what it was in the past. Whereas previously there was great store set by full awareness of impending death, complete with final confession, last rites, and death bed words to survivors, now a good death is thought of as a death that is hardly noticed: 'He died tonight in his sleep: he just didn't wake up' (Ariès 1987: 587).

After death, also, great care and expense are taken to disguise the realities as much as possible. The corpse is taken to a mortuary where undertakers embalm it in such a way as to make it look as much like a living, sleeping body as possible: only then are family and friends invited to come and 'view' the body. 'To create a pleasing and comforting setting for a farewell to the dead, in the modern American funeral "home," evisceration, embalming, and cosmetology are all raised to a high art to guarantee that the realities of death remain unseen, for the brief space of time needed, and that what is seen appears in a reassuring light' (Tatum 2003: 19). Cemeteries resemble huge, beautiful gardens filled with trees and flowers, with tombstones recording the names of those who are buried there. 'What lies beneath the durable marble headstone that loved ones like to visit and decorate with flowers? . . . a body subject to unpleasant changes that no one wants to think about. Attention has been shifted, in a kind of metonymy, from the contents to the vessel' – to the grave and the garden around it (Vincent 1991: 267). In England where cremation is commonplace it is possible to remove traces of death even more completely, retaining only photographs and memories of the person now dead. The fear and dread of death evidenced by modern tactics of evasion, and efforts to render death invisible, indicate anxieties about death far beyond what is necessary for respectful and sanitary disposal of corpses.

Watch your language

The very words we use betray our deathly preoccupations. If we look at actual speech patterns in current use, it is striking that everyday language is suffused with imagery of death, often violent death. We might be 'dead worried' at a bad turn of events, or 'dead chuffed' by some good news. We 'kill' things in our society which should not be there, or even things (like emails) that we have dealt with. Any newspaper will carry accounts of a 'battle' against some foe: a battle against poverty, against cuts in bus services, against erosion of the countryside. New educational techniques are 'weapons' against illiteracy; an 'arsenal' of new drugs is developed to 'fight' diseases. The causes are laudable, but the language is the language of violence. There is a 'fight' against cancer, or unemployment, or child abuse, or whatever is seen as the current 'enemy', not noticing that the metaphors of warfare and violence may be singularly inappropriate – as, for instance, in 'battle against child abuse'. The ways in which we routinely construct the world linguistically as if it were filled with enemies whom we seek to exterminate both reflects our deathly symbolic and also reinforces it. The formation and retention of a cultural habitus is related to its narratives and symbols, its myths, jokes, figures of speech and cultural icons, but also to its ordinary language by which daily existence is articulated. The tropes of death and warfare in our everyday vocabulary inscribe and reinscribe patterns of thought and behaviour which are normalized by the very fact that they come to be routine and conventional. Gradually they determine what is morally thinkable.

In more specialized contexts the vocabulary of death and violence is even more apparent. From computer games, to film and television or the lyrics of pop music, popular entertainment is saturated with images of violence and warfare, often interlinked with love and sex. In popular and 'high' culture, in musical compositions, novels, paintings, and sports writing, even children's television (like 'Tom and Jerry') there is a preoccupation with violence and death. It is impossible to make a thorough investigation of all of these manifestations here; but a glance through the daily papers with this issue in mind readily illustrates both the superficial and the underlying symptoms of necrophilia in post/modernity.

The language of death and warfare is just as prevalent in philosophical writing as it is in popular culture. In later volumes I shall discuss the ways in which necrophilia shapes philosophical thought as it shapes other master discourses of modernity; but we can see at a glance that in philosophical terms post/modernity is premised on the death of God ('and we have *killed* him'), which leads directly to ideas of the death of 'man', the death of the subject, the death of the author. . . . For all the controversy surrounding all these notions, it is striking that the suitability and function of death as the central metaphor is rarely challenged.

Perhaps that is because intellectual discussion and even philosophy itself has taken an adversarial stance as its normal procedure, at least since the early nineteenth century. German idealists used the terminology of thesis, antithesis and synthesis: any position generates its opposite, and out of the conflict a new position is established, and the process begins again. This concept of conflict as the way in which intellectual (or indeed historical) progress is achieved is especially associated with Hegel, even though he did not actually use the terms 'thesis', 'antithesis', 'synthesis'. In the *Phenomenology of Spirit* (1977), Hegel's construction of the moves from the material to the spiritual, from art and ethics and religion to the absolute knowledge he claims for the vantage point of philosophy, all turn on conflict: without conflict no advance would occur. The trope is made vivid in his famous image of the battle to the death between master and slave: it encapsulates his whole system. Yet for all that his system depends upon it and could not get started without it, Hegel never analyses conflict and violence as a trope. It is a classic case of a philosopher who extends rationality against mythology and metaphor, yet nevertheless uses a metaphor on which his system depends even while he denies or evades it (as Michelle Le Doeuff has pointed out in another context in relation to Kant (1989: 8)).

Few philosophers in the Anglo-American analytic tradition would subscribe to Hegelianism; yet the adversarial method is just as deeply inscribed in their procedure, and rarely challenged. As Janice Moulton has shown in her now classic essay, 'A Paradigm of Philosophy: The Adversary Method' (1983), intellectual aggression has taken a central role in analytic philosophy. It is taken for granted that philosophy is about making truth claims, and that these claims must be watertight. Accordingly,

> it is assumed that the only, or at any rate the best, way of evaluating work in philosophy is to subject it to the strongest or most extreme opposition. And it is assumed that the best way of presenting work in philosophy is to address it to an imagined opponent and muster all the evidence one can to support it.
>
> (1983: 153)

The language standardly used in philosophical writing bears out Moulton's claim, though she does not refer to it. Metaphors of violence abound. Positions are advanced, attacked, defended, embattled, or shot down in flames, as though philosophy consisted of intellectual warfare. And indeed the hostility and aggression of much philosophical engagement, often covered by an urbane veneer, is well encapsulated in these metaphors of violence. Analytic philosophy, instead of working cooperatively and creatively to open up new insights and risking the possibility of mistakes, is too often content with 'blowing holes' in 'opponents' arguments, or else in 'mounting a defence' of ever dwindling and more boring positions.

My central claim in all this is that the language of violence whether at academic or popular levels, is indicative of structures of a symbolic within which violence and death are unthinkingly chosen as apt metaphors for a vast range of causes and activities. Now, whatever the precise philosophy of metaphor or psychoanalytic account of verbal behaviour, it is clear that the choice of language, especially when it seems natural and automatic, both reflects and reinforces entrenched collective patterns of thought. The ease with which metaphors of violence are used, the way in which both speaker and hearer take such metaphors for granted and seldom challenge them, indicates, when we stop to notice it, a shocking obsession with death. If the language we use indicates what we are and shapes what we become, then the ubiquitous language of violence is a worrying symptom of the necrophilia of modernity.

Gender and the maternal body

Another significant aspect of the western habitus symptomatic of the necrophilic symbolic is the connection of death with gender. It will become apparent as we proceed that whereas men have been overwhelmingly linked with violence and aggression in western culture, women have been linked with death. The symbolic connects death, sex and the female, while systematically silencing women and ignoring or suppressing the significance of natality. The dimensions of these linkages will be demonstrated throughout these volumes; it will help to maintain clarity if I sketch the direction of argument here with respect to the importance of gender in the western habitus.

To begin with the obvious, women have been underrepresented in situations of power and esteem in western history, while men have been overwhelmingly overrepresented not only in situations of power but also in aggression and violence. Aggressive sports like football are heavily male dominated. So also is the army. As for violent crime, this is almost entirely male: where women are involved they are usually involved as accomplices of men, seldom on their own. Women comprise less than 10 per cent of the prison population of any western country.

Everyone knows these things. And yet, though they must be significant for any attempt to understand violence and work toward a more peaceful world, these facts are often suppressed. Thus for example Jonathan Glover, in his book *Humanity: A Moral History of the Twentieth Century* (2001) shows how warfare and aggression took increasingly ugly forms in the twentieth century, and shows also the increasingly banal and unworthy collusion by many an intellectual. Yet although much of what he says has obvious gender markings, he never discusses the bearing of gender on the aggression he seeks to analyse, even when, as in his presentation of the attraction to men of close combat and the exhilaration of danger (ch. 8), his account cries out for gender analysis. Glover writes as though men are normative for what counts as human, and so he does not notice the fact that the other half of the human race was *not* taking part in the aggression. I am not suggesting that all women are peace loving: there are more forms of hostility than overt violence, and western women are very good at some of them. But we can hardly hope to understand, let alone transform, our death-dealing world unless we acknowledge that aggression and gender are interlinked.

This generates a further consideration. As will become clearer in the chapters that follow, the preoccupation with death that I have been discussing earlier in this chapter is largely a male preoccupation. Women have been concerned about death too, of course; but as we shall see, it was predominantly men who structured the symbolic with its obsessive concern with death and other worlds. I have begun in these introductory remarks to develop an analogy between intellectual effort and therapy. If we now carry the therapy analogy forward, one question it brings to mind is a question of displacement. A phobia about one thing (e.g. spiders, dirt) is often actually a deeply unresolved complex about something else, to which the ostensible object of fear is related. Indeed the actual source of fear is repressed, silenced, precisely by this displacement, whereby the substitute becomes the focus of attention and anxiety. Thus in Freud's account of Little Hans, the boy's phobia about horses was a disguised complex about his father and masculine sexuality. Once he was able to acknowledge the real source of his fear and deal with it, his phobia about horses resolved itself.

What suggests itself, then, if we follow the therapy analogy, is that the obsession with death characteristic of the western symbolic may be a displacement of something to which it is related but which renders it invisible, silenced within the symbolic structure. From what I have already said about gender and the silencing of the maternal in the masculinist obsession with death and violence, an obvious candidate for the real locus of the problem is the maternal body, and female sexuality more generally. Could this be the repressed centre of the fear of death, the site which must be silenced and controlled at all costs? Michelle Walker (1998), in her study of silence, has shown how the maternal body and especially its reproductive fecundity has been cast as the enemy of the masculine logos in western philosophical discourse, its creative capacities both feared and appropriated by writers from Plato to Deleuze. If we add to her analysis the ubiquity of preoccupation with death, then the question presents itself: are the death-dealing structures of the western symbolic, discernible from Homer to the master discourses of post/modernity, attempts to silence and control the mother, and all the other (m)others who might bring the central fear to mind: the earth, its beauty, its peoples, its unpredictable life? Is the suppression of natality part of a deep fear of gender? The suggestion requires careful working out; but already it is clear that if we are working toward a redemptive imaginary, gender will necessarily be a major consideration.

The idea that the preoccupation with death is at least to some extent displaced anxiety about the maternal body is reinforced by the regularity with which women and death are linked in discourses from philosophy to music, which just as regularly ignore birth. At the level of physical reality, all women die just as all men do. But the western tradition has regularly portrayed men as concerned with their own mortality, not with women's death; indeed women have frequently been represented as the *cause* of (men's) mortality. Thus as we shall see, Odysseus gains everlasting fame by conquering the (female) sea and its seductive creatures: his mastery of death is his mastery of the females who would cause it, in all its various guises. Plato attempts to 'give birth like a man', appropriating natality to men and displacing beauty to an eternal realm. Roman men, in their efforts towards manliness, take violence as one of its key features, linking the penis and the sword; and dread the idea of being womanly. In later volumes I shall explore how in the Christian tradition, too, the stress on death (which was portrayed as punishment for sin) was closely linked with the female. It was Eve, the first woman, who had been tempted to sin; Eve who had brought death to humanity. Though this is not the only way in which the Genesis story could be read, centuries of chris-tendom have linked women and death in a multitude of ways. Not only is death as punishment for sin taken to be ultimately the fault of women; woman is also portrayed as the source of temptation for men, especially, of course, sexual temptation.

Many of the cultural masterpieces of modernity, whatever their other themes and no matter how different one from another, make regular use of the linkage of women, love and death. Shakespeare's plays, from *Romeo and Juliet* to *Othello* and *Hamlet*, portray women who die (or are murdered) for love. These plays become models not only for drama but also for opera, in which the passion of love and the linkage of women and death are seldom far apart. In Mozart's *Don Giovanni* the promiscuous hero (for that is how he is presented) accepts death rather than renounce his lecherous ways: women are simply too seductive. Beethoven's *Fidelio* rings the changes on the ever popular tale of the woman who sacrifices herself to rescue her husband. Classical music of all sorts regularly plays on the theme of women and death, either women as the cause of death of their lover, as in Schubert's famous song cycle *Winterreise* or as women dying or being murdered by their lover, as in Berlioz' *Symphonie fantastique*.

The symbolic connection of women with death will need to be substan-tiated in detail; but if for the moment we assume that it is along the right lines, then this raises another consideration. Is it not the case that a phobia, if it is expressive of an unresolved complex, indicates not only deep fear and dread but also unacknowledgeable longing and desire? If that is so, or even partly so, what desire lies deep within the symbolic of necrophilia/phobia? Freud as we shall see took the death drive at face value: he postulated *Thanatos* straightforwardly as a desire for stasis. But underlying that, as Freud also sometimes recognized, is there not a repression of longing for lost unity – lost unity precisely with the maternal? The identification of the womb and the tomb is a trope in western representation from Plato's myth of the cave to the medieval understanding of a monastery or an anchorhold: from Francis Bacon's forcible 'wooing' of nature and the 'masculine birth of time' to William Blake's 'Daughters of Albion', and the lyrics of con-temporary pop music. Moreover it is a commonplace of psychoanalytic theory that the infant longs for unification with its mother, and enters the (masculinist) social and linguistic symbolic only by repressing that unassuageable loss. Now if, as I would argue, that symbolic is necrophilic, then the complex which underlies it is at least in part an unacknowledged longing for the maternal, a longing repressed by death-dealing strategies of control.

In many respects these ideas are not new: a considerable body of feminist writings has concerned itself with repressed longing for the maternal and the silencing of women as a tactic of repression (cf Irigaray 1985; Walker 1998). I suggest, however, that the silencing of the maternal body includes other silences that have been less noted: in particular the silencing of birth and the displacement of beauty. The underlying aim of my project is, as I have said, to help effect a change in the western imaginary by showing how natality and beauty have been repressed and displaced, and thus restoring them to focus as a resource for newness and redemption.

Transformative practice: the therapy of philosophy

Now, if I am correct in characterizing the deathly symbolic of post/modernity as rooted in and reinforcing necrophilia/phobia, if I am correct, that is, in treating it as an obsession or psychic disorder of the social realm, then it will not be changed by arguing against it. Appeals to rationality will not bring about the desired change, any more than it would help to tell a person in the grip of a neurosis what it is that they are repressing. Such strategies only bring out stronger resistance, ever more clever rationalizations, deeper anger and control. The task of the intellectual in the transformation of the present cannot therefore be simply didactic or exhortatory. Neither is the intellect alone sufficient to bring about human flourishing: this requires substantial change in material as well as discursive conditions, changes in behaviour as well as in thought.

However, this is not to say that careful analysis, genealogies, archaeologies, and deconstructions are useless: it does mean that it is necessary to think through what their use is and what it is not. As I have said, it is not likely to be effective in the case of a society deeply invested in the symbolic of modernity and unwilling to recognize at a deep level the problems which that habitus generates. However, these problems are coming more and more to the fore. To take only three examples, recent years have witnessed barbarically violent international and internecine conflicts, 'ethnic cleansings', and some of the preliminary consequences of global warming; and it is becoming apparent to many that we cannot go on with our death-dealing habitus and expect humanity to survive. There are therefore many who are actively seeking ways of thinking otherwise.

Now, it is usually a necessary step in any effective *individual* therapy that the client should come to explicit consciousness of the ideas that have been shaping problematic responses and behaviours, and see where those ideas came from. The same, I suggest, is true at a *cultural* level. Although rational argument on its own is unlikely to change action, it is a crucial part of understanding the provenances of the symbolic (and its changes and variants) and of recognizing the responses it generates. This then enables one to consider the question of whether we really want to continue to have our actions and thoughts controlled by these unconscious motivations or how we might find release from them.

Only patient investigation and analysis can develop adequate responses to the violent habitus. It is tempting for those who seek solutions to the ills of post/modernity to move quickly to strategies, policies or plans of action, recognizing the urgency of the need to put things right. It is no part of my project to minimize the urgency, let alone to dismiss all proposed strategies. However, what we can learn from the therapeutic model is that to the extent that the problems of post/modernity are consequences of acting upon a destructive cultural symbolic, strategies and policies to change behaviour are unlikely to be effective unless the underlying patterns of thought are changed. Moreover for this to happen it is necessary to bring those patterns, the cultural symbolic, to consciousness, and this, in therapy, means probing its sources and history. Once the contours of the symbolic become clearer it becomes easier to see what is involved in its transformation and why it is necessary to go through the massive process of tracing its past in order to redeem the present. This is therefore the critical aspect of these volumes: an effort to bring to consciousness the layers of violence in our habitus, to see where they came from, and not to let them remain unchallenged.

I shall return to that in a moment; but first I wish to point to another important facet of the therapeutic model. It is, ultimately, highly optimistic. Resources for change come not from outside the client but from within. As it becomes clear what has been repressed and why, and how the patterns of thought and behaviour have been distorted, fissures and fractures appear which, when probed, allow alternatives to be discerned, lifted up, and examined for their creative potential. No one else can impose healing; but the resources are not lacking. What I shall show in this project is that the same is true at a cultural level. As we trace the preoccupation with death and its violent manifestations, we will gradually see how this preoccupation has displaced life-giving possibilities: beauty, natality, flourishing. What these come to, and how they can become transformative in redeeming the present, it is the aim of these volumes to bring to light. In the next chapter, therefore, I shall discuss the critical dimensions of its methodology, and in the final chapter of this introduction I shall begin a discussion of the creative poetics of natality.

Chapter 3

Denaturalizing death

> The starting point of critical evaluation is the consciousness of what one really is, and is 'knowing thyself' as a product of historical process to date which has deposited in you an infinity of traces without leaving an inventory. It is important therefore to make an inventory.
>
> (Gramsci 1971: 324)

The inventory which this project makes is of the 'infinity of traces' which have sedimented in our cultural symbolic to form a habitus of violence: in this first volume I focus on the immense influence of classical civilization upon the habitus of the west. Our culture is, I believe, in the grip of something analogous to a neurosis, and in urgent need of healing. Yet I have also pointed out that such healing cannot come, at either individual or collective level, by a simple decision to change, even when the problem is acknowledged. Therapeutic practice can only succeed as the traces that have sedimented into psychic structures are examined and challenged: the 'natural' must be problematized. It is necessary to see that the present is not inevitable; other choices could have been made; things could have been different. Only by seeing this is it possible to recognize also that the pattern of these choices need not be repeated forever: it is still possible to find new ways of thinking and living, and be free of the neurosis in which we have been gripped.

This project as a whole is a study of the layers of choices which have formed our violent habitus, and an attempt also to attend to the voices which urged other choices, voices which were silenced and repressed but which could yet offer resources for freedom and newness. There is, however, a major objection that is often raised, a block to the whole process; and that is the contention that what I am calling necrophilia, an obsession with death and violence, is not a 'neurosis' at all, but rather is essential to the human condition. It is, in short, natural. Although Bourdieu may be correct in his assessment of the naturalization of other aspects of life, with respect to death and violence, its naturalness is not a result of social construction but rather is rooted in the very constitution of what it is to be human.

In this chapter I wish to address this objection and show how it can be overcome. In order to do this, I shall discuss two accounts that root violence within the human condition: a Freudian psychoanalytic account, and a biological account reaching back to Darwin and modified by genetic theory, and shall argue that neither of these substantiate the claim that violence is innate or natural. Rather, both can be used as rationalizations for necrophilia. I shall then draw upon Foucault's work in which he destablized other 'natural' categories and show that the same can be applied to death. Death also has a genealogy.

Naturalizing necrophilia

'All men are mortal': with this announcement as a first premise of philosophical reasoning, death is placed squarely at the centre not only of rationality but also of what it is to be human. Moreover, the premise implicitly carries other assumptions that have determined how this human condition of mortality is to be understood. Underlying the assertion of mortality is an acceptance that there are universal truths, and a metaphysical assumption that there is one single reality which it is the job of philosophy to understand. From Plato and Aristotle onwards, there has been a widely shared 'metaphysical assumption that the object of scientific knowledge is the one, essential, intelligible structure of the one reality' (Addleston 1983: 170). To know the nature of a thing is to know its essence, its constitutive or defining characteristics which are true of every instance of that thing. To know the nature of humankind, therefore, on this model is to know that we are mortal. Death is a universal attribute of human nature.

But it has also been long recognized that 'nature' is a notoriously tricky term, not least when what is at issue is 'human' nature (see Soper 1995). Although it often stands for 'essence', an inescapable and constitutive reality, it equally often stands as a moral category, about which we have choices. More confusingly still, its moral implications can cut in diametrically opposite ways. Thus for example on the one hand civilization is sometimes said to be that which raises us 'above nature': here 'nature' is assumed to be inadequate or even immoral. Such a view is reflected and transmitted in the Biblical view of the 'natural man': that is, the sinful person whose 'nature' must be transformed by the supernatural. Here 'nature' is linked with an idea of original sin. Yet on the other hand, in many discussions of morality 'nature' is taken as the standard, and acting 'against nature' is synonymous with acting immorally. In recent centuries all sorts of things from homosexuality or interracial marriage to the education of women have been alleged to be 'contrary to nature', in other words, immoral.

What can frequently be observed in such appeals to 'human nature' is a slide from a non-moral assertion of nature as essence or constitutive characteristic to a moral judgement or exhortation. Thus, human beings are 'naturally' – that is, in essence – heterosexual and therefore ought not to engage in homosexuality; women are 'naturally' – biologically – constituted for reproduction and there-fore ought not to be taught mathematics which will induce in them hysteria, a

wandering of the womb. Such a slide is obviously confused. If a particular characteristic is in fact essential or constitutive, then it can neither be transcended
nor contravened: if it were *constitutive* of 'human nature' to be heterosexual, then
homosexuality would be impossible.

The slippages in the idea of 'nature' raise the possibility that similar confusions
may surround the assumption that death is 'natural'. At a biological level it is
obviously true that every human being is mortal. Each of us will die: nothing is
more certain. But upon this fact a whole inventory of cultural, moral, and religious
constructions have sedimented, often purporting to be as constitutive of human
mortality as the biological fact itself. In this way, I would argue, not only death
itself but also violence and the obsession with death has been assumed to be rooted
in 'nature'. Necrophilia has been naturalized.

Homo homini lupus

One of the most influential instances of such naturalization in modernity is to
be found in psychoanalytic theory. In *Beyond the Pleasure Principle* Freud introduced his famous distinction between the life and death drives, which he later
labelled Eros and Thanatos. As he then understood it, organisms are governed by
something like a principle of entropy; they have an inherent 'urge . . . to restore
an earlier state of things' which stills all tension or excitation (1984: 308).
Although the life instincts press an individual to growth and progress, ultimately
their function 'is to assure that the organism shall follow its own path to death,
and to ward off any possible ways of returning to inorganic existence other than
those which are immanent in the organism itself.' In Freud's account, death is not
a part of life; it is the end of life as birth is its beginning. It is in a sense more
fundamental than life. The inanimate underlies the animate, and 'the aim of life
is death' (311). It must also be noted that in Freud's account the connection with
gender is never far away: the drive to return to a prior, tensionless state can be
read as a longing for the womb from which life has been ejected. But the womb
is, as it often is in western cultural representations, a trope for the tomb: 'Dust
thou art, and unto dust thou shalt return.'

Freud's characterization of the life and death drives in terms of what are in effect
thermodynamic theories of quantum physics has not found universal favour
even among psychoanalysts. However, the idea of death as fundamentally linked
with separation, loss, and longing to return to the mother has found much greater
acceptance. Already in Freud, the young boy's separation from his mother is
effected in the Oedipal stage through fear of castration, a dismemberment which
is perceived as an analogue of death: 'the fear of death [is] . . . a development
of the fear of castration' (1984: 400). Because this feared event can be averted
only by the renunciation of the desire for the mother, that desire is repressed out
of consciousness. The result, however, is that it returns in a tendency to aggression
and violence, especially by men against women, or against other men for the
attention or favour of women. It can be acted out by individuals in destructive,

even sadistic ways; or it can be turned inwards in masochism or melancholia (1984: 394–401). At a societal level, it can be released in war (1991: 358; cf Rose 1993: 15).

In his 'Civilization and its Discontents', Freud put the matter starkly:

> Men are not gentle creatures who want to be loved, and who at the most can defend themselves if they are attacked; they are, on the contrary, creatures among whose instinctual endowments is to be reckoned a powerful share of aggressiveness. As a result, their neighbour is for them not only a potential helper or sexual object, but also someone who tempts them to satisfy their aggressiveness on him, to exploit his capacity for work without compensation, to use him sexually without his consent, to seize his possessions, to humiliate him, to cause him pain, to torture and to kill him. *Homo homini lupus.*
>
> (Freud 1985: 302)

'Man is a wolf to man.' Freud was deeply influenced by Darwin (Ritvo 1990), whose theory I shall come to in a moment. For Freud, ultimately biology and psychology were inseparable; and at their heart lies the instinct of aggression, as primary and inescapable as instincts of self-preservation. Violence and mutual hostility are as inevitable as eating, sleeping and sex: 'the inclination to aggression is an original, self-subsisting instinctual disposition in man' (Freud 1991: 313).

Freud, therefore, considers how this aggressive instinct is to be satisfied without destroying humanity. Aggression turned inwards, in guilt or depression, is unhealthy. But if the aggression is turned outwards, 'the organism will be relieved and the effect must be beneficial' – at least for the organism itself. Because of its instinctual nature, moreover, 'there is no use in trying to get rid of men's aggressive inclinations' (1991: 358). The only question is how they can be deflected in such a way as to be containable within civilization; whether the instinct of Eros, which stands in the balance against this destructive death instinct, will be strong enough to enable humanity to sublimate their destructive impulses.

Psychoanalysts after Freud have disagreed among themselves about how the death drive should be understood, but most agree that it is linked with tendencies to aggression and destruction (which may be turned inwards). Melanie Klein is noted for her linkage of aggression to the 'bad breast', the infant's experience of separation and loss (Klein 1988). In Lacan, aggressivity is closely connected with the fragility of the subject's self-construction in the mirror stage, and the rage against any threat to that construction (Lacan 1977: 8–29; cf Brennan 1993). The death drive is taken to be manifested in the attempt to repeat that which gives meaning and satisfaction (Ragland 1995: 88–90). Julia Kristeva is yet another psychoanalyst who echoes the Freudian linkage of death, castration, and women: in *Black Sun* she writes that 'the feminine as image of death' mirrors anxiety about castration and is acted out in a matricidal drive which, unless it is sublimated, 'would pulverize me into melancholia if it did not drive me into crime' (1989: 28). It is not putting it too strongly to say that for all these thinkers, civilization is built upon the repression and sublimation of the death drive and its attendant aggression.

It will be important in a later volume of this project to explore more fully the centrality of the death drive in psychoanalytic theory, one of the master discourses of modernity. What I want to emphasize here is that these psychoanalysts, and writers who follow them, present the death drive and aggressivity as constitutive of 'human nature', whether or not they use that term. In their thinking, to become a subject, to enter the human world of language and the symbolic, is always already to have a structural desire for death. Though this is repressed into the unconscious, it is no cause for surprise that it erupts ever and again in the necrophilic symptoms and the gendered violence, individual and collective, that has characterized the west: indeed if these analysts are correct, then aggression must characterize all of humanity throughout time and space.

The survival of the savage

Of all the discourses naturalizing aggression and violence, perhaps the most influential upon late modernity is that of Darwin and his followers, especially as it is developed in genetic theory. According to Darwin's account in *The Origin of Species*, the variety of flora and fauna have come about by a principle of natural selection working over vast periods of time. All of life is a struggle for existence, species against species but also often individual against individual. Applying Malthus' theory of the increase of populations if left to reproduce without check, Darwin argued,

> A struggle for existence inevitably follows from the high rate at which all organic beings tend to increase. . . . As more individuals are produced than can possibly survive, there must in every case be a struggle for existence, either one individual with another of the same species, or with the individuals of distinct species, or with the physical conditions of life.
>
> (Darwin 1968: 116–17)

Darwin's reference here to 'physical conditions of life' suggests that the struggle for existence should not be equated with aggression and violence: it might equally be the enhanced ability to manage with little water in a dry place. Nevertheless, Darwin lapses easily into the language of war. In his restatement of his theory in his later book, *The Variation of Animals and Plants under Domestication* Darwin returned to the Malthusian idea of population increase, and said:

> The inevitable result is an ever-recurrent Struggle for Existence. It has truly been said that all nature is at war; the strongest ultimately prevail, the weakest fail . . . the severe and often-recurrent struggle for existence will determine that those variations, however slight, which are favourable shall be preserved or selected, and those which are unfavourable shall be destroyed.
>
> (Darwin 1868: I.5–6)

In a situation where 'all are at war' aggression will be an advantage for survival, and it is therefore consistent with natural selection to assume that aggression will be bred into those who survive as central to their nature.

In fact, that conclusion goes beyond what Darwin himself said, and perhaps beyond what he would have been happy with, but it was accepted by the proponents of Social Darwinism from Herbert Spencer onwards, who were willing to use Darwin's theory of the survival of the fittest to validate every sort of conquest from the colonial appropriation of Africa to the unification of German states under Prussia. It became taken for granted that aggression and violence are hard-wired into the human psyche: in more recent terminology, it is sometimes claimed that there is a 'gene' for violence, or, more circumspectly, that human beings are genetically predisposed to violence. Moreover (in something of a reversal of Darwinian theory which presumably would imply that aggression should increase over time as a selective advantage) aggression became associated with primitive cultures. The rise of civilization involved finding ways of dealing with aggression in ways that did not harm society: sports like football and fox hunting; vicarious participation in violence through film, video and games; and from time to time the necessary blood-letting of war (cf Mennell 1992: 140–58; Elias 1994: 156–68).

Denaturalizing violence

In the face of such authority it may seem foolish to resist the claim that aggression is innate and violence inevitable, that humanity is ruled by *Thanatos*. The best we could hope to do is try to channel it into the least destructive ways; though even that is an endless and possibly unachievable task. If aggression is instinctual, on a par with the need for food or sex, then pacifism is at best like virginity: perhaps a few can choose it, with varying quotients of liberation and personal cost, but it is neither possible nor desirable for humanity as a whole. Social conditioning can teach us to eat with a knife and fork, and to behave sexually within socially sanctioned parameters, but it would be futile to forbid eating or sexual expression. If the urge to violence is similarly natural – an innate part of human nature – then it is just as futile to bewail it. We would do better to find a 'knife and fork' for aggression, a channel for its expression which does the least amount of damage.

Against all of this, I suggest that it is not the case that violence is natural. My claim is rather that violence saturates the western habitus, and that those who see violence as innate have not made their case. Rather, they have reflected their violent habitus, built it into their theories, and thereby reinscribed it in western thinking and practice. It is a classic example of Bourdieu's theory of history being produced on the basis of history, the habitus reinscribing itself at an ever deeper level. To substantiate this claim, I offer the following considerations.

First, there is the question of evidence. The claim that aggression is innate or natural is presumably meant to be an empirical claim. As an empirical claim it can ground the theory which is built upon it. But it can only do so if it is itself true; and its truth is dependent upon evidence that confirms it. Yet neither Freud nor Darwin (nor their followers) evaluates the empirical evidence for their premise that aggression is natural. What they do instead is look around them at all the aggression and violence in the world, and move directly from the perceived ubiquity of violence (sometimes, as in Freud, acknowledging that they find it in their own hearts also) to the assumption that it is innate. Now it is of course obvious that the world is full of human-produced violence, and important not to pretend otherwise. But if what is in question is whether that violence is rooted in innate aggression or whether it is better understood as a result of social formation, an expression of our habitus, then a simple appeal to the sheer prevalence of violence proves nothing one way or the other. So far, the evidence is compatible with either hypothesis. It is therefore unwarranted for the theorists of modernity simply to assume that violence is innate.

To reconsider that assumption we might begin with the simplest question: *who* is violent? It is noteworthy that violence is much less equally distributed in the human population than is the instinct for food or sex. In the first place, as we saw in chapter 2, violence is strongly gendered. By and large it is men who make war; men who commit violent crimes such as rape or murder; even men who play football or engage in other aggressive sport-substitutes for violence. This is not to say that women are never violent: some of them are. Neither is it to argue that women are morally superior to men. There are other moral evils besides violence; some of them arguably worse. But the incidence of *violence* is heavily skewed to the male.

The implication is obvious. One can hardly allege in one breath that violence is part of human nature and in the next breath say that it applies to only half of humanity: think of the parallel with food or sex. If women are very much less aggressive than men, then aggression cannot be a human instinct or innate to human nature. At most it could be argued that aggression is instinctive to *male* human nature. Both Freud and Darwin are notorious for their views of women; and, Freud's concern about what women want notwithstanding, they mostly proceed as though *male* nature is *human* nature, or putting it another way, they take the male as normatively human and render the female invisible, at least in their considerations of death and aggression.

Now, one response is to retreat to essentialism, either biological or psychoanalytical. The biological version links aggression to testosterone; the psychoanalytical to the way a little boy must negotiate his Oedipal complex. In either case, aggression is or becomes rooted in the male body or psyche in a way that does not apply to females. But again the logic does not stand up to scrutiny. For the argument to be persuasive, it would have to be possible to measure testosterone levels, or grade the negotiation of the Oedipal complex, or identify particular genetic segments, and correlate the findings with violent behaviour over a large experimental cohort, complete with a control group. Only if the correlates were strong could the hypothesis have credibility. Once again the argument is based on assuming the very thing that is in question: the innateness of aggression. First it is assumed that men are violent by their very nature, and then some gender-specific explanation for that violence must be found. The logic does not bear examination.

Moreover, not all men are violent. Very many men are gentle, and abhor aggression. That is observably true of many individual men in western societies; it is also true of whole societies and cultures in other parts of the world. The aboriginal peoples of Australia and North America, for example, seem to have lived in relative peace before European contact, as also did many Asian and African peoples. Some, but by no means all, tribes and peoples have been warlike. Once European contact generated insecurity and introduced alcohol, guns, and measles, the propensity for warfare increased, though even then it is noteworthy how hard many aboriginal peoples tried to keep their peace-loving ways (Wright 1993).

Because so much of what counts as history has traditionally been written by European men for whom wars and conquests have been of central importance, there has been less notice taken of peaceable societies in which 'nothing happened'; but this is yet another inscription of a violent habitus. The case should not be overstated or romanticized: it would certainly not be true that all precontact societies were peaceable (or indeed that war is the only kind of violence) (Keeley 1996). Nevertheless, it is demonstrable that the idea of the 'savage' was largely a European invention, projected on to peoples who were being subjected to European behaviour much more deserving of the term (Dickson 1984).

The point of this for present purposes is that the existence of largely non-violent societies, and of non-violent men in western society, drives a coach and horses through the argument that violence is part of (male) human nature. Of course it is always possible to narrow the argument: one can move from 'violence is part of human nature' to 'violence is part of male nature' to 'violence is part of a sub-group of male nature', but this dwindles to the claim that violence is innate to those who are violent, and only the violence itself can be adduced as evidence. In spite of the fact that the master discourses of modernity naturalize violence, the arguments for such naturalization simply do not hold water.

I suggest, in fact, that naturalizing violence acts as a rationalization, in a way parallel to the rationalization of other forms of obsession (think of the excuses that any alcoholic can adduce). If violence is 'only natural', if gendered aggression can be shrugged off with the comment that 'boys will be boys', if war is taken as inevitable, then ultimately non-violence cannot work: the wolf will at best be chained and sooner or later will break loose. It is true that Freud looked for ways in which civilization might sublimate aggression; but even he conceded that periodic blood letting was inevitable and probably healthy. We see in his writings a theme that is latent in much modern thought: if violence is naturalized it is partly justified; if it can't be helped it must be condoned.

If, however, the assumption that violence is natural is destabilized, then so also is that rationalization. We have no choice but to take responsibility for it, no let-out from the task of critical evaluation and re-formation of our habitus. The assumptions that form our habitus and the violent language, practices, and theories which entangle it must be brought to light, not left buried underground where they will spring up into new batches of war and terror.

It is inescapable that the habitus of the west is violent, and that western history, including its most recent history, is a reenactment of this violence which has been internalised to such an extent that in any situation requiring response violence seems natural, the only alternative. Violence has so colonized our habitus that we have collectively lost the capacity to imagine other sorts of response. In the global context this is regularly expressed in military terms: from the Gulf War to Bosnia, from Kosovo to Afghanistan and Iraq, the alternatives are presented as either 'doing nothing' or military bombardment. Since there is a felt moral and political need to do something, the west, claiming God and goodness on our side, goes to war.

Yet it is not war, worrying though that is, upon which I think our attention should be focused. Many thoughtful people deplore war – sometimes all wars, sometimes specific wars as unjustifiable morally or tactically – and would hold that the values of western society are and should be fundamentally peaceable. But if I am anywhere near right, war is no more than an explosive symptom of the systemic violence which spreads its underground tentacles throughout our cultural habitus. Susanne Kappeler, in her book *The Will to Violence* puts this point starkly:

> War does not suddenly break out in a peaceful society; sexual violence is not the disturbance of otherwise equal gender relations. Racist attacks do not shoot like lightning out of a non-racist sky, and the sexual exploitation of children is no solitary problem in a world otherwise just to children. The violence of our most commonsense everyday thinking, and especially our personal will to violence, constitute the conceptual preparation, the ideological armament and the intellectual mobilization which make the 'outbreak' of war, of sexual violence, of racist attacks, of murder and destruction possible at all.
>
> (1995: 9)

Once we are alert to it, we can see violence everywhere, expressing and reinforcing our habitus in ways that seem entirely natural, taken for granted, but that are in fact continuous reenactments of necrophilia, reproducing history on the basis of history. How, then, can we denaturalize necrophilia, show that it is not part of the universal essence of what it is to be human, in such a way that we may be freed from its grip upon our habitus?

A genealogy of death?

The recent thinker who has done most to destabilize the hegemony of putative universals is Michel Foucault. All through his writings Foucault worked to undermine the idea of fixed identities or essences, whether of rationality and madness, health, delinquency, or sexuality. He showed that things were always more complicated than could be captured by any sense of essence; and indeed that strategies of naturalization are covert technologies of power. Foucault summarized his method as 'a systematic scepticism with respect to all anthropological universals,' such as madness, crime, or sexuality. As he put it,

> In the realm of knowledge, everything presented to us as having universal validity, insofar as human nature or the categories that can be applied to the subject are concerned, has to be tested and analysed.
>
> (Foucault 1994: 317)

Although Foucault does not apply his method to the notion of death as a universal, it is not difficult to make the extension. That, of course, does not amount to the denial of death, any more than Foucault's work denied sex or sexuality. As Foucault says,

> To refuse the universals of 'madness', 'delinquency', or 'sexuality' [or 'death'] does not mean that these notions refer to nothing at all, nor that they are only chimeras invented in the interests of a dubious cause. Yet the refusal entails more than the simple observation that their content varies with their time and circumstances; it entails wondering about the conditions that made it possible. . . . The first methodological rule for this sort of work is thus the following: to circumvent anthropological universals to the greatest extent possible, so as to interrogate them in their historical constitution.
>
> (Ibid.)

Thus, famously, Foucault wrote a history of madness (and by implication of rationality), showing how what has counted as madness has gone through significant shifts which betoken changes in what has been deemed the 'essence' of rationality. He applied the same method of problematizing central ideas of the western symbolic, ideas that had been thought to indicate universals of human nature, such as health, crime, and sexuality, in such a way that it became apparent that concepts that seemed obvious or natural in one time or place seem highly questionable or absurd in another.

To proceed by Foucault's methodology, then, would mean that rather than accept mortality as an unchanging and natural 'essence' of what it is to be human, a universal that is always at the core of human nature, an appropriation of his thinking would extend it to consider how death has been characterized and how this characterization has varied according to the historical context. How has the category of death *functioned* as a way of circumscribing human subjectivity and society?

What David Halperin says of Foucault's approach to sexuality offers great possibilities for a critical rethinking of mortality. Halperin argues that Foucault shows the importance of asking, not about the *essence* of sexuality but about its *function*: what role does it actually play in society?

> The effect of Foucault's inquiries into that latter set of questions about sex is to reconceptualize sexuality as a strategic device, as the linchpin of a complex socio-politico-scientific apparatus. Foucault thereby converts sex into the basis for a radical critique of, and political struggle against, innumerable aspects of modern disciplinary culture.
>
> (Halperin 1995: 120)

We can reread that passage, substituting 'death' or 'violence' for 'sexuality' or 'sex'. When we do so, we begin to see that while death, like health or sex, is at one level a biological reality for all human beings, at another level its naturalizing function must be challenged. Death, I shall show, is a concept multiply inscribed in the western symbolic, its meanings and implications sedimented into our subjectivities so that our habitus is deathly. The platitude that 'all men are mortal' is not simply a statement of fact; it is part of a construction of human subjectivity which preoccupies western culture and saturates our habitus in self-perpetuating necrophilia.

In this project, therefore, I make it my business to examine the ways in which death and violence have functioned. Instead of colluding in the assumption of an essence of death, of mortality as a simple given of human nature, and violence as its inevitable manifestation, we should investigate how mortality has functioned and the roles it has played in concept and experience in western history. We would then begin to see how mortality has served as a 'linchpin of a complex social-political-scientific apparatus' of the disciplinary cultures of the west. Once we grasp that the category of death, what it means to be mortal, has a genealogy, this insight then opens up the recognition of the heavy regulatory hand that it has laid upon western history. The genealogy is the task of this project, but we can readily anticipate some of its contours, from Plato's prisonhouse of the soul and the christendom of late antiquity to the medieval emphasis on the mortification of the flesh and the preoccupation with heaven, hell and purgatory, to the modern visions of death and other worlds ranging from colonial conquest and space exploration to the meting out of violence in the name of political or religious righteousness. In all of these, I suggest, necrophilia plays a regulatory function, kept in place by a rationalization built on a naturalization of death. If we denaturalize necrophilia, recognize mortality as socially constructed, what new possibilities are opened up?

A history of the present

For Foucault the painstaking archival work that was necessary to develop the genealogies of madness, punishment and sexuality was necessary as a means for posing 'the question of the present as a philosophical event incorporating within it the philosopher who speaks of it', as he said in an essay on Kant (1986: 89). It is we ourselves, our own central ideas, our habitus that must be problematized, brought to consciousness and held up to scrutiny and thus shown to be rooted neither in nature nor biology nor necessity but in the sedimentations of historical and social construction. As he put it in another essay, what he was trying to develop was a 'critical ontology of ourselves' as

> an attitude, an ethos, a philosophical life in which the critique of what we are is at one and the same time the historical analysis of the limits that are imposed on us and an experiment with the possibility of going beyond them.
>
> (1984: 50)

In this way Foucault presents his genealogical method as a contribution to a transformative practice of philosophy. It is a method that helps to show the contours of the present habitus, how those contours were formed, and how they can, where necessary, be reformed.

One of the things that this implies is that the onus for reconfiguring the habitus is not left with those who are already too often its victims. It is certainly true that 'dissident speech' often arises out of the life experience of members of oppressed groups; and those who are in positions of economic and cultural privilege need to learn much from those who are not (Meyers 1994: 56). However, I suggest that Foucault's approach also invites those of us who are in privileged positions to problematize *ourselves*, to call into question our own habitus. Paul Rabinow, following Foucault, has written of the need to develop an anthropology, not of exotic others, but precisely of ourselves, to become aware of how peculiar we are: we need, he says, to

> anthropologize the West: show how exotic its constitution of reality has been: emphasize those domains most taken for granted as universal (this includes epistemology and economics); make them seem as historically peculiar as possible; show how their claims to truth are linked to social practices and have hence become effective forces in the social world.
>
> (Rabinow 1996: x)

A fine recent example of what this comes to is Richard Dyer's book *White* (1997). Rather than lay the burden of developing alternative and positive figurations of blackness upon Blacks, Dyer shows what an odd notion 'white' is as an image of a racial category. A person whose skin was actually white would be very ill indeed: we who are classed as white are various shades of pink, cream, tan – 'flesh colour', as it is tellingly called. Yet we link up images of whiteness as a putative skin colour with cleanliness, with purity, and with goodness: sin and evil are dark and black and dirty. When we stop to think of it, this is not only very odd but also morally chilling. And Dyer *does* stop to think of it. He looks at how the imagery of whiteness works in the media, in novels and film, in the history of christendom and colonialism, and he destabilizes its taken-for-granted status and thus its grip on the habitus. I am not suggesting (and neither is Dyer) that we should prob-lematize whiteness without listening to the dissident speech of Blacks: certainly both are necessary. But what is important about the idea of problematizing ourselves is that it does not exoticise others or leave the whole burden of changing the habitus on those who already bear the brunt of it.

Moreover, it enables us to see how our multiple positioning can be a help in transformative thinking. Most people who are able to write or read books of this sort are simultaneously privileged and oppressed. All of us who are in academic life are culturally and economically privileged, some more than others. Yet those of us who are women are members of what is still in many respects the 'second sex'; and for both women and men our skin colour, sexual orientation, age, and dis/abilities position us variously in relation to privilege. But what is most significant in terms of this project is the way in which gender positions us in relation to death. At a biological level, women and men are equal in relation to death: each of us is mortal. But I have already suggested that at a symbolic level women are more particularly linked with death than are men. Men, on the other hand, are linked in the symbolic with aggression and violence, but also with immortality and other worlds.

What Foucault's genealogical strategy and Dyer's example show is how an awareness of multiple positioning of gender, privilege and status is involved in the development of a transformative imaginary. A genealogy of death brings to consciousness the inventory of traces which have formed us, and in bringing it to consciousness loosens its grip and destabilizes its hegemonic control of our habitus. When we begin to see the contours of our own symbolic and the genealogy of its present shape, then we can also begin to see what it might be like to think otherwise, what might be developed as transformative possibilities. The central tropes that frame the habitus of the west are so familiar that we have to work hard to notice them. They shape our thought and actions even while remaining outside our conscious focus. A history of the present, a genealogy that exposes the symbolic at stages of its formation, opens up unacknowledged assumptions and offers an opportunity to reshape the habitus.

As the work of Foucault shows, a genealogy is not a history in the sense of telling a complete story; it is a selection that reveals a particular shape. Even more important, a genealogy does not assume progress, as though the constructions of the past have been improved upon so that the present has been reached. Just as in a genealogy of a family, there are often significant influences to be discerned down the generations; but this does not imply that later generations are better. Moreover, a genealogy as I propose to develop it in relation to death, gender and beauty must occupy a strange situation in its perspective on the western habitus. Because I am examining formative aspects of the necrophilic symbolic, I shall look at figures and events who have been of great influence in shaping it: Homer, Plato and the Stoics will take up a good deal of the present volume. But because I am seeking ways of thinking otherwise, possibilities of transformation, I shall also pay particular attention to those whom these dominant figures have silenced or marginalized – Sappho, the goddesses of ancient Greece, the early Christian martyrs – and to ambiguous murmurings of dissent, including the Greek tragedians and Ovid. What are the contours of necrophilia's others?

It is in its movement towards transformative possibilities that Foucauldian strategy reconnects with psychotherapeutic practice. A genealogy of death, tracing its imbrication with gender and beauty, shows that the violence which is symptomatic of the present and threatens the very possibility of the future, is like a destructive trajectory in an individual's life. The very fact that necrophilia has a genealogy already indicates something of its social construction, and thus destabilizes the notion of its inevitability. Part of the therapy of an individual is the gradual awareness that the destructive impulses which underlie symptomatic behaviour patterns have a history, probably reaching back to childhood. They may have very deep roots and tentacles, but they are not innate, not part of the very essence of the self. Similarly, a history of the present is a history that reveals the successive patterns of deathliness which enact and reinforce the necrophilic habitus. A first stage for liberation from this pattern is thus to see that it *is* a pattern, imposed and reimposed, but not impervious to challenge or change. It is this recognition, brought about by sometimes painful and painstaking analysis of the traces of sedimentation, that suggests possibilities of difference, shows how choices can be made otherwise, so that newness can enter the world. In the next chapter I turn to this vision of hope, before embarking, in the following parts, on the inventory of the western habitus that began in the classical world.

Chapter 4

Towards a poetics of natality

If any therapy is to succeed in releasing an individual from an obsession, the time must come when, having patiently explored the events and experiences of the past which have sedimented into the neurosis, the individual arrives, however hesitantly, at a point of freedom, where a fresh start is possible. This new start does not, of course, obliterate the old; rather, it begins the task of redeeming and transforming the past without repeating its destructive patterns. It is an openness to hope. In this chapter I want to move towards such a hope, in which creativity rather than violence could shape our habitus, and a poetics of natality could replace the necrophilia of the western symbolic.

Natality

As I have been emphasising, throughout the western tradition, mortality – the fact that we all die – has been taken as central to our self-understanding. In this focus on mortality, our natality – the fact that we are all born – has been largely ignored. What would happen if that balance were redressed? Why not sometimes replace 'All men are mortal' as the first premise of the first syllogism of logical thinking with 'All people are natals'? What if we were to treat natality as seriously, as a philosophical and cultural category, as mortality has been treated, taking natality as equally crucial to our understanding of what it is to be human? The suggestion may at first cause bewilderment – itself a symptom of the extent to which natality has been ignored. I propose to explore its potential to subvert and reconfigure the western habitus of violence into patterns of creativity and hope.

We may begin at the most basic and concrete level: the actual physical birth of babies. What would the world be like if births decreased dramatically or ceased altogether? In recent years several novelists have made that question the premise of a book, notably Margaret Atwood in *The Handmaid's Tale* (1987) and P.D. James in *The Children of Men* (1992). For all the differences between these two books, both paint a chilling picture. In Atwood's novel, the reason for the decrease in births is that most women, especially in the upper classes, have become infertile. The few women who might bear children are made slaves of the rich and powerful, to breed for them, in a state system that couples the most extreme form of Orwellian totalitarianism with a Christian fundamentalism: the land is called 'Gilead' and the breeding women are 'Handmaids' to the rich; from time to time all join in a 'Prayvaganza' which includes ritual execution of those who deviate. In P.D. James' scenario, it is the men who are infertile. Without children and young people, the world sinks increasingly into depression punctuated with violence. Above all, there is no hope: no hope for the world, no hope for a future, no newness entering the world. There is novelty, yes: ever more clever technology and gadgetry chiefly used for oppressive purposes. But real newness, real creativity of thought and action, has ceased. Death is all there is left. When we have allowed ourselves to sink into a scenario of a world without births, a world in which new life does not appear, the significance of natality as a category in our lives and our symbolic structures begins to emerge.

Natal features

But what does it mean to be natal? If to be mortal means that we shall die, then at the most elementary level, to be natal means that we have been born. Each of us has come into the world through birth. But just as mortality is more than physical or biological, and has become also a category of our cultural symbolic upon which many layers of meaning have sedimented, so, I suggest, natality carries significance. I shall here sketch some of the most important features of natality, each of which destabilizes the preoccupation with death and mortality which has characterized the western tradition. It is no part of my project to create a fresh set of binary oppositions; but it is heuristically useful to draw broad brush strokes of contrast between features of natality and mortality. These features will be refined and qualified as the project proceeds; but it is helpful to have a preliminary glimmer of the hope which natality offers.

First, then, natality entails embodiment. To be born is to be embodied, enfleshed. The significance of this emerges by contrast with mortality. Throughout western culture, shaped by a mixture of Platonism and christendom, death has often been thought of as in some sense the separation of the soul from the body, even if soul and body are thought to come together again in a resurrection for final judgement. The soul is what is important. This has had several consequences. First, it changes the focus to the eternal destiny of the soul, in some *other* world, away from the flourishing of the whole person in *this* world. Second, and connected with this, it means that the religious emphasis is on salvation of the soul for this other world, rather than on the welfare of human beings in this one. Third, in the west, the soul has been closely linked with the mind, with rationality, which has been valorized as humankind's most godlike attribute. It has also gone along with a construction of gender in which maleness is associated with rationality and the soul, while femaleness has been linked with bodiliness and reproduction. Since detachment of the soul from the body, or at least from bodily desires, has been linked with rationality and salvation, it is not hard to see how these constructions tend toward a denial of the significance of the body, the earth, and human justice and flourishing, while emphasising a rationality and spirituality somehow separate from the body and the physical. Moreover, in much of the focus on mortality in the western tradition, and on the mortification (literally 'putting to death') of the flesh as spiritual discipline, there has been a deep undercurrent of misogyny.

An emphasis on natality subverts all that. Without denying the possibility of life after death, and certainly without denying that we will die and the importance of taking death seriously, a focus on natality shows the significance of embodiment and of our bodily life here and now. It shows that the flourishing of human beings requires that bodily needs must be met, and therefore that it is wholly misguided to bypass issues of justice and liberation and appropriate distribution of the world's resources in favour of a spirituality focused on salvation of a soul for some other world.

Moreover, the idea that rationality is akin to godliness, let alone the idea that rationality can be detached from bodiliness, is undermined. Our embodiment is to be celebrated not denigrated, and the embodied flourishing of all our fellow natals must have a high priority in our ethical and political stance. Neither does a focus on natality allow for the gender distortion whereby men are kept from being in touch with their bodies and emotions, while women are treated as sex objects and kept from exercising their rational capacities. Natality as a conceptual category requires a positive attitude to bodies and materiality, to the flourishing of this world in all its physical richness.

The emphasis on embodiment indicates a second feature of natality: all natals are gendered. Whereas with death gender ceases to matter, for embodied natals gender is inescapable and of great importance. It is instructive to remember what happens whenever we hear that someone has had a baby. One of the things we want to know – even if the people are strangers, friends of friends, and nothing to do with us – is, 'Is it a girl or a boy?' Why do we want to know? Why is that question one of the first we ask, second only to the health of all concerned? Or again, it is a common experience to be walking down a street or sitting in a train and finding oneself taking a hard second look at someone – a total stranger – because their gender had not been ascertained at first glance. Why should it matter? And yet we find gender and gender identification important: it is central to embodiment and human personhood, whether in biological or psychoanalytical terms. Indeed it is one of the more convoluted ironies of the west that even when we do not need to do so for warmth, we wear clothes for 'decency', at least enough to cover our genitals, even though gender signals are among the most insistent that we give and receive, and mistakes can cause deep confusion.

This leads to a third characteristic of natality, linked to its particularity. It is possible to die alone, but it is not possible to be born alone: there must be at least one other person present, and she, in turn, was born of someone else. To be natal means to be part of a web of relationships, both diachronous and synchronous: it means, negatively, that atomistic individualism is not possible for natals. For all our particularity, we are particular and special primarily in relation to one another, not by ourselves alone. We could not survive, as infants, if we were not held and cared for in a human nexus. But it is not just as infants that we require relationships for our very survival: humans are social. Even the most solitary of persons looks for some variant of solidarity with others, whether through books or even through memory. It is no accident that prolonged solitary confinement is considered one of the worst forms of punishment. In modernity in the west there has been a strong emphasis on independence and self-sufficiency, especially emotional self-sufficiency, as a mark of (masculine) adulthood. And yet to be natal means to be in a web of relationships; and if natality is emphasised, then it becomes important to attend to that web, to work for its flourishing. Violence, which disrupts such flourishing, is problematized.

Fourth, the most significant feature of natality is that it allows for hope. Whereas death ends all possibilities, with each new infant, new possibilities are born, new freedom and creativity, the potential that this child will help make the world better. Freedom, creativity, and the potential for a fresh start are central to every human life and are ours in virtue of the fact that we are natals. Hannah Arendt, pondering natality, saw it as the aspect of the human condition which allows for the possibility of making new beginnings, fresh starts whether large or small. One of her favourite citations was from Augustine's *City of God*, which she translated as, 'That a beginning might be made, man was created, before whom nobody was' (1996: 147). She argued, as I do here, that 'because he *is* a beginning, man can begin; to be human and to be free are one and the same. God created man in order to introduce into the world the faculty of beginning: freedom' (1977: 167; cf Jantzen 1998: 145). Arendt is here appealing to Christian theology; but her point does not depend upon it. What is crucial is the potential for making fresh starts, for acting creatively; and this is grounded not in our mortality but in the newness that enters the world with each birth. Our embodied, gendered selfhood, situated in the social and cultural web of relationships, delineate our natality; and it is out of this natality that creativity emerges. If violence is linked with death-dealing and destruction, creativity is linked with natality. If we wish seriously to pursue alternatives to necrophilia, then the greatest resource is that it is birth, at least as much as death, that characterizes what it means to be human, natality that signifies a future and a hope.

The necrophilic habitus of the west has, as I shall demonstrate, frequently repressed the voices of natality and flourishing, finding such voices a threat to gendered power. But the repressed returns. In the margins, in the sidelines, in the voices of dissent it is possible to find creativity and beauty, offers of alterities. These voices were too often silenced, sometimes brutally, sometimes by ignoring or distorting them. But by careful listening, it is possible to hear them again; and by exploring their possibilities, find resources for transforming and redeeming the present and bringing newness into the world.

The displacement of beauty

Because of the integral connection of natality and creativity, the silencing of natality and the maternal body is, I believe, interwoven with the displacement of beauty in western culture, in such a way that beauty either is pressed into the service of death or else is itself silenced or marginalized. Indeed, as violence is a central symptom of necrophilia, so, I suggest, beauty and its creation is central to natality. However, although beauty and creativity is crucial to natality, it has too often been appropriated by the powers of necrophilia or subverted to the causes of violence. Again, this theme will be worked out in detail throughout the project. Here, therefore, I shall do no more than give a few examples and a brief discussion to demarcate the theme in an introductory way.

As early as Homer's *Iliad*, beauty is identified with death: those who fight courageously and die in battle are reckoned as beautiful because they will be forever youthful. It is a theme that runs throughout western culture and is still repeated at the cenotaph in London every Remembrance Sunday. Whatever the horrific realities of wartime death, beauty is pressed into its service: the dead are said to be more beautiful than those whom 'the years condemn'. Such an attitude to death can easily be pressed into the service of the state, and made to serve ideological purposes: I shall show for example how Augustan Rome appropriated beauty for its own violent ends.

Alternatively, beauty can be linked with death by serving as the ladder upon which one must climb to immortality, as we shall see in Plato's *Symposium* or Plotinus' quest for unity with the One. An individual beautiful body is taken as interchangeable or commensurable with other beautiful bodies; and the experience of these beauties leads the soul to 'beauty itself', a beauty not available to the senses or bodily experience but only to the incorporeal immortal soul. This ladder from the corporeal to the beatific vision is frequently invoked in medieval christendom. Though its rungs are placed differently by different writers, beauty is linked with the spiritual and the eternal, the world beyond death, not with this life and this world and our bodily experience within it. Beauty is displaced, in a necrophilic symbolic, away from human flourishing into eternity, a realm where bodies and birth have been overcome.

In modernity the displacement of beauty takes different forms, often characterized more by repression than by shunting beauty to an after-life. For this, I believe that protestant christendom bears a heavy responsibility. If we compare the centrality of beauty in the religious writings of late antiquity and the medieval mystics and theologians with its virtual absence in contemporary christian theology and philosophy of religion, the contrast is startling. In premodern writing there were many who placed beauty squarely in the centre of such a conversion of the imaginary: 'Late have I loved you, O Beauty, so ancient and so new, late have I loved you!' wrote Augustine (*Confessions* X.27; 1984); and it was the discovery of this Beauty and this love that released him to his real longings and helped him to find a way forward in his tangled sexuality. Augustine, to be sure, struggled with the relationship between this Beauty and his sensory experiences, often relegating the former to the strictly spiritual, as though beauty can have nothing to do with the body. In this he was following through on the Platonic legacy of dualism in which the soul sought an incorporeal and immortal beauty released from the shackles of the body: it was a legacy severely in tension with a christian doctrine of incarnation, as we shall see. Augustine bequeathed his struggle, on this as on sexual matters, to medieval thinkers in the west, who were often torn, as he was, between *concupiscentia oculorum*, ocular desire for beauty that diverts from spiritual concern, and a recognition that in painting, architecture, music, illumination of manuscripts, and the physical world itself the soul can be drawn to the wonder of God (Miles 1985). With the Reformation, however, and the emphasis (at least in Protestant countries) upon the Word, visual representation was often taken to be less important, even idolatrous (Jay 1994, ch.1); and belief replaced beauty as the mode of access to the divine. The emphasis on beliefs and their justification in Protestant theology and philosophy of religion almost completely obscures consideration of beauty and its centrality in inspiring and focusing longing and desire.[1] No wonder that so much theological and philosophical writing in modernity is boringly ugly, both in presentation and in consequence.

In the secular counterpart of religion in modernity, the march of technology and the military–industrial–information complex has little room for beauty, which is relegated (with mystical experience) to the private realm, not of public importance. It is of course true that there is great interest in 'fine arts', as well as intense holiday pressure on the countryside; but here again we find the features of modernity, of slipping into commodification and being a private 'leisure' activity, not part of the serious business of everyday life. It could be argued that contrary to what I am suggesting modernity in fact shows a heightened awareness of beauty, as evidenced by the establishment of museums, national parks, art galleries and concert halls. Welcome as these are, however, I suggest that the very need for them partly proves my point: if areas of the countryside were not set apart for conservation they would be gobbled up as building sites; but we do not have to worry about the converse, that factories or motor ways will be destroyed because of increasing demand for unspoiled country. Similarly art and artefacts are gathered into museums and galleries, partly to conserve them, partly to render them commodities for cultured consumption; but it would be hard to argue that before the existence of museums people were less involved with beautiful things or cared less about their preservation.

One way to see how the displacement of beauty configures the post/modern western symbolic is to consider common attitudes toward its absence. We would (rightly) feel that we could not live with integrity if we did not care about truth. Yet we are much less clear that we cannot flourish if we are content with ugliness. We live with light pollution and cannot see the stars. We live with noise pollution and cannot hear birdsong or insects or the wind in the trees. Most people now live in cities, often crowded and dirty, where it is seldom possible to watch the dawn or the sunset, or wonder at the beauty of the world. When this is the case for us, we may feel that it is a pity, of course, a matter of regret that we try to remedy as best we can by holidays or weekends in the country, but we don't let it stop our lives and careers. Suppose we tried the same tactic in relation to truth: 'well, it's a pity, but I'll just have to live in untruth; I regret all these lies, of course, but they are necessary for my career. I do try for truthfulness in my own home or at weekends. . . . ' It is of course preposterous. A person evincing such an attitude would be deemed mad or immoral, certainly not to be trusted. Yet if people are deprived of beauty or show no sensitivity to it, such belittling of beauty can be dismissed with a shrug.

Indeed, much of the world as it is organized by a free market economy effectively excludes many people from the beauty of nature, in part by actively destroying it through environmental degradation, and in part by making it an economic necessity that most people live in cities. Thus sensitivity to birdsong and wild flowers increasingly becomes a privilege of the wealthy. The beauty of art and music, too, is skewed to those with the leisure and education to develop an appreciation for them. These material and economic realities are important indications that 'beauty' is not a straightforward term. It has been defined in many ways; and what has counted as beauty is not unrelated to who has had the power to do the counting. But the complexity of the notion of beauty is not a reason to dismiss it. Again the parallel with truth is instructive. Truth, like beauty, is obviously not a straightforward notion: it has preoccupied thinkers for millennia, as they have tried to develop epistemologies and logics that do justice to rationality. Beauty, surely, calls out for at least as much attention. It should not be sidelined into a marginal area of philosophy known as 'aesthetics', but pondered in relation to its centrality for human flourishing.

What this indicates is that beauty itself is a candidate for genealogy: it cannot rightly be discussed as a natural or universal essence. I shall develop some sketches towards such a genealogy in this project, as I probe the interconnections between a necrophilic symbolic and the displacement of beauty; but again some introductory remarks will perhaps be helpful. First, it is important to note that attitudes to beauty, like attitudes to death, are clearly tied to gender. In modernity, for example, beauty has been linked with the feminine, as in the writings of Burke and Kant; and with the emotional; whereas sublimity was seen as masculine, awe-inspiring and ultimately rational. Considerable attention has been focused on the sublime, perhaps precisely because it has been constructed as rational and masculine, whereas (feminized) beauty was more easily dismissible as mere prettiness (De Bella 1989). Thus Derrida, in *The Truth in Painting*, discusses the claim that 'the sublime cannot inhabit any sensible form' (1987: 131) and therefore unlike beauty, cannot be presented or occur in natural configuration. Such unrepresentibility of the sublime is taken even further by Lyotard, who valorizes the sublime precisely as the feeling of incommensurability, the shock of impossible juxtaposition, linked with desire, but desire best glossed as violent (1984: 78; 1989: 196). Beauty and its attracting power is ignored or dismissed as naive consolation. Throughout the modern and postmodern discourse on the beautiful and the sublime, the interconnections with gender and death are convoluted and in tension, but never far away.

Part of my reason for lifting up beauty for reconsideration is to reveal something of these tensions and their background in the western symbolic. But even more importantly, I wish to suggest that attention to beauty opens a way to redeeming the present, transforming the imaginary from its necrophilic obsessions to a celebration of natality, a celebration that includes the acceptance of death as the end of life but not its goal. Beauty, I shall argue, links longing and desire with natality, and both with the divine. Elaine Scarry, in her recent book *On Beauty and Being Just*, points out that recognition of beauty 'seems to incite, even to require, the act of replication' (1999: 3): if we see a beautiful landscape (or person, or painting) we paint a copy, if we can, or take photographs, or write a poem or an entry in a journal or send a postcard to a friend describing the beauty we have experienced. We long not only to retain the experience of the beautiful but also in some way to re-create it. Yet the recreation is not just mindless copying (unless it is mere commodification: a thousand bookmarks and mugs printed with Wordsworth's 'Daffodils'), but can often be a creation of beauty in itself, as a Mahler Symphony creates a musical rendition of light upon a mountain. Thus beauty demands the enactments of one of the central features of natality, which above all else, is the potential for newness, fresh beginnings, while at the same time requiring its own preservation. Scarry points out how often we remark of a beautiful thing: 'I never saw/heard/etc. anything quite like it': it both presents itself as newness and also leads to fresh creativity. 'The beautiful thing seems – is – incomparable, unprecedented; and that sense of being without precedent conveys a sense of "newness" or "newbornness" of the entire world' (22). As Simone Weil wrote,

> The love of the beauty of the world ... involves ... the love of all the truly precious things that bad fortune can destroy. The truly precious things are those forming ladders reaching toward the beauty of the world, openings on to it –

and Weil immediately speaks of books and education, along with the kestrel hovering on the air currents, as having potential to develop in us such openings (1951: 115).

But putting this another way, is there not here an indication that attending to beauty could help to change the imaginary? If the necrophilia of modernity is an obsession, to be understood as I have suggested as a collective neurosis, then even if we accept this diagnosis, I have pointed out why rational argument and analysis will not get us out of it. Only by catching glimpses of a better way, of delight, of freedom and joy, can those struggling with neuroses find the courage and incentive to liberate themselves from the structures of control, and claim instead that which meets their true desires. To change the necrophilic symbolic of modernity and its discursive and material practices, might it not be an effective strategy to seek, in the counter discourses of natality which give the lie to the omnipotence and fearfulness of death, the beauty that draws us spontaneously to yearn towards it?

Part II

Out of the cave

Introduction

So and such they were, these men – worthy of their city. . . . They gave her
their lives, to her and to all of us, and for their own selves they won praises that
never grow old . . . their glory remains eternal in men's minds, always there on
the right occasion to stir others to speech or to action.

(Thucydides 1954: 149)

Thus says Pericles in Thucydides' account of his funeral oration in 430 BCE for
the men who died at the beginning of the Peloponnesian War. Pericles' speech is
in praise of these men, and is given in the presence of their families and friends.
But it is also a speech in praise of Athens, a city worthy of the lives of the men,
just as they were worthy of her. Their glory, Pericles says, remains eternal; and so,
surely, does the glory of Athens.

As Pericles represents Athens in his speech, she is a model of what a city should
be, with the most worthy ancestors who have established her empire, the best
political system of democracy for the whole people and equality before the law,
personal tolerance and responsibility, and the beauty of public buildings like the
Parthenon. Pericles proclaims,

Mighty indeed are the marks and monuments of our empire which we have
left. Future ages will wonder at us, as the present age wonders at us now.

(148)

And so indeed they have. Athens of the Periclean 'Golden Age' became the
model of civilization for the west; its ideals of democracy, tolerance and civic
responsibility were set as a foundation for western public life. Classical Greece,
more broadly, has been taken as a paradigm for civilization emerging out of the
cave of barbarism. Post-Enlightenment Germans modelled themselves on Greeks
(Schmidt 2001); while in England the classical thought patterns learned by boys
in every public school saturated the habitus and influenced everything from
athletics and the administration of the colonies to the architecture of the City of
London (Jenkyns 1980). In any inventory of the traces that have shaped the

trajectory of the west, Greece must have a very large part. Although, strictly, it was Plato who developed the 'myth of the cave' which we will consider in chapter 10, in a broader sense the modern world looks back on the whole of classical civilization as the civilization that emerged from barbarism into the sunlight of reason, philosophy, democracy and culture, and formed the foundation of the western world. Pericles' speech has been taken as celebrating precisely that emergence, putting into microcosm the debt which the west owes to Greece.

It should not be forgotten, however, that Pericles' speech was a *funeral* oration; it was a speech in praise of dead men. Moreover, they were not just any dead; they were men who had died violently, in a war whose justification was hotly disputed even at the time. Their glory was to be 'eternal', but it was an eternity premised on violence. The same was true of Athens itself. Its architectural glories were built on the revenues of the treasury funded by the tribute-paying Athenian empire (Boardman 1996: 143). Pericles himself was proud of this: 'our adventurous spirit has forced an entry into every sea and into every land,' he says; and the memorials left behind are 'everlasting' (Thucydides 1954: 148). He never pretends that those memorials were not built upon blood; indeed according to his speech the deaths upon which they were erected is part of their eternal glory.

Pericles also makes a direct link between death and gender. 'To me it seems,' he says, 'that the consummation which has overtaken these men shows us the meaning of manliness in its first revelation and in its final proof' (ibid). They may have had their faults in their private lives; but in their fighting they were willing to stand their ground rather than give way; and in so doing 'they have blotted out evil with good'. Manliness is linked with fighting and with a refusal to submit. On the other hand, the 'duties' of the widows of these men, Pericles says in the conclusion of his speech, is 'not to be inferior to what God has made you, and the greatest glory of a woman is to be least talked about by men' (151). Women should not call attention to themselves; should never be in the limelight. Even as widows, their place is that of submissive domestic devotion.

If the habitus of the west has incorporated the classical symbolic, then it is no cause for surprise if it, too, valorizes gendered violence. In the rest of this volume, therefore, I shall examine several specific aspects of this violence and the praise of death which characterized classical civilization, sediments of the necrophilic cultural habitus of the west. I shall pay particular attention to the gendered nature of death and violence, both in terms of significant shifts in the symbolic, and in terms of protest and dissent. This part will be devoted to aspects of ancient Greece, and the following part to Rome, not in a bid to write a new history of the classical world, but to uncover something of the genealogy of death and to discern possibilities of natality.

The necrophilia of the classical world can be characterized, I suggest, as a tense continuum between violence and eternity. Pericles' funeral oration illustrates this. On the one hand, the men who died, and Athens itself, are to have eternal glory. Yet on the other hand the men are *not* eternal; they have met their final, violent end. Death is accepted for the sake of eternity; eternity is premised on death. They appear as contradictories, but they are locked in a tense interdependence. It is an interdependence which, I shall argue, characterizes the culture of classical Greece and Rome as surely as does the tension between Being and Becoming or the One and the Many, themes that are much more often discussed by historians of classical thought.

In the following chapters I shall trace out some of the dimensions of this tension of violence and eternity, paying particular heed to its gendered nature, and looking always for alternatives. In chapter 5 I shall discuss the Homeric idea of beautiful death, the glory of war as portrayed in the *Iliad*, and in chapter 6 some of the ways in which that idea was destabilized but also taken forward in the *Odyssey*. Chapters 7 and 8 take that destabilization further, in the works of the fifth century tragedians, who question the valorization of violence and reveal the gendered nature of its tragedy, though without suggesting alternatives. In chapter 9 I shall discuss Parmenides and other presocratic philosophers, who shifted the attention on death away from warfare and towards immortality. Their intention was not to inflict death but to be united with an eternal truth upon which neither death nor women could gain a purchase. In Plato, whose work I shall examine in chapters 10 and 11, I suggest that the tension is intensified: on the one hand he looks for eternal truth and beauty in an immortal and changeless realm; yet on the other hand he is concerned with politics and warfare, and indeed would banish the poets from his republic lest they diminish the appetite for violence among prospective soldiers. A similar tension is found in Aristotle, though it is expressed differently: he is the teacher of Alexander the Great, arguably the man who perpetrated the most violence in the history of Greece; yet Aristotle looks to a life of contemplation as the best kind of life and the nearest to the eternal gods. Aristotle seems, in fact, to stand against necrophilia with his insistence on the notion of flourishing; it is, however, always important to ask who flourishes, and at whose expense?

There are, of course, many qualifications that must be made in this characterization: all the thinkers I shall discuss are far too profound and complex to fit neatly at any one point in a continuum from violence to eternity. However, the two ideas serve as poles in relation to which the habitus of gendered death and its symptoms of violence and the displacement of beauty can be brought into sharper focus: both the focus and the qualifications will emerge as I proceed. Moreover, there are voices which fall outside this tense continuum. Most significant for this part is the recurring voice of Sappho, to whom I pay attention not in terms of her sexuality (which has received more than enough comment already) but in terms of her insistence on beauty and natality. Indeed I shall suggest that she is a more significant figure even for the understanding of Plato than has usually been allowed; she presents a vision of beauty otherwise, beauty that destabilizes the preoccupation with death and brings newness into the world.

There are many other figures and events of the ancient world which could have been discussed, some of them of great importance for the ideas of death and natality: I make little mention of Orpheus and the Underworld, for example, or of Demeter, or of the mystery religions. But I hope that in the chapters that follow some of the most significant of the sediments that make up the inventory of our violent cultural habitus are opened to scrutiny, and some of the voices of dissent and newness can be heard, beginning with those of classical Greece and continuing, in the next part, with 'eternal' Rome.

Chapter 5

The rage of Achilles

Rage – Goddess, sing the rage of Peleus' son Achilles,
murderous, doomed, that cost the Achaeans countless losses,
hurling down to the House of Death so many sturdy souls,
great fighters' souls, but made their bodies carrion, feasts for the dogs and the birds,
and the will of Zeus was moving towards its end.

(77)[1]

The story of western culture begins with gendered violence. Achilles is furious. He is encamped with the Achaean army before the walls of Troy, where they have been fighting inconclusively for ten years. Agamemnon, the leader of the Achaean army, has required Achilles to yield to him a girl, Briseis, who had been given to Achilles as booty after a raid. Under duress Achilles gives her up; but is so angry that he refuses to fight with Agamemnon's army and plans instead to go home with the troops under his command.

The *Iliad* is Achilles' story. It is the story of how he sulks and remains aloof while the Trojans inflict heavy losses upon the Achaeans. It is the story of how his friend Patroclus pleads with him to rejoin the fight, and at last goes into battle wearing Achilles' own armour, only to be killed by the Trojan hero, Hector. More enraged than ever, Achilles now goes into battle against Hector. When he kills him, he drags his body round and round the grave of Patroclus, consumed with grief and venom. Although the poem does not complete the story of Troy, we know, and all Homer's ancient listeners knew, that Hector's death is the signal for the fall of Troy and the end of the war. It is also, however, the signal for Achilles' own death, foretold by his mother Thetis when she brought him new armour for his fight: 'hard on the heels of Hector's death your death must come at once' (470).

But if the *Iliad* is Achilles' story, and that of the Achaean and Trojan heroes, it is also the story of the immortals, gods and goddesses of ancient Greece. The 'will of Zeus' is over all that happens. Apollo, Hera, Thetis and the rest of the Olympian pantheon not only look down upon the earthly events but intervene directly, sometimes resorting to intrigue and conflict among themselves as they do so. Sometimes, as when Thetis brings Achilles a new suit of armour forged by Hephaestus, the mortals are aware of divine intervention; often they are not. Nevertheless, the *Iliad* is the story of divine involvement, for good and ill, in human affairs. The poem itself is presented from the very first line as the song of the Goddess.

The *Iliad*, moreover, is *our* story. It is deeply inscribed in the cultural history of the west. Over millennia it has been memorized, copied, translated into Latin and into modern languages. It has served as a model and standard for countless works of literature, a resource for painting and drama. Its heroes have been part of the repertoire of educated people through the centuries. Indeed its very familiarity can have its dangers: as Jean-Pierre Vernant (1991) has argued, the culture of the Homeric world is in crucial respects different from our own; and the actions and attitudes of Homer's gods and mortals must be interpreted within that ancient system of meaning. Yet to interpret at all is necessarily to interpret from our own cultural perspective, even while actively looking for those alterities that call our complacencies into question. 'To make the ancients speak, we must feed them with our own blood' (Williams 1993: 19; attributed to Tycho von Wilamowitz). And feed them we have, with an assiduous reverence second only to the vener-ation of the Bible in the west through the centuries. Even while we find some of the actions and assumptions of the Homeric world strange, it has shaped our attitudes and cultural habitus in ways of which we are barely conscious. Some of those ways are deathly.

I propose, therefore, to begin my examination of the genealogy of death in western culture with the *Iliad* and, in the next chapter, the *Odyssey*. This is not to say that the Homeric writings were the first or only ancient writings in which death played a major part. The ancient Egyptians, for example, thought much about death; so also did the Babylonians as evidenced by their *Epic of Gilgamesh*. I shall consider Babylonian and Egyptian ideas of death in the next volume, in connection with early Hebrew writings which, like the Greek, are deeply formative of western culture. History can never begin at the beginning; we are always already in the middle. No matter how far back we go there was always something preceding it.

My aim in this chapter is to show how, in the *Iliad*, death – violent death – has been valorized in ways that have had incalculable influence on the western symbolic. I shall discuss the connection between heroic excellence and death, and show how this distinguishes mortals from the immortals. For mortals, beauty is epitomized in youthful violent death. But I shall also show how this beautiful death is gendered; and how an alternative, life-affirming beauty, was available. It was, however, a way not taken; and I shall conclude the chapter with a discussion of how Alexander 'the Great' appropriated Achilles, and was in turn appropriated, so that the *Iliad*'s standards of death, beauty, and violence reverberate through western culture.

Death and glory

For three-quarters of the *Iliad*, Achilles sulks in his tent while the tide of battle goes against his countrymen. His anger, though it is occasioned by having to give up his slave girl Briseis, is not primarily due to grief for her. Rather, it is his loss of honour that stings. Agamemnon, by requiring Achilles to give up Briseis, has humiliated him: indeed that is why Agamemnon demanded her, as he himself admits:

> . . . I will be there in person at your tents
> to take Briseis in all her beauty, your own prize –
> so you can learn just how much greater I am than you. . . .
>
> (83)

Stung to the quick, Achilles is prevented from killing Agamemnon there and then only by the intervention of goddesses, Hera and Athena. But he swears he will never again help Agamemnon fight.

> What a worthless, burnt-out coward I'd be called
> if I would submit to you and all your orders,
> whatever you blurt out. Fling them at others,
> don't give me commands!
>
> (87)

It is his honour that he is concerned about: and it is this, not anything to do with love for Briseis, that he pours out to his mother, the goddess Thetis.

> Mother!
> You gave me life, short as that life will be,
> so at least Olympian Zeus, thundering up on high,
> should give me honour – but now he gives me nothing.
>
> (89)

Nor does Achilles relent even when Agamemnon, having recognized the cost of offending Achilles, sends a deputation offering gifts of restitution. The only thing that moves Achilles back to reconsider is an even greater affront to his honour than was the loss of Briseis, the death of his friend Patroclus. This must be avenged. Achilles' response to Patroclus' death returns him to the battle, and brings about his glory and his death.

The incident with the slave girl shows a great deal about Homeric[2] attitudes to gender, to which I shall return; but first I want to explore more fully Achilles' attitude to honour and its link with violence and death. This attitude is closely linked with its cultural context, which places the worth of individuals not in their internal integrity or the depths of their heart, but in what others think of them.

It is what anthropologists call a 'shame culture', a culture in which 'each person exists as a function of others, in the gaze and through the eyes of others' (Vernant 1991: 85). In such a culture, honour is all-important; shame or dishonour is worse than death.

Thus, when the deputation from Agamemnon tries to persuade Achilles to rejoin the fight, Achilles, in a moment of reflection, weighs up the alternatives:

> If I hold out here and I lay siege to Troy,
> My journey home is gone, but my glory never dies.
> If I voyage back to the fatherland I love,
> my pride, my glory dies . . .
> true, but the life that's left me will be long,
> the stroke of death will not come on me quickly.
>
> (265)

Which will it be: glory and an early death, or a long, ordinary life? He cannot have both. In this passage Achilles seems to favour returning home and living a long life. But, as we know, he stays after all, and helps to win the victory against the Trojans, though it costs him his life just as he had predicted. What is important is that Homer presents this heroic glory as far more excellent than a long but quiet life. It wins for Achilles the immortality of celebration, the poet's song, for which life is well lost. Everlasting glory, the immortality of fame, is more desirable than length of days. Thus death – heroic, violent death – is given precedence: it is the mark of a hero to choose glorious death rather than peaceful life.

The Greek word in Homeric writings indicating the highest aim for mortals is *areté*, often translated 'excellence'. True excellence is imperishable. It is glorious, with a glory that will be celebrated in poems that sing ever and again of the heroic deeds. This, indeed, is the way in which immortality can be won. Homer did not think of immortality in terms of everlasting life in heaven or hell, even though he did believe in some form of survival: as we shall see later on, the 'shades' or spirits of the dead continue a ghostly existence in Hades (see Sourivinou-Inwood 1995: 70–92). But for Homer, such nameless survival is pitiable. The shades of Hades have passed out of the gaze of others, and therefore have lost that which gave them worth, indeed that which made them individuals. To die quietly, without special honour, is to pass into oblivion, to be forgotten, without fame. The immortality that is glorious, on the other hand, is the immortality that is gained by becoming the subject of a bard's song so that one will never be forgotten. This can only be achieved by doing heroic deeds, and doing them spectacularly.

As we see from the example of Achilles, in the *Iliad* the type of heroic deed that qualifies above all for imperishable glory is violence and killing, bravery on the battlefield where youthful warriors are slaughtered. Achilles is by no means the only hero of which the poet sings: all the main warriors on both the Achaean and the Trojan side are immortalized for their valour. Hector, the greatest of the Trojans, has a few moments away from the battle, talking with his wife

Andromache and their baby son. She begs him not to go back into the fray, foreseeing that he will be killed. But Hector replies,

> All this weighs on my mind too, dear woman.
> But I would die of shame to face the men of Troy
> and the Trojan women trailing their long robes
> if I would shrink from battle now, a coward.
> Nor does the spirit urge me on that way.
> I've learned it all too well. To stand up bravely,
> always to fight in the front ranks of Trojan soldiers,
> winning my father great glory, glory for myself.
>
> (210)

Hector is not without pity for his wife and infant son: his tenderness towards them contrasts poignantly with Achilles' unappeasable rage. But in the end, both Hector and Achilles deem glorious death preferable to a life that would win them no place in the poet's song.

The glory of the hero derives in the *Iliad* from his ruthlessness and determination on the field of battle. It is a masculine glory, a glory of violence and slaughter: as Moses Finley says, the *Iliad* is 'saturated in blood' (2002: 110). When Patroclus leads the Achaeans into battle against Hector's Trojans, Homer describes the scene in long sequences of savagery and gore: brains spilling from broken heads, splintered spears and splintered bones, roaring and tumult, efforts to desecrate the bodies of the enemy. Yet it is precisely these fallen warriors who are represented as paradigmatically and beautifully heroic; these are the men who by their killing justify their own existence (Knox 1990: 35) and by their valour win for themselves the immortality of celebration in the songs of the bard.

The hero might also be commemorated in other ways which extolled his glory. It was important to the Greeks to hold proper funeral rites in which the dead would be celebrated; whereas refusal to allow burial was a huge and vengeful insult to the dead. Thus Achilles builds a great funeral pyre for Patroclus, slaughters oxen and sheep for him, and at last gathers up his ashes in a golden urn which he places in a barrow. But he refuses to allow the Trojans the body of Hector. In his grief, Achilles would

> yoke his racing team to the chariot-harness,
> lash the corpse of Hector behind the car for dragging
> and haul him three times round the dead Patroclus' tomb,
> and then he'd rest again in his tents and leave the body
> sprawled facedown in the dust.
>
> (589)

Not until the Olympian gods, outraged at such indignity to one of their heroes, order Achilles to allow Hector's body to be taken away by his old father King Priam who comes to Achilles as a suppliant can the situation be resolved. The *Iliad* ends with the burial of Hector and his funeral rites.

Heroes, both Achaean and Trojan, were due honour in death: an honour that concerned itself with the deceased body rather than with the fate of the soul. Heroes would be honoured by the Greeks with sacrifices, votive gifts, and perhaps grave monuments such as the one for Kroisos, found in a cemetery near Athens and coming from about the middle of the sixth century BCE. The beautifully proportioned young male body bestrides the tomb; and the inscription reads, 'Stop and grieve at the tomb of the dead Kroisos, slain by wild Ares in the front rank of battle' (Boardman 1996: 84). The glory of the hero is extolled in the monument: he was no coward; he died with honour in the 'front rank' just where Hector means to be; and his glory would be commemorated once a year on the festival calendar (Burkert 1985: 203–8). Thus the *mnēma*, the memorial of the tomb, fixes in the memory of the living the heroism of the deceased: it is the counterpart of the epic song. Both the song and the statue inscribe on social memory the glory and beauty of the hero, which, as Vernant puts it, 'one can ensure for oneself only by losing them. [They] become eternal possessions only when one ceases to be' (1991: 69).

Thus it is valour on the killing fields that brings glory, *areté*, to the Homeric heroes. The immortality that is prized is the immortality of celebration, both in the funeral monument and the bard's song. Glory is achieved, ultimately, by heroic death. Here, then, is the irony that stands at the foundation of western culture. Immortality is gained through dying, eternity through violence; and both are more excellent than a peaceable life. Although the shame culture of archaic Greece is in many ways different from the culture of the west, it is important to ask: to what extent does western culture build upon these ancient sediments of valorized violence? It is a question that will run through all the chapters to come.

On being mortal

There is a very close connection between the heroes and the gods and goddesses of Mount Olympus. Some heroes, like Achilles, are born of one divine and one human parent. Others are particular favourites of a god or goddess. Odysseus, for instance, is cared for by Athena; Apollo and Aphrodite are especially concerned for the Trojans; while Hera and Athena are on the side of the Achaeans. And so it goes on. Moreover, for all their extraordinary powers, the gods of the Homeric writings are very like humans: certainly more like humans than would be countenanced in religious systems like Judaism or Christianity. The Greek gods were born; they had bodies and ate and drank, made love, slept, travelled, worked and played. They held council and often argued amongst themselves. They were capable, just as were the heroes, of immoral, treacherous and vindictive conduct, and also of great care for those in their charge.

If the gods are like humans, the heroes are like gods. Time after time in the Homeric writings individuals are spoken of as *dios* or *isotheos*, translated 'divine' or 'godlike' (see Griffin 1980: 81–102): *dios* in particular comes to be something of a 'filler epithet' to make the verse run smoothly. In the *Iliad* Achilles is often referred to as godlike. In the *Odyssey* the term is used frequently for Odysseus or his son Telemachus. What makes the heroes godlike is not moral goodness as we would think of it, but precisely their *areté*, their excellence of valour and glory. When old King Priam goes to see Achilles to plead for the body of Hector, Priam kneels beside Achilles,

> clasped his knees
> and kissed his hands, those terrible, man-killing hands
> that had slaughtered Priam's many sons in battle . . .
>
> (604)

and calls him, without irony, 'great god-like Achilles'.

A bronze statue, now known only in copy, is thought to represent Achilles: he is young, a muscular, perfectly proportioned man, glistening with strength. Though the original dates from somewhat later than the Homeric writings, it retains the ideals of the beauty of the young warrior who went to fight with Hector. His shining body, full of energy, seems to capture that moment 'when, for an instant, the brilliance of divinity seems to fall on a mortal creature, illuminating him . . . with a little of that splendor that always clothes the body of a god' (Vernant 1991: 36). It was such glory that Priam saw in Achilles when he went begging for Hector's body. The poet says that Priam

> gazed at Achilles, marvelling
> now at the man's beauty, his magnificent build –
> face-to-face he seemed a deathless god. . . .
>
> (609)

But Achilles is *not* deathless. Neither are the other heroes. This, indeed, is represented as the crucial difference between gods and humans. In Greek writing from Homer onwards, the gods are the 'immortals' while the humans, no matter how godlike, are simply 'mortals'. Humans die. Gods do not die. It is this distinction between immortality and mortality rather than inequalities of power or wisdom or goodness that marks the definitive characterization of gods and humans respectively. The gods, powerful and cunning as they are, are not defined by these attributes but by their immortality. They are 'the race of the blessed ones who live forever,' the 'blessed immortals' who live on snowy Olympus' peak, the 'deathless ones'. Humans, by contrast, are spoken of not as the embodied ones, or the rational ones, but simply as mortals.

Moreover, mortal bodies show their mortality all their lives. Humans regularly must refresh themselves with food and rest; their mortal condition is one in which energies are always being depleted and must be replenished; and even so they decline into an increasingly fragile old age. In Greek mythology, *Hupnos* (Sleep) and *Thanatos* (Death) are twins; and Hunger, Fatigue and Old Age are part of the same family. Mortals are known as 'eaters of bread'; the gods, by contrast, feed on nectar and ambrosia, not out of hunger or need but simply for pleasure. The link between food and death, for humans, is poignantly displayed on the great shield of Achilles, forged for him by Hephaestus after Hector removed Achilles' original armour from the dead body of Patroclus. On that shield Hephaestus forged two cities. One was a city at war, under siege from an encircling army. The other was a city at peace, going about the events of ordinary life. There was also rich ploughland, a plenteous harvest, a great ox slaughtered for a feast, a thriving vineyard with luscious purple grapes – plenty of food and wine for all (xviii.572–688). In one sense the contrast between the two cities could hardly be greater. Yet in the Greek symbolic both indicate mortality, the first through violence and possible heroism, the second through the needs of the human body for food and drink, needs which reveal human fragility and mutability.

In the Homeric writings humans are sometimes envious of the gods' immortality, but the gods jealously guard it for themselves. Achilles and Hector are evenly matched in their fight; both of them are men of 'god-like' beauty and valour, and both are favourites of one or other of the gods. Zeus suggests that Hector should be spared, plucked from death.

> But immortal Athena,
> her grey eyes wide, protested strongly: 'Father!
> Lord of the lightning, king of the black cloud,
> what are you saying? A man, a mere mortal,
> his doom sealed long ago? You'd set him free
> from all the pains of death?
> Do as you please –
> but none of the deathless gods will ever praise you'.
>
> (547)

Zeus immediately acknowledges her words, and gives Athena permission to intervene and thus bring about Hector's defeat. There can be no relaxation of the rule that separates humans from the gods. Humans are mortals. Death is that by which human life is defined from the earliest literature of western civilization.

At one level this is hardly puzzling. After all, it is accurate. Humans, without exception, die; and it is reasonable that death should be taken seriously. No poet who did not ponder death would be worthy of serious attention. The characterization of humans as mortal only becomes puzzling when we note how this *one* fact of human existence, and not other characteristics, comes disproportionately to define what it is to be human. The representation of humans as 'mortals' and gods as 'immortals' is adopted without hesitation or suggestion that other characteristics might be more central or might complicate the picture. Although death is constructed in ever changing ways in the western cultural symbolic, the basic assertion that 'all men are mortal' comes to stand as the basic definition of what it is to be human. It is assumed without argument or qualification from the moment that Homeric writings are taken as a primary source for western culture. Yet is it really the case that, finite though we are, death is the single most significant characteristic of being human? Is this *the* crucial contrast between humans and the divine? Should humans be *defined* by death?

Beautiful death

One of the striking aspects of the representation of death in the *Iliad* is its close association with beauty. There is beauty in mortality; beauty, especially, in early heroic death. The fight between Achilles and Hector is represented as a fight between two strong, beautifully proportioned young heroes, both of them worthy of admiration. Old Priam, Hector's father, foresees his son's doom and at the last moment begs him not to fight. Yet even in this extremity, Priam recognizes that the death of young warriors is beautiful. Only early death will preserve forever the beauty of a manly body, delivering it from the ugly indignities that come with age. Priam says,

> For a young man all is decorous
> when he is cut down in battle and torn with the sharp bronze, and lies there
> dead, and though dead still all that shows about him is beautiful;
> but when an old man is dead and down, and the dogs mutilate
> the grey head and the grey beard and the parts that are secret,
> this, for all sad mortality, is the sight most pitiful.
>
> (Lattimore trans. Homer 1960: 437)

When Achilles kills Hector in revenge for the death of Patroclus, it is this manly beauty that he most wants to destroy. As he stabs Hector and stands over him in rage, Achilles shouts,

> I smashed your strength! And you –
> the dogs and birds will maul you, shame your corpse
> while Achaeans bury my dear friend in glory!
>
> (552)

But Achilles and the Achaeans are not willing after all to leave the desecration of Hector's corpse to the dogs and the birds. They,

> . . . running up around him,
> crowded closer, all of them gazing wonder-struck
> at the build and marvellous, lithe beauty of Hector.
> And not a man came forward who did not stab his body . . .
>
> (553)

They try to make sure that the beauty of a youthful corpse would not be granted to Hector; they set about mutilating his body so that the beauty of his youthful death should be obliterated. But the gods thwart their intentions. Even though Achilles drags Hector's body in the dust round and round the tomb of Patroclus, the gods preserve the beauty of his body 'fresh as dew . . . and no sign of corruption' (602) until King Priam comes to claim the corpse. The dead body of a hero is the paradigm of beauty. His is a beautiful death, a *kalos Thanatos*. He will never have to deal with the indignities of aging, nor will he ever pass into oblivion. His heroism, culminating in his death in battle, guarantees that he will never be forgotten. He has achieved *areté*, excellence, an excellence that is 'actualized all at once and forever after in the deed that puts an end to the hero's life' (Vernant 1991: 51). This, for the Greeks, is the paradigm of beauty, the imperishable glory of the poet's song in which the glow of youth never fades. Whatever the realities of the blood and filth of the battlefield (and Homer portrays them in gruesome detail), the idealized corpse of the youthful warrior preserves its radiant beauty forever.

For the ancient Greeks from Homer through the classical period until the fourth century BCE and beyond, the ideal of beauty is a perfectly symmetrical well proportioned young male body. War, death and beauty are interlinked: the most beautiful body of all is the body of a dead young warrior. Men whose shining youth gives illusions of god-like immortality march to killing fields, the symmetry of their limbs matched by the discipline of their columns and the gleam of their weapons. Indeed the ancient sculptor who made the famous statue of the Spearbearer, Polyclitus of Argos, explicitly argued that perfection comes about through exact *symmetria*, an ideal of beauty 'projected upon that most powerful of all Greek images, the warrior' (Stewart 2000: 14).

Although the male body was normative, women were also sometimes described as beautiful in the *Iliad* (and even more often in the *Odyssey*, as we shall see in the next chapter). Indeed, the whole story of the *Iliad* depends upon the beauty of a woman, Helen, whose loveliness so captivated Paris of Troy that he stole her away from her husband, the Achaean Menelaos, and thereby precipitated the Trojan War. And behind the whole episode stands the goddess of beauty, Aphrodite. Moreover, we recall Briseis, the slave girl who was at the centre of the quarrel between Achilles and Agamemnon, described as beautiful (83, 89); as also is Chryseis, the captive girl she replaces in Agamemnon's tent (82). But in the *Iliad* these descriptions are little more than conventional formulae, carrying nothing like the weight of meaning that is involved in the beauty of the male warrior, especially the warrior who has died the 'beautiful death'. Archaic sculpture reflects this distinction. While statues representing males are nude and meticulously crafted, states of women were, in the words of one modern commentator, 'little more than clothes hangers,' even their faces no prettier than those of men (Boardman 1996: 86).

If women get little attention in terms of beauty, the physical world gets even less. There are some descriptions of the physical world in the Homeric writings which to a modern reader suggest beauty: for example the often-repeated formula, 'the rosy-fingered dawn'. Mount Olympus, also, is beautiful: in the *Odyssey* it is described as the place where

> the gods' eternal mansion stands unmoved,
> never rocked by galewinds, never drenched by rains,
> nor do the drifting snows assail it, no, the clear air
> stretches away without a cloud, and a great radiance
> plays across that world where the blithe gods
> live all their days in bliss.
>
> (169)

But the portrayal of Mount Olympus is not so much a celebration of natural beauty as it is a provision of a fitting setting for the gods. It is not the physical world with its unsymmetrical variations that is represented as beautiful but the well-proportioned male body in its shining youthfulness, preserved forever in an early death.

Part of what is involved here is that beauty is strongly associated with the immortals. They are, above all, radiant with glory; their immortality is represented as shining splendour that never dims. In consequence, it is not surprising that specifically *youthful* human bodies are deemed paradigmatically beautiful, since the youthful body does not yet show signs of age and inexorable mortality. The young heroic warrior, in particular, appears god-like, invincible. The fact that humans are mortal is the great enemy of beauty: mortality itself is ugly to the ancient Greeks. The signs of mortality are transience and decay, the diminishment and ultimately the obliteration of beauty – just the opposite, in fact, of the 'shining immortals'.

Indeed it is sometimes suggested that the gods are not meant even to look upon the dead. In Euripides' tragedy *Hippolytus*, the goddess Artemis whom the hero has always revered, comes to meet with him one last time; but as his death draws near she quickly takes her leave, saying:

> Farewell, I must not look upon the dead.
> My eye must not be polluted by the last
> gaspings for breath. I see you are near this.
>   (Euripides 1953: 127)

Euripides wrote several centuries after the *Iliad* was composed, but the idea that the gods would be polluted by the sight of a human corpse was still current. The bodies of the beautiful, the bodies of perfect proportion whose shining youth gives the illusion of immortality, are the bodies of young heroes, favourites of the immortals.

The irony is biting. Only early death will preserve the beauty of the body, which by its youthful demise will never have to submit to the ugliness and indignities of aging. Yet the gods cannot look upon death. The very death that confers ever-lasting beauty and immortal fame also banishes the hero forever from congress with the gods: immortality for mortals is achieved precisely by the loss of that life which makes them god-like. And even the beauty of the dead youth is rhetorical rather than real. The Greeks and Trojans alike were very concerned to commit the corpse to the funeral pyre before decomposition set in; but even in the best case, everybody knows that what actually happens to a corpse, including a youthful, well-proportioned corpse, is not eternal preservation of beauty. Beauty and death are connected by denial. Violence, rather than being represented as destructive and brutal, is portrayed ultimately as glorious: it confers beauty and immortality upon its perpetrators and victims, and becomes the ideal of manly excellence. But that it does so can only be maintained at the price of an ideology of death which refuses to recognize the abjection of destruction and decomposition. Death, killing, displaces beauty from an actual lived body to the realm of memory. Only there can the dead be glorious.

Beauty otherwise

The Homeric ideas of death and beauty, and the valorization of violence, have had a very long run in western culture. I shall trace some of their transmission and transmutations later. But from very early, there were alternatives to Homeric themes. The fact that violence was lifted up as a cultural value was not inevitable; neither was the linkage of beauty with death. In the lyric poetry of ancient Greece, particularly in the poetry of Sappho, a quite different set of values obtained. Beauty, and indeed life itself, was configured differently.

Sappho lived on the Greek island of Lesbos towards the end of the seventh century BCE. Her work is the earliest that survives of any woman writer. Her poems were highly regarded in antiquity: she was known as one of the nine great lyricists of ancient Greece or, sometimes, as the tenth Muse. The latter description sees her as a goddess, one of the immortals. But already there is a difficulty. To describe someone as a goddess is a 'grand gesture', as Margaret Williamson points out, but 'as well as paying her an extravagant compliment, it may also indicate a difficulty in thinking of real women as poets' (Williamson 1995: 15). In the writings of Aristotle, the gender bias is plain. Sappho, he says, was honoured 'although she was a woman' (*Rhetorics* 1389b12).[3]

To contemporary readers, the very names 'Sappho' and 'Lesbos' indicate issues of sexuality; and this, indeed, has been a preoccupation of readers of her work, often distracting attention from the themes of her poetry. Vast quantities of ink have been spilled over questions of whether Sappho was or was not erotically attracted to other women; if she was, then whether or not she acted on it; if she did (or did not), then what effect it had on her poetry . . . (see Greene 1996a; 1996b; Wilson 1996). As Judith Hallett observes, this absorption with questions of Sappho's sexuality has meant that she has received 'different (and increasingly inequitable) treatment from that given Greek male lyric poets' (1996: 128). It has also meant, as I shall argue, that her reconfiguration of beauty with all that it might have meant for western civilization has been effectively sidelined.

If, however, we start from the other direction, if we make her poetry itself and not her sexuality the primary focus, what emerges is a quite different configuration of beauty and death from what we have observed in the *Iliad*. Here is the beginning of one of Sappho's poems.

> Some say a host of horsemen, others of infantry,
> and others of ships, is the most beautiful thing
> on the dark earth: but I say, it is what you love.
> > (Trans. du Bois 1996: 80; see also
> > Rayor 1991: 55)

The most beautiful thing is what you love. Sappho is quite deliberately rejecting the Homeric preoccupation with the fast black ships of the Achaeans, the horses and weaponry of the fighters, or even their youthful male bodies as the standard of beauty. The military ethos and its violence, the heroism and its accoutrements of glory and immortality: all these are dismissed by Sappho. For her part, it is love – love for a particular woman – that is the source of meaning and the standard of beauty. She thinks of the beautiful Helen, the alleged cause of the Trojan war; and thinking of her, she is reminded of another woman, 'Anactoria, far away . . .'

> Her lovely way of walking, and the bright radiance
> of her changing face, would I rather see than
> your Lydian chariots and infantry full-armed.
> > (du Bois 1996: 80)

When Sappho thinks of beauty, what comes to her mind is Anactoria, now absent. It is she whom Sappho longs to see, with all the individual features that make her just the person she is: her particular gait, the 'bright radiance of her changing face'. This, for Sappho, would be far more beautiful than a display of military hardware and men equipped to do violence.

Who was Anactoria? Was she one of Sappho's 'students' in the 'school for young ladies' that has sometimes been woven into stories of Sappho's life, as though seventh-century Lesbos was an early precursor of a nineteenth-century ladies' finishing school? Was Sappho's love for Anactoria the affection of a teacher for an apt student? Or did it go further: were they lovers? And was Sappho heart-broken because, in the manner of archaic Greece, Anactoria has now been taken away, married off to some man, possibly against her will? All these fantasies and many more have been spun out at great length on very slender threads.

But surely the central point is that Sappho is offering a different understanding of beauty from that which is predominant in the Homeric writings. This is beauty otherwise. Nor is it simply a question of finding different things beautiful, as though it were a matter of subjective taste: Homer likes ships and horses and armour; Sappho prefers women. Rather, it is a different conceptualization of beauty, which rejects both poles of violence and eternity. For Sappho, beauty is involved with love, not with violence. And love is always love of the particular. It is cherishing the specific individual characteristics that make the beloved not a mirror of oneself but the unique person she is. Moreover, in Sappho's writing beauty is not displaced to some eternal realm beyond death with its fiction of perpetual youth. Her love is centred in this present life and its vicissitudes, not in some immortal or deathless realm. Anactoria is 'far away', and her loss is keenly felt; but she is not dead and her beauty is not contingent on heroic poetry, let alone on grave monuments. The pain of absence gives rise to lament, but not to fantasies of death or other worlds. Here is a celebration, even in pain and longing, of beauty and love, not as abstract or idealized but as embodied in Anactoria. It is in this particular flesh and blood woman, not in heroic military adventures as in the *Iliad*, nor in daring adventures on the sea as we will find in the *Odyssey*, nor in some all-encompassing One or fragmenting Many that concerned the preSocratic philosophers, nor in the eternal unchanging Beauty Itself that would preoccupy Plato that Sappho finds excellence and 'the most beautiful thing'.

Sappho struggles to make this different conceptualization of beauty, a beauty that is not premised upon death, plain to her readers. She reads Homer against himself, pointing out (in a manner worthy of Derrida!) that although the beauty that is exalted in the *Iliad* is the beauty of male warriors and the weapons and deeds of violence, yet even in the *Iliad* the whole story could never even begin were it not precisely for the different sort of beauty which she, Sappho, is presenting: the beauty of a particular woman. It was Helen, who 'far surpasses all mortals in beauty,' without whom the Trojan war would never have begun. Indeed it is Helen who puts Sappho in mind of Anactoria, one beautiful and much loved woman reminding her of another. This, Sappho avers, should be easily enough 'understood of one and all'; it is after all the repressed premise of Homer's song. If that premise is brought to consciousness, then it points to just the configuration of beauty that Sappho advocates: beauty premised not on violence nor on eternity but on this life and this love.

The theme of particular beauty runs through Sappho's poetry, though its precise meaning is often difficult to discern because of the fragmentary nature of the poems. Sappho writes, for example,

> I have a beautiful child, her form
> like golden flowers, beloved Kleis
> whom I would not trade for all of Lydia
> or lovely –
>
> (Rayor 1991: 72)

and there the fragment breaks off. Again, scholars have woven fantasies around these lines, some holding that if Sappho has a daughter then she must be heterosexual after all, while others point out, first, that such a conclusion hardly follows; and second, that there is no certainty that 'I' in this poem or any other refers to its author. ('Here I lie' on a grave monument does not refer to the engraver.) But once again, arguments about Sappho's sexuality miss the point of the poem. In this fragment as in the poem about Anactoria, Sappho is offering an ideal of beauty that is centred on a beloved individual, this time a child. For this she would not trade 'all of Lydia': wealth and luxury are no more to be compared with 'beloved Kleis' than military equipment with Anactoria.

Sometimes Sappho links the beauty of the beloved one to the beauties of nature, in a way that is never found in Homeric writings which, as already pointed out, offer little comment on the loveliness of the world. Part of one of Sappho's fragments runs:

> Now she stands out among
> Lydian women as after sunset
> the rose-fingered moon
> exceeds all stars; light
> reaches equally over the brine sea
> and thick-flowering fields,
> a beautiful dew has poured down,
> roses bloom, tender parsley
> and blossoming honey clover.
> (Rayor 1991: 61)

The lines carry a high erotic charge, as do many of Sappho's poems; but whether the desire they portray is Sappho's own or someone else's, real or fictional, it is impossible to say. What is clear, however, is Sappho's delight in the beauty of nature, and her representation of beauty in terms of love and delight rather than violence and death. The end of one poem, the body of which is too fragmentary to interpret, says,

> . . . passion for the light
> of life has granted me splendor and beauty.
> (Rayor 1991: 66)

Again, 'me' might or might not be autobiographical. But whether it is or not, there can be no doubt that the poet is linking together light and life and beauty, not valorizing death.

Although Sappho says that her construction of beauty is 'full easy' to understand, however, it was the Homeric picture, not Sappho's, that became prominent in western culture. Sappho was marginalized. When she did receive attention, the focus was not on serious appreciation of her thought, but, as I have said, on her allegedly 'deviant' sexuality. It is worth taking a little time to see how this occurred, as a specific instance of how a symbolic is reinscribed (and otherness erased) in the cultural habitus, as discussed in the previous chapter. In early modern England Sappho was discussed as an example of female homosexuality. Although she was recognized as an excellent poet and a model for women writers, attention was not focused on the content or meaning of her poems but on the ways in which good English ladies should *not* emulate her. Thus the seventeenth-century poet Abraham Cowley wrote:

> They talk of *Sappho*, but alas the shame
> Ill Manners soil the lustre of her of her fame.
> (Quoted in Andreadis 1996: 113)

When women writers began to take Sappho seriously, their attention too was on her sexuality, defending her purity from what they saw as the slanderous attacks of the male scholars.

Even more telling is the reception of Sappho in the development of German nationalism after Napoleon. Joan DeJean (1996) has shown how the most influential German thinkers of the time – Schiller, Schelling, Hegel, Goethe – were all Graecophiles, and all were influenced by the male homophilic aesthetic theories of J.J. Winckelmann. In his books on ancient art, Winckelmann had argued that Greek ideal poetry was formative of Greek national identity. Moreover, he held with the Homeric writings that ideal beauty is, paradigmatically, 'beautiful virile youth'. As DeJean says, Winckelmann 'treats in great detail the types of male beauty glorified by the ancients, while dismissing the value of the female body as an artistic model in summary fashion: "Few observations can be made about the beauty of women"' (DeJean 1996: 125). Philologists who studied Sappho in the light of Winckelmann therefore minimized her importance: as a woman, she could hardly have contributed to the great ideals that formed the Greek identity. Women would never be able to know or participate in the highest forms of love or beauty. That was the prerogative of heroic young males. The work of these scholars shows a deliberate choice of the Homeric ideals of manly beauty associated with violence and death, rather than Sappho's alternative view, that the beautiful is linked with love and life. And this for them is not merely a claim about how to understand ancient texts. For them, the Germans are to become the new Greeks: as Goethe once famously said, 'I, too, am an Achaean'. German greatness as a nation would come about by translating Greek ideals, most importantly ideals of beauty, into German culture. Thus the marginalizing of Sappho in their philological works by treating her in terms of her sexuality rather than her ideas was of a piece with their efforts to develop a virile German nationalism whose ideals of beauty were linked with violence, war and death. A very similar move occurred in England: Shelley, echoing Goethe, said 'We are all Greeks'; and English Victorian culture was saturated with Greek ideals (Jenkyns 1980).

The development of psychoanalytic theory is a telling example of the selective appropriation of Greek ideals. Page du Bois has shown how Freud reads the Greeks not for their differences from us but for their similarities, finding in them confirmation for his ideas of the psyche (du Bois 1988: 18–24). Thus he looks to Oedipus, and to Empedocles' notions of love and strife (which I will discuss in a later chapter) as precursors of his own insights. Sappho again is side-lined. But as du Bois stresses, the erasure of Sappho's ideas is not inevitable; it is a choice, and the choice could have been made differently. By repressing the memory of Sappho's ideas and her presentation of this-worldly, particular female beauty rather than beauty premised upon violence and death it is possible to present a narrative of western culture that centres on the necessity of aggression and death, the Greek *Thanatos* becoming the Freudian death-drive; while even *Eros* is presented as aggressive. Delimiting the story of culture in this way, du Bois argues,

> turns 'the Greeks' into our ancestors, within the terms of a certain narrative trajectory originally, visibly, obviously devoted to misogyny and control of women, and to a program of philosophical self-mastery. To begin the history of the West with classical [and Homeric] Greece . . . is a polemical choice that determines the subsequent course of the narrative of Western civiliza-tion, and the place of 'the Greeks' in that narrative. In the beginning were men –
>
> (1995: 131)

men whose heroic violence and investment in early, glorious death was taken as the ideal of beauty and excellence. And thus, as we shall see, the west has constituted itself. How much of Sappho's work was destroyed in the process, how many others left work that has forever disappeared, how many women who could have produced significant work but were silenced because of their gender, we cannot know. What we do know is that Sappho left sufficient material to serve as a basis for an alternative imaginary, and that it was sidelined by the device of focusing instead on her gender and sexuality. As Walter Benjamin once said, 'when forces of oppression prevail, not even the dead are safe' (Benjamin 1969: 255).

But the repressed returns. Fragments remain. And in their very fragmentary and jagged nature they disrupt the smooth narrative of western self-constitution. How if we were to take Sappho seriously, with her assertion that the beautiful is that which one loves? How if we were to valorize not violence and death, but the beauty and love of life? We cannot undo the history of the west. But by challenging its alleged inevitability, by looking as far as we can down the roads not taken, we can become clearer about the ways in which power and knowledge have forged a violent and deathly narrative that could have been otherwise.

And we can refuse to reinscribe it. Early in the literature the west claims as its own, the woman Sappho celebrates this world, not some other, love, not war, particular embodied women, not heroic ideals of manliness and death. Her voice, though repressed, has not been wholly erased; and from her we can begin a dream of what an alternative history might be. It is, of course, a utopia, a history that never was. But, as Richard Wolin has said, 'philosophical contemplation must draw its strength as much from hopes inspired by what has never yet been as from that which merely is' (Wolin 1994: 28). It is by the destabilization of the deadly trajectory of the west that an imaginary of life and beauty may emerge.

Appropriating Achilles

Sappho did not get her wish. Achilles did. If immortality is to be found in the song of the poet, then Achilles is indeed immortal. Pindar, one of the most significant of the fifth-century BCE poets, reflects on Homeric themes, and writes,

> The wave of death comes over us all.
> It breaks unexpected; it comes if you look for it also.
> Fame is theirs
> for whom the god makes the legend flourish after their death.
>   (*Nemea* 7, 30–3; trans. Lattimore 1976: 120)

Pindar did much to promote the fame of the Homeric heroes, to whom he likened the subjects of his 'victory odes', poems written in honour of the winners of competitive games. And Pindar accepted the Homeric view that it is precisely the fame of poetry which gives immortal status to the victors: 'it is worthy to describe the noble ones in the most beautiful songs, only this will make it equal to the privileges of the immortals, while every noble deed dies when it sinks into oblivion' (Frag.106b, cited in Tatarkiewicz 1970: I: 40).

Oblivion was not the fate of the heroes of the Trojan war. Though the *Iliad* may initially have been part of an oral tradition, it was written down on papyrus scrolls or, later, on parchment, and preserved through the centuries. In what remains of the great library of Alexandria, established in the third century BCE, nearly half the copies are of Homer's works, with the *Iliad* by far the most numerous (Finley 2002: 7). Already from the fifth century BCE it had been a standard part of Greek education, with great passages learned by heart. The heroes of Achaia and Troy were taken as ideals for life and conduct by the schoolboys of Greece and, later, of Hellenistic Rome.

Not everyone thought this was a good idea. Plato, as we shall see, banished Homer and other poets from his ideal republic because Plato held that Homer told falsehoods about the gods and heroes and thus was an inappropriate teacher of the young (see *Republic* iii.383c; 387b; *Laws* ix.858e).[4] But Plato did not practice what he preached. He quotes both the *Iliad* and the *Odyssey* dozens of times in his writings, often to illustrate his point, or as an approved authority; and calls Homer the greatest master of tragedy (*Theaetetus* 153e), the 'best and most divine' of poets (*Ion* 530b), the one whom Socrates would most like to meet in the immortal life he looks forward to after his execution (*Apology* 41a–c). I shall discuss Plato's ideas of death and immortality in chapter 10; the point here is that even for Plato, despite his criticisms, Homer's *Iliad* was canonical.

Aristotle takes up the praise of Homer, calling him the 'poet of poets, standing alone not only through his literary excellence, but also through the dramatic character of his imitations;' he is also the unsurpassable master of epic (*Poetics* 1448b35). Aristotle is particularly insistent that imitation is central to art: artists, he says, show the virtues and vices of people and actions, representing them as models for imitation (*Poetics* 1448a5). Imitation, Aristotle holds, is how we learn to live: mimesis is 'natural to man from childhood' and one of the 'greatest pleasures not only to the philosopher but also to the rest of mankind' (1448b20). So if it was Homer who presented the noblest of characters and actions, then Homer should be venerated and his heroes imitated.

Throughout the Greek and Hellenistic world, Homer was regarded as having set the standard for excellence, not only of literature but also of morality. There is a marble relief statue from about the second century BCE which shows Homer, seated, holding his staff of office in a vigorous grip, while female figures representing the World and Time place a crown upon his head. It is of course impossible to trace the incalculable effects of Homer and his ideal of heroic excellence and beautiful death: such a study would be a study of the whole of western culture. Yet it is useful to gain some concrete purchase on the influence of his ideals; and to do so, I shall sketch something of its effects on just one man, Alexander of Macedon, and the commemoration of Alexander by later commentators.

Alexander of Macedon, often called 'the Great', took seriously the Aristotelian notion of mimesis; indeed, he may have learned it from Aristotle himself. Aristotle was appointed by King Philip of Macedon, Alexander's father, to be tutor to his son. In a legend known as *The Romance of Alexander*, King Philip says to Aristotle, '"Take this son of mine away . . . and teach him the poems of Homer," and sure enough, that son of his went away and studied all day, so that he read through the whole of the *Iliad* in a single sitting' (Fox 1997: 47). As Robin Lane Fox who recounts this tale observes, 'in spirit, this charming fiction comes near to life'. Alexander, true to the idea of mimesis, modelled himself upon Achilles, going so far as to foster the myth that he was his reincarnation.

Alexander did not merely venerate the *Iliad* as great literature; he tried to live by it. While still a boy, he took for himself the nickname 'Achilles', and called his friend Hephaistion 'Patroclus'. Aristotle helped Alexander prepare a special text of the *Iliad*, which the latter treated as his most valuable possession and his guide to excellence in his conquests: 'the *Iliad* was Alexander's guide to the art of war, and its hero, Achilles, his exemplar of heroic virtue' (O'Brien 1992: 21). Every night Achilles slept with this book and a dagger under his head. When as a young man he went on a major campaign against the Persians, early successes against its king, Darius, resulted in Alexander's soldiers looting Persian treasure. One of the most precious of Darius' treasure chests was brought to Alexander. He asked his friends to suggest what they thought particularly valuable, to put into the chest for safe-keeping. 'Various suggestions were made, but he himself said he would put the *Iliad* there' (Plutarch 1998: 335). As far as he was concerned, the *Iliad* was the most precious thing he had.

Plutarch, the second-century CE writer who recounts this story, continues: 'Homer was no sleeping partner on his campaign, but made a positive contribution' (336). Plutarch had his own reasons for telling the tale; but what he gets across is that Alexander's veneration for the *Iliad* and for Achilles upon whom he modelled himself was an incorporation of a symbolic in which excellence consists in violence, heroic courage, and glorious deeds in a field of slaughter. It is the choice of an early, violent death rather than a long but uneventful life. All these things, Alexander copied.

In his military adventures Alexander tried to re-enact scenes from the Homeric writings. His first destination when he sailed from Greece to subdue Asia was Troy, by that time only a village with a temple to Athena. As Peter Green, a biographer of Alexander, points out, 'Few men can ever have given such solid embodiment to their private myths. [Alexander] was the young Achilles, sailing once more for the windy plains of Troy' (Green 1991: 165). Once landed, Alexander sacrificed at the graves of the Achaean heroes and invoked their favour for his coming campaign. He had himself crowned with a golden crown; and then, 'anointing himself with oil, he ran naked among his companions to the tombstone of Achilles and honoured it with a garland, while Hephaistion did likewise for the tomb of Patroclus' (Fox 1997: 101). Then, just as Achilles had given his armour to Patroclus and received a new suit of armour from Athena before embarking on his killing, so Alexander sacrificed his own armour to the goddess and took from the priests at her temple weapons and a shield purported to have come from the Trojan war.

But Alexander's efforts to model himself upon Achilles and even to rival him, to live his life as a Homeric hero, went far beyond imitating the rituals of sacrifice at Troy or basking in a nickname. Alexander took with utmost seriousness the Greek ideal of excellence as personal glory won in violent combat. Alexander is at his most Homeric in some of his most notoriously cruel actions. Example after example can be given. In Alexander's campaign against Persia, he encountered opposition at Tyre. When at last it fell after a prolonged siege which used cunning strategies (imitating Odysseus at the siege of Troy), his army took 30,000 people as slaves, killed 8,000, and then Alexander ordered that 2,000 more be crucified. That accomplished, he sacrificed in thanksgiving to Heracles and consecrated the sacred ship of Tyre: clearly Homer was never far from his mind.

Next he came to Gaza, which offered intense resistance but eventually fell. Here he slaughtered all male citizens and enslaved all women and children, just as had been done by armies in Homeric writings. Even more telling is the account of what happened to Batis, the governor of Gaza. His ankles were tied and the thong was lashed to the back of Alexander's chariot; he was then killed by dragging him backward around a defeated city: 'a grim variant on Achilles' treatment of Hector's dead body in the *Iliad*' (Green 1991: 267; see also Fox 1997: 182–3). The Homeric prototype was not an inconsequential literary fantasy nor a cultured gentility for Alexander: it was a symbolic structure which shaped his attitudes and behaviour with catastrophic consequences for those who opposed him.

And as Achilles had been a model for Alexander, so Alexander himself became a model for later centuries. Plutarch, in his famous *Parallel Lives*, presented his readers with biographies of paired sets of Greek and Roman figures: prominent among them is Alexander, paired with Julius Caesar who like him used violence and ruthlessness to forge an empire. Alexander was the great measuring rod against whom the Roman Caesars were evaluated. The ambitious Trajan, for example, undertook military expeditions in emulation of Alexander, whose praise, as Edward Gibbon has it, was 'transmitted by a succession of poets and historians' and 'had kindled a dangerous exaltation in the mind of Trajan' (Gibbon 1960: 8; Gibbon, of course, had his own preoccupations around Homeric/Alexandrian ideas of greatness). Through the Middle Ages, histories and legends of Alexander proliferated: along with King Arthur he was celebrated in the troubadours' songs of courtly love in the twelfth century. He was invoked in the fourteenth century by writers as various as Marguerite of Porete in her mystical treatise *The Mirror of Simple Souls* (1993: 80) and Chaucer in the Monk's Tale of the *Canterbury Tales*, who says of Alexander:

> Even now no comparison can be made
> With him and any other conqueror;
> Before him the whole world once quaked with dread.
>   (Chaucer 1998: 214)

(For the popularity of Alexander in the Middle Ages, see Ross 1956.)

But it was with the revival of classical humanism in the west that Alexander and his Homeric prototype were again studied in detail. Northern humanists like Erasmus, Budé, Colet and Thomas More used Alexander (in a sanitized, legendary form drawn largely from Plutarch) as an exemplar of an ideal prince (Skinner 1978: I: 228–34). Francis Bacon drew on Plutarch's examples; Shakespeare lifted chunks from an English translation for his Roman plays; Goethe and Schiller avidly read Homer, Plutarch, and all things Greek in their efforts towards German nationalism, as we have seen. The ideals of mastery and conquest, of manliness as consisting of courage and violence, thus were reinscribed ever and again in the symbolic of western modernity, with Alexander serving as an exemplar of an ideal heroic prince.

Yet Alexander posed some problems for the humanists, since they could not overlook the fact that, ideal though he was, he was hardly a Christian. Some of the humanists, moreover, abhorred warfare and gratuitous violence. Nevertheless, they continued to admire him, and managed to preserve their regard for him by selective interpretation. Scholars like Budé and Erasmus made much of the fact that Alexander was taught by Aristotle and knew his Homer. This for them was the civilizing influence, and shows, according to Budé, 'the honour and great glory which arise out of a study of good letters' (cited in Skinner 1978: I: 243). Francis Bacon, in his enormously influential *Advancement of Learning* a century later, similarly exalts Alexander, 'of whose virtues and acts of war there needs no note or recital, having been the wonders of time in that kind;' and proceeds to attribute much of his greatness to the high esteem for Homer which Aristotle had taught him (Bacon 1973: 48). Montaigne, continuing the humanist tradition in sixteenth-century France, returns frequently to the theme of Alexander and his greatness. For Montaigne, only Christ himself was greater than Alexander: the latter was 'the greatest man who was simply man' and not God incarnate; and he is, like Christ, 'our example' of how to live and die (Montaigne 1991: 93–4). Moreover while Montaigne admires his learning, it is precisely his courage and willingness to venture all that Montaigne finds exemplary: Alexander is 'the supreme model of daring deeds'; there is in his heroism 'a beauty shimmering with lustre' (145). Indeed, Montaigne sees that it is because of his love for Homer and emulation of Achilles that Alexander was heroic. When Montaigne retells the story of Alexander choosing to keep the *Iliad* in the treasure chest that had been plundered from the Persian king, he asserts that finding a cultured man without Homer 'would be like finding one of our priests with no breviary' (852) – the *Iliad* has become a holy book which gives access to the divine; and it is worthy to be stored in a precious casket like a reliquary. But surely it is high time to ask: worship of what God of gendered violence and death is inculcated by such veneration?

Yet the ambivalence of the humanists to Alexander's violence returns. They were aware of Augustine's censure (drawn from Cicero) which in its context renders Alexander and his armies a 'gang of criminals on a large scale':

> For it was a witty and truthful rejoinder which was given by a captured pirate to Alexander the Great. The king asked the fellow, 'What is your idea, in infesting the sea?' And the pirate answered, with uninhibited insolence, 'The same as yours, in infesting the earth! But because I do it with a tiny craft, I'm called a pirate: because you have a mighty navy, you're called an emperor'.
>
> (Augustine 1972: 139)

Thus for all that Erasmus held up Alexander as a model prince civilized by Homer through Aristotle and lacking only christendom to be ideal, Erasmus could also be critical of his ambition to rule the world. Erasmus continues the parallel between Alexander and Julius Caesar that Plutarch had begun, but with a different emphasis: What did they not endure, he asks, in order to rule the world?

> He [Alexander] obtained it, but his soul found no rest there; he yielded before the worries and the consciousness of his crimes, because of the pressure of his mind, and sought death because of his dissatisfaction with life, a death he did not expect.
>
> (Erasmus 1964: 356)

There is a striking difference in this Erasmian characterization of death as the end of disillusioned life from that of the portrayal of the heroic warrior finding excellence in slaughter: I shall discuss in a later volume what happens to the configuration of death when it is held that the vanity of this world is revealed by the realization that there are other worlds to conquer and that the crimes of this life will impact upon that one. For the present, it is significant to note that, critical as Erasmus is of Alexander's crimes, he nonetheless continues to valorize him. He was effective. He conquered. Thus Hellenistic civilization, which Erasmus so much admires, was spread.

The same ambivalence can be found in acute form in Montaigne's essay 'On the most excellent of men': this time he places Homer first and Alexander immediately after. Montaigne begins in adulatory mode, but gradually history intrudes on hagiography and his praise becomes increasingly anxious:

> for his character seems to have justly been beyond reproach, though not some of his rarer, untypical isolated actions . . . his destruction of Thebes and the murders . . . of so many Persian prisoners in one stroke, of a troop of Indian soldiers (not without impugning his pledged word), of the Cosseians, including their children, are ecstasies a little hard to excuse.
>
> (Montaigne 1991: 854)

Montaigne squirms his way through, interpolating general high-flown praise of Alexander's virtue, glory and excellence with specific instances of cruelty, duplicity, and violence which utterly destabilize the claim to greatness of character. Montaigne's ambivalence shows through even in the structure of his prose. A single sentence goes on for nearly two pages, with a clause on Alexander's virtues followed by a recognition of his vices in convoluted succession. In the end Montaigne says of his flaws, 'well, that kind of thing seems pardonable to me in a man of his age and his strangely prosperous Fortune' and will be 'excused' by any who 'reflect on his many military virtues' (854). What it comes down to is that Alexander is admired because he won. It is success that reveals heroism: glory lies in conquest.

Many more examples of Alexander's grip on the western symbolic could be given: there are poems by authors from Chaucer to Dryden, operas like Handel's 'Alexander's Feast', military histories that laud his exploits. Each decade sees another biography of Alexander; every schoolchild learns of Alexander sighing for new worlds to conquer. And with each valorization of Alexander, the Homeric ideals of heroic manliness are also lifted up, and the beauty of an early death. Thus from its archaic past, the western symbolic is saturated with an idea of death, glorious death in manly bravery, before age has made the body ugly. Death preserves and displaces beauty.

In the remaining chapters of this book and in the volumes that follow, I shall explore many changes in the genealogy of death and its relation to beauty. Yet for all the changes, in some respects western culture retains the Homeric ideal of the beauty of an early, heroic death, violence as a basis for eternity. Every year on Remembrance Sunday in a solemn service at the Cenotaph in London the words of a poem by Laurence Binyon are solemnly intoned:

> They went with songs to the battle, they were young,
> Straight of limb, true of eye, steady and aglow . . .
>
> They shall not grow old, as we that are left grow old:
> Age shall not weary them, nor the years condemn.
> At the going down of the sun and in the morning
> We will remember them.
>
> (1972: 831–2)

One can almost hear Achilles applaud.

Chapter 6

Odysseus on the barren sea

Sing to me of the man, Muse, the man of twists and turns
driven time and again off course,
once he had plundered the hallowed heights of Troy.

(77)[1]

The man is Odysseus; the Muse is the same goddess who was invoked at the beginning of the *Iliad*. In the *Odyssey*, the same goddess who inspired the bard to sing of rage and battle and beautiful death is now asked to inspire the tale of the homecoming of Odysseus, one of the Achaean warriors who survived victorious at the fall of Troy. But will the song have the same tune?

Odysseus is the hero of the *Odyssey* as Achilles is of the *Iliad*; but he has a very different character. Whereas Achilles relied on his rage and violent courage, Odysseus is a wily strategist who makes his way as much by wit as by force. Just as the Achaeans had already fought for ten years against Troy when the *Iliad* begins, so in the *Odyssey* Odysseus and his companions have been journeying for ten years trying to get home. And just as in the *Iliad* the gods and goddesses intervene in the course of events, so in the *Odyssey* their anger impedes Odysseus and makes him lose his way on the sea. It is the intervention of Athena that eventually secures his successful return to his wife Penelope and his son Telemachus, just as Athena had intervened to ensure the defeat of Hector and the fall of Troy.

In spite of these parallels, however, the *Odyssey* portrays death and its relation to beauty and gender in different and more complex ways than we find in the *Iliad*. In this chapter I shall discuss some of these complexities. I shall reconsider the relationship between excellence (*areté*) and death, and examine how the *Odyssey* configures the gender of death and its relationship to beauty at a somewhat different point of tension between violence and eternity. I shall look for hints and repressed promises that destablize the *Odyssey*'s gendered narrative of death, the life-affirming alterities hidden in the masculinist text which invite us to think – and live – otherwise. I shall conclude this chapter as I did the previous one with a sketch of some of the ways in which the gendered configurations of the *Odyssey* have shaped western modernity, when even ventures to outer galaxies are called 'Space Odysseys'.

What is excellence?

Odysseus' journey was not to outer space but across the seas from Troy to his home in Ithaca. Odysseus and his men proved their valour in the battle against Troy, but they lived to return. They did not, therefore, achieve the glorious immortality of death in battle, eternity bought by violence. The *Odyssey* tells of another kind of excellence, an excellence that also involves flirting with death, but death through the dangers of the sea rather than in warfare. In this way also immortality can be won – at least by Odysseus himself. His undifferentiated men die in various gruesome ways and are not remembered by name, even in the poem.

Early in the *Odyssey* excellence, *areté*, is portrayed just as it was in the *Iliad*. Telemachus, Odysseus' son, is grieving at his father's long absence, not knowing what has become of him. His grief is as much about the absence of fame as it is about his father's disappearance:

> I would never have grieved so much about his death
> if he'd gone down with comrades off in Troy
> or died in the arms of loved ones,
> once he had wound down the long coil of war.
> Then all united Achaea would have raised his tomb
> and he'd have won his son great fame for years to come.
> But now the whirlwinds have ripped him away, no fame for him!
> He's lost and gone now – out of sight, out of mind – and I . . .
> he's left me tears and grief.
>
> (85)

The fame of the bard's song, and the enduring grave monument: these are the elements of immortality that Telemachus craves for his father.

But as the Odyssey goes on, although immortality is still obtained through the excellence of heroic deeds, the idea of what these deeds consist in is gradually widened. Odysseus confronts the challenges of the sea itself, its storms and calms, the winds of Zeus blowing him off course, 'a howling, demonic gale, shrouding over in thunderheads the earth and sea at once' (213). Shipwrecked, and 'cringing at death', Odysseus and his men heroically refuse to give way. With dogged perseverance they struggle on, mastering the elements. When at last Odysseus reaches land at Phaeacia and is welcomed to the court of King Alcinous his bravery at sea becomes part of his song of heroic excellence as significant as was his part in the victory over Troy.

So also do his encounters with various dangerous creatures of the sea: the Lotus-Eaters, Polyphemous, the Sirens, Circe, Scylla and Charybdis. We shall see a little later how dangers represent death, and how Odysseus' triumph is configured as immortality. Here I want simply to make the point that heroic excellence is construed in terms of victory not just in warfare, but also over these creatures, sometimes through violence, but also sometimes through cunning and cleverness and Odysseus' sheer determination to return home. Mastering the elements, mastering the creatures of the sea and its islands, mastering also himself and the temptations placed in his way, Odysseus achieves heroism that reveals his excellence and is worthy of poetic fame just as surely as is excellence in battle and heroic death. The point of tension between violence and eternity has shifted slightly.

A telling example is Odysseus' encounter with the goddess Calypso, who has detained him on her island and taken him for her lover. With her, Odysseus has every good thing. Calypso offers him the opportunity to remain with her and 'preside in our house.' She gives him the amazing offer to make him immortal like herself, 'ageless, all his days', if only he will stay and give up his desire to return home (156). But Odysseus refuses. The immortality Calypso offers, though it is indeed the everlasting life of the Olympians, is not the immortality of imperishable glory sung by the poets. If Odysseus stays with Calypso he himself will live forever; but nobody will hear of him, no bard will tell of his exploits. This is too high a price to pay, even for everlasting life.

Immortality without fame is unworthy; indeed it is presented in the *Odyssey* as temptation. In this respect it is very like the temptation Achilles faces in the *Iliad* when he has a choice either to go home and have a long but unheroic life or to stay and fight and die a glorious death. Only this time it is the determination to go home that is heroic; by contrast, choosing Calypso's offer of immortality would forfeit glory. Seth Schein, commenting on Odysseus' refusal of Calypso's offer, points out the importance of the parallel with Achilles in the *Iliad*:

> In effect he [Odysseus] chooses to be remembered as the hero of the *Odyssey* over the oblivion among mortals that would accompany his existence as Calypso's husband. The choice is every bit as significant as Achilles' decision to die at Troy and achieve 'imperishable glory' rather than return home to a long life with no glory. In each epic the hero chooses, in a different way, to be a hero, and so chooses life (in heroic song) over death (through being forgotten).
>
> (Schein 1995: 20)

Yet the irony is that this is also a reversal of what is actual life and death. The immortality Calypso offers is 'ageless'; Odysseus chooses instead a life which will bring on the indignities of old age rather than preserve the youthful beauty prized by the Greeks. Moreover the 'life' in heroic song which both Achilles and Odysseus choose is actually physical death, mortality; while the 'death' of being unremembered is actually a long life of physical ease. 'That is, by choosing death . . . you choose life . . . and by choosing immortality . . . you end up choosing death' (Doniger 1999: 200). The very act of choosing death rather than life is presented as excellence, since only death can bring immortal glory through the poet's song. In the *Iliad* such a choice was always in the context of violence and battle; while here in the *Odyssey* the range of heroic deeds extends to other ways of choosing life and death and glory. It is a first clue to a shift in the configuration of death.

Moreover there is a greater recognition in the *Odyssey* than in the *Iliad* that women, too, are capable of excellence (*areté*). While Odysseus masters the elements and the creatures of the sea through courage and cunning, his wife Penelope is using her wits at home to fend off a crowd of suitors. The excellence she achieves thereby is, to be sure, ambiguous, dependent in large measure upon her conformity to male expectations derived from her identity as the sexual possession of Odysseus. The double standard is glaring. Penelope is expected to be chaste in spite of Odysseus' twenty-year absence, while it is taken for granted that Odysseus will take sexual pleasure with whatever women or goddesses are available to him. Penelope, moreover, is expected to be obedient to male commands, including those of her son Telemachus, and to do traditional women's work.

All of this notwithstanding, Penelope also can gain excellence, and can gain it precisely by being clever, determined and skilful. Now, these are the very terms by which her husband's excellence also is achieved in the *Odyssey*. Penelope evades the suitors who press her to marry one of them by postponing the choice until she has finished her weaving project; meanwhile she unravels by night what she had woven by day. Thus her faithfulness to Odysseus is translated into clever strategies; and the excellence of her doings is such that she also will be accorded the immortality of fame usually reserved to men. In the final book of the *Odyssey* the ghost of Agamemnon praises Penelope in an address to Odysseus:

> What good sense resided in your Penelope –
> how well Icarius' daughter remembered you,
> Odysseus, the man she married once!
> The fame of her great virtue will never die.
> The immortal gods will lift a song for all mankind,
> a glorious song in praise of self-possessed Penelope.
>   (474)

Penelope is honoured for her prudence and constancy. There is in the representation of Penelope a subversion of the notion that imperishable glory is for men only; and that it can be attained only through violence, whether by flirting with death in battle or on the high seas. Penelope demonstrates that it can be obtained also by a woman's 'mental toughness and faithfulness' (Schein 1995: 23), in ways that partly reinforce but also partly go beyond stereotypes of female sexuality and women's work. I shall return to this.

The ghost of Achilles

The genealogy of death in the *Odyssey* is moved onward in other ways besides the widening of what counts as excellence. Although there are passages in which the glory of youthful death in heroic battle is assumed, there are other passages which call that assumption into question. One such passage is the account of Odysseus' meeting with Achilles' ghost. Odysseus, in quest of the fame that will make him the immortal subject of heroic song, is sent on a visit to the underworld to speak with the dead. There in Hades Odysseus meets the ghost of Achilles who had been killed in the battle for Troy. Odysseus discovers that Achilles has been made king of the underworld just as he had been a master and leader of men during his life. Odysseus seems at first to suggest that Achilles' lot is not too bad. He says,

> But you, Achilles,
> there's not a man in the world more blest than you –
> there never has been, never will be one.
> Time was, when you were alive, we Argives
> honoured you as a god, and now down here, I see,
> you lord it over the dead in all your power.
> So grieve no more at dying, great Achilles.
>
> (265)

But Achilles will have none of Odysseus' consolation. It would be preferable, he insists, to be a poor hungry slave in the living world than to reign as a king among the dead. He protests,

> No winning words about death to *me*, shining Odysseus!
> By god, I'd rather slave on earth for another man –
> some dirt-poor tenant farmer who scrapes to keep alive –
> than rule down here over all the breathless dead.

Achilles seems to have forgotten all about the immortality of glorious fame. He draws no comfort from the honour he receives among humankind for his heroism on the battlefield. Almost, one might think, Achilles regrets the decision he made at Troy. Nor is there any indication at this point in the text that Achilles' lament is puzzling. It is full of the pathos of one who finds, too late, that any human condition, even slavery, would be preferable to death. When Odysseus talks with the ghosts of the other dead warriors, they echo Achilles' sadness. All of them deplore their state, even though their glorious death has ensured them the immortality of the bard's songs. The assumptions of the *Iliad* are seriously undermined.

But then they are reinforced again, though with the additional twist that heroism can come not only on the battlefield but also in other forms of mastery. Indeed in this passage Odysseus is shown to be the master even of death and the underworld, venturing into its interior and emerging alive, unlike any other mortal. One of Odysseus' encounters in the underworld is with his deceased mother, Anticleia. He longs to embrace her.

Three times I rushed toward her, desperate to hold her,
three times she fluttered through my fingers, sifting away
like a shadow, dissolving like a dream, and each time
the grief cut to the heart, sharper.

(256)

Odysseus pleads with her; asks why she will not accept his love. Anticleia answers that what is happening is not rejection; rather, the state in which the dead find themselves makes embrace impossible:

this is just the way of mortals when we die.
Sinews no longer bind the flesh and bones together –
the fire in all its fury burns the body down to ashes
once life slips from the white bones, and the spirit,
rustling, flitters away . . . flown like a dream.

Although Anticleia presents this as the state of all the dead regardless of gender, it is surely no accident that the explanation occurs in the context of the encounter of a male hero and his mother. In the thwarted embrace is a foreshadowing of the linkage of the woman/mother with the (now dissolved) body and death, the womb and the tomb, the place of birth and death. As Page du Bois has explained,

Traditionally, the invisible world of the Earth that lies beneath the surface of the earth, in the space of burial, was associated with the mother, the woman's body. As a vessel, a container, a body filled with an interiority itself full of potential for holding, for entreasuring or warming, the woman's body was seen as analogous to the earth, with its caves and cuirasses, openings into an invisible world from which the living emerged, into which the dead departed.

(du Bois 1991: 78)

Odysseus is not defeated by his journey into the underworld. He cannot be held by his mother's embrace, even though he desires it. He emerges from Hades victorious, reborn. He comes forth as none other has out of the land of death: when he emerges he and his crew are hailed by the goddess Circe:

Ah, my daring, reckless friends!
You who ventured down to the House of Death alive,
doomed to die twice over – others die just once.

(272)

Again, his immortal fame is secured by flirting with death; but it is not the death of the battlefield. It is Hades itself, and his mother's arms.

Death, the interior space of the earth, place of burial, of the interiority of the
female body, the goddess earth whom the Greeks called 'mother of all',
represent darkness and oblivion . . . [Hades'] place is that of the unseen and
the unseeable, like the inside of the earth, like the inside of the body,
especially the mysterious cavities of the female body.

(du Bois 1991: 81)

It is this space of death which Odysseus must master and from which he must
come forth victorious. He conquers the female body and its cavities and emerges
reborn from the mother who cannot hold him. By this he is prepared for the
rest of his impending voyage and its dangers. By victory, his immortal glory is
assured.

Only the ghost of Achilles sounds a discordant note. But who would listen to
a ghost?

The gender of death

Who would listen to a ghost? Perhaps only cowards and women; and in the
Homeric writings a hero worthy of immortal fame must overcome both. Only
Penelope is an exception; and even her excellence is construed in relation to
that of her husband and son. If we read the central texts of archaic Greece with
the question of the gender of death in mind, it becomes clear not only that the
configuration of death changes, but also that each of the changes is related to
gender. While 'beautiful death' is the prerogative of men, its sad realities are
associated with women: women are the ones who do the work of laying out the
dead and are involved in ritual mourning. Most importantly, death is in some sense
women's fault.

In the *Iliad* this is overt. The immortality that can be won by heroic deeds
is immortality for men only, men who march off to battle and excel in violence.
And the *cause* of all the fighting is a woman, the beautiful Helen. Her beauty is
the death-trap of sexual attraction, represented as the precipitating cause of the
war. It is taken for granted by both sides in the battle that Helen is to be possessed
by males; the question is only which set of males will have her. The same is true
of the girl Briseis over whom Achilles and Agamemnon quarrel: no one asks her
whom she would prefer. Without her wishing to be, she is the cause of the deaths
of many heroes.

Homer is not alone in attributing the cause of death to women. In *Works and
Days*, Hesiod, writing in about the eighth century BCE, tells of the creation of
Pandora and her box, who was sent to live among men in punishment for
Prometheus having brought them the gift of fire. The woman was made beautiful
as 'an immortal goddess', a 'lovely figure of a virgin girl'; but into her were placed
'sly manners and the morals of a bitch'. She was then presented to the race of men
who lived in an idyllic (and single-gendered) Golden Age.

Before this time men lived upon the earth
Apart from sorrow and from painful work,
Free from disease, which brings the Death-gods in.
But now the woman opened up the cask,
And scattered pains and evils among men.

(Hesiod 1973: 61)

There is slippage in the text between Pandora and the cask that she brings. Sometimes it seems that it is the cask which holds rancour and disease and death; sometimes on the other hand it seems that these are in Pandora herself. Indeed in some sense Pandora is the cask, just as she is all women – the beautiful, enticing, death-bearing virgin, who, once she is 'opened', brings death and disease to men. She is 'this ruin of mankind' (82). 'When women did not yet exist – before Pandora was created – death did not exist either. . . . Death and women arose in concert together' (Vernant 1991: 98).

When we come to the *Odyssey*, it initially appears less misogynist. It is not about violent men fighting over sexual possession of women, like the *Iliad*, but rather about Odysseus' struggles to return to his faithful wife Penelope, who is portrayed as the complete opposite of Pandora. But when we look more closely, we find in the *Odyssey* more subtle misogyny which strongly genders death as female and the hero who attains immortality as male. On the face of it Odysseus is a hero because by a mixture of courage, craft and the help of the gods he survives his adventures at sea and gets back home to Ithaca. But two things must be noted. First, in the *Odyssey* the sea is symbolic of death, the extreme limit against which finitude is tested. Second, the sea is gendered female. It is worth looking at each of these in a little more detail.

First, then, the sea in the *Odyssey* (and elsewhere in the writings of ancient Greece) is associated with danger and death. It is presented as a limit of finitude, much as violence and battle are presented in the *Iliad*. The hero must master it: conquer or die. At one point, Odysseus is shipwrecked and thrown into heavy surf, 'roaring breakers crashing down on an ironbound coast' (165). Odysseus is in despair. He can find 'no spot to stand on my own two legs and battle free of death'. But just as in the *Iliad* the battles which were fought by men were also on another level arguments among the gods and goddesses, so in the *Odyssey* Poseidon and Athena struggle over whether Odysseus shall live or die. Athena wins. And in Odysseus' desperation, just in time, Athena the 'bright-eyed one' comes to his aid.

He lunged for a reef, he seized it with both hands and clung
for dear life, groaning until the giant wave surged past
and so escaped its force, but the breaker's backwash
charged into him full fury and hurled him out to sea . . .
A heavy sea covered him over, then and there
unlucky Odysseus would have met his death –

against the will of Fate –
but the bright-eyed one inspired him yet again.
(165–6)

Thus Odysseus is saved to continue his journey, mastering the waves with the aid of the immortals. 'Shipwrecks, routes, points of arrival, traversing a "newness" that offers itself over and over as an occasion of death' (Cavarero 1995: 21) – all this is necessary to establish his heroism. It is precisely because of the deadly possibilities of the sea that overcoming it is worthy of bardic celebration. Unless the sea was as dangerous a place as the battlefield there would be nothing to sing about when it is vanquished.

Second, this deadly sea which the hero must overcome is gendered female. This is so first of all at the simple grammatical level. The Greek word for 'sea' is *thalassa*, and takes the feminine article. In the Homeric writings the femaleness of the sea is often further specified by ascribing to it adjectives relating to female reproduction, most frequently 'barren', salt rather than fresh water. 'The barren sea', the sea whose womb/tomb is voracious, who does not bring forth life, but rather threatens death, is so recurrent a strain in the *Odyssey* that by sheer frequency of use one can miss its fomulaic significance. It is the 'deadly gulf of the barren salt swells' (194); the 'barren sea' across which Odysseus gazes from Calypso's island (155): the formula is repeated on page after page.

Moreover, it is precisely in the liquidity of the sea, a liquidity associated with femaleness, that its deadly danger consists. Jean-Pierre Vernant has shown how, in archaic Greek writing, fluid is a mark of gender. In a man, the humid element is construed as his vital force, his reserve of energy. That humid vitality can drain away in tears, or in the sweat of exertion (as in battle), leaving a man exhausted. In death it dries up completely. Love is like death for a man. As long as he retains his semen he remains hard, vital, full of the energy of desire; but when he ejaculates he loses his liquid force and is depleted and limp. And it is the woman and her liquidity – the moisture of her gaze, her soft sexual allure – that draws this from him. But there is a gender difference in the fluidity of sex. In love-making, 'a man dries up, losing his freshness and his juices while the woman, all liquidity, flows all the more. . . . Femininity acts like death' (Vernant 1991: 101). Vernant does not make the further association to the danger of the (female) sea in the *Odyssey*, but the implication is clear. The sea is an 'unreliable liquid element'; its waves are 'voracious' (Cavarero 1995: 21); it is enticing and treacherous. It behaves, in short, like the stereotype of an insatiable woman who threatens to exhaust a man utterly, even to his death. Heroic mastery of the sea, riding upon the sea and flirting with the death she threatens but emerging unscathed, is metonymically also mastery of the female. It is an ominous development in the genealogy of death; its repercussions reverberate down the centuries.

In the linkage of the sea with death and with the female, it is significant that the temptations, pleasures and dangers which Odysseus encounters on his journeyings across this barren sea are for the most part figured female, and their danger often lies in their sexual enticement. I have already discussed Calypso, who dwells on 'a wave-washed island rising at the centre of the seas' (79): in Greek the island is the 'navel' of all the waters. Calypso, as we saw, offers Odysseus immortality if he would remain with her and be her lover; but the immortality is a living death. As long as he is with her, his liquid forces drain away at night in forced lovemaking, and during the day in tears, as Odysseus sits

> on a headland, weeping there as always,
> wrenching his heart with sobs and groans and anguish,
> gazing out over the barren sea through blinding tears.
>
> (155)

Calypso's island is called Ogygia; it has been argued that Ogygia is, symbolically, a Land of the Dead and that Calypso is a goddess of death; thus her offer of immortality is the making of Ogygia into 'an Eden of Hell' (Porter 1962: 1–20, citing Güntert 1919), a trap in the all-encompassing liquidity of the sea.

Even more deadly than Calypso is the bewitching nymph Circe. She also lives on an island; and when Odysseus and his crew make landfall upon it and he sends a platoon to scout the island Circe gives them a warm welcome to her house. But into the wine that she offers them she mixes a potion which turns them into pigs.

> Once they'd drained the bowls she filled, suddenly
> she struck with her wand, drove them into her pigsties,
> all of them bristling into swine – with grunts,
> snouts, even their bodies, yes and only
> the men's minds stayed as steadfast as before.
> So off they went into their pens, sobbing, squealing
> as Circe flung them acorns, cornel nuts and mast,
> common fodder for hogs that root and roll in the mud.
>
> (237–8)

Odysseus, going to find out what has happened to his men, narrowly escapes the same fate. He is saved only by the intervention of the god Hermes, who gives him a counter-potion. When Circe gives Odysseus her magic brew, it does not work. Instead, Odysseus recounts,

> I drew my sharp sword sheathed at my hip
> and rushed her fast as if to run her through.
>
> (240)

As this incident is portrayed in a Greek black vase painting, the movements are vividly sexual. The naked pig/crewman reaches forward with the same thrust as Odysseus' sword; Circe, even while fleeing, reaches backward with an enticing gesture. And indeed Circe immediately invites/commands Odysseus to her bed. The only way he can rescue his men and enlist her help for his onward journey is by refusing to make love to her until she swears a binding oath to set them free. Even when she has done so, he is detained by her for a year of ease and feasting and love-making in 'that luxurious bed of Circe's' (245); and when at last the Greeks are allowed to depart it is only on condition that they sail not for their home in Ithaca but for Hades, the Underworld: we have already seen his encounter there with his mother.

Perhaps the most seductive of all the female figures of Odysseus' voyages are the Sirens, enchanters of men, 'creatures who spellbind any man alive, whoever comes their way' (272). They lure men to them by their sweet singing. They sit in a meadow (which in Greek thought symbolizes female sexuality); but although it seems alluring, actually they have around them 'heaps of corpses rotting away, rags of skin shrivelling on their bones' (273). Again, what Odysseus has to do is not just escape from them but master them. By his cunning (and the advice of a goddess) Odysseus manages to hear their singing and still come away unscathed, thus getting the better of them. He has himself tied to the mast of his ship, puts beeswax into his crewmen's ears so that they cannot hear the singing, and gives them orders to row past the Siren's island and not to heed his desire to be released until they are safely past. Like the other island goddesses, the Sirens are female figures of the sea, sources of danger and death precisely because of their female sexuality. The sea is 'a realm in which . . . the unruliness of women seems to stand for the challenges of the sea itself, the element with which Odysseus must contend and over which he must achieve mastery' (Murnaghan 1995: 65).

Another way in which the sexual danger of the deadly female sea monster/goddess is represented is in terms of being swallowed up (as the sea itself would do), eaten alive: it is a thin disguise of the recurrent male fear of a voracious womb. Most terrifying of these goddesses are the twin monsters Scylla and Charybdis. Scylla is 'a grisly monster' whose body from the waist down is a hollow cavern, a figure of a terrifying and all-consuming womb.

> She has twelve legs, all writhing, dangling down
> and six long swaying necks, a hideous head on each,
> each head barbed with a triple row of fangs, thickset,
> packed tight – and armed to the hilt with black death!
> She shoots out her heads, out of that terrifying pit –

and snatches passing sailors whom she gobbles up alive like little fishes writhing in her mouth (274). Scylla is a nightmare rendition of the 'vagina dentata', the devouring womb that has haunted men in western culture.

No less terrible is her opposite, the monster Charybdis, who sucks the sea water into herself, creating the whirlpool beside her crag. The goddess warns Odysseus about Charybdis:

> Three times a day she vomits it up, three times she gulps it down,
> that terror! Don't be there when the whirlpool swallows down –
>
> (274)

Charybdis is another devouring female of the sea, in turn sucking and vomiting until the whole sea is boiling turbulence.

All these deadly female monsters of the sea must be overcome by Odysseus, the normative male, the mortal hero. As Seth Schein summed it up in his study of gender in the *Odyssey*:

> These females, to hear Odysseus tell of them, are often monstrous, and their menace is literally or symbolically sexual – specific instances of the general danger of being swallowed, engulfed, concealed or obliterated, against which he constantly struggles. In this respect they are vividly imagined versions of the sea itself in which Odysseus is lost, through which he struggles to return home.
>
> (Schein 1995: 19)

The immortality of glorious fame which in the *Iliad* was achieved through heroic death on the battlefield is won in the *Odyssey* through overcoming the barren sea, mastering her deadly and often sexually demanding creatures with heroic manliness. The violence is less overt. Is it less misogynistic?

What happened to beauty?

The changes between the *Iliad* and the *Odyssey* in the configuration of death are paralleled by changes in the configuration of beauty, which becomes more complex, especially in relation to gender. This is not to say that the paradigm of heroic beauty, the dead young warrior, is rejected. On the contrary, it is assumed throughout the *Odyssey* that heroic manliness is as near to the beauty of the immortal 'shining ones' as is possible for mortals. But just as the excellence that would merit a place in the bards' songs is widened to include heroic mastery in other contexts than the field of slaughter, so these heroes also are beautiful with a beauty that relates them to the gods.

Young Telemachus, growing up to be a hero worthy of his absent father Odysseus, journeys to the house of Nestor to see whether the old man knows anything about what might have happened to his father after the defeat of Troy. Through the course of his journey, and listening to Nestor's reminiscences of the Trojan war, Telemachus gains in maturity. In the ritual of his departure, he is given a bath by Nestor's youngest daughter.

> Rinsing him off now, rubbing him down with oil,
> she drew a shirt and handsome cape around him.
> Out of his bath he stepped, glistening like a god.
>
> (122)

And from that point onwards his beauty is a mark of his heroic valour that by the end of the *Odyssey* will join him with his newly returned father to defeat the suitors that have been plaguing their household.

Beauty, similarly, is given to Odysseus – no longer youthful – when he at last returns to Ithaca. But to make the point more sharply, Odysseus is first deliberately made ugly by Athena, so that he will be unrecognizable to the suitors who clog his palace vying for his wife. This ugliness gives him an opportunity to assess the situation and plan his course of action. The ruse works. Odysseus gets the measure of the suitors and kills them in a bloody battle. Victorious, he is given a bath by his old nurse, in a passage echoing the bath of Telemachus:

> The maid Eurynome bathed him, rubbed him down with oil
> and drew around him a royal cape and choice tunic too.
> And Athena crowned the man with beauty, head to foot,
> made him taller to all eyes, his build more massive,
> yes, and down from his brow the great goddess
> ran his curls like thick hyacinth clusters
> full of blooms. As a master craftsman washes
> gold over beaten silver . . .
> so she lavished splendour over his head and shoulders now.
> He stepped from his bath, glistening like a god.
>
> (460)

just as his son Telemachus had done. Heroism is rewarded by the immortals with beauty like their own. Such heroism is attained only by courageous encounter with death, this time in the slaughter of the importuning suitors, but also in the mastery of the barren sea.

While the category of manly beauty is widened with the category of heroism in the *Odyssey*, a change is also happening to the configuration of female beauty. This change, however, is altogether more sinister. In some passages, female beauty continues to be described in the terms conventional in the *Iliad*. Just as in the *Iliad* Helen is described as the most beautiful of women, so in the *Odyssey* her daughter is

> the breath-taking Hermione,
> a luminous beauty gold as Aphrodite.
>
> (125)

Similarly Nausicaa, the young daughter of the king and queen of Phaecia whose court Odysseus visits on his journeys, is described as 'a match for deathless gods in build and beauty' (169).

However, as early as Odysseus' encounter with Calypso there is an indication that something different is going on. While Calypso is trying to persuade Odysseus to stay with her and accept her gift of immortality, she points out sharply that she is surely more beautiful than Penelope who awaits her husband at home:

I just might claim to be nothing less than she,
neither in face nor figure. Hardly right, is it,
for mortal women to rival immortal goddess?
How, in build? in beauty?

(159)

Odysseus immediately concedes the point. Penelope, he says,

falls far short of you,
your beauty, stature. She is mortal after all
and you, you never age or die.

The point is that in this passage beauty – female beauty – is construed as a danger, a temptation which the female uses to tempt the male off his course. Just as Calypso's island is an island of death and the immortality she offers is a living death, so female beauty is linked with death. But this is a very different linkage of beauty and death than the beautiful death on the battlefield. Whereas that was to be welcomed as a basis for the immortality of song and monument, this would be the death of oblivion, the dreaded, unremembered death. It is this oblivion, this death, to which female beauty can entice. Beauty is the allure of female sexuality, a deadly beauty fraught with danger.

The deadly beauty of Calypso foreshadows that of the other female figures of the sea whom I have already discussed. Circe, who turned Odysseus' crewmen into pigs, is described as 'the nymph with lovely braids', singing with beautiful voice and weaving a web on her loom of 'shimmering glory' (237). The Sirens, too, are seductive, singing their enchantment that makes men reckless with desire. All these creatures of the sea develop the association between death and female sexuality; what I am emphasizing here is that this association comes precisely by a reconfiguration of beauty. Already in the *Iliad* Helen's beauty precipitated the Trojan War and all its slaughter. But there the battle was represented as glorious, heroic. By contrast, the beauty of the female figures of the sea is dangerous, a deceptive enticement that lures men to a death that is horrible and unheroic.

In the dreadful monstrosity of Scylla and Charybdis the deception is revealed. Here the female face is repulsive, terrifying with a terror of voracious, all-consuming sexuality. In Greek mythology this is the face of the Gorgon, whose gaze means death. Just a glance from the Gorgon turns a man to stone, all his liquid frozen. Her slavering tongue and sharp teeth, her eyes, one wide and staring, the other closed in cunning, all bespeak an urgency to devour her hapless victim. In the *Odyssey* all the female figures of the sea culminate in Scylla and Charybdis, Gorgon-like in their terrifying features. The beauty and erotic attraction of the nymphs and goddesses are collapsed into a hideous nightmare. Female beauty, though sometimes alluring, is in reality savage and murderous, seducing men to hideous and nameless death. The hero must resist and master such seduction, not by denying his own sexual desires (Odysseus takes sexual pleasure with some of

these female creatures) but by doing so on his own terms, never allowing himself
to be emotionally bound to them. He must above all never give way to the fatal
beauty that would turn him to liquid or to stone, unremembered.

But if the erotic is deadly, death is eroticized. In the *Iliad* the attraction of death
is focused on the youthful hero, whose beautiful death preserves him forever
in memory. In the *Odyssey* also, heroism, and with it immortality, is available only
to those who flirt with death: we should not forget that although Odysseus
eventually leaves both Calypso and Circe, he does not do so until he has spent
many nights in the arms of these goddesses of death. The willingness to be half
in love with death, to eroticize death and make it an object of desire to be taken
on the hero's own terms, is portrayed differently in the two Homeric books; but
in both of them, death is central. As Adriana Cavarero has observed of the
Homeric writings:

> Death defines its dominion in the wars, the sorrows and the fury of heroes.
> It is always present insofar as it is always challenged, functioning as a measure
> of the challenger's excellence. In the Homeric world of mortals, only legend
> can win over finitude and save humans for eternity, but only the challenge of
> this finitude can become legend.
>
> (Cavarero 1995: 26)

Thus death, desire and gender are woven together in these early texts whose
preoccupations with violence and eternity have formed western culture. Death's
presence is a necessary condition for excellence; the mark of a hero is its mastery.

Weaving subversion

But there is another kind of weaving going on in the *Odyssey*, a weaving that
unravels the web of death and mastery which is the epic's predominant pattern.
This is the weaving done by Penelope. What Penelope is weaving as she works at
her loom all day is a shroud, a continuous *memento mori*. She resists her impor-
tunate suitors with the insistence that this shroud, which she is weaving for her
father-in-law, must be finished before she can think of marrying any of them.
Preoccupation with death must take precedence over the pleasures of life. She
admonishes them:

> go slowly, keen as you are to marry me, until
> I can finish off this web . . .
> so my weaving won't all fray and come to nothing.
>
> (96)

And they believe her. They leave her alone, waiting until she had finished her
work, 'the weaving finespun, the yarns endless' (96). But it is a ruse:

> by day she'd weave at her great and growing web –
> by night, by the light of torches set beside her,
> she would unravel all she'd done.

The shroud that she works at all day she undoes by night, unravelling the pre-occupation with death that pervades the *Odyssey*. And as we have seen, Penelope is represented as excellent, worthy of immortal glory just as is Odysseus, for tough-minded cunning determination. If we take this recognition of Penelope's excellence as an invitation to read against the grain, it is possible to figure Penelope in a way that destabilizes the preoccupation with death and suggests other possibilities. It is as though there is a bare hint here of an alternative imaginary, a recognition that from a woman's point of view things might look very different.

Adriana Cavarero has taken up this hint, and reads it back imaginitively into the story of Penelope. She imagines Penelope, in a break from her weaving, going to stand on the shore of her island and looking out across the waters. Yet Penelope does not go out to sea to contest with death, as though that were the most important thing to do. 'Penelope knows that the sea belongs to Odysseus, and she allows him to measure his deeds and story on the yardstick of death. She allows the legend to recount wards, sorrows and fury. . . . She allows him to test the sense of his own living in the power of death' (1995: 21). For her own part, however, Penelope has better things to do. Although men have configured death as the measure of life, this configuration is a perverse and violent reversal of reality. Life is dependent upon *birth*. Without birth there would be no life, no adventure, no possibilities for action. It is birth, not death, that gives us our lives. Birth is the repressed premise without which the *Odyssey* and its flirtation with death could never get under way. Penelope, suggests Cavarero, 'speaks of birth and rootedness, rather than death and adventure. . . . This first horizon of belonging leaves masculine industry elsewhere, in the realm of death that it has chosen as its measure, and as the farthest point on its blood-soaked horizons' (22).

This is not to say that Penelope denies death or pretends that it does not happen. It is after all a *shroud* that she is weaving. Death comes; it is inevitable; it is a condition of finitude. And it is better to prepare for the end of life, to have one's shroud ready, than to pretend to be immortal. But there is a very big difference between recognizing death as the inevitable *end* of life and taking it as the *measure* of life. In Odysseus' adventures, as also in the battles of Troy, death is made to be constitutive of life: the excellence of life is measured in terms of death. Thus death must be continually sought out, flirted with, encountered. Death becomes an obsession; violence and mastery a way of life.

I suggest that to raise up death as the source of life, the measure of its excellence and the standard of its beauty, bespeaks a denial of reality so deep and perverse as to raise the most fundamental questions of repression and projection. It indicates a need to suppress the centrality of birth, and the dependence of all human life on women. We have seen how the womb, and the nourishment and mutuality offered by women are presented in the *Odyssey* as horrific and all-consuming, death-dealing rather than life-giving. In subsequent permutations in the western symbolic we shall see how the preoccupation with death continues to be entangled with the body, gender and sexuality; and through the influence of christendom the love of suffering and death becomes religious duty and devotion, especially for women. But already in the Homeric writings the basis is laid for a gendered obsession with death, violence and mastery. And already in the *Odyssey* there is just a hint that some women are elsewhere, thinking otherwise.

In the *Odyssey*, the representation of Penelope as a countervailing possibility is no more than a tiny chink in otherwise overwhelmingly masculinist writing. For the most part, the story belongs to the men; and most of the female figures, as we have seen, are made to represent death. Even Penelope is on the whole portrayed according to masculinist stereotypes, meekly subservient to her husband and even to her son whose orders to her are brusque and harsh. It would be going too far to say that the writer of the epic is consciously subverting the masculinism of the text and its gendered preoccupation with death. To the contrary, he is inscribing it in a way that will be decisive for western culture (see Nagler 1993). And yet the chink is there; the seeds of destabilization are sown. It is as if the male writer cannot quite evade the glimmer of recognition of what he has repressed: that life and death, beauty and excellence could be configured otherwise.

As the western symbolic proceeds, it is the masculinist tradition that wins. Death, violence and mastery become the story of western culture. Yet time after time in the western genealogy of necrophilia we will see the return of the repressed, the emergence of natality as an alternative imaginary, Penelope unweaving the shroud. Ever and again it is silenced, trampled upon by masculinist structures threatened by repressive desires for the womb, memories of natality, possibilities of relationships built upon mutuality rather than domination. But still it reappears, offering the possibility of new beginnings, a possibility that is the very hallmark of natality.

The returns of Odysseus

Odysseus does return home. With the help of Athena he arrives at last in Ithaca, and in a scene of unbridled violence slaughters the suitors who have been consuming his goods while vying for Penelope's favour. He makes himself known to his son Telemachus and is reunited with his wife. But even before they go together to the bed for which they have both been longing for twenty years, Odysseus tells Penelope that he will be leaving again, sailing once more across the barren sea and confronting further trials.

> Dear woman . . . we have still not reached the end
> of all our trials. One more labour lies in store –
> boundless, laden with danger, great and long,
> and I must brave it out from start to finish.

So the ghost of Tiresias prophesied to me,
the day I went down to the House of Death.
(463)

It is as though Odysseus is determined not to be detained by a home that he has struggled so long to reach. Before he can enjoy his homecoming he must announce a new departure. He presents it, to be sure, as a duty laid upon him by the gods, bringing as little joy to him as it does to his wife. Yet is he not itching to be gone again, flirting once more with death rather than making love to his wife? Significantly, it is in the House of Death itself that he has learned this: death has dictated the shape of his life. Penelope can only sigh and resign herself to the inevitable.

In western culture, too, Odysseus returns. His voyage, his mastery of the barren sea overcoming all the trials and tribulations of his journey until at last he reaches his home, became one of the constitutive myths of the western symbolic. Plato, in fifth-century BCE Athens, acknowledged that Homer was 'the educator of Greece' (*Republic* x.606e); and from Greece his influence spread through the Hellenized world of Alexander of Macedon and then throughout the Roman Empire. Homer was held to have had a special grasp of truth, given to him by the gods, so that his books were a source not only of literature or of history but also of morals and knowledge of the divine. To be sure, not everyone was content with this. Heraclitus, for example, writing around 500 BCE, said that 'Homer deserved to be . . . thrashed,' presumably for portraying false ideas about gods and morals (Waterfield 2000: 38). In some moods Plato agreed, at least to the extent of wanting to banish Homer from his ideal republic (*Republic* iii. 386–96).

Most philosophers (including Plato himself in different moods) took a different line, however. They came instead to hold that those sayings of Homer that caused theological or ethical problems if they were taken literally could be taken allegorically. There was a long succession of Greek and Roman scholars whose delight was to discover (or invent) the allegorical or symbolic meaning in Homer's texts: as they said, 'if Homer had not spoken in allegories, then he would have advanced all sorts of impieties' (cited in de Lubac 2000: 2.2). Thus for instance Odysseus' voyage is an allegory of the journey of life; the creatures he contends with are the struggles and temptations that must be mastered. As monotheism took an increasing hold, the various gods and goddesses came to be seen as symbols or attributes of a single god. In this way popular beliefs and superstitions could be refined into a sophisticated ethical or philosophical system for the elite, while the masses could continue to enjoy the poetry (Pelikan 1971: 28).

All of this was ready to hand when the early Christian writers came on the scene. Many of them were well educated; and good education was almost invariably grounded in the Homeric writings. Some of them, to be sure, rejected Greek culture as evil or even demonic when they became Christians. Tatian, for example, wrote vigorous scholarly condemnations of the poetic myths. At a more popular level, the hymn writer Romanos the Melode wrote a hymn for Pentecost in which he first praises the Spirit for making fishermen wise, and then contrasts this Spirit-given wisdom with the foolishness of those whom the Greeks thought clever:

> Why do the Hellenes bluster and drone on? . . .
> Why do they go astray in the company of Plato? . . .
> Why do they not realize that Homer is an idle dreamer?
> (Lee 2000: 257)

But many others, using a method of allegorizing or spiritualizing the Homeric writings, saw them as a primitive revelation, and combined them with stories from the Hebrew Bible to make a Christian point. Indeed some early Christians like Justin believed that the ancient Greeks had borrowed their myths from the Bible: the Homeric episode of the Giants was a distortion of the Biblical account of the Tower of Babel; the virgin birth of Jesus foretold by the prophets was echoed in Greek writings; and in regard to Christ's birth and ascension, Justin claimed, 'we [Christians] introduce nothing new beyond what you say of those whom you call sons of Zeus' (Justin 1977: 170).

The most important writer to bring the *Odyssey* into Christian thinking was Clement of Alexandria (150–215 CE). Clement draws countless parallels between Homeric and Biblical stories. The former, he holds, are borrowed from the latter and have often been distorted in the process (see Daniélou 1973: II, ch. 3, 'Homer in the Fathers of the Church'). The cunning Odysseus himself is, for Clement, an allegory or 'image of the prudent Christian who is acquainted with both human knowledge and divine wisdom' (Daniélou 1973: II.94). It is worth considering an extended passage from Clement where Clement repeatedly quotes from the story of Odysseus, conflating Charybdis and the Sirens and allegorizing the elements of the story to make it fit for Christian exhortation.

> Let us then shun custom; let us shun it as some dangerous headland, or threatening Charybdis, or the Sirens of legend. Custom strangles a man; it turns him away from truth; it leads him away from life; it is a snare, and abyss, a pit, a devouring evil. 'Wide of that smoke and wave direct, O helmsman, thy vessel' (*Od.* 12.219–20). Let us flee, comrades, let us flee from this wave. It belches forth fire; it is an island of wickedness heaped with bones and corpses (12.45–6), and she who sings therein is pleasure, a harlot in the bloom of youth, delighting in her vulgar music: 'Hither, renowned Odysseus, great glory of all the Achaeans; bring thy ship to land, that a song divine may entice thee' (12.184–5). She praises thee, sailor, she calls thee renowned in song; the harlot would make the glory of the Greeks her own. Leave her to roam among the corpses. . . . Sail past the song; it works death. Only resolve, and thou hast vanquished destruction; bound to the wood of the Cross, thou shalt

live freed from all corruption. The Word of God shall be thy pilot, and the Holy Spirit shall bring thee to anchor in the harbours of heaven.

(*Protrepticus* XII.118.1–4; quoted in Daniélou 1973: II.94–5)

In this long passage, as in many others in Clement, the allegorical identification of Homeric ideas with those of Christianity is assumed and heightened. Odysseus is the Christian; the journey is life; the destination is home/heaven. The mast to which Odysseus is tied to escape the seductions of the Sirens becomes the Cross of Christ; and the wind that blew him onward is the breath of the Spirit. Although Clement does not explicitly make the connection in this passage, it is easy to read the boat as the Church, which, conflated with the story of Noah, becomes the ark of salvation, the only means by which to cross the deadly barren sea and escape its many temptations.

The important point here is not just that Clement and other early Christian writers appropriate Homer and allegorise him for their purposes: that has already been studied in depth (Daniélou 1973; de Lubac 2000). What I want to emphasize is that it is precisely the Homeric preoccupation with gendered death in the *Odyssey* that is taken up in Christian thought, thus reinforcing its symbolic of death and making it constitutive also of christendom. We can see this beginning to happen in the above passage, even though Clement himself may not have been aware of it. The sea is life; but it is deadly. Moreover to be on this sea, that is, to be alive, is to be in exile: life is a journey and this world is an alien place full of tempests and struggles. Home is eternal heaven; but it will be arrived at only after death. Death therefore becomes the goal: it is the arrival at a place where love and peace are gained at last, the place of feasting and music and reunion with loved ones, like Odysseus' return to Ithaca. Thus in two senses death is given priority over life. Heaven – the other side of death – is the goal that confers meaning on life: life is significant and its events have meaning not in themselves but precisely insofar as they are a preparation for death. But second, the temptations and struggles of life are exciting adventures, because they are always engaged in the effort to master the 'sea of life' and its monsters, that barren sea which would swallow the unwary in a deadlier death, and foreclose arrival on the heavenly shore.

Moreover in christendom as in the *Odyssey*, the seductions and temptations that must be mastered in that great voyage of life are regularly configured female and sexualized. Clement explicitly connects Pandora with the creation of Eve, a connection echoed by Tertullian and Origen. In early Christian literature the troubles caused by women – especially women's beauty and sexual allure – are spoken of by movement between Helen of Troy, the story of the fall of the angels, Pandora, Eve, and the female creatures of the sea (Daniélou 1973: 90–5). All of these are amalgamated into a notion of the sexual female as the allegorical type of temptation and destruction for the Christian, who by implication is normatively male. In the long passage from Clement quoted above, the Siren is the harlot and her song works death: not the longed-for death of the heavenly arrival, but the unremembered death of the hero in the voracious barren sea. The extent to which the symbolic of gender and death can be mapped on to the lives and deaths of actual men and women in christendom is of course a further question; but it is already apparent from this sketch that the Homeric presentation of gendered death is deeply constitutive of western religious thought.

The theme of the Odyssean hero undertaking great ventures, flirting with death in order to achieve a haven of peace and fulfilment, became a standard trope of western literature. From the *Song of Roland* in the eleventh century to John Bunyan's *Pilgrim's Progress*, and from Tasso's account of the First Crusade in *Gerusalemme liberata* to James Joyce's dubious hero *Ulysses* and Tolkien's *Lord of the Rings*, the idea of male adventurers going out to face insuperable difficulties and temptations in order to undertake some quest whose achievement brings great (heavenly) reward is deep in the western imaginary. Actual women are usually left at home (Bunyan) or hardly enter the story at all (Tolkien), while the male heroes flirt with death. The struggles are often presented in gender-specific ways. Woman, beauty, seduction and death are metonymically linked, while at the other extreme there is often an idealized lady love, patterned after Mary the immaculate virgin who helps the hero on his way or receives him to his blessed reward. And it is the hope of that fulfilment, that reward, which can be obtained only after the journey of life is over, that gives meaning to life. Life is defined by death: Odysseus returns.

And he returns again. From the extent to which Odysseus was taken up as an allegory of the prudent Christian struggling towards his heavenly home, one would hardly expect that Odysseus would also be read as a prototype of secular Enlightenment man. Yet this is just what happened. Theodor Adorno and Max Horkheimer, for example, in their book *Dialectic of Enlightenment* (1989) see the *Odyssey* as 'the basic text of European civilization' (46) in which the conflicts and struggles of Odysseus can be seen as parables that reveal the self-destructiveness of modern rationality. The parables begin with the fact of the journey itself. As Adorno and Horkheimer read it, the *Odyssey* is a journey of self-discovery, 'the way taken through the myths by the self' (46). As the monsters of the sea are mastered one by one, their god-like power is removed and the world becomes secularized. The gods need no longer be feared. Odysseus tackles each new adventure, each flirtation with death as a modern experimenter, determined to squeeze out of each situation all that it can teach him about the mastery of the world.

> The adventures of Odysseus are all dangerous temptations removing the self from its logical course. He gives way to each allurement as a new experience, trying it out . . . the knowledge which comprises his identity and which enables him to survive, draws its content from experience of multitudinousness, from digression and salvation; and the knowing survivor is also the man who takes the greatest risks when death threatens, thus becoming strong and unyielding when life continues.
>
> (47)

He is therefore able to come home as the conqueror; he has lost himself in order to find himself. Just so do the masters of modernity penetrate and conquer the forces of nature and make themselves rulers over the earth, their home.

Adorno and Horkheimer take the story of the Sirens as especially illuminating of modernity: their reading of it could hardly be more different from that of Clement of Alexandria. For Adorno and Horkheimer, the songs the Sirens sing are songs of the past; their allurement is the temptation to stay in the past rather than confront the dangers of the future, to refuse to accept fully rational maturity. And their song is genuinely beautiful, something Odysseus/modern man wants to hear. As Adorno and Horkheimer present it, Odysseus' cunning is the prototype of Enlightenment rationality: it bifurcates the world. On the one hand, he dominates his crewmen, forcing them to work twice as hard, and plugging their ears with wax so that they are immune to the beauty of the Sirens' song: these are the workers who, in modernity, make capitalism possible. On the other hand, Odysseus arrogates to himself the privilege of the master. He listens to the music, is enraptured by its beauty, but at the price of making himself impractical. Thus in modernity beauty becomes art, 'a mere object of contemplation' for the privileged, while the world of manual labour becomes devoid of beauty, doggedly practical (34).

In this and other stories of the *Odyssey*, they argue, Odysseus masters nature and disempowers its gods, but at the cost of rendering the world disenchanted, without beauty. Rationality is reduced to calculation, practicality, the utilitarian. But the consequence is that rationality becomes rigid, dis-spirited: it is, in Adorno and Horkheimer's words, 'mimesis unto death' (57). As Douglas Kellner summarizes their account,

> Homer's text is read as an allegorical journey in which Odysseus overcomes primitive natural forces (immersion in pleasure, sexuality, animal aggressivity and violence, brutal tribalism and so forth) and asserts his domination over the mythic/natural world. In his cunning and deceit, his drive toward self-preservation and refusal to accept mythic fate, his entrepreneurial control over his men and his patriarchal power over his wife and other women, Odysseus is presented as a prefiguration of bourgeois man who reveals the connections between self-preservation, the domination of nature, and the entanglement of myth and enlightenment.
>
> (Kellner 1989: 91)

Different as is their reading from that of the Christian writers, Adorno and Horkheimer, like their Christian counterparts, appropriate Homer's preoccupation with gender and death. The sea of life, the natural world, is itself rendered deathly by calculative rationality; and beauty, identified with the feminine, is regressive. This is not to say that Adorno and Horkheimer are happy with the post-Enlightenment world: quite the reverse. Neither should their reading of Homer be designated as 'true' or 'accurate' any more than that of Clement or Tolkein:

Homer himself might for all we know have been surprised by any of these readings. The point, rather, is that as the Homeric writings have saturated the symbolic of the west, so that the preoccupation with gendered death is assimilated into western culture, returning with every return of Odysseus to work itself out in violence and the displacement of beauty.

Sometimes, indeed, Odysseus returns even when he does *not* return. His story of alienation from home, his wandering and adventure, is taken up in ways that preclude a return to Ithaca. Emmanuel Levinas finds the Homeric account of Odysseus unsatisfactory precisely because in the end Odysseus gets safely back to his starting point: indeed this return had been his intention all along. Levinas, like Adorno and Horkheimer, reads Odysseus as a parable of western culture, especially philosophy. Unlike them, however, he de-emphasizes the extent to which Odysseus has been changed by what he went through. Rather, in Levinas' view Odysseus is little better than a tourist collecting adventures and experiences, only to return to the safety of the known. He gathers up all that he has experienced into a systematic and fully integrated unity, a philosophical photo-album, the One or Absolute of western metaphysics from Parmenides to Hegel. This is his philosophical home, his metaphysical source and return (Levinas 1969a: 102). But by this pre-determined assimilation of everything to the safe and known, genuine life-changing encounter with the other is precluded. Even while ostensibly travelling far and wide, there is no scope for alterity, for thinking otherwise. Like the worst of tourists collecting photo-opportunities in exotic lands but never actually being open to people and situations in all their difference, western metaphysics treats the foreign simply as material for its own after-dinner talk, not as something that could threaten its identity or destabilize its totalizing assumptions.

Levinas makes an alternative suggestion, drawn from the Hebrew Bible. 'To the myth of Odysseus returning home,' he says, 'we wish to oppose the story of Abraham leaving his fatherland forever for a land yet unknown' (Levinas 1986: 348). Abraham's ancestral home and its idols are put behind him. There is no hope of return. Yet neither is there any assured destination. All there is is the voice of God and the face of the Other, which, Levinas says, 'puts me into question, empties me of myself' (350) in an encounter with radical alterity. It is this willingness to renounce the safety of the known with its perpetual return only to itself, this willingness to be open to the Other, to think otherwise – at an angle, on the margins, in a different space – that Levinas prescribes for philosophy, and in his own work enacts by giving ethics priority over ontology (Levinas 1969a; 1987; see also Peperzak 1995).

Like Adorno and Horkheimer, Levinas sees the Odyssean rationality of modernity as destructive and violent, invested in death; and like them, too, he is acutely aware of its masculinity. He writes,

> The world in which reason becomes more and more self-conscious is uninhabitable. It is hard and cold . . . true with the truth of calculation and

brought into the anonymous realm of the economy that proceeds according to knowledgeable plans which cannot prevent though they can prepare disasters. There it is – spirit in its masculine essence. It *lives outside*, exposed to the fiery sun that blinds, to the winds of the open sea which beat it and blow it down – on an earth without inner recesses, removed from its home-land, solitary and wandering.

(Levinas 1969b: 33)

As Odysseus is taken up into the western symbolic, the linkage of the masculine with mastery and violence is ever and again reinforced (see also Derrida 1978).

Now, there is much in Levinas' insistence on openness to alterity, to thinking otherwise, that runs as a deep thread through my account of the genealogy of death and its displacement of beauty in western culture. For each instance in which death and violence have configured the symbolic and the lived reality of western history, I am lifting up a theme or figure from the margins, a silenced or repressed voice – a Sappho, a Penelope – that shows that the investment in death was a choice, not a necessity, and a choice which could have been made otherwise. That theme, which obviously draws much from Levinas, will continue in the chapters that follow, so that cumulatively resources are developed for a new imaginary.

Yet for all my indebtedness to Levinas, some caveats must be entered. It would take us too far afield in the present volume to show how Levinas' own philosophy is also preoccupied with death – the face of the Other is, before all else, the face that forbids *murder* – and its identification with gender, especially the feminine (Levinas 1969a: 197–201; see also Charlier 1991; Irigaray 1991; Jantzen 1998). To the point here, however, is Levinas' assumption that for Odysseus to return home is for him to be unchanged, to have simply assimilated all that he has experienced into a predetermined One: hence Levinas' preference for Abraham. It is of course possible for this to occur, for a traveller or for a philosopher. But it is also possible, through actual or intellectual journeys, to be changed by the encounters, so that although the traveller returns 'home', that home is no longer perceived in the same way. The place of origin is both reached and not reached. It is utterly re-evaluated. Indeed if it were not the case that origins could thus be reencountered, there would be no possibility of radical (i.e. 'from the roots') transformation, because the roots could never be exposed to be configured differently. If the violence and preoccupation with death that shapes western culture is to be transfigured, this can only come about by confronting *both* its deep genealogical structures *and* the possibilities of alterity: the latter without the former cannot bring about change. Only when we bring otherness home and learn to live with it, destabilizing the assumptions that have hitherto characterized our point of origin, does it enable us to think – and live – otherwise. It is the way to bring newness into our world.

But this is to get ahead of myself. The story of Odysseus is a story in which the hero returns; and as we have seen, the return of Odysseus (and his flirtations with death along the way) has been a central theme in western culture. Yet, strikingly, the most influential of all the appropriations of the Homeric epic is one in which the hero does *not* return: it is Vergil's *Aeneid*, written about 20 BCE. Vergil takes up the journeys of Odysseus, incorporates parts of the *Iliad*, and fuses them into a story to serve his own political purposes: a story of the founding of Rome and the legitimation of the Roman Empire.

'I sing of arms and the man,' says Vergil in his famous opening, the man 'fated to be an exile, who long since left the land of Troy and came to Italy' (1990: 3). That man is Aeneas. Aeneas is modelled on Odysseus, though he is also unlike him in important ways. Like Odysseus, Aeneas is portrayed as sailing with his men for ten years after the sack of Troy, 'driven by the Fates to wander year after year round all the oceans of the world' (4) because of conflicts among the gods. Like Odysseus, too, he overcomes the hardships of the sea and the temptations and challenges of its female creatures – the Sirens, Scylla and Charybdis – by a mixture of courage, determination, and divine help. Indeed the gendered dimension is heightened in the *Aeneid* by the story of Aeneas' affair with Dido, Queen of Carthage, whom he abandons to despair and suicide without a word of explanation in his determination to reach Italy. Like Odysseus also, Aeneas must visit the underworld and only then can emerge to victorious conquest of the land of Lavinium and the foundation of the Roman race.

But Aeneas is also unlike Odysseus. He is not an Achaean but a Trojan, who escapes with his father and his young son from the sack of Troy, never to return to his home. Indeed there is no home left for him to return to. At least in the early books of the *Aeneid*, Vergil is alive to the pathos and devastation of war, its ugliness and cruelty, even if the later books celebrate violence and battle in graphic, bloody detail. Rather than return to his wife (who is left behind and dies at Troy), Aeneas' aim is to get to Italy, there to found a state in which the Roman people can achieve their destiny (Williams 1987: 12–19).

Vergil wrote during the reign of Augustus Caesar, and his purpose was to praise his ruler and the ideal of empire: the *Aeneid* is not a politically neutral book. The most respected literature of the Hellenistic world, the Homeric epics, are taken up by Vergil; and their stories of events that had taken place hundreds of years previously are forged into an account representing the establishment of the Roman people, the line of Augustus himself, and the empire over which he presided, as we shall see more fully in chapter 15. The *Aeneid* is thus deliberate ideological fabrication. It is not without nuance (see Spence 1998: ch. 2); nevertheless its overarching aim is to provide a literary and symbolic underpinning for an ideology of dominance for the Roman Empire.

It worked. The *Aeneid* (together with literary works by Cicero, Livy and others) became retrospective justification and rationalization of the Roman Empire, which was represented as uniquely fitted to rule the whole world because of its goodness and benevolence and superior civilization. Had not Jupiter himself foretold its destiny? When Jupiter explains his plans for Aeneas and the Trojans to his daughter Venus, Vergil has him say of the Romans, 'On them I impose no limits of time or place. I have given them an empire that will know no end. . . . From this noble stock where will be born a Trojan Caesar to bound his empire by Oceanus at the limits of the world, and his fame by the stars. He will be called Julius . . . he too will be called upon in prayer' (Vergil 1990: 12). The text of Vergil, written as it was in praise of Augustus and his ancestor Julius Caesar, and according them divine status, was thus used to give underpinning to the authority of their line and to the expansion of the Empire throughout the known world. Every school child learned Vergil, often by heart. Public buildings in Rome, like the Forum of Augustus, had portraits of rulers going back through Julius Caesar to Aeneas (Blagg 1990: 724). It was this lineage that indicated his divinity and thus the propriety of his worship: it was to cause much difficulty for Christians (Ferguson 1990: 766). And with every recitation of the text of Vergil, every march of the Roman legions to the farthest outposts of Europe and Asia, every libation poured to the emperor, the symbolic of violence and gendered death were reinscribed. Manliness, in this case Roman, is configured by flirting with and mastering death. Even by not returning, Odysseus/Aeneas returns: comes back, in another place and time, to preoccupation with violence and eternity.

And he keeps on returning. One of the most influential of all books of christendom is Dante's *Divine Comedy*, which explicitly takes Vergil as a guide to the worlds of death: hell, purgatory, paradise. Politically, the Holy Roman Empire modelled itself (at least rhetorically) on Rome. So did the Napoleonic Empire. So did the British: and it is no accident that the British public school system which educated boys to run the Empire placed Latin – indeed the *Aeneid* – at the centre of its curriculum. The United States of America takes the Roman eagle as its national symbol, just as Napoleon and the Holy Roman Empire did. Time and again, the barren sea must be mastered and the strange creatures who are encountered on the journey must be subdued, as 'new' land is claimed upon which to establish a home away from home, a return without return. Vasco da Gama's voyages were modelled on the *Odyssey* and the *Aeneid* by Camoens in his epic poem *Lusiads*; the Pilgrim Fathers began a homeland in a territory wrested from (feminized) Native Americans; the 'manifest destiny' of the United States to possess the continent from sea to sea echoed in phrase after phrase the rationalizing justifications for the expansion of the Roman Empire. In the name of bringing a higher civilization it brought genocide and destruction, a preoccupation with death and gendered violence. If Odysseus as a symbol of European bourgeois man is the one who returns to his starting place, Aeneas is the one who, in ostensibly going elsewhere, actually remakes the other in the image of the same. He returns by not returning, obliterating the otherness of those he conquers, supplanting it with his own 'superior' civilization. There is reason to think that Vergil himself might have protested at this appropriation of his work (Spence 1988: ch. 2). Nevertheless, whatever Vergil's intentions, the effect of his book was to provide a textual foundation for a symbolic of gendered death that had endless implications for western culture.

On we go, amigos . . .
down the ages way across the watery world,
and yearning, yearning for my home,
as you do, as we do, though we can't go home,
never again.
            (Judith Kazantzis, in Hartog 2001: vii)

Chapter 7

'The murderous misery of war'

Apollo, whose immortal hand
Reared the strong towers and walls of Troy! . . .
Why did you dishonour what you had made,
Surrender the work of your own hands,
Unhappy Troy, unhappy Troy,
To the murderous misery of war?
(Euripides 1972: 178)[1]

Thus sings the Chorus of Phthian women in sympathy with Andromache, the widow of Hector, who according to Greek tradition had been dragged off as a slave when Troy was conquered. Although Euripides who wrote these lines borrowed much from Homer, for Euripides war was not glorious. It was tragedy.

The Chorus continues:

By the river bank on the Trojan plain
Many a horse was harnessed well,
Many a man you summoned
To the trial of strength and valour;
But the prize was death and the garland blood.
And the princes of Troy have gone to the home of the dead,
And the altars of Troy are cold,
The smoke of incense vanished,
And the holy flame quenched.

According to Euripides, war is not the theatre of manly excellence and youthful beauty which Homer valorized. War is brutal and horrible. It is destructive folly unworthy of human intelligence and decency. Its consequences should be measured not in terms of valour and victory but in terms of devastation and death and the diminishment of the human spirit. Men die. Women are violated. Children's futures are destroyed. The victors as much as the vanquished are losers, for they have become the sort of people who can inflict cruelty and still live with themselves. Even the gods lose out according to Euripides: their altars are cold.

Indeed Euripides implies here and elsewhere in his writings that if the gods tolerate or even command war, that is reason enough to doubt them: how could a god worthy of the name countenance something so horrible?

Euripides revealed on stage the 'murderous misery of war', rather than the glory of violence. His plays raise questions about the moral legitimacy and even the manliness of becoming a soldier, a man whose purpose is to inflict death or to die. Moreover, many of Euripides' plays reveal the tragic effect of war on women and children. An intelligent observer of Euripides' plays would come away with a whole new set of questions: questions about justice and vengeance; questions about political corruption and the hypocrisy of the rulers; and questions about the ways in which the powerful invoked the immortals to excuse or legitimize their own moral hypocrisy. Set against Homer, Euripides can be read as voicing powerful dissent to the valorization of violence of the *Iliad*. Violence is not countenanced by the immortals; nor should it be seen as heroic, leading to immortal fame.

Similar themes can be found in the two other most famous tragedians of fifth-century Athens, Aeschylus and Sophocles. Like Euripides, they drew upon Homeric epics and the myths of archaic Greece, and like him they reworked the ancient material for their own purposes. Each of the three had different themes and emphases, but all were concerned to call Athenian society to account, most particularly in relation to war and violence, justice and vengeance, and issues of gender. All of them require a reconsideration of mortality, especially in relation to the immortals. Together, they effect a disruption of the Homeric exultation in gendered violence, placing it differently in the light of eternity.

The writings of the tragedians can be read in many different ways, and have had an incalculable impact upon the western cultural symbolic. Without denying the validity of other readings, my purpose is to consider them in relation to the genealogy of death, reading them in comparison and contrast with the Homeric writings. It will quickly become apparent that the sort of death which captures the attention of the tragedians is violent death: murder, child-sacrifice, suicide, war. Very few of the characters of these dramas die peacefully in their beds (Loraux 1987). It is in their portrayals of violence that the tragedians hold up a mirror to society, a mirror into which those who glorified Homeric violence would find it uncomfortable to look. In this chapter I shall focus particularly on their portrayal of war. In the next, I shall investigate more closely their portrayal of war's consequences upon its victims, and the ways in which this shaped their understanding of death. In many respects, however, the themes intertwine; and the two chapters should be read together as an investigation of the tragedian's representations of violent death for the western cultural symbolic. In these dramatists the swirling currents of violence, death, beauty and gender go through shape-shiftings which have had enduring effects on western culture.

Commentators on the great tragedies of fifth-century Athens often remark upon how pertinent their themes are for our own time (e.g. Rehm 1994: 128). It will become apparent that this is particularly true in relation to violence. Their treatment of warfare and of the rhetorical legitimation of violence holds up a mirror not only to fifth-century Athens but also to the western world of the twenty-first century. Part of the reason for this is the sheer brilliance of the tragedians in their presentation of human characters and their interaction: as Adrian Poole has said, 'The power of Greek tragedy to outline the local conditions of its original production depends on the quality of the challenge which it once offered to those local conditions' (1987: 12). But implicit in this, paradoxically, is careful anchoring *within* those local conditions. To understand the tragedies in relation to warfare and violent death it is necessary to know something about the violence and warfare with which Athens was involved during the century that the plays were produced, the so-called 'Golden Age' of Athens. The themes of the tragedians are closely related to the rapidly changing political happenings of their time (see Podleci 1966; Meier 1993).

At the beginning of the fifth century Athens was a minor city ruled by an aristocracy. Next to Sparta, it was the most powerful city in Greece; but in relation to the might of Persia it seemed insignificant. However, in the first quarter of the century Athens and Persia engaged in warfare. Athens trounced Persia, and began a meteoric rise to imperial power, setting up external shock waves and internal ferment. The military success of Athens brought about immense social and political changes which were in turn interconnected with cultural and intellectual upheavals. For several decades Athens seemed unstoppable.

But the tide turned. The alliances Athens had built up began to crumble, fractured by jealousy, treachery and hatred, often brought on by Athenian arrogance. The empire began to break up. War, initially with Sparta and eventually spreading through the Peloponnesian peninsula, dragged on in a series of defeats, exacerbated by an outbreak of plague in 430. By the turn of the new century and the end of the Peloponnesian War, the empire had disintegrated and the Athenian Golden Age had collapsed. All was in turmoil, a turmoil that can be symbolized by the trial and execution of Socrates in 399. All of Plato's writings were still to come (Samons 1998; Meier 2000; Hornblower 1991).

It was in this turbulent fifth century that the tragedians produced their major works. Aeschylus (525–456) participated in the rise and development of Athens, and celebrated it in his writings, though not without qualification as we shall see. Sophocles (496–406) saw both the rise and the decline of Athens, and though he was a congenial and venerated Athenian his plays frequently call Athens back to its stated ideals of freedom, justice and generosity. Euripides (484–406) went further: he dramatized the horror and stupidity of war and revenge, destabilized gender assumptions, and questioned religious tradition. So controversial did Euripides become that in 407 he moved to voluntary exile in Macedon. Aristotle was to call him the 'most tragic' of the dramatists.

'The murderous misery of war'

The deaths that permeate all three of the tragedians are seldom far removed from war and violence; and all of them prompt reflection that casts doubt on the received opinion about the glory or even the justification of war. Each of the three increases the level of questioning regarding war and its legitimacy.

Aeschylus in *The Persians* (performed in Athens in 472) presents Queen Artossa and the Elders of Persia waiting for news of the battle against the Greeks – a battle which had actually been fought about eight years before, and in which many of the viewers of the play, including Aeschylus himself, had participated. Curious about the city that her son Xerxes has gone from Persia to fight, Queen Artossa asks, 'But tell me, where, by men's report, is Athens built?' (Aeschylus 1961: 129). Athens is so insignificant a place, by her reckoning, that the Queen has never taken it seriously enough to learn its geography. Aeschylus represents the Persians, at first, as filled with confidence: they are by far the greater power, with the larger army and navy. The Chorus recites the list of all those who have joined Xerxes in his campaign against Greece:

> From every realm of Asia
> The east in arms pours forward;
> The king's dread word is spoken:
> A million sabres hear.
>
> (124)

Xerxes had achieved the remarkable feat of making a bridge across the Hellespont by lashing boats to one another so that his army could march across; and had built up his navy ready for an encounter with the Greeks.

> See his thousand oars advance!
> See ten thousand arrows fly!
> . . . Persian arms no strength can stay;
> Persian hearts no fear can sway.
>
> (125)

But a note of uncertainty creeps into their song. The army has been away for a long time; moreover, as the Chorus tells the Queen, there is historical precedent for Greeks defeating an invading Persian army. At the Battle of Marathon in 490, Greek soldiers had for the first time defeated the Persian army; it was in part to reverse that defeat that Xerxes mounted this new campaign. Above all, human life and human fortune are unpredictable, they reiterate: the decrees of the gods are inscrutable.

> Yet, while Heaven with tortuous plan
> Works its will, what mortal man

Can elude immortal guile?
. . . There man pays his mortal debt:
Doom has caught what death will keep.

(125)

The Persian Elders and their Queen anxiously await news, their sense of dread
and foreboding steadily increasing. They are right to fear. The news, when it
comes, is disastrous. A messenger arrives, running to bring his word, and gasps
out what they most dreaded: 'Persians, our country's fleet and army is no more'
(130).

Aeschylus' audience knew it already, of course; and from a very different
perspective. Among the Athenians who watched the play, many had participated
in the Battle of Salamis, the famous naval encounter in which the Athenian
triremes had roundly defeated the Persians. Greek allies had then pursued the
Persian land army as they tried to make for home, decimating their ranks as they
chased them. Aeschylus' play could be taken as a celebration of the Athenian
victory: they could gloat to hear the Persian messenger exclaim,

What name more hateful to our ears than Salamis?
Athens – a name of anguish in our memory!

(131)

The messenger is then made to recount the whole story: the trickery that
started the sea battle; the destruction of the heavy Persian ships by the more
manoeuvrable Athenian fleet; the butchery of the Persian army on an island
where they had waited to assist their navy; the disarray of what was left of army
and navy struggling to get home, hungry, thirsty, exhausted; only a handful actually
returning, among them Xerxes himself, his tattered clothes and pitiable state
betokening the shattered Persian might. The Chorus greets him:

Alas for Persia's honoured name!
Alas for all that noble host,
The flower of manhood, Asia's boast,
By gods condemned to deadly shame! . . .
They followed the dark road and died;
A thousand thousand are no more.

(147)

The fate of the warriors who had marched with Xerxes is rehearsed one by one:
some are drowned, some slaughtered, none have returned to the wives and families
waiting for them.

How did Aeschylus' Athenian audience respond to his drama? At one level it
was of course a triumphal celebration of Greek victory, a victory that had been

won against long odds by sheer single-mindedness and courage on the part of the Athenians. Since that victory nearly ten years earlier, Athens had gone from strength to strength, emerging as a growing, self-confident power, sure of its moral as well as its military superiority. For some in the audience, as they watched the recitation of events, it must have been an occasion of pride and self-congratulation: how easily it might have turned out the other way!

Yes – but was that not precisely Aeschylus' point? By setting his drama in Persia rather than in Athens, he structures the action in such a way that those who are announcing Athens' victory are lamenting their own defeat, grieving for lives lost and hope destroyed. And the dramatist shows that those lives are very like the lives of the audience: courageous, steady, faithful to their country and its leader. The men who died had women and children at home who depended upon them as surely as Athenian families depended upon the men who now watched the drama. In all the killing and conquest Athens had emerged victorious, true; but those whom they killed were not beasts or monsters but ordinary people like themselves. Xerxes may have been vain and weak, but he was not a bad man, and neither were his followers or his people. They were foreign, but they were not evil. Were Persian lives not worth mourning? Was this war not tragedy? – a tragedy for the Persians, obviously; but perhaps a tragedy for the Athenians too, who had slaughtered and maimed their fellow human beings and were now prepared to *congratulate* themselves for it?

Athenians heard from the stage the voice representing Darius, Xerxes' father, saying from beyond the grave,

> dead heaped on dead
> Shall bear dumb witness to three generations hence
> That man is mortal, and must learn to curb his pride.
> For pride will blossom; soon its ripening kernel is
> Infatuation; and its bitter harvest, tears.
> Behold their folly and its recompense; and bear
> Athens and Hellas in remembrance.
>
> (145)

Intelligent listeners would have got the message that exactly the same applies to Athens: if Athens on the strength of her victory over Persia now extends herself in imperial might, her pride also will lead to disaster; the same defeat will come to her. And if Athenians indulge in self-congratulatory gloating over the Persian dead, they make themselves unworthy. The military tragedy is Persian, but it is triumphalist Athens that is in danger of moral tragedy.

If this theme is implicit in *The Persians*, Aeschylus brings it to the fore in a subsequent drama, *Seven Against Thebes*. Here the main contestants are not foreign, but rather two Greek brothers, Polyneices and Eteocles, the sons of Oedipus, each at the head of an army, each slaughtering the other. At one level the killings are portrayed as fate, the fulfilment of a curse on the brothers pronounced by their father long ago. Yet at another level Aeschylus suggests that they do have choices; they do not have to attack and kill one another. It is they who choose violence and battle. As they do so, the terrified Chorus of Theban women pray desperately to the gods for protection, and bewail the pity of war.

> The madness of Ares [the god of war] masters men in masses . . .
> Man faces man and falls before the spear.
> Stained with blood, mothers of new-born infants
> Cry for their young slaughtered at the breast;
> Roving bands tear apart those of the same family . . .
>
> (1961: 98)

And so it goes on, in a litany of destruction, 'pain and never-ending tears' (99). Who is victorious – what could count as victory – at such a price? As the Chorus exclaims, 'At the end of the day victory belongs to the Curses' (116).

'This violent passion'

Towards the end of the century, when the victory over the Persians was a distant memory and Athens was moving inexorably towards defeat and humiliation at the hands of Sparta (her erstwhile 'brother' and ally), Euripides presented his own version of the tragedy of Polyneices' and Eteocles' mutual murder. Whereas for Aeschylus a central concern had been to explore the question of human choice over against fate or the will of the gods, in Euripides' reworking of the story the gods play a much less central role. Rather, Euripides is concerned to expose the motives and excuses that propel men into violence. In his plays, everyone knows that war is destructive folly. Everyone professes not to want it. And yet the protagonists move steadily to mutual slaughter, rejecting all efforts towards reconciliation, each blaming the other.

Euripides' play, *The Phoenecian Women* (so named for the Chorus), begins with Iocasta (Jocasta) explaining the background. Oedipus her husband and erstwhile king of Thebes had cursed their two sons, Polyneices and Eteocles, saying that they would 'divide the inheritance of their father's house with sharpened steel' (238). The brothers were appalled. To try to prevent such a dreadful outcome, they made a pact that Eteocles would rule Thebes for one year while Polyneices went into voluntary exile; at the end of the year they would exchange places. But when the year was up and Polyneices returned as agreed, Eteocles refused to give up his rule: 'once firmly on the throne, Eteocles would not budge' (239). Enraged, Polyneices gathered an army and prepared to take by force the throne that his brother denied him. As the play opens, Iocasta has summoned her two sons under a truce to come and meet with her: her plan is to effect a reconciliation between them. They are after all brothers. They lead armies of fellow human beings. Is any grievance so severe that it justifies slaughter? – and in any case would slaughter resolve the grievance?

Polyneices arrives first. He protests that the impending war is not of his making: he is the victim. 'What a foul, fearful thing, mother, is enmity within a family!' he exclaims (248). However, he has mustered a huge army, who have agreed to help him fight for his throne, and he feels that he can hardly turn back now without losing their respect.

> . . . for my sake they give
> Their service – I've no choice but to accept, though this
> Distresses me, for I march against my own city.
> And I call heaven to witness that I come in arms
> Against my kin and country most unwillingly.
>
> (251)

But how unwilling is he really? Would someone who is serious about not wanting to fight raise a huge army? As for the excuse that he will lose face if he were to disband his forces, what sort of rationale is that? If the viewer of the drama begins to feel sceptical, the scepticism is soon confirmed, as Polyneices admits the real reason for his aggression:

> . . . the thing
> That gets most honour in this world, and wields more power
> Than anything else, is money. That's what I've come here
> To get, with twenty thousand spears to press my point.
>
> (251)

In order to acquire wealth Polyneices is willing to destroy a city and kill his brother along with all the others, army and civilian, who will be caught up in the fighting. Formally, he has justice on his side; his brother has broken their agreement. But what sort of justice is it that allows him to kill his brother, and his fellow human beings, for wealth?

Eteocles comes next to Iocasta. He is outraged that Polyneices has come to Thebes with an army, expecting him to negotiate under threat: if Eteocles were to accede now it would looks as though he had done so out of fear. He says,

> It was a mistake, mother,
> For him to seek a settlement by force of arms;
> Everything that a military attack could gain
> May well be achieved by conference.
>
> (253)

By threatening violence Polyneices is courting violence, preempting the possiblity of peaceful resolution. And yet Eteocles' own sincerity is also in question. Would he really be willing to negotiate if Polyneices were to disband the army? Or would he simply continue as before? He has after all already reneged on their agreement. Moreover, he admits to Iocasta,

Mother, I'll be quite open with you. I would go,
If it were possible, to the regions of the stars,
Explore the sunrise, probe the depths of the earth, to win
That greatest of all goddesses, absolute power.

(253)

So much for his protestations of willingness to compromise. He himself says flatly
that he will never relinquish power.

I will not give up
My throne to Polyneices. In all other matters
Piety is well; but since there must be wickedness,
There is no nobler pretext for it than a throne.

(253)

The possession of power has corrupted Eteocles' integrity, made him cynical
about religion, and willing to destroy even his own family in order to retain his
throne.

Iocasta points out the folly of their ways to each of her sons. To Eteocles she
says,

Oh, son, why set your heart
Towards the most evil of divinities, ambition?
She is a corrupt power; shun her . . .
Why set so high, so extravagant a value on
Sovereignty – this injustice crowned by good fortune?
Is admiration precious? It is an empty gain.

(254)

The sheer lust for power and domination which Eteocles thinks makes him
great in fact demeans him. It makes him less of a man, unable to make a proper
assessment of (or even to care about) the consequences of his action on his city
or on his own family. As for wealth as a motivation, Iocasta points out that that
is equally senseless.

This wealth you long for – what advantage comes with it?
For a mere name, it brings you endless trouble. Enough
To supply need contents the man who knows himself.

Through Iocasta's exchange with her sons, Euripides neatly demonstrates the
utter destructive folly of war. Both sides claim right and justice; both sides claim
that the other has wronged them. Yet Euripides shows that even though they are
both partly right, what is really driving the conflict is not a desire for justice. Both
brothers are in the grip of far less worthy desires. Iocasta pleads with them:

Both of you, cast away
This violent passion, let it go! When headstrong fools
Meet two together, the outcome is most horrible.

(255)

The willingness to nurse hatred and grievances, to refuse to negotiate or compromise, to look to violence and ultimately to control rather than to mutual trust as a solution, and to use the rhetoric of justice as an excuse for violence can lead only to a situation in which everybody loses. In the drama Eteocles and Polyneices fall to the level of exchanging insults, and soon are fighting each other to the death. Both are killed; many men are slaughtered. Too late, Polyneices realizes that it has all been wrong. As he lies dying, he says to Iocasta,

Mother, my life is finished. I am sorry for you,
And for my sister, and my dead brother. For he was
My brother, and became my enemy, yet was still
My dear brother.

(284)

Though he was the more wronged of the two, in the end he shows greater under-standing and generosity of spirit: the man who had become his enemy was still his dear brother. All the killing was a tragic mistake; warfare solved nothing.

Justice: a bound to mercy?

The audience in Athens who watched the drama of the tragedians must often have had their conscience stung. Repeatedly it was made plain on the stage that the motives for the violence, war and killing which they had inflicted in their bid to acquire and retain imperial dominance might be cause for shame rather than glory. The lust for power or wealth easily slid into hypocritical piety and invocation of a high moral ground, which closer examination showed to be self-interest. In the genealogy of death, the glorification of killing is hardly a chapter of which to be proud.

This much was relatively easy to show. But if the ambition for dominance or wealth, once acknowledged, are poor motivations for war and violence, that is hardly the end of the matter. As Athens increased in power during the fifth century, and in its own estimation was the most advanced and civilized polity of the Mediterranean, it began to use this self-perception as a rhetorical justification for war. To put it simply, Athens invoked justice. When other city states, especially Sparta, contravened the conditions Athens set down for it, Athens was indignant. Sparta must be brought to justice; wrongs must be avenged. The gods must be on the side of Athens: the immortals could be invoked so that violence could be seen as a religious duty. Later, as the Peloponnasian War went increasingly against

Athens, the appeal to justice was additionally linked to an appeal to self-defence as the legitimation for war.

All three of the tragedians ponder deeply the relationship between justice, violence, and the immortals, and in all three the themes are interlocked with gender and the genealogy of death. They take it as axiomatic that justice requires that wrongs be dealt with: someone who has done evil should not be allowed to get away with it. As Electra puts it in Sophocles' play named after her,

> if the unhappy dead
> Are nothing but the dust in which they lie,
> And blood not paid for blood,
> There is no faith, no piety, in any man.
> (Sophocles 1953: 76)

Piety, morality and religion require – do they not? – that killing be avenged, that justice be done. But is vengeance justice? The question demands more intricate formulation: what (if any) modes of vengeance are just? What are those who place themselves on the side of justice to do in the face of great evil?

In the genealogy of death in the western symbolic, much death has been inflicted in the name of justice: defending the weak, putting a stop to great evil, punishing murderers. Often religion is invoked. But is this pious rhetoric every-thing it seems? As in the case of less worthy motivations for violence, the three tragedians reflect deeply upon the rhetoric of justice as a legitimation of violence. All three of them wrote plays starting from Homeric material representing the sequel to Agamemnon's sacrifice of his daughter, Iphigenia. We can trace the shifts in their thinking about the relations between justice and the infliction of death, by considering in turn how each of them portrays the story.

The Homeric tale upon which all of them draw is that Agamemnon returns to his home victorious after the battle of Troy, a war that is itself revenge for the Trojans' capture of Helen. Agamemnon is met by his wife Clytaemnestra. While he has been away she has taken a lover, Aegisthus. She is deeply embittered by her daughter Iphigenia's death at her father's hands. Together, Clytaemnestra and Aegisthus kill Agamemnon. Iphigenia had a younger sister, Electra, and a brother Orestes. Orestes had been sent away as a young lad. He returns a grown man; and urged on by Electra he kills Clytaemnestra and her lover Aegisthus in retribution for their father's death. But now Orestes in turn has become a killer of his own mother, and is pursued by the Furies who drive him mad. What can deliver him from madness? And what can stop a spiral of violence? The topic was ripe for pondering in the fifth century as Athens first rose to victorious supremacy through warfare and then was involved in a seemingly endless cycle of violence in mutual retaliation of injustices, real and perceived.

'Violence longs to breed'

Aeschylus' *Oresteia* is a play cycle in which, uniquely, all three of the original dramas have been preserved, and which together present the cycle of violence and the playwright's solution. In the first play Aeschylus presents the story of Agamemnon's return. Before Agamemnon arrives on stage, the news comes that the Greeks have been victorious; Troy has fallen. All should be celebration; but the Chorus, waiting for him to arrive, comments darkly that a just household 'is blessed with radiant children,

> But ancient Violence longs to breed,
> new Violence comes
> when its fatal hour comes, the demon comes
> to take her toll – no war, no force, no prayer
> can hinder the midnight Fury stamped
> with parent Fury moving through the house.
> (1976: 131)

However, this ominous note is swept aside when the king enters triumphant. The gods have given victory to the Greeks, ruin to Troy, in just retribution. Agamemnon exults:

> For their mad outrage
> of a queen we raped their city – we were right.
> Our thanks to the gods.
>
> (133)

Agamemnon presents the rape and slaughter as simple justice, with the gods on their side. 'We were right,' he says flatly, and thanks the gods.

Yet even as he says this, the audience knows that Clytaemnestra is about to kill him in just retaliation for his sacrifice of Iphigenia, 'act for act, wound for wound' (166). But although Clytaemnestra is confident that she has right on her side, the Chorus voices its disquiet: where will it end? 'But now if he must pay for the blood of his father's shed, and die for the deaths he brought to pass, and bring more deaths to avenge his dying . . . ' how can there ever be release from the cycle of violence? (158). The drama ends with no answer to the question it has raised: how can justice be achieved without degenerating into endless mutual destruction?

It is this dilemma with which the second drama of Aeschylus' trilogy opens. Electra is praying at her father's grave, and asks the accompanying Chorus of women for advice: what should she pray for? They encourage her to pray for the murderers that 'the one who murders in return' should come upon them. Electra protests,

How can I ask the gods for that
and keep my conscience clear?

But the Chorus replies, 'How not, and pay the enemy back in kind?' (182–3).
When Orestes arrives bent on murdering Clytaemnestra in revenge for his father's
death, the Chorus sees it all in terms of justice.

Justice turns the wheel.
'Word for word, curse for curse
be born now,' Justice thunders,
hungry for retribution,
'stroke for bloody stroke be paid.'
(192)

Orestes declares that the god Apollo himself has ordered him to kill his mother.
He does so; but immediately finds himself conflicted: 'she – I loved her once and
now I loathe – I have to loathe – ' (222). Though he feels it is duty to loathe her,
he loves her still, and having killed her is consumed with guilt that takes for him
the shape of Gorgons, 'swarming serpents' that pursue him and drive him mad.
Was his action just, a manifestation of the god Apollo?

Or should we call him death?
Where will it end? –
where will it sink to sleep and rest,
this murderous hate, this Fury?
(226)

In the third play of the trilogy the Gorgons/Furies have pursued Orestes to the
Acropolis in Athens, where he falls before the shrine of Athena. Orestes cries out
for vindication: it was after all by Apollo's command that he had murdered his
mother. Why then do the gods allow the Furies to pursue him so relentlessly?

And now a new theme emerges: Aeschylus introduces a new way of resolving
conflict. Rather than an ongoing cycle of violence, there will be a court of law.
It will decide what should be done, and the court's decision must be accepted.
Vengeance will thus be replaced by justice; more accurately, the concept of justice
is itself changed from being defined in terms of personal revenge to being defined
as the prerogative of the polis. The decision will rest with a group of independent
citizens who will cast their ballot as they see fit on the basis of the evidence
presented to them.

Orestes and Apollo are on one side; the Furies are on the other. Ten citizens
are chosen to be judges. Athena herself presides over the hearing. The Furies,
acting now as prosecutors, question Orestes about what he has done and why:
Orestes appeals to Apollo for vindication. Apollo speaks; the judges cast their
ballots. A cycle of revenge is replaced with the due process of law. It is a theme of

immense importance for western civilization. Aeschylus and Athens can be read as celebrating, in the resolution of this trilogy, the emergence of a new form of political consciousness in which the court of law, not the desire for revenge, is the source and measure of justice (see Rocco 1997, esp. ch. 5). Whereas in the earlier plays justice had been defined as revenge, from this point onwards justice rests with a court of law, and personal vendettas become by definition unjust (Fagles and Stanford 1966). The locus of legitmated violence is removed from the individual and becomes the prerogative of the polis, with the decision resting not on personal grievance but on majority vote on the basis of evidence. Death – the right to inflict death – is the prerogative of democracy, not of the individual.

This enormously important theme is, however, tangled up with another: the misogynist nature of the whole process. The Furies are grotesque female figures, monsters entwined in serpents:

> black they are, and so repulsive.
> Their heavy, rasping breathing makes me cringe.
> And their eyes ooze a discharge, sickening.
>
> (1976: 233)

They are altogether revolting. Over against them is Apollo, glorious male god. The Furies speak for the women: for Clytaemnestra, the mother whom Orestes had murdered, and for Iphigenia the daughter, whose death she was avenging. Apollo, on the other hand, stands up for Agamemnon, the father/husband whom she had killed, and for the son who killed her. Apollo invokes Zeus 'the Olympian Father' on the side of the males: he says,

> This is *his* justice, omnipotent, I warn you.
> Bend to the will of Zeus. No oath can match
> the power of the Father.
>
> (259)

In Apollo's eyes fathers and sons are more important than mothers and daughters.

But the Leader of the Furies scorns this. 'Behold, Justice!' she says scathingly. How can a son murder his mother with impunity? Apollo's speech in reply is breath-taking:

> The woman you call the mother of the child
> is not the parent, just a nurse to the seed,
> the new-sown seed that grows and swells inside her.
> The *man* is the source of life – the one who mounts.
> She, like a stranger for a stranger, keeps
> the shoot alive.
>
> (260)

To prove his case, Apollo points to Athena herself, who in Greek mythology was not born of a woman, but sprang directly from the head of Zeus.

> The father can father forth without a mother.
> Here she stands, our living witness. Look –
> Child sprung full-blown from Olympian Zeus,
> never bred in the darkness of the womb.
>
> (261)

Therefore to kill a father in revenge for a daughter requires retribution in return; but to kill a mother in revenge for a father is justice. The asymmetry is glaring.

Nevertheless, in Aeschylus' play Apollo's speech is decisive. Athena, who has been presiding over the hearing, has just been made the chief exhibit. She speedily draws proceedings to a close, making an issue of the way in which a court of law has replaced individual action as the locus of justice. The judges go to cast their ballots. The vote is equally split. So Athena herself casts the deciding vote – and votes for Orestes' acquittal on specifically gendered grounds.

> I will cast my lot for you.
> No mother gave me birth.
> I honour the male, in all things but marriage.
> Yes, with all my heart I am my Father's child.
> I cannot set more store by the woman's death –
> she killed her husband, guardian of their house.
> Even if the vote is equal, Orestes wins.
>
> (264)

So Orestes is set free, vindicated. Athena pacifies the Furies, who are outraged at the verdict: she persuades them to renounce their inclination to incite civil war and destruction.

> Let our wars
> rage on *abroad*, with all their force, to satisfy
> our powerful lust for fame . . . – my curse on *civil* war.
>
> (269; my emphasis)

The whole play – indeed the whole trilogy – is presented as the emergence of law and democracy over individual wilfulness and internecine strife. A concept of justice has been born worthy of such a polis where 'neither tyranny nor anarchy' rules. Only the polis through its courts has the right to inflict death: no individual can take it into their own hands. Athenians watching the play would be celebrating their city and its institutions, congratulating themselves on the emergence of justice worthy of a free people.

Or would they? At whose expense was this justice? What was suppressed when this understanding of justice came to the fore? As Aeschylus presents it, the triumph of justice is also a triumph of father-right over mother-right, of male over female, and of civil peace at the expense of foreign war: was this meant to be celebrated? The answer turns on the extent to which the utterances of Apollo and Athena represent Aeschylus' own views. It can of course not be assumed that a character in a drama is an unequivocal mouthpiece for its author. Indeed it has been argued that Aeschylus is at pains to indicate his refusal of the misogynist and xenophobic stance of the gods as he represents them (Rehm 1994: 54–6). Might Aeschylus at some level have been signalling that the arrogation of the right of death to the male citizens constituting themselves as a court of law actually engendered injustice even while asserting justice? If males have the sole right of deciding on death, who in fact will die? In the play, the answer is plain: women's deaths do not count for as much as men's deaths when men are doing the counting; neither are foreign deaths important. Democracy takes to itself the exclusive right to kill, and calls it justice; but the result is that men kill and women and foreigners die. Is that the sort of justice that should be celebrated?

Can this be justice?

Whatever Aeschylus intended, those in his audience with ears to hear would perhaps have pondered such questions. One member of his audience was probably Sophocles, who some years later wrote his own play[2] on the stories of Orestes and his family. In Sophocles' *Electra*, Clytaemnestra and Aegisthus have been ruling triumphantly since their murder of Agamemnon. Electra, who continues loyally to mourn for her father, is vilified by her mother and her lover, is forbidden to marry, and is treated as 'a menial drudge' in the house that had been her father's (1953: 74). At the beginning of the play Electra comes out of that house, in distress at her father's death, utterly isolated and longing for her brother Orestes to return. Her loyalty is to her father's tomb. Yet this very loyalty and insistence on justice is also its opposite: love for her father is constituted in Electra as hatred for her mother; fidelity to justice turns into the bitter poison of revenge.

Sophocles' play turns on these reversals, which are also reversals of life and death, male and female. More insistently than Aeschylus, Sophocles reveals how easy it is for someone persuaded of their own justice to turn to evil. Violence, he shows, destroys the very structures of the society that it was undertaken to preserve. His play is at one level a psychological study of individuals and family relations, and has often been studied as such; but in fifth-century Athens it must surely also have been a statement on the bitter antagonism between members of the 'family' of Greek city-states that erupted in the disastrous Peloponnesian Wars. It was a searing meditation upon the soul-destroying narrowness of self-righteous insistence on justice as vengeance. As Sophocles says in another play,

> You must not let your violent will persuade you
> Into such hatred as would tread down justice.
>
> (1953: 63)

It is of course all the more dangerous when coupled with religion and self-deception, so that hatred can masquerade as piety and love, as when Electra represents to herself her hatred for her mother as love for her father, and her lust for revenge as fidelity to justice.

Symbolic of these reversals in Sophocles' play is the oscillation between house and tomb. The former should be the place of life, the latter the place of death; but the opposite is the case. The house, the home, is the place in which Electra feels herself deadened. She is kept from marriage and the new life of children, and made into a menial slave as her mother and Aegisthus try to force her away from her loyalty to her dead father. Her house has become a tomb in which she has been buried alive. By contrast, her father's grave and her hope of revenge is the focus of her life. At a point of despair in the play she calls the house 'hateful' and swears never to enter it again.

> Can this be justice? No, I will not go back,
> Nor ever set foot in the house again. Here,
> Here at the door I will lie and starve to death,
> For I have no friend in the world.
> Let them come and kill me
> If they hate me so; to kill me would be kindness;
> Life is all pain to me; I want to die.
>
> (93)

Sophocles draws pity from his audience for Electra's suffering. Yet mingled with the pity is unease. Electra clutches the suffering to herself, forges her identity in victimhood. As the Chorus says of her, she hoards her grief and finds distorted satisfaction in self-torture (75). From making a virtue out of being a victim, it is only a small step for her to turn the perceived injustice into revenge. As the Chorus warns her, 'your sullen soul breeds strife unending' (75).

A little urn signifies the reversals (Segal 1981: 277–9; 1995: 124–5). Electra has been longing for the return of her brother Orestes; Clytaemnestra has been dreading it. Both of them expect that when he comes he will exact revenge. A messenger arrives to announce that Orestes has died in a chariot race, and that he bears his ashes in an urn. From the Prologue, the audience knows what Clytaemnestra and Electra do not, namely that this urn of ashes is a ruse and that the messenger is none other than Orestes himself, alive and well. Electra weeps and wants to hold the urn in her hands: 'this little pot of dust' which is all that is left of her darling who is now 'dust and a shadow' (104).

> Death lay in the way you had to walk, and I
> Must die, must die with your death. O my brother,

> Let me come home with you, dead with the dead,
> To stay with you forever . . . let me die
> And be where you are . . .

ash in a small urn. Electra clings to the urn, to death and to the love that she had for the dead, transformed now into hatred for the living; while Orestes, unrecognised, tries to persuade her to give it up because he is alive. It is only when Orestes shows her their father's signet ring, the symbol of male power and possession, that Electra is willing to relinquish the urn, the womb-like container that holds only (pseudo) death. It is that deathly womb/urn that parts Electra and Orestes irrevocably from Clytaemnestra who gave them birth, while their dead father's signet ring unites them.

The urn thus indicates yet another reversal that works itself out through the play: that between mother and daughter. Electra presents herself as being on the side of justice and loyalty, but by her own admission she is so overwrought as to be beside herself (75). When Clytaemnestra first makes her appearance she seems by contrast quite reasonable and not nearly the ogre that Electra's account of her would have led us to expect. Yes, Clytaemnestra admits; she did kill Agamemnon. But she argues that she had justice on her side: no father who is willing to sacrifice his own child in order to lead an army could be a 'sane and prudent parent': she might even be implying that murdering him saved Electra and the other children. 'You would do well to make sure of your own ground before condemning others,' she concludes (85).

Electra, however, will have none of it. She has a different interpretation for Iphigenia's sacrifice, based on an appeal to divinities, and refuses even to consider her mother's reasoning. 'If life for life be the rule,' Electra insists, then 'justice demands *your* life before all others' (86). Yet as Aeschylus had already pointed out, by that argument Electra herself, an accomplice in her mother's murder, would be next in line: revenge never stops. Electra rages at her mother:

> call me what you will –
> Vile, brutal, shameless – if I am all these,
> I am your true daughter!
>
> (86)

In a savage twist, Clytaemnestra goes to prepare the urn for burial; and as she does so, Orestes kills her, while Electra shrieks, 'strike her again, strike!' in paroxysms of hatred and revenge. Death, gender and justice go through multiple inversions as the urn/womb is harbinger not of Orestes' death but of their mother's murder; and what has seemed like loyal love shows itself to be uncontrolled violence.

Electra becomes what she hates. She never doubts that she is the victim and has justice on her side; but by the end of the play it is in fact her mother who has become the victim, dead because of Electra's rage, while Electra has become savage in the passion of her hatred. Sophocles reminds his viewers that though Electra has indeed been wronged, as has Agamemnon, so also have Iphigenia and Clytaemnestra. Electra's unselfcritical righteousness is portrayed as suspect, deeply unattractive and dangerous; and in the end she herself is so consumed by it that all she can do is scream for Aegisthus' murder without pity and without so much as proper burial or funeral rites.

> Kill him at once,
> And throw his body to the gravediggers . . .
> No other punishment can pay his debt
> For all that I have suffered.
>
> (116)

No longer is there an appeal to justice or retribution on behalf of her father, which up until this point has been the reason (or at least the rationalization) of Electra's insistence on the killings. Here it is her own suffering, her own sense of victimhood seeking revenge that is screaming for blood. Her suffering has been real enough; moreover Aegisthus in the play is a thoroughly despicable character. But Sophocles shows that hatred and violence are no way to deal with the problems: they only breed more of themselves in the very person or society bent on rooting them out. It was a sharp message to deliver to the Athenians, who just at this time were setting themselves up as the moral policemen of the Greek world.

The folly of revenge

In Aeschylus' *Oresteia* the gods have a significant role; in Sophocles' *Electra* they are much less to the fore. By the time Euripides wrote his own *Electra* and *Orestes* his message is that revenge is *always* folly; and that attributing the desire for revenge on to the deities is weak-minded projection that refuses its own moral responsibility (Vellacott 1972: 10; 1963: 12). This is so in spite of the fact that in many of Euripides' plays, including the two which retell the story of Electra and Orestes, the gods come on stage and speak for themselves at the end of the play: even then Euripides invites his audience to be sceptical.[3]

In Euripides' play, Electra has been married off to a poor but upright peasant who treats her with dignity. Electra herself, however, nurses her grievances as devotedly as she does in Sophocles' drama, but with even greater emphasis on the immortals. She repeatedly calls on the gods to bring back Orestes to avenge their father's death.

> Zeus, O Zeus, hear me! Let Orestes,
> Wherever he be, land on the shore of Argos
> And punish the murderers of our father!
>
> (1963: 109)

The Chorus of country women suggest that she ought to pray 'piously' rather than spending her time in 'sighs and groans'; but Electra replies, 'Electra the wretched prays, year after year . . . but no god hears' (111).

But perhaps they do hear after all. Immediately after Electra says this, Orestes and his friend Pylades actually do arrive, just as she had asked, though Electra does not recognize them. Is this an answer to her prayers? The Chorus seems to think so: they sing,

> God is with us, Electra;
> God leads us in our turn to victory.

Electra herself, however, is bent wholly on revenge; and, not content with their return, makes vengeance a new test of the gods.

> We can never again believe in gods
> If wickedness is now to triumph over right.
>
> (125)

What this amounts to is saying that the gods must conform to her expectations of them, expectations which have become distorted with hatred and self-pity.

Electra and Orestes now plot to murder their mother and her lover. The plot does them no credit. Aegisthus is to be killed while he is making a sacrifice: as he presides over it he is to become the unsuspecting victim. That is bad enough; but the plan for the murder of Clytaemnestra is worse. Electra proposes to send word to her mother that she has had a son; she is confident that Clytaemnestra will come to celebrate the new arrival. And indeed she does come, showing concern and care for her daughter. Even more than in Sophocles' *Electra*, Clytaemnestra is nothing like the evil woman that Electra has made her out to be. Early in the play we are informed that she has saved Electra's life at least once; and now she falls for Electra's deception like any grandmother wanting to see the new baby and looking for some way to make peace with her daughter. Electra confronts her with all her stored up accusations and the old refrain that justice demands revenge. Clytaemnestra replies with great restraint, putting the most charitable possible construction on Electra's tirade; she even shows remorse for killing Agamemnon.

> My child, your nature has always been to love your father.
> It is natural; some children love their fathers best,
> And some their mothers. I'll forgive you. I do not,
> In fact, exult unduly over what I did.
> With what insensate fury I drove myself to take
> My grand revenge! How bitterly I regret it now!
>
> (142)

But Electra dismisses this regret; and instead of reconciliation she lures her mother into the house to celebrate the 'birth'. There, she and her brother murder their mother; the pretended birth turns into real death.

What makes the murders of Aegisthus and Clytaemnestra all the more disturbing is the religious aura with which Electra and Orestes surround themselves. When they have made their treacherous plans, and before they begin to carry them out, they have a prayer meeting, raising their petitions to Zeus and Hera, praying for victory and vengeance. They are sure that they have the gods on their side; they never think it possible that they might be mistaken. But the Chorus strikes a more cautious note. After several stanzas in which they tell the old story in the usual form in which Zeus rewards good and punishes evil, they suddenly stop in their tracks, and say,

> That is the story. But I can hardly believe
> That the golden sun turned his face,
> Changed his burning course,
> To help a mortal's misfortune
> And requite a human sin.
>
> (130–1)

By contrast, Electra is incapable of such healthy scepticism. So also is Orestes when he returns triumphant with the corpse of Aegisthus: 'Name first the gods . . . as accomplishers of this good fortune,' he says, 'and give your second praise to me, who am the gods' . . . instrument' (135–6).

When it comes to killing Clytaemnestra, however, Orestes becomes far less confident. He protests that although he and his sister had a legitimate feud with Aegisthus, killing their own mother is different. Even if Apollo himself commanded it, it is 'blind brutality'. But Electra argues with him, urges him, asserts that not to murder is to 'defy the gods'. Orestes hesitates: 'Some fiend disguised as god commanded me,' he says. Electra is scornful: how could a fiend impersonate Apollo? But still Orestes doubts: his moral conscience struggles to assert itself over self-regarding piety. 'I can't believe that what the god told me is right' (138). Exasperated, Electra abandons religious appeals and accuses him of cowardice. With this accusation Orestes is defeated: he is indeed cowardly, for he cannot stand up to her; but that is not what she meant. 'Let it be done,' he says, 'Heaven cannot help my agony' (139).

It is only when the murder has been accomplished that things change. Suddenly, having killed their mother, Orestes and Electra become like lost children needing a parent. Shocked and weeping, Electra says,

> Tears, my brother – let tears be endless.
> I am guilty.
> I was burning with desperate rage against her;
> Yet she was my mother, I her daughter.
>
> (146)

Orestes, too, is in torment. In contrast to their former certainties, neither of them now know what to do. And the Chorus affirms this state of mind.

> Your mind has returned to itself,
> And blows now with the wind of truth.
> Now your thoughts are holy;
> But then they defied the gods.
>
> (146)

And now, when it is too late to change anything, the gods Castor and Polydeuces appear on stage. They pronounce the injustice of the murders and the punishment for the sister and brother. The two will be parted forever; Orestes will be tormented by the Furies. The spectator can hardly escape increasing levels of scepticism: what a fine time for the gods to show up! As Charles Segal has shown in relation to other plays of Euripides, the gods are revealed to be remote from participation in actual dilemmas of justice; 'human actors are left alone, to work out their own solutions to the evil and degradation around them' (Segal 1993: 224), and only when it is all over do the gods make an appearance. The piety that projects hatred, retribution and revenge on to the divine and uses religion as a justification for killing is utterly flawed, and can lead only to further cycles of evil and destruction. Euripides does not deny the gods, though he makes them ambiguous (Gould 1990: 171–88). What he does insist upon is that people must take moral responsibility for their own actions, and that revenge is never justice.

Killing in self-defence?

It is possible – indeed conventional – to read the tragedians, especially Sophocles and Euripides, as offering deep psychological insights into individual conflicts and unconscious motivations: we need only recall the use Freud made of Sophocles' *Oedipus*. Since the time of the Greek comedian Aristophanes, Euripides has been credited with special insight into female psychology and the effects upon women of the masculinist culture of violence and possession (Vellacott 1963; 1972; 1975; but see also Rabinowitz 1993). I have been suggesting, however, that the plays should also be read in their political context, and thus as offering analyses not only of individual psychology but also of social and political affairs.

Athens and Sparta with their respective allies had been at war since 431, but in 421 they agreed to the Peace of Nicias by which hostilities were officially at an end. Both sides, however, used the Peace only when it was convenient to them. Both continued to behave aggressively and each claimed justice on their side when they pursued revenge in a spiral of violence that could hardly fail to escalate. If *Electra* was performed in 418 or soon after, as is generally agreed, then its audience would have been no strangers to the cycle of revenge and whipped-up hatred and violence that the drama portrays. They would have been experiencing or participating in just such a cycle in relation to Sparta, and, like Electra, waiting for the opportunity to take complete and murderous revenge. They could see themselves as victims and portray their aggression as self-defence. But Euripides poses questions for them. What happens to people who cling to victimhood as their self-identity? Is revenge really justice? Can those who see violence as just retaliation in fact claim the eternal gods on their side? What of their own moral responsibility? Is it possible that they might be mistaken?

These questions became even more insistent in 417. In that summer, Athens 'made an expedition against the island of Melos,' as Thucydides states starkly (Thucydides 1954: 400). Melos is a small island in the Aegean Sea. During the first phase of the Peloponnesian War it had been neutral, though as it had initially been settled by Spartans its sympathies lay with Sparta, especially after Athens 'had brought force to bear on them by laying waste their land'. Athens' arrogant political and economic exploitation during its imperial period gave rise to festering resentment throughout the Aegean; especially because with the Peace of Nicias of 421 such exploitation should have ceased. Peace or no peace, Athens under the leadership of the flamboyant and self-regarding Alcibiades was spoiling for a fight: for Alcibiades it was actually an opportunity to consolidate his political power at home. Athens was stirred up into resentment at Melos' neutrality, which they chose to portray, improbably, as a danger to Athens and a threat to the peace of the region. So they, in 'self-defence', sent against Melos the expedition that Thucydides describes – a force of 3,000 troops, probably twice the size of the entire Melian male population – and ordered Melos to surrender without condition.

As Thucydides presents it, the Athenians proceed with complete cynicism. They pretend to negotiate, claiming the voice of reason; but the Council of the Melians see through this perfectly well. The Athenian proposal to negotiate is a fig leaf barely covering their lust for battle; since as the Melians point out,

> What is scarcely consistent with such a proposal is the present threat, indeed the certainty, of your making war on us. We see that you have come prepared to judge the argument yourselves, and that the likely end of it all will be . . . war.

> (401)

The Melians are right; Athens is brandishing reason and negotiation but is actually using it as a weapon. Although Athens prides itself upon being the civilization built on freedom of speech and rationality, they actually reject any appeal to justice, and assert instead that 'the standard of justice depends on the equality of power to compel and that in fact the strong do what they have the power to do and the weak accept what they have to accept' (402). The Melians try to find a compromise, pointing out that even in terms of Athenian self-interest Athens should accept their neutrality rather than insist on their humiliation, which in the long run is sure to bring instability to the whole region. But Athens replies that they are not interested in the long run: they want power and they want it now. Above all, they want to be *seen* to have power. The eyes of the world are upon them and concessions would look like weakness.

The Melians, fully aware that their adversary is vastly superior in military might, can only appeal to the gods to help them: 'we trust that the gods will give us fortune . . . because we are standing for what is right against what is wrong' (404). But the Athenians brush off this idea, claiming that they themselves have the gods on their side: *their* theology is the correct one, and it gives them the right to force the Melians into submission. And with that they lay siege to the city and blockade the island; and when in due course it falls, as it inevitably must, the Athenians behave with extreme brutality, killing all the men, selling the women and children into slavery, and eventually recolonizing the island with people of their own choosing. Thucydides presents it baldly, without comment; but it is clear that although Athens is militarily victorious, the defeat of Melos is for Athens a moral disaster: one of a series which culminates at last in the decline of Greek civilization.[4]

Now, if Euripides' *Electra* was performed in 416–415 then the audience who watched it were the same people as those who had gone to war against Melos.[5] How would they hear the assurance of Electra that she had the gods and justice on her side? What about her refusal to take seriously any effort at explanation or negotiation that her mother offered? And would they not have been uncomfortable with the appeal to the gods of Electra and Orestes? There were of course important contrasts as well as parallels between the characters of the play and the political drama between Athens and Melos: for example, in the play Clytaemnestra and Aegisthus are unquestionably guilty of crimes of which the Melians were never accused. But in the immediate situation that could only make the Athenian appeal to justice and to the gods appear even more brazen. And if a longer view was taken, a view which identified Melos with Sparta, then both sides had been guilty of treachery and atrocity. How could Athenian violence masquerade as superior morality?

Euripides did not stop with *Electra*. In 415, when the Athenians had the annihilation of Melos fresh in their minds, he produced another play, the *Women of Troy*. Its setting is the time immediately after the fall of Troy when the victorious Argives are about to sail for home: it is an obvious parallel to the victory over Melos. But the focus of the drama is not on the Argives, but on the Trojan women who bear the brunt of the defeat. Their husbands, brothers and fathers have been slaughtered, and they themselves are waiting to be taken away into slavery by the conquering Greeks. It is a lottery. Cassandra is to go to Agamemnon; her sister Andromache goes to Neoptolemus; and their aged mother Hecabe is assigned to Odysseus: they are likely never to see one another again. The women are in despair. Hecabe laments,

> Shear the head, tear the cheek,
> Beat the brow! . . .
> Weep for me, and veil my head;

> Hope is dead; today I know
> The last throe of misery!
> (1973: 99)

The Greek messenger, Talthybius, who comes to tell them their fate, is both callous and stupid: 'strange how intolerable the indignity of slavery is to those born free,' he says (100). Strange? The Athenian audience, remembering their treatment of Melos, should have cringed. Hecabe continues her lament, aware of the fate of slaves. She has seen her husband the king killed, and all her sons including Hector. She has had to watch her daughters being assigned to the Greeks.

> Now comes the last, the crowning agony; that I
> In my old age shall go to Hellas as a slave.
> This will lay on me tasks to humble my grey head –
> Answering the door, or keeping keys, or cooking food –
> I, who bore Hector! I shall lay my shrivelled sides
> To rest, not in a royal bed, but on the floor;
> And wear thin, faded rags to match my skin and mock
> my royalty. O misery!
>
> (106)

There is even worse to come. Andromache breaks the news to Hecabe that her youngest daughter, Polyxena, has been killed, slaughtered by the Greeks as a virgin sacrifice at Achilles' tomb. And then, when it seems that the women can bear no more, the dreadful Talthybius returns with the Greek demand that Astynaenax, the infant son of Hector and Andromache, should be taken from her and killed, 'thrown from the battlements of Troy.' As he announces his demand, he insists, 'Now, accept this decision and be sensible. Don't cling to him' (114). But what mother would *not* cling to her child rather than let him be taken to slaughter? Who would be able to watch this drama without revulsion at what the conquering Greeks were counting as 'sensible'? Hecabe cries out,

> O city, dead, deserted, I weep for you.
> Home where my babes were born, this is your end:
> Who would not weep? City lost, children lost,
> All lost! Was there ever heard such a chorus of pain?
> When were such tears shed for a murdered house?
> Can even the dead see this, and forget to weep?
>
> (110)

And could even the Athenians watch it without shame at their own similar behaviour at Melos? When all is at its worst, Menelaus, the Greek captain, strides on to the stage with the words, 'How gloriously the sun shines on this happy day!' (118).

As in his other plays, Euripides raises inescapable questions about how the events he portrays relate to the gods: the tension between violence and eternity. As Hecabe is about to be dragged off to the ship that will bear her to slavery, she cries out, 'Gods! Gods! Where are you?' But then she adds in despair, 'Why should I clamour to the gods? We called on them before, and not one heard us call' (131). And the Chorus puts the lingering question:

> Zeus, God, farewell! . . .
> Firm in your heavenly throne,
> While the destroying Fury gives
> Our home to ashes and our flesh to worms –
> We ask and ask: What does this mean to You?
>
> (125)

What indeed? They get no answer. Is the suffering really the will of the gods, or is it the evil cruelty of selfish men who claim the gods on their side? The Trojan women 'ask and ask'; but at the very beginning of the play Euripides has given a clue. Poseidon and Athena between them have agreed to whip up storms that will make the homeward journey of the Greeks 'unfortunate': we know before the action begins that most of the Greeks, for all their victorious swagger, are soon to perish. Even then, however, Euripides is ambiguous. Poseidon says,

> When a man who takes a city includes in the general destruction
> Temples of the high gods and tombs that honour the dead,
> He is a fool: his own destruction follows close.
>
> (93)

Yes; but what is the sacrilege to which the gods are objecting? In the drama, it seems that all they are concerned about is the insult to themselves, to their temples. But is not the whole destructive war, its slaughter and its slavery, sacrilege? What is Euripides saying about such savagery masquerading as civilization, whether in his play or in his city? For the Athenians to break the peace, to bully and slaughter the Melians, and then claim the gods on their side could be seen as the sort of 'victory' of which they should be deeply ashamed. Those with eyes to see and ears to hear in Euripides' audience must have been most uneasy about Athens' behaviour at Melos. It can be no great surprise that a few years later, as Athens was sliding further into moral decline and eventually military disaster, Euripides fled to Macedon (where he died in 406), conscious that there were those in Athens who would react with guilty rage at the mirror he held up to them.

In the genealogy of death in the western symbolic the tragedians occupy a special place. Although in such matters as the place or state of the dead they largely echo the conventional thought of the time, they each in their own way confront death – and force their audiences to confront death – as tragedy. The deaths that occur in their dramas are violent: sacrifice, murder and war. Women bear the brunt of it. The tragedians are intent on showing the misery of war, the folly of revenge, the hypocrisy of confident and self-serving appeals to justice and religion. They insist on making their audiences aware of the gendered cruelty and suffering caused by war and violence. In a political context in which Athens wanted to celebrate its moral and military superiority, they do not allow the Athenians to escape the knowledge that there is much for which shame would be a far more appropriate response.

Chapter 8

Whose tragedy?

The great tragedians of the Athenian Golden Age, I have argued, represent violence and war, not as glorious, or as a platform for eternity, but as brutal, foolish and evil. In contrast to a Homeric view of the manly heroism of a beautiful death, or the immortal glory achieved by flirting with mortal danger, the tragedians emphasise ever and again the futility and misery of war. Even if there is alleged legitimacy for war, even when it purports to be about justice, war undermines the very moral values in whose name it is fought. War is tragedy.

But whose tragedy is it? I suggest that that question can be explored at several levels. The great dramas of the fifth century can be read as the tragedy of Athens itself, not only in her downfall, but even more profoundly in her embrace of values and behaviour that were unworthy of her professed ideals. That tragedy, however, fell unequally, as all tragedies do: again and again in the works of the tragedians we find heightened the effects of the tragedy on women, on foreigners, on refugees, on asylum seekers. More broadly still, the tragedy of Athens can be read as tragedy for western culture. From Alexander the Great to Napoleon, and from Julius Caesar to contemporary USA, the west has refused to learn the lessons the tragedians sought to convey, but rather has taken for itself violence, vengeance and patriarchal power appropriated in the name of death-dealing gods whose pseudo-credentials the tragedians had laid bare. The modern west venerates the tragedians as great dramatists; but they are set into a realm of 'culture' separated from 'politics'; and their efforts to challenge the death-dealing of a violent society are, now as then, too often side-lined. In this chapter I want to lift up their early protest at the trajectory of necrophilia which even then was gaining ascendancy in what would become western culture. I want, also, to ask what could have served as an alternative, and suggest one reason why they did not find it.

'There is enough death'

Death – violent death – is the very stuff of tragedy. To understand the work of the tragedians it is necessary to understand their underlying assumptions about death, assumptions that are different from the Homeric writings on the beauty of glorious death, or from what we will find in Plato with his belief in the immortality of the soul. The portrayals of death and violence in their dramas are intercon-nected with issues of gender, beauty and religion, as they are in Homer and Plato; but they use these themes, I suggest, to challenge received opinion.

The tragedians take for granted that death is to be feared, dreaded and mourned. They retain much of the mythology of death and the afterlife that is found in Homeric writings: Hades is the god of Death, and his dwelling is the place of shades; Charon is the 'ferryman of the dead' leaning on his pole and summoning souls to 'the home of the dead' (Euripides 1953: 50–1). But while they retain this mythology, they give a different evaluation of it than we find in Homer. We have already seen this in relation to warfare; but it applies more broadly. There is very little in the tragedians about glorious death. Some lip service is paid to the notion; but the deaths that happen in the dramas are far more often horrific rather than glorious, like Jocasta's suicide when she learns that Oedipus is both her husband and her son (Sophocles 1982: 236), or the vengeful murder of Agamemnon and his mistress/slave Cassandra by his jealous but equally adulterous wife and the chain of revenge killings in which that murder is one of the links (Aeschylus 1976); or Medea's crazed slaughter of her own children (Euripides 1963: 57). There is nothing to suggest that any of these deaths are beautiful or glorious. They are horrible. Nor is there any notion in these dramas that death is simply stepping out of the prisonhouse of the body into a new realm of incorporeal truth, as we will find in some of Plato's dialogues. The fifth-century tragedians on the whole saw death as evil: indeed without that assumption their plots hardly get a purchase.

> Men who live for a day
> Are a race doomed to suffering, endless suffering.
> Fate we know to be inevitable;
> And when we meet it, it is evil.
> (Euripides 1972: 415)

Death, especially youthful death, cuts off life and its possibilities, curtails the potential of the future. In Sophocles' *Oedipus the King*, the Chorus graphically sets the grim context for the plot and reveals assumptions about death in its despairing cry about the plague that is ravaging the city of Thebes:

> Death
> so many deaths, numberless deaths on deaths, no end –
> Thebes is dying, look, her children
> stripped of pity . . .
> generations strewn on the ground
> unburied, unwept, the dead spreading death . . .
> Thebes, city of death, one long cortege . . .
> (Sophocles 1982: 169)

There is no hint here that such deaths are anything but tragic: they are certainly not beautiful.

That does not mean that there was unanimity about death, either between the tragedians or even within the surviving plays of any one of them. In Euripides' *Women of Troy* there is a sad exchange about whether in some circumstances death is preferable to life: the women of the defeated city are captives about to be dragged away into slavery, and one of their number, Polyxena, has been killed. Her sister Andromache tries to console their mother:

> It is over now. Yes, it was terrible; and yet,
> Being dead, she is more fortunate than I who live.

Hecabe, however, is not convinced.

> Not so, my daughter; death and life are not the same.
> Death is extinction; but in life there is still hope.

But Andromache insists that she is right.

> To be dead is the same as never to have been born,
> And better far than living on in wretchedness.
> The dead feel nothing; evil then can cause no pain.
> . . . For Polyxena it is as though she had not been born;
> In death she recalls none of her past sufferings.
> > (Euripides 1973: 111)

Not everyone would have agreed that the dead had no memory or feeling: the shades of Hades were sometimes represented as having a ghostly existence like that of Achilles in the *Iliad*, an existence which might include the possibility of showing themselves in apparition to the living, complete with memory and intelligence, as does Darius king of Persia in Aeschylus' *The Persians* (1961: 141). Nevertheless the dead are deeply mourned, while the living console one another as best they can with the thought that at least the dead no longer suffer.

'Count no one happy until they are dead'

One of the frequently repeated themes of the tragedians is the uncertainty of life, the many ways in which a life of comfort and happiness can suddenly be transformed into misery. Until a life is complete – that is, until a person has died – it is premature to pronounce that life a happy one, since a sudden reversal could overturn the verdict (see, for example, Aeschylus 1976: 138). It was Solon, a law-giver and reformer of sixth-century Athens, to whom the actual saying was attributed; the characters of tragic drama made it their own.

It is, for example, the last line of Sophocles' great play *Oedipus the King*, and (in a reading different from that made familiar by Freud) it can be seen as the summation and moral of the tragedy. Oedipus had risen from obscurity to become king, had solved the riddle of the Sphynx to the great benefit of the city and had married the Queen Jocasta, widow of the former king. All was in his favour. And then, in his effort to bring justice to the city and his determination to leave no stone unturned in his investigations, he discovers that a man he had killed in a skirmish had in fact been his father, and that the Queen he married was his mother, even though he had been removed from his parents at birth to try to prevent just such a happening which had indeed been prophesied. Appalled at what had happened through their ignorance, Jocasta hangs herself, and Oedipus takes her brooch and with it puts out his eyes. After he is led away in a pitiable state, the Chorus concludes:

> People of Thebes, my countrymen, look on Oedipus.
> He solved the famous riddle with his brilliance,
> he rose to power, a man beyond all power.
> Who could behold his greatness without envy?
> Now what a black sea of terror has overwhelmed him.
> Now as we keep our watch and wait the final day,
> count no man happy till he dies, free of pain at last.
>   (Sophocles 1982: 251)

And there the play ends. In Sophocles' tragedies, the uncertainty of life is linked to the inscrutable dealings of the gods with mortals. Oedipus' murder of his father and marriage to his mother had been prophesied; and both he and they had done all they could to try to avert it. But they could not escape their fate. They were foredoomed. The eternal gods hold the world, and the lives and deaths of mortals, in their power.

In the sequel to *Oedipus the King*, *Oedipus at Colonus*, Sophocles portrays Oedipus as a pitiful, blind old man, saying resignedly to Theseus who has granted him refuge:

> Oh Theseus,
> dear friend, only the gods can never age,
> the gods can never die. All else in the world
> almighty Time obliterates, crushes all
> to nothing. The earth's strength wastes away,
> the strength of a man's body wastes and dies –
> faith dies, and bad faith comes to life,
> and the same wind of friendship cannot blow forever . . .
>   (Sophocles 1982: 322)

The gods are in charge. They turn human fortunes around unpredictably, without correlation to good or bad behaviour. Oedipus had tried to do right, and his very efforts were his undoing.

The same uncertainty is emphasized by another of Sophocles' heroes, Philoctetus, a character drawn directly from Homer. Philoctetus, gripped by illness, has been abandoned and left all alone on an island, because his fellow Greeks did not want the bother of caring for his noxious wound. However, he has in his possession the bow and arrow of Heracles. This is the bow which the gods have said will be necessary to conquer Troy. So Neoptolemus, son of Achilles, is sent by the Greeks to take it away from Philoctetus.

Philoctetus, seeing a human being at last, begs in vain for help.

> You must have pity
> If you but think how all our mortal lives
> Are set in danger and perplexity:
> One day to prosper, and the next – who knows?
> When all is well, then look for rocks ahead;
> Look well to your life, when life runs easily;
> Death may be waiting for you.
> (Sophocles 1953: 179)

In his case, too, fortune and misery are held to be in the lap of the gods: it was a serpent's bite in a temple of the goddess Chryse that had caused his stinking wound. But whereas Oedipus had resigned himself to the fate that the gods handed out to him, Philoctetus rages against it in helpless fury.

> Does nothing evil ever die? . . .
> I think the gods delight to turn away
> All deep-eyed villains from the door of death
> And hale in all the good men. Why, then, why
> Praise the gods, when, even while we praise,
> We find them evil?
> (178)

Philoctetus' frustration is not an expression of disbelief in the gods, or even of doubt that they ultimately control human affairs. Rather, it is a protest at their unfairness: what happens to Philoctetus can hardly be said to be justice. Although each of Sophocles' tragedies raises issues of human choice and responsibility – is Philoctetus' fate the result of divine decree, or of the callousness of the Greeks? – the gods are still said to be in charge of human destiny. The exhortation to count no one happy until they are dead is a reminder that it is impossible to know what the gods might have in store.

In another of Sophocles' plays, *Women of Trachis*, the action opens with the words of Solon. This time they are spoken by Deianeira, wife of Heracles, who is eagerly awaiting her husband's return; and their import is destabilized. Deianeira tries to remember the words, but seems uncertain, slightly scatty, unable to recollect exactly how his saying goes.

> Call no man happy, unhappy . . . you cannot tell
> Till the day of his death. The proverb is old and plain.
> It may be true. I know I'm still alive
> And I have had sorrow and suffering in plenty.
> (Sophocles 1953: 119)

It is an amusing sequence, as the woman takes the solemn words of the law-giver and muses that 'it *may* be true'. But if we are meant to be amused by her dithering, the amusement quickly turns to bitter irony as Deianeira doubts Heracles' continuing love for her and, in an effort to ensure his affection, inadvertently sends him a poisoned robe which causes him to die in torment. Again the responsibility is attributed to the gods. The Chorus presses home the point in the shocking final words of the play:

> Women of Trachis, you have leave to go.
> You have seen strange things,
> The awful hand of death, new shapes of woe,
> Uncounted sufferings;
> And all that you have seen
> Is God.
> (161)

But is it? The question could hardly be avoided.

In Euripides, the same Solonic refrain is pointedly used *without* reference to the gods. It is not divinity but human violence which is to the fore, for example, in Hecuba's misery in *The Women of Troy*. Like Sophocles, Euripides is dramatizing incidents from Homer, in this case the effects upon Hecabe (Hecuba) and her daughters of the fall of Troy to the Greeks. All that the women can now look forward to is violence: rape, slavery, or (at best) death. Before, they had lived in comfort; now their fortunes are reversed.

> The soft proud days of Troy are past; lead me
> To find my hard slave's pallet and my pillow of stones,
> And die under the lash of tears. Good fortune means
> Nothing; call no man happy till the day he dies.
> (Euripides 1973: 107)

The grief and misery Hecabe now experiences are not attributed to fate or to the gods but to the ways in which men conduct warfare and to their brutal behaviour towards captive women.

In drama after drama, Euripides shows the devastating consequences for women of the perpetual violence of men, especially the way in which men who are victorious in battle take for granted that the women of the defeated city are lawful booty, for them to treat as they please. In *Andromache*, Euripides expands the theme, using the same old phrase from Solon. Andromache is by now in exile, captive to Neoptolemus to whom she has borne a son; but she is only a slave mistress. Neoptolemus has married Hermione; and Andromache, as slave woman, is treated with contempt by the wife. Andromache can do nothing but 'cry her griefs to heaven'. All women do the same, she says,

> But *my* griefs
> Clamour unending for lament: my city gone,
> Hector my husband killed, this harsh and joyless life
> To which I've been bound fast since first I left my palace
> To become a slave. How wrong it is ever to call
> Any mortal happy until he's dead, and you have seen
> In what condition he passed through his final day
> Of life, before departing to the world below.
>
> (Euripides 1972: 148)

We might well wonder what it must have been like for Athenian men to hear these words of one of their own venerated ancestors spoken by a woman who was bearing the brunt of Greek conquests. Did they get the message? Would they have been outraged? At the very least, Euripides was confronting those with ears to hear that their practices of war and violence had brutal consequences for people just like themselves, especially for women.

Themes of gender are constantly interwoven in fifth-century tragedies (Rehm 1994; Rabinowitz 1993). Euripides rejects the idea that the misery that women suffer as a result of war is simply fate or the will of the gods; he shows that the responsibility for their suffering rests squarely on human shoulders. By placing the famous words of Solon into the mouths of women who are bearing the brunt of Greek conquest, Euripides removes the phrase from stock conventional piety and turns it against the very people who might have wanted to claim the gods as their own. In such a context, where death cannot be blamed on gods or on forces outside of human control, tragedy must be assessed differently. Tragedy – war – arises out of human action. Not only is death tragic rather than glorious, but its tragedy is a result of human folly or wickedness, of the evils of war and, as we saw in the previous chapter, of revenge hypocritically masquerading as justice.

The lesser evil

That is why, although death is tragic, it is not the worst of tragedies. One of the themes emerging in the writings of the tragedians is that there is a standard of physical and moral integrity without which life is not worth living. Aeschylus dramatizes this in relation to physical torment in *Prometheus Bound*, where unbearable pain is seen as worse than death. Prometheus is a god, one of the Titans. He is being punished by Zeus for giving gifts, including the gift of fire, to human-kind. Prometheus is shackled to a rock. Each day an eagle comes to tear out his liver; each night it grows back again, so that his agony is perpetual. He is visited by Io, a mortal woman, who is also being tormented by the gods: they send an enormous gadfly whose sting literally drives her crazy. This affliction is visited upon her by Hera, wife of Zeus, out of jealousy because Zeus desired Io. Both the god Prometheus and the woman Io find their suffering intolerable. It brings about a striking exchange between them. Io says in despair,

> Why should I go on living? Why not hurl myself
> At once from this rocky cliff, be dashed to pieces,
> And find relief from all my pain? Better to die
> Once, than to suffer torment all my living days.

But that option is not available to Prometheus: he is immortal; he cannot die. He replies:

> Then you would find it hard to bear *my* agonies,
> Since I am fated not to die. Death would have brought
> Release; but now no end of suffering is in sight.
>
> (Aeschylus 1961: 42)

We have seen how in the Homeric writings the immortality of the gods is the feature that distinguishes them from humans/mortals, and makes the gods enviable. By a deft twist Aeschylus shows that there are circumstances in which the desir-ability of god-like immortality is problematic to say the least.

There are other instances as well in which death is portrayed as preferable to physical and moral suffering. In Aesychlus' *The Suppliants*, the fifty daughters of Danaus vow to die rather than to submit to rape and brutal marriage. Sophocles' *Ajax* is the story of a man who acts out a fit of jealous madness; when he comes to himself he chooses to fall on his sword rather than live with the shame of what he has done.[1] Death may be evil; but it is not the worst evil.

It is, in fact, in situations of moral intolerability that the choice of death is presented most tellingly as the lesser evil. The most famous example of one who deliberately chooses death as the inevitable price that she must pay to achieve her moral and religious goal is Sophocles' Antigone, in his play by that name. Antigone is determined to fulfil the burial rites for her brother, even though the king has forbidden her to do so on pain of death. She insists,

> Die I must, I've known it all my life –
> how could I keep from knowing? – even without
> your death-sentence ringing in my ears.
> And if I am to die before my time

> I consider that a gain. Who on earth,
> alive in the midst of so much grief as I,
> could fail to find his death a rich reward?
> So for me, at least, to meet this doom of yours
> is precious little pain. But if I had allowed
> my own mother's son to rot, an unburied corpse –
> that would have been an agony!
>
> (Sophocles 1982: 82)

There have been many modern analyses of Antigones' action in terms of the tension between the family and ritual piety to the state, and the role of gender in that tension (see Hegel 1977: 266–78; Irigaray 1985: 214–26; Rehm 1994: ch. 4; Mills 1996: 59–88). The point I am making here is simply that Sophocles is representing a woman who sees death as less evil than failure to do what she takes to be her moral duty. Death can be chosen as a necessary or inevitable price to pay for sticking with a conception of duty or good, without which human life is considered without value. In this representation, self-sacrifice or martyrdom first becomes thinkable: we will find this repeated both among the Stoics and in the amphitheatres of the Roman empire.

Although Sophocles' Antigone is represented as making an individual choice in which she sets the values of home and family against those of the city, in the context of the time the play also raises political questions. Creon, the ruler of the city, represents his refusal of the burial of Polyneices as appropriate revenge necessary for the good of the city; but as the play progresses it becomes clear that his motivations have at least as much to do with defending his own mastery and manliness as with justice. The results are disastrous, not only for Antigone but also for Creon and his family, and ultimately for the city, whose civic structure is undermined as it is left unstable and leaderless, its political continuity destroyed with the destruction of Creon's household. Was this the justice that Creon sought? What is the price of self-righteousness? What are the limits of tolerance? Antigone's choice of death, set against Creon's choice of unbending mastery, both of them represented in terms of justice, would raise for viewers questions about what sort of values, what sort of city, would be worth living for? The play represents the possibility of situations of such moral intolerability that death is preferable to acquiescence.

Again, Euripides takes this theme further, and in doing so raises awkward questions for his audience. Whereas Sophocles' Antigone is willing to accept death because of her love for a member of her own family, Euripides in several of his plays overtly depicts young people willing to be sacrificed as the price the gods demand for some supposed good of the larger community. Thus, for example, in *Phoencian Women* Creon's son Menoeceus gives his life as a blood sacrifice required by the oracles to assure the victory of Thebes (Euripides 1972: 271); and in *Hecabe* Polyxena goes willingly to be ritually killed in order to give the Argives a fair wind for their homeward journey: in her case the self-sacrifice is also a welcome escape from a life of slavery, which would have been the alternative (Euripides 1963: 69). In each drama, however, Euripides can be read as raising questions about such sacrifice. Without undermining the nobility and even the martyrdom of the young people who give their lives, he prompts the viewer to wonder about the status of the oracles and their use as a political tool. Should they be taken at face value? Did the immortals really speak? Are the deaths of young people really necessary to achieve the desired ends? Or might it be the case that the powerful are using religion, including the sincere piety and patriotism of these young people who are willing to give their lives for their country, as a cynical and calculating measure to foster their own ends?

These questions emerge again in Euripides' *Children of Heracles*, in which the young woman Macaria offers herself as the sacrifice which the 'experts' have said is necessary for Athens to win a battle in which they are engaged. There is a bitter twist to this, in that Macaria is a refugee seeking asylum in Athens together with her brothers. The king of Athens refuses to sacrifice any of his own citizens, but is willing to accept the death of an asylum seeker to whom he has a duty of hospitality. Macaria the 'barbarian' in fact shows a good deal more generosity than the Greek king. She says,

> Before you bid me, Iolaus, I am myself
> Ready to die, and give my blood for sacrifice.
> . . . Here I am: lead me to the place where I must die;
> Garland me if you will; perform your ritual.
> Defeat your enemies. Readily, not reluctantly,
> This life is offered; here I pledge myself to death.
> Because I did not count my life dear, I have won
> This dearest prize of all – to meet death gloriously.
> (Euripides 1972: 120–1)

The echoes of Homer here only add to the irony. The 'glorious death' is not that of a warrior but of a refugee woman.

Macaria goes on to voice scepticism about conventional piety, again starting with an Homeric echo: she asks for a 'glorious tomb' which will be her reward

> – if there is a world
> Below the earth; I hope there is none. For if we
> Whose short life ends in death must there too suffer pain,
> I do not know where we can turn; since death has been
> Thought of as our great remedy for all life's ills.
> (123)

At one level Macaria's self-sacrifice can be read as an act of generosity which puts Athenians to shame with their assumptions about foreigners and women, and their ideas of their own status as the most civilized of peoples. But the questions go even deeper: is there really 'a world below the earth'? And if that can be questioned, perhaps it is also possible to question the gods themselves, or at least to challenge the idea that they demand sacrifice? Once *this* question is raised, then the possibility emerges that the whole system of oracles and conventional piety is a mantle of hypocrisy, used by rulers to further their own ends. Macaria the foreign woman is sceptical and generous; the Athenians in the play are pious and selfish. It is not hard to imagine the affront this contrast might have caused to its fifth-century audience.

In Euripides' late play, *Iphigenia in Aulis*, the contrast is drawn even more tellingly between simple, generous piety that accepts self-sacrifice, and its cynical manipulation by men of power. The theme of the drama is again taken from Homer. This time it is Agamemnon's ritual sacrifice of his daughter Iphigenia in order to persuade the gods to send the fleet a fair wind to sail to Troy for the commencement of the Trojan War. Calchas the seer has pronounced that the goddess Artemis requires the blood of a virgin. Agamemnon has therefore sent for his daughter, on the pretext that she is to be married to Achilles. Before she arrives, however, he is already vacillating, regretting what he has sworn to do.

> Gods aren't blind; they're well aware when oaths are taken foolishly
> Or upon compulsion. But for me – I will not kill my child.
>
> (Euripides 1972: 381)

But he does not stick to this decision either. Under pressure from his brother Menelaus, Agamemnon is afraid that he would lose his supreme position as commander of the army if he did not now carry out the sacrifice: he actually portrays himself rather than his daughter as the victim. As for Iphigenia, at first she pleads with her father; but when she sees that it will be no use, she resolves to die nobly. Iphigenia, not her father, is the one who in fact takes the oracle at face value; and in simple piety chooses to give her life for the goddess and for the Greeks. She says,

> . . . indeed I have no right to cling to life so passionately . . .
> and if Artemis has laid a claim
> On my body, who am I, a mortal, to oppose a god?
> This I cannot do. To Hellas, then, I dedicate myself.
> Sacrifice me; take and plunder Troy.
>
> (419)

This, she says, is 'only fair and just'.

Agamemnon should have died of shame at the contrast: it is obvious that he is murdering his own child in order to retain a grip on power and to satisfy the blood lust of the army. What kind of gods would condone – let alone command – such action? The Chorus puts it succinctly: 'Events fester, and divinity is sick' (419). The drama is a tragedy, but whose tragedy is it? Is it the tragedy of Iphigenia, who dies young, murdered by her own father? Is it the tragedy of Agamemnon, who betrays not only his daughter but his own humanity in stooping to such a craven and self-regarding act? Or is it the tragedy of the whole Greek army – and by implication of the Athenian theatre audience – who would demean themselves and their religion by using it in the service of violent power? Euripides shows how in the genealogy of death, religion, self-sacrifice and manipulation are perilously intertwined.

Beauty as curse

All three tragedians hold up a mirror to Athens in which Athenians would sometimes see themselves from uncomfortable perspectives. Although especially in Aeschylus and Sophocles there is also much that can be read as a celebration of Athenian polity and civilization, even in their work there is, as we have seen, criticism more or less explicit of Athens' policies of killing and cruelty, and of the effects of war, especially upon women. In the later plays of Euripides, as the Peloponnesian War dragged on and it became obvious that Athens could not win, the critique became sharper and more pointed. Even more than military tragedy, the dramatists showed their audience the moral tragedy of a proud civilization behaving in ways unworthy of its ideals.

And yet apart from recalling Athens to its ideals – which is of course of enormous significance – the tragedians did not set themselves to offering ways forward, alternative visions of the social and symbolic structure such as can be discerned, even if only in fragments, in Sappho. The tragedians are passionately concerned with the moral integrity and reform of society; but they want Athens to live up to the ideals it already professes; they are not trying to replace those ideals with different ones. They accept that there will be wars, and that those who are defeated will be killed or enslaved, even while they expose war's savagery and its gendered consequences.

But then what? They could hardly be asking for non-violent war, or for humane slavery. They can and do expect less hypocrisy by the conquerors and more respect for the victims. That is no small thing to ask. But is it enough? If the Athenians took seriously Aeschylus' portrayal of the vanquished Persians, or Euripides' representations of captive women, would it not be necessary for them to look not just for a reform of warfare and slavery but for alternatives to them? If war is both foolish and evil, and its violence such that no divinity worthy of the name could countenance it, then must there not be ways of living that renounce the preoccupation with death? Such questions seem obvious; but they do not arise for the tragedians.

Now there is another question that does not arise, and that is the question of beauty. There is almost no discussion of beauty in the extant plays of the tragedians. The only exception is the beauty of women – especially Helen of Troy – which is virtually always a matter of their sexual attractiveness to men. I shall examine this further in a moment. But first I want, tentatively, to raise a question: is their failure to discuss beauty related to their failure to offer an alternative vision for their society? The question is of course unanswerable. It would depend upon many factors, not least how beauty was conceptualized: as we have seen from Homeric writings, it is possible to conceptualize beauty in such a way that it actually glorifies the very violence which the tragedians often tried to decry. On the other hand, if beauty is conceived of as fragile, particular and precious, as in the poems of Sappho, then focus on beauty calls for the construction of a society which preserves and cherishes the beauty of natals and enables them to flourish, a society in which the destructiveness of war and the indignity of slavery could have no place. I shall discuss the idea of flourishing more fully in relation to Aristotle, and again in later volumes of the project. Here, I want to look at what the tragedians actually say about beauty, and suggest that its relative insignificance in their writing may be interpreted as a missed opportunity.

When the tragedians do talk about beauty it is, as already indicated, most frequently in relation to women's sexual attractiveness to men, and often in a context which sets it in a negative light. Thus for example Deianeira, in Sophocles' *Women of Trachis*, expresses anxiety about the beauty of a young slave girl whom her husband has brought into their household. 'I know, I see how it is: the one with youthful beauty ripening to its prime, the other falling away. . . . This is my fear' (Sophocles 1953: 137).

It was above all Helen of Troy, appropriated from the Homeric writings, who served the tragedians as the paradigm of beauty and sexual attractiveness. Upon her beauty was blamed the destruction of the Trojan War.

> Helen the wild, maddening Helen,
> one for the many, the thousand lives
> you murdered under Troy . . .
> Once in the halls she walked and she was war,
> angel of war, angel of agony, lighting men to death.
> (Aeschylus 1976: 164)

In the Homeric writings Helen had been carried off to Troy by Paris: there is ambiguity about whether she was kidnapped or was a willing accomplice, but in either case she was hardly a warrior. Yet here she is accused of murdering a 'thousand lives'. Men's lust and sexual violence, even war itself, is blamed on women. Female beauty is made to carry the weight of guilt for multiple murder. Rather than the warriors taking moral responsibility for war, they project the burden of blame upon Helen, and more particularly upon her beauty.

Sometimes the projection goes beyond Helen to the goddesses themselves. According to Greek mythology the story of Helen had its origins in a competition between Hera, Aphrodite and Athena; and the Trojan War was the result of the goddesses' continuation of that competition, now using human pawns. Thus the young Iphigenia is portrayed by Euripides as piously accepting the old myth before she is sacrificed: the three goddesses, she says, came 'to compete for a prize of beauty' but the result was 'to doom me to death'. But even Iphigenia's piety has limits: 'My curse, my curse on Helen,' she says, 'And on the fate that linked us' (Euripides 1972: 414). Yet it is perfectly obvious (and surely Euripides intended his audience to notice) that it is actually her father Agamemnon, not Helen, who is about to kill Iphigenia, and that it is the men's desire for sex, power and war that drives on the action of the drama.

As usual it is Euripides who lifts up the myths to the most critical scrutiny. In his *Women of Troy*, Helen, in self-defence, blames the Trojan War on the goddesses, reciting again the old myth of their competition. In fact Helen goes so far as to present herself as the actual victim who should be shown 'pardon and sympathy,' since she was 'sold for (her) beauty'. It is Aphrodite, not Helen, who should therefore be the target of indignation. But the aged Hecabe pours scorn on Helen's argument.

> I don't believe
> Gods to be capable of such folly . . .
> Why should they indulge in such frivolity
> As travelling to Mount Ida for a beauty-match?
> What reason could the goddess Hera have for being
> So anxious about beauty?

The whole idea is ridiculous. And Euripides through Hecabe drives home his lesson: 'To cloak your own guilt, you dress up the gods as fools' (1973: 122).

The whole episode of the Trojan War is presented as a farce by Euripides in his drama *Helen*: not a farce that mitigates its tragedy and bloodshed but a farce in the sense that all its bloodshed was based on a false assumption. Helen was never at Troy. She had been wrapped in a cloud by Hermes and carried off to safety in Egypt. Meanwhile Paris, who thought he was taking Helen to Troy, was in fact tricked by the gods into taking only 'a living image compounded of the ether in [Helen's] likeness.' So Helen explains, 'Paris believes that he possesses me: what he holds is nothing but an airy delusion' (Euripides 1973: 136). It is, however, a delusion which the Greeks accept as fully as do the Trojans; and for that delusion the Trojan War was fought, with all its death and suffering.

Though she is safely in Egypt, Helen in this play knows all about 'the pestilence of war' that is being fought about her, and repeatedly bemoans her beauty as its cause. It is her beauty 'if so great a misfortune can be so named' that had been used to attract Paris (136). Her beauty has been a 'millstone' hung around her neck; it has been the cause of all her own suffering and has made her a curse to others. 'Beauty,' she says, 'torments me'. Though it is a blessing to other women, its effect on Helen has been to drive her to desperation.

> My cursed beauty damned with deadly power
> Trojan and wandering Greek to sufferings untold.
> (147)

The drama has a happy ending, as Menelaus, the Greek husband from whom Helen had initially been taken by Paris, is cast up by a storm on Egyptian shores on his way home from the sack of Troy. In some comical scenes, Helen and Menelaus are brought to recognize one another and eventually they escape from Egypt, sailing off into the sunset. The gods appear and appease the king of Egypt who had hoped to marry Helen himself; and everyone lives happily forever after. It is a much more lighthearted play than most of Euripides' extant dramas.

In its very lightheartedness, however, it reinforces Euripides' theme of the utter folly of war. It was presented in 412, as the Peloponnesian War was dragging to its disastrous end. In this play as in many others, Euripides uses Homeric themes of the Trojan War to comment on current events. And the underlying message of the play is that the whole Trojan War has been fought over a phantom. Helen never was at Troy. Moreover, as the Chorus says, 'reasonable words could have solved the quarrel for Helen' (171); instead, many men 'lie deep in the lap of Death,' and the world is filled with greater bitterness than before.

> You who in earnest ignorance
> Would check the deeds of lawless men,
> And in the clash of spear on spear
> Gain honour – you are all stark mad!
> If men, to settle each dispute,
> Must needs compete in bloodshed, when
> Shall violence vanish, hate be soothed,
> Or men and cities live in peace?
>
> (171)

When indeed? As Athens played its increasingly inglorious part in a war with Sparta that was by now more about phantoms than reality, more about anger and vengeance than about any just cause, Euripides, having attempted to use more conventional tragedies as a mirror for what he saw as Athenian folly, now tried showing them just how ridiculous the whole idea of war is. There was plenty of pain behind the laughter. And beauty was only ever spoken of in terms that would make it complicit with violence. Was there any way out?

The tragedians did not suggest one. Although they challenged the valorization of violence, and decried the idea that it was the will of the immortals, they wrote tragedies, not essays on flourishing and natality. But during the Golden Age of Athens while the tragedians were writing, there was another current of thought swirling in that great city: the first philosophers of the west were developing ideas of eternity which would put violence in quite a different light, and be a further sedimentation in the western genealogy of death. Would their thought provide a way forward? In the next chapter I begin the investigation.

Chapter 9

Parmenides meets the goddess

My carriage was drawn by the mares which carry me to the limits
Of my heart's desire; they took me and set me on the renowned way
Of the deity [goddess], which takes a man of knowledge unharmed
    through all.

(28B1; 56)[1]

Parmenides is on a journey. Like Odysseus, he is an intrepid adventurer, going
as far as his heart's desire will take him. But unlike Odysseus, he writes his own
epic; he is the hero of his own story. Instead of a ship and oarsmen, Parmenides
has a carriage drawn by mares; instead of crewmen, maidens, daughters of the
Sun, escort and guide him. And instead of the waters of the earth, Parmenides'
journey is a journey into the realms of Truth. If the Homeric writings extol the
hero who gains immortal fame through valiant conquest of death, Parmenides
begins a long line of philosophers who construe their thinking as valiant exploits
in a realm of thought, often represented as dangerous, and certainly not suitable
for ordinary mortals. As Achilles gave his life at Troy, and as Odysseus mastered
the barren sea and all its monsters, so the intrepid philosopher pursues truth and
becomes its master. It is a trope that runs through western philosophical thinking
from Parmenides to Heidegger: the great heroic philosopher-poet is the one who
ventures the abyss and gains insight beyond the grasp of lesser mortals (see
Heidegger 1971: 91–142). And from Parmenides to Heidegger, the conquest of
truth is linked with gender, death and beauty.

But there are also differences from the Homeric model. Although philosophy
is often presented as strife or warfare by ancient thinkers, its violence is at least
not overt. Rather, Truth (with a capital 'T'), the preserve of philosophers, is
conceived of as immortal and unchanging, whereas opinion, fluctuating and
unstable, belongs to ordinary mortals. Parmenides was born about 515 BCE, and
was active at the same time as the tragedians were producing their plays. There is
no indication that he was directly influenced by them; nevertheless it is instructive
to read his work in relation to theirs. Rather than emphasising the violence which
has so large a place in Homer and which the tragedians decry, Parmenides seeks
unchanging Truth. In the polarity between violence and eternity, Parmenides

insists on eternity. It will be the work of Plato to struggle with the complexities and tensions between the two poles, as we shall see in the following chapters.

Again, gender considerations are crucial. Although at first sight it seems that Parmenides, in presenting the goddess as the one who reveals Truth to him, is honouring her, I shall argue that this is not the case. Instead, he is effectively silencing all female voices and placing himself in the position of the mouthpiece of the divine. Carried to its logical consequences, this means that the goddess can drop away altogether, as she does in commentaries on Parmenides. Eternal Truth thus becomes a configuration of a masculinist symbolic deeply invested in mastery of death.

Parmenides' goddess

As Parmenides is drawn forward in his carriage he arrives at huge gates which guard the paths of day and night. Controlling these gates is Lady Justice, who holds the key. The maidens escorting Parmenides persuade her to unlock the gates, which swing wide open.

> Then the maidens steered the carriage
> And the horses straight through the gates and down the road.
> The goddess received me kindly. Taking in her hand my right hand
> She spoke and addressed me with these words: 'Young man,
> You have reached my abode as the companion of immortal charioteers
> And of the mares which carry you. You are welcome.
> It was no ill fate that prompted you to travel this way,
> Which is indeed far from mortal men, beyond their beaten paths;
> No, it was Right and Justice. You must learn everything
> Both the steady heart of well-rounded truth,
> And the beliefs of mortals, in which there is no true trust.
> Still, you shall learn them too, and come to see how beliefs
> Must exist in an acceptable form, all-pervasive as they altogether are.
>
> (28B1; 57)

The first thing that stands out in this Prologue to Parmenides' philosophical poem is the preponderance of female figures who help Parmenides to the truth. First there is the goddess herself, whom I shall consider more fully in a moment. But there are also the 'maidens' who lead the way, the 'daughters of the Sun' who drive the carriage. These maidens are the ones who persuade Justice, also personified as female, to unlock the gates. Even the horses pulling the chariot are mares. Other than Parmenides himself, no male figure is introduced.

Parmenides continues a line of thinkers begun with Homer's invocation of the Muses who appeal to the goddess or her female representatives as the source of their wisdom – Empedocles' goddess, Plato's Diotima, Boethius' Lady Consolation, Dante's Beatrice: with the advent of christendom there is often an assimilation to the Virgin Mary. Sappho, too, had called upon the goddess: she pleads with her to come down

> in your chariot yoked with swift, lovely
> sparrows bringing you over the dark earth . . .
> asking again what have I suffered
> and why am I calling again.
>
> (Rayor 1991: 51)

There are important parallels between Parmenides' and Sappho's invocations of the goddess; but there is also a striking contrast. Sappho wants the goddess to come *down* in her chariot drawn by sparrows, to deal with this earth and with her own pain. Parmenides, and the thinkers who follow him, seek rather to go *up* to the goddess and to an eternal realm, leaving this world and its suffering behind. It is a small but significant clue. I shall argue that the same male thinkers who reverently invoke female figures often treat actual women (and often, also, ordinary men) with contempt. It is a reverence and contempt, moreover, which parallels and is of a piece with their reverence for the world of the mind, which is linked with immortality and with the divine, and their contempt for this actual world of time and change, this world which they see not in terms of life but in terms of death. Thus in the case of Parmenides, the world of true Being is opened up to him by an immortal goddess, but as we shall see, actual women and men are dismissed as mortals who never leave the beaten paths of deceptive appearance. Parmenides' division of the world into Truth and Opinion, into those who know and those who do not know, turns out to be a momentous step in the gendered genealogy of death.

Before we turn to what Parmenides meant by the 'way of Truth' it is therefore helpful to look a little more closely at the Prologue to his epic. Why does Parmenides choose to people his Prologue entirely with females, all of whom, even the goddess, serve him, the only male? When we turn to commentators on Parmenides to get some light on this question, it turns out, astonishingly, that they have very little to say. Plato was the first to write a book engaging with Parmenides' thought, but he never so much as mentions the goddess or the other female figures. Instead, in his *Parmenides* Plato concentrates entirely on the way of Truth.[2] Modern commentators follow Plato in the suppression of the female characters. The serious study of Presocratic philosophy in modernity begins with Hegel's *Lectures on the History of Philosophy* in 1840. Hegel interprets the 'maidens' of Parmenides' Prologue as allegories of the senses, and the 'daughters of the sun' as the eyes; he says nothing whatever about the goddess herself, even though he quotes the Prologue extensively (1995: I.251).

Twentieth-century English commentators take the same line. F.M. Cornford points out that Parmenides' invocation of the goddess is similar to that of Hesiod, who claimed that he wrote what the goddess (Muse) taught him (1939: 29). Cornford begins his exposition using phrases like 'the goddess says' or 'the goddess teaches', but very soon he reverts to 'Parmenides says' or 'Parmenides teaches', even though in Parmenides' poem *all* the teaching is attributed to the goddess. The same slippage occurs in virtually all subsequent commentaries. W.K.C. Guthrie, like Cornford, accepts that Parmenides is 'plainly allegorising', borrowing from Hesiod and Homer (1965: II.12). Yet although Guthrie asserts that 'as a mere literary device, nothing could be more unsuited to the main content of the poem, which would have been much better conveyed in plain prose,' he is uneasily aware of the poem's religious roots.[3] Guthrie recognizes that for Parmenides his poem is a 'spiritual odyssey', a philosophical parallel of the *Odyssey* of Homer. But Guthrie never thinks through the significance for Parmenides or his readers of the representation of the search for truth as a religious quest, or of the importance of the goddess in his work.

Cornford and Guthrie became the standard sources for English analyses of Parmenides, and are cited by virtually every subsequent commentator. The goddess is routinely suppressed; while the teaching of the poem is attributed directly to Parmenides himself. Frederick Copleston (1962: I), though he discusses Parmenides as one of the most significant of the Presocratic philosophers, never mentions the goddess at all. Karl Popper identifies her with *Dikē* (Justice), but otherwise takes no interest in her (1998: 77, n2). Neither does Scott Austin (1986) even though he is particularly interested in the relation of Parmenides' teaching to (Christian) theology. Jonathan Barnes, in a manner typical of Anglo-American analytic philosophy, dismisses the invocation of the goddess and any other female figure as mythological and therefore (!) of no philosophical interest (1979: I.156). Robin Waterfield mentions that the goddess might be identified as either Necessity or Persephone, and, like Guthrie, supposes that her invocation suggests that Parmenides might have been 'a shaman of some kind': her teaching, however, is 'devilishly obscure' (2000: 50). Mourelatos (1970) spends a whole chapter discussing the Prologue, but is chiefly interested in discerning parallels to other aspects of Greek mythology without discussing their significance; he then devotes the rest of the book to a study of 'Parmenides'' teaching. And so it goes on. Among modern commentators, only Heidegger stands out as an exception. He thinks that the usual dismissal of the goddess is too hasty because in his view it is important to ponder the representation of truth (*aletheia*) as divine, personified by a goddess. In spite of this insistence, however, Heidegger pays no attention whatever to her gender, or to that of the other female characters of the Prologue.

Instead of thinking further about the goddess, all of these modern interpreters focus steadfastly on the central theme of her teaching (which they routinely attribute to Parmenides himself). That theme is the distinction between the 'path of Truth' and the 'path of confusion' which leads mortals astray (28B2; 28B6; 58). The way of Truth is the way of Being, of Reality: it reveals the things that are. It also shows that 'nothing is not'; and that there can be no passing back and forth between what is and what is not. Philosophers from Plato onwards have been intrigued by this obscure teaching. Whatever is meant by the contrasting ways of truth and confusion, it appears that the 'way of truth' will be very different in this presentation from ordinary human experience. Ordinary life as it is lived by 'mortals' is in error. In Parmenides' poem, the true constitution of Being can be learned only from the goddess.

But then why do commentators ignore her? And what is really going on in Parmenides' poem? Modern commentators see Parmenides as laying the foundations of western logic and rationality, as well as setting out the crucial metaphysical problem that came to be known as the problem of 'the One and the Many'. Later in this chapter I will explore what this means, especially in relation to gender and death. It will be my contention that the erasure of the goddess typical of his commentators is first effected by Parmenides himself; and that in his heroic journey to Truth we have a self-constitution of philosophy which founds itself upon the masculine appropriation of the female and in preoccupation with death, as surely as Homer figured Odysseus' immortal fame as the mastery of the barren sea and her female monsters. The collusion of modern commentators in the refusal to treat the goddess seriously shows just how effective the mastery of the female has been.

Now, my suggestion may at first seem perverse. Is it not the case that Parmenides presents the goddess as the teacher of immortal truth? How then can I say that he is engaged in a conquest of the female? Whatever may be the case for his commentators, surely Parmenides himself was honouring the goddess, not mastering her? This, indeed, is the position taken by scholars like Guthrie (1965) and Mourelatos (1970) who take his teaching to be based upon sincerely held religious experience (which they then ignore).

But I wonder. It is important to remember that what we have in Parmenides' poem is not a female voice but a male representation of a female voice, not a goddess but a (male) representation of a goddess. I suggest that what we need to look for in his poem is neither divine revelation nor women's wisdom. Rather, we need to ask what it is that Parmenides was trying to achieve by putting his teaching into the mouth of a female, and a divine female at that. What is gained (and what is lost) in the strategy of having an immortal goddess, upon whom time and change can have no purchase, express eternal Truth? *Who* gains? Why did Parmenides not speak in his own voice? And if not, why did he choose *this* ventriloquism? Why a goddess?

To formulate an answer to these questions is, I believe, to begin to see how the philosophy of western culture is shaped in relation to gender and death, and how natality is supplanted. To see what Parmenides was up to, it is important to take into account something that philosophical commentary routinely ignores, namely the goddess worship of early Europe which his work was both drawing upon and supplanting. Only then can we see how his account of Truth is related to a preoccupation with death; and how he configures philosophy – the 'love of wisdom' – as war. Putting these themes together will make clear both why Parmenides uses a goddess figure and at the same time how he supplants her with a masculinist and necrophilic rationality that denies beauty and life; and will show his importance in the tension between violence and eternity. But it also makes clear that once again his stance is a choice; there was nothing inevitable about it. Indeed in a renewed interest in goddesses some contemporary feminists have found resources for thinking otherwise.

The goddess before Parmenides

It is widely accepted that in the Bronze Age culture of the Aegean, the chief deity was a goddess, or perhaps several goddesses with different names and attributes. In this respect early Greek culture was similar to other cultures of the Near East and probably borrowed from them (Burkert 1979: ch. V; Gimbutas 1982; 1991). Many clay statues of female figures have been found, sometimes in shrines and temples, in Crete and Mycenae, as also in other areas of southern Europe. While some of these were goddesses, there were also many carved representations of mortal women pursuing various activities (Teubal 1997): indeed it is not always possible to be sure whether a particular statue is a figure of a goddess or a mortal woman. Marija Gimbutas has taken female statues, which considerably outnumber statues of male figures of the period, as evidence for a cult of a Great Goddess across the Near East, a cult which she believes was part of a peace-loving matriarchal society. When Parmenides put his teaching into the mouth of the goddess, was it this Great Goddess he had in mind?

Unfortunately things are much more complex. Some feminist scholars have been eager to follow Gimbutas in her assertion of a Great Goddess revealed under the specific aspects of birth, life and death, the same across vast tracts of space and time, and violently supplanted by the male god of patriarchal warrior culture (Baring and Cashford 1991; Christ 1997). But this is probably too broad a claim. There were after all great differences among the cultures of the Near East: assimilation of all the traces of goddesses into one Great Goddess who presided over one matriarchally structured world is neither historically credible nor does it show respect for the alterity of ancient societies. Moreover, as the archaeologist Margaret Ehrenberg points out, although the preponderance of female over male figures must be significant, it is hard to say exactly what the significance is. Female representations might be goddesses, but then again they (or some of them) might be fertility charms, items used in sympathetic magic or sorcery, objects for initiation or instruction, or even children's toys (1989: 74).

Yet even allowing for the complexity, it is obvious that the ancient Greek pantheon reflected by Hesiod and Homer had many goddesses of great power and status, among them Hera, Athena and Demeter/Persephone; and that although 'the power of the female god [sic] was immense . . . it was ultimately circumvented by that of the male gods' (Price 1999: 19). Athens itself was dedicated to Athena; and across Greece various festivals in honour of goddesses such as Hera or Artemis were yearly events (Clark 1998; Cole 1998). Among the so-called 'Mystery Religions', the Eleusinian Mysteries, which honoured Demeter and her daughter Persephone, counted among the most prominent (Godwin 1981: 32–3). The goddesses of ancient Greece cannot all be collapsed into one 'Great Goddess' (let alone 'Great Mother') without doing violence to the texts that show plurality and difference (Loraux 1992); neither can one move directly from goddess worship to the status of women (wives, courtesans, prostitutes, slaves) (Patterson 1991; Clark 1998). However there can be no denying that in ancient Greece the divine was female as well as male. All the gods, according to Hesiod, had descended from 'broad-bosomed Earth' (*Gaia*), who first brought forth Heaven (*Ouranos*) and then either with him or on her own, generations of gods and goddesses (Hesiod 1973: 26–8). Although Hesiod's *Theogony* was not normative for ancient Greece in the way that, say, the Bible was for the European Middle Ages, nevertheless from at least his time onward through the Hellenistic period there was widespread popular veneration of goddesses. The divine was female as well as male. Gradually, however, the male gods gained mastery. It was within this context that Parmenides wrote, and was read. The maidens and the mares do not bring the goddess to earth, but take him to the goddess, a goddess who Parmenides represents as a source of Truth, even while he takes that Truth over as his own.

But which goddess would this be; and how should she be understood? Robin Waterfield, as I have mentioned, thinks it may have been Persephone, or at least that this identification would spring to the minds of Parmenides' contemporaries; and as we shall soon see, there are reasons why that might be so. However, I suggest that something much more radical was going on. It seems to me that Parmenides was taking up extant associations to goddess worship in Greek myth and religion, perhaps especially those of the Eleusinian Mysteries, and then reshaping them for his own purpose, simultaneously appropriating their authority and utterly transforming them. In this conquest of the goddess, philosophy constituted itself. Moreover, it did so by a radical denial of birth and death, and a displacement of beauty from this world of our experience to an 'other' world, incorporeal and immortal. It is of course impossible to ascertain whether or not this was Parmenides' deliberate intention: my argument is not about his conscious purposes but about the effects of his writing for the sedimentation of the western cultural symbolic.

To explain the basis of my claim it is necessary to take a step or two backwards. Marija Gimbutas in her monumental study of ancient statues of goddesses and female figures makes a strong case for the identification of the goddess with the earth, an identification which holds even though the idea of a single 'Great Goddess' cannot be sustained. The male god, often, is the sky god, a distant god who might visit the earth but who is other than it, perhaps its creator. The goddess, however, is Mother Earth, manifest in nature, in things that are born and grow and live upon the earth and in the seas. She was also the one who received the dead back into herself again. As womb and tomb, life-giver, nourisher, and final resting place, the goddess allowed for a holistic picture of life and the world, and an acceptance of birth, life and death that did not require denial of the experiences of people. As Gimbutas reads the statues, art work and inscriptions of southern Europe before the Bronze Age, all nature was taken as revealing her power and life-giving presence; it was, in fact, her body. Thus

> The Great Mother Goddess who gives birth to all creation out of the holy
> darkness of her womb became a metaphor for Nature herself, the cosmic giver
> and taker of life, ever able to renew Herself within the eternal cycle of life,
> death, and rebirth.
>
> (Gimbutas 1991: 222)

The societies that emphasized goddesses seem, at least sometimes, to have been
more peaceful and earth loving than those which were developing patriarchal
social and religious systems. Baring and Cashford, for example, discuss the case of
ancient Crete, from which a great many artifacts have been preserved, many
of them portraying goddesses and female figures (1991: ch. 3). From the studies
that have been undertaken, it appears that this was a less violent society, in which
'human nature was not war-like' (144) and the divine was not thought of as a
warrior king. More generally, Sabina Teubel has studied the relationship between
female images and female reproduction control from the Upper Paleolithic to the
Stone Age, and argues that the prevalence of female images corresponds to a
higher status for women and more egalitarian communities (1997: 282).

All such studies must be approached with great caution, to be sure. Nevertheless,
the caution should equally be applied to archaeological stereotypes based on
masculinist assumptions. The importance of even-handed critical assessment
becomes clear in the careful work of Margaret Ehrenberg. While denying any
monolithic religion of a 'Great Goddess' with a matriarchal society to match,
she argues that in prehistoric societies women did have a higher place than
subsequently. She also has an explanation for the decline of this higher status.
Ehrenberg begins by calling into question the assumed centrality of 'man the
hunter' in prehistoric societies, pointing out that in fact survival depended on
women gathering food. Hunting meat supplied extras which would have been very
welcome, but could not have sustained life. As she puts it,

> The term 'Man the Hunter' is . . . commonly used, and the implication is that
> man's principal food is meat, and his principal occupation hunting; this has
> been assumed to be invariably a male task which gives men a high status.
> It has been shown, however, that this view is not entirely correct, and may
> be largely a reflection of the interests and preconceptions of nineteenth-
> century Western male anthropologists and of the status of hunting as an
> upper-class pastime in nineteenth-century Europe.
>
> (1989: 51; cf Dahlberg 1981)

Ehrenberg points out that in so-called 'primitive' societies today, and in past
societies which can be studied by archaeologists, meat forms only a very small
proportion of the diet (except among those like the Inuit who live in extremely
cold conditions); and women are almost always those who forage for food and
are the main providers. Women also are primarily responsible for rudimentary

agriculture and economic developments such as bartering and marketing. Ehrenberg argues that the stereotypes of gender prevalent in descriptions of prehistoric society have less to do with evidence than with the assumptions of modern interpreters projected back on to early peoples. The evidence of females as principal providers 'contrasts sharply with the traditional picture of the male as protector and hunter, bringing food back to a pair-bonded female. That model treats masculine aggression as normal, assumes that long-term, one-to-one, male–female bonding was a primary development, with the male as the major food provider, and that male dominance was inherently linked to hunting skills' (50) – which were also connected with warfare. It is an anthropological variant of the naturalization of violence discussed in chapter 3.

If women had a much greater role in prehistoric societies, when and how did things change? Ehrenberg suggests that the decline began with the invention of the plough, possibly augmented, as Gimbutas (1991) has argued, by attacks on agricultural societies by more nomadic groups. Though in Ehrenberg's opinion the plough was probably invented by women, it required greater muscular strength than the hoe, and was gradually taken over by men. Moreover, the plough enabled larger crops, which could feed greater herds as well as more people. As herds grew, so did cattle raiding and the increase of warrior status among men: women, meanwhile, became more domesticated with the weaving of wool from the larger herds. As raiding continued and men became more aggressive and more dominant, not only cattle but also women were raided and traded, and women lost their respected position in society. If the society had worshipped goddesses, this might now be suppressed in favour of a Father God more congenial to masculinist society; alternatively the goddess herself might be made into a voice for the suppression of women.

As I have already insisted, there were many prehistoric societies, not just one; and this account need not hold for all of them. It is therefore of particular interest that classicist Page du Bois has from a quite different range of evidence argued for a very similar progression in the actual stages of the conceptualization of women in the society of ancient Greece, and has shown how the changes were linked with changes in agricultural practice. Du Bois focuses on the eighth to the fifth centuries BCE, and considers both texts and artifacts. She begins by showing how Hesiod and Homer preserve traces of a pre-agricultural society, using metaphors of the earth which indicate the earth's generosity, giving without stint plants and trees that provide food. Parallel to these spontaneous gifts from the earth is the generosity and 'spontaneous', perhaps parthenogenic, reproduction of humankind by women: moreover women, the earth and the goddess are conceptually linked. As du Bois says,

> The analogy between the goddess/body and the earth is probably very ancient; the theme of male death or sleep after intercourse may refer to the male loss of semen and of force, which is thus sacrificed to the earth in order to ensure its continued productivity. The goddess and earth are undiminished by their

intercourse or by reproduction. Giving birth and receiving the dead seem to replenish them, while the male suffers only loss.

(1988: 54)

This view of the generosity of the earth, the goddess and the woman's body, all of which produced fruit either of itself or by the simple sowing of the seed, underwent a major shift with the development of agriculture in which seed was not simply scattered but was sown carefully in a field. Similarly, the male 'ploughed' the woman's body; and women 'are now seen as cultivated furrows' (65), the property of her husband as the field is the property of its owner.

As already said, the goddess most readily identifiable with Parmenides' project is Persephone; and in the myths surrounding her many of these themes come together. Demeter is the goddess of fertility and the fruitfulness of the earth; Persephone (also called Kore) is her daughter, who is tricked and abducted by Hades, king of the underworld and taken by him to be his wife. Demeter is distraught at what has happened to her daughter; consequently women do not conceive, crops do not grow, and the earth becomes sterile. To avert catastrophe, Hades is persuaded to allow Persephone to rejoin her mother for half of each year. During this time the earth warms up and is fertile; but when she returns to Hades it is winter and things stop growing.

The myth is of course a myth of the changing seasons and patterns of growth. But as Adriana Cavarero points out, it also illustrates how the patriarchal gods are linked with death and gendered violence: Hades is the god of death; and his capture of Kore severs the maternal bond. 'With the complicity of other male deities, Hades kidnaps Kore and deports her to the realm of death. . . . No symbology is more explicitly bipolar in its design: an order of birth marked as feminine is opposed to an order of death marked as masculine' (1995: 65). Moreover, Cavarero argues that to read this myth *only* as a myth of the seasons, and erase its gendered rendition of death and natality, is to repeat the rhetorical violence which it perpetuates.

In the myth itself, and as it was probably celebrated in the Eleusinian Mysteries, the goddess continues to have significant influence over the earth and its fruitfulness, though Hades is clearly gaining in power. In goddess worship, it is fertility, birth and life that is the focus of meaning. *This* world, not some world after death, is the goddess's domain. Death is not denied; but neither does it become the defining moment of life. Rather, death is contained within the whole, as a natural ending but not as a goal or purpose of life. The Eleusinian Mysteries would have been quite unsuitable for the warriors of the Homeric writings, or even for Odysseus, whose focus was not so much on life and its experiences as for the fame and immortal glory that their heroism would bring them after death. As we shall see, it would also be quite unsuitable for philosophers like Plato, who treat fertility of the body with contempt and valorize death as the rite of passage which releases the soul from the prisonhouse of the body.

With this awareness of the mythology of the goddess in mind, Parmenides' visit to the goddess and his attribution to her of the teaching of Being calls out for reconsideration. Although goddesses continued to be venerated by the populace during his time, the people and their opinions were derided by the men who are now taken as the founders of western rationality: philosophers were working towards a rationality which valorized the (male) mind over against the body, and the sage against the masses, in what modern commentators often describe as their 'progress' to monotheism and ultimately to monotheistic rationality. For example, the sixth-century BCE philosopher Xenophanes famously rejected any anthropomorphism in his theology: even oxen and horses and lions would, if they could, portray the gods in their own image (21B15; 27). He moved, rather, to an idea that God is One, or that the One is God: if Aristotle is right that Xenophanes was the teacher of Parmenides this is a significant formulation. Xenophanes 'one god' is able to 'see all over, think all over, hear all over' (21B23–4; 27). While this god is far from what the masses believe in, it is a recognizable precursor to the god of the western philosophical tradition. But for the goddess, no place is left except as a tool by which Parmenides' conceptions can be expressed.

Like Xenophanes, Heraclitus, who was Parmenides' older contemporary and in many respects his opposite had harsh words to say about popular religion, especially the mystery rites: 'the secret rites which are in use among men are celebrated in an unholy manner' (22B14; 46). Since those secret rites prominently included the Eleusinian mysteries, we see once again a suppression of the goddess and popular religion in favour of elite rationality. Heraclitus certainly had no great opinion of the intelligence of ordinary people: 'For the many do not understand such things when they meet with them; nor having learned do they comprehend, though they think they do' (22B17; 37).

So, although in the fragments that remain of these philosophers they do not make direct reference to goddesses, there can be little doubt that they are pressing for a rationality that excludes them. In this context it is a very clever move on the part of Parmenides, after he has disparaged the masses as those who hold only inferior 'opinion', to place Truth in the mouth of the goddess. This is no goddess of popular worship. The secrets which she tells Parmenides initiate him into mysteries of Being, but stand in complete contrast to initiation into the mysteries of the Eleusinians. Ordinary people who hold to such things are treated by 'her' with a mixture of pity and contempt, 'for helplessness guides the wandering thought in their breasts; they are carried along deaf and blind alike, dazed, beasts, without judgement' (28B6; 58). It is as though Parmenides is offering an alternative mystery initiation, a teaching which runs far contrary to ordinary experience or daily life but which puts in place a detached, disembodied rationality that is, however, linked to the masculine. By placing this teaching into the mouth of a goddess, he uses a goddess as his method of condemning the religious beliefs and practices of the masses, or at least dismissing them as useless opinion. Thus a female figure is used by a male philosopher to establish his variety of rationality, a rationality of eternal truth linked with the male, to suppress the female.

Parmenides, while ostensibly learning from the goddess, actually stuffs his own teaching into her mouth and chokes her with it. Once he has done so, he has effectively silenced her and eliminated anything she might have wished to say for herself. The goddess, in philosophical terms, can therefore be allowed to drop out of consideration: she is extraneous to what now becomes simply *his* teaching. The lack of attention to the goddess by modern commentators shows the success of Parmenides' strategy. Her conquest was effective. Yet the goddess could never be erased completely: in various ways an imaginary of the goddess repeatedly haunted the masculinist symbolic, and we will greet her again in subsequent chapters as we trace how things are and might not have been, and how they might yet be different.

'The way that it is': Parmenides' One

But could things really have been different? According to Parmenides' teaching (attributed by him to the goddess) 'there is the way that it is and it cannot not be' (28B2; 58). The 'way of Truth' which Parmenides describes is as mysterious as any initiation into a mystery religion. Central to it is his concern with birth and death, and a denial of both.

> Now only the one tale remains
> Of the way *that it is*. On this way there are very many signs
> Indicating that what-is is unborn and imperishable,
> Entire, alone of its kind, unshaken, and complete.
> It was not once nor will it be, since it is now, all together,
> Single and continuous . . .
> That is why Justice has not freed it,
> Relaxing the grip of her fetters, either to be born or to perish;
> No, she holds it fast.
>
> (28B7; 59)

Justice (or Necessity) is personified as guaranteeing the unchanging unity of all that is. Change and chance belong to the misguided experience of ordinary mortals. The heroic philosopher, however, receives special insight and knows that that-which-is could not be subject to change: could not be born, cannot die. Thus in an ironic twist which has been lost on commentators, Parmenides has the goddess herself rule out the dimensions of human life – birth and death – with which she had traditionally been regarded as most concerned, eliminating the reasons for her own existence.

According to what the goddess tells him, the world of the senses, of coming into being and passing away, is unreal. But if that is so, then birth and death are also negated: 'birth has been extinguished and perishing made inconceivable' (28B7; 60). Reality is other than what is experienced; it transcends bodies and births and deaths, and is eternal and immutable, the realm of truth and pure thought. The things which ordinary mortals experience

are no more than names –
Both birth and perishing, both being and not being,
Change of place, and alteration of bright colouring.

(Ibid.)

Now, how should Parmenides' efforts to deny the obvious realities of embodied
life be understood? Modern philosophers read this as the intellectual cost of strict
fidelity to logic, and honour Parmenides for it (e.g. Mourelatos 1970: ch. 2; Meijer
1997). But I suggest that from a post-Freudian perspective another interpretation
is possible, one which we shall find running all the way through the history of
western philosophy: namely that reason and logic can be used as an escape from
the realities of birth and death, which are experienced as unbearable. Such a
reading is confirmed by the teaching Parmenides presents as the 'way of opinion',
the alternative to the way of Truth. In it, he speaks of birth and begetting as 'vile'
or 'hateful' and, intriguingly, links such 'hateful birth' directly with the goddess
(though it is not clear whether this is the same goddess who teaches him the two
ways). According to this picture of the world, there are rings of fire and of night
around the earth.

> In the middle of these is the goddess who steers all things, for she is the
> beginner of all hateful birth and all begetting, sending the female to mix with
> the male and the male in turn to the female.
>
> (28B12; trans. Robinson 1968: 122)

It is not clear what Parmenides intended by these cosmological speculations;
but for my purposes it is the vocabulary and the attitude expressed in it that is
instructive. It would seem that for Parmenides, birth, begetting and erotic attraction are troubled notions. By his insistence on strict logic, they, and death with
them, can be eliminated from the world of true Being. Logic makes it possible to
escape from the world of ordinary experience.

Parmenides' teaching becomes clearer by contrasting it with that of his older
contemporary, Heraclitus. Heraclitus is famous for his teaching of flux, of all things
passing into their opposites, everything in continuous change. His most frequently
quoted saying is preserved by Plato, who writes of him:

> Heraclitus . . . says that everything moves on and nothing is at rest; and,
> comparing existing things to the flow of a river, he says that you could not
> step into the same river twice.
>
> (22A6; Plato *Cratylus* 402a)

or in Heraclitus' own words, 'On those who step into the same rivers ever different
waters are flowing' (22B12; 41). Not only is human life and experience always
changing, but the elements of the universe themselves are continually coming
into being and passing away, like 'an ever-living fire flaring up in regular measures

and dying down in regular measures' (22B30; 42). Thus sea and earth and fire are in reciprocal and continuous exchange: 'Everything is a compensation for fire, and fire is a compensation for everything, as goods are for gold and gold for goods' (22B90; 42). Heraclitus finds the lived experience of change parallel to the endless play of opposites, in which all things are mutable and all things are interdependent. For Heraclitus, the *logos* shows that all things are impermanent: we find in him no celebration of an eternal or fixed world order.

This is very different from Parmenides. In Parmenides, such unceasing change belongs only to the way of becoming, which is mere opinion, not the way of Truth. Clear thinking, according to Parmenides, shows that true Being cannot change, whatever the appearances to the contrary. He might have had Heraclitus in mind when he wrote that 'coming into being and passing away' or 'being and not-being' are false opinions. The fundamental difference between them is that for Parmenides the real world is the unchanging world of reason, not the world of ordinary life and experience, while for Heraclitus the *logos* offers insight precisely into our experience of change and opposition.

Philosophy as war

There is another more subtle theme, however, which is shared by Parmenides and Heraclitus for all their other differences: namely their emphasis on war and strife. In spite of the fact that Parmenides looks to eternal Truth, he shares with Heraclitus the notion that the philosophical venture is a parallel to the heroic adventures of Homeric epic. In the case of Heraclitus, it is evident from his fragments that he does not consider the continuous reciprocal exchange of elements to be a matter of smooth transition but of opposition and war. He says,

> It is necessary to understand that war is universal and justice is strife, and that all things take place in accordance with strife and necessity.

> For fire lives the death of earth, and air lives the death of fire; water lives the death of air, and earth that of water.
>
> (22B80; trans. Robinson 1968: 93)

and again,

> War is the father and king of all.
>
> (B53)

Although he is aware that there are those who pray that strife might be eliminated, Heraclitus says that if strife were to end, the whole world would perish (A22). He thus assimilates the transformation of the elemental opposites with war and conflict between people; violence is a fundamental principle of the universe.

Parmenides, for his part, represents the goddess as setting the way of truth and the way of opinion in sharp opposition to one another. Parmenides' follower, Zeno, takes Heraclitus' ideas of war and strife and applies them to the conduct of philosophy itself. Zeno was an enthusiastic champion of Parmenides' teaching that change is impossible; neither can there be plurality. It is to Zeno that we owe such conundrums as the paradox of the arrow that can never hit its mark, and Achilles who can never catch the tortoise. Much ink has been spilled over these; but the point I wish to make is not about the content but about the style. It is significant that in the presentation of his paradoxes, Zeno was polemical, carrying the dispute to the 'enemy', attacking first. As Robinson characterizes it, for Zeno '"dialectic" was the verbal counterpart of war. The weapons are words; skill, the ability to secure the desired admissions; success, the defeat of one's opponent' (1968: 138). As the Achaeans had measured themselves and found immortal glory in physical combat with the Trojans, so the followers of Parmenides engage in intellectual combat, using dialectics as the counterpart of battle. Thus philosophy constitutes itself as adversarial, based on a metaphor of violence.

For Robinson and for many other modern philosophers, this adversarial method is of central importance to philosophical advance. Seeing argument and the pursuit of truth as a battle in which positions are set up, attacked, defended, held or demolished became standard methodology in philosophical writing; and the model of battle gives philosophy some of its most significant metaphors. As Robinson says,

> to the extent that European philosophy is Greek, it is inherently polemical. . . . For the mode of Greek thought is contentious; the *agon* or contest for the prize of victory is central to it; and this spirit has entered into the very texture of the philosophical tradition which is the creature of that impulse.
>
> (Robinson 1968: 139)

Many contemporary philosophers, particularly in the Anglo-American analytical tradition, take for granted that this adversarial approach is the method of philosophical thinking, and if pressed will argue that it is the best way for errors of reasoning to be exposed. The violence and death-dealing of western philosophical procedure has roots deep in Greek soil where intellectual combat became the philosophical version of Homeric warfare and its pursuit of fame through glorious death, even while aiming for eternal truth.

Strife and death

Greek thinkers who followed Heraclitus and Parmenides tried to deal with the latter's rejection of ordinary experience of time, change and motion; those who are singled out as forming the history of western philosophy retained his rejection of death and birth. They combined it, however, with the notion of philosophy as war, seeing strife as central to all that exists. Empedocles, who lived in fifth-century Sicily, appealed to a notion of aggression reminiscent of Heraclitus as a fundamental principle of his cosmology, but combined this with a Parmenidean rejection of birth and death as impossible.

> For to come to be out of what is utterly inexistent is inconceivable, and it is impossible and unheard of that what is should pass away . . . there is no real coming into being of any mortal creature, nor any end in wretched death, but only mingling and separation of what has been mingled, and 'coming into being' is merely a name given to them by men.
>
> (31B12, B8; trans. Robinson 1968: 158)

Empedocles postulated four unchanging elements, earth, air, fire and water, which mingled and separated to form and reform the universe. The forces which caused them to do so, Empedocles called Love and Strife. These are the two unchanging principles, in the physical world as in human life, from which everything else derives (Wright 1997: 182–3). Thus for Empedocles as for Heraclitus, hostility and violence do not represent an aberration or a problem. On the contrary, strife is naturalized, represented not merely as part of the natural order of things but as one of the root causes, without which there would not be a world at all. It can hardly, therefore, be a matter for moral censure. Empedocles describes the world-processes in terms of these two forces, Love and Strife:

> I shall tell a two-fold tale . . . at one time all coming together into one through Love, at another each being borne apart again through the hostility of Strife.
>
> (31B17; trans. Robinson 1968: 158–9)

It is only through hostility and violence that there is a world order at all: if all were love, there would be no separation upon which individuation depends.

In this way Empedocles connects the principle of Strife with apparent coming into being and passing away. Interestingly, it is not Love which produces birth, but Strife; birth for Empedocles as for Parmenides is grievous, hateful. This world is a place of delusion, joyless, in which we are 'exiled'; it is not our true home but rather the place to which we are sent in successive incarnations under the sway of Strife. In some respects it is reminiscent of Odysseus in his 'exile' on the sea during his long journey home. Yet the shift from the Homeric writings with their pleasure in earthly life and the great and valorous deeds of the body is immense. From this point onwards the notion of the earth as a place of exile recurs in the genealogy of death. It is obviously connected with a rejection of the body, which is material and linked to the earth, and a valorization of a (non-material) mind or spirit. Since the earth was linked to the Mother Goddess, and the body was connected with the mother, this notion of embodied life on earth as exile from our true, spiritual, and implicitly male home carries strong gender overtones, and continues Parmenides' project of suppressing the goddess. At the same time, the idea of exile, and successive mortal forms, allows Empedocles to deny the reality of birth and death. As M.R. Wright puts it,

> Birth and death in Empedocles' theory are merely names, to be understood in reality as the mingling and separating of eternally existing elements, which are subject on the cosmic and the human scale to the alternating control of Love and Strife. . . . Birth is not to be considered as generation from what was not there before, nor death the annihilation of what now is.
>
> (1997: 201)

We find here a configuration of violence, misogyny and preoccupation with (a denial of) death that is repeated with variations on many occasions in western philosophical thought and goes deep in the cultural symbolic: we will meet it again in Plato. Indeed one might read the history of pre-Socratic philosophy (including such figures as Pythagoras and Anaxagoras) as a series of attempts to develop a cosmological system that would allow for the denial of death; as though the preoccupation with death was the driving motive of philosophical thinking, and rationality was founded upon its erased centrality.

The logic of the mind and the experience of the body

In an obvious sense, all this denial of birth and death is utterly futile. Whatever philosophers may pronounce, people are born and people die. And yet from Parmenides onward, and especially through the paradoxes of Zeno, the 'way of Truth' was so sharply structured upon a logic that denied change and motion, that not only the goddess but also actual experience could be dismissed as nothing but the 'way of opinion'. Ordinary human beings would walk this lesser way, but true philosophers, instructed by divinity itself, could deny all such ideas in their grasp of a higher rationality. Thus actual physical death is hardly recognized in their systems of thought, even though from the point of view of the 'way of opinion' of ordinary experience the reality of death might be thought to reduce those systems to absurdity.

From such an elitist conception of rationality and contemptuous dismissal of 'ordinary' experience it is but a short step to the idea that death is a gateway to this other world of eternal being, at least for the elite who are in the know. There is no evidence that Parmenides himself held such a view. However, his teaching is in some respects a response to that of the Pythagoreans, and they, it is clear, did teach the immortality of the soul. In their thought, also, it was overtly connected to gender.

Pythagoras himself left no writings, and his followers seem at first to have formed a secret group. However, many other ancient writers described Pythagorean teaching:

first, his claim that the soul is immortal; second, that it changes into other species of living things; third, that past events happen again in specific cycles, and that nothing is simply new; and fourth, that we should regard all ensouled creatures as akin.

(14A8a; 98–9)[4]

Whereas in the Homeric writings and the fragments of Milesian philosophers the difference between immortal and mortal was the difference between gods and humans, with Pythagoras it is the difference between soul and body. The line is drawn differently. The gods and the human soul share the space above the line; the body and the material world is left below it. The body is mortal. So, if death is to be denied, it follows that something other than the body must be the real person. In the fragments of Parmenides' poem nothing is said of this; but later philosophers like Empedocles and Anaxagoras who struggled with the problems left by Parmenides' denial of change were able to appeal to the division of mind or soul from body as part of their solution.

The enormity of this shift in the relation of body and soul had consequences for the whole understanding of human life, the gods and the physical world. If the soul, like the gods, is immortal, what exactly is its relationship to the mortal body? What is its relationship to the gods? The Pythagorean account of soul and body is as different as could well be imagined from the Homeric exultation in bodily vigour and courage. For the Pythagoreans 'the soul has been yoked to the body as a punishment of some kind, and . . . has been buried in the body as in a tomb' (44B14; 97). Embodiment is not a cause for rejoicing but rather that which impedes the soul. Indeed, the soul should strive to be as little ensnared by the body's needs and desires as possible. Of Pythagoras himself it was said

> that he was satisfied with honey alone, or a bit of honeycomb or bread (he did not touch wine during the day); or, for a treat, vegetables boiled or raw. Seafood he ate but rarely. His robe, which was white and spotless, and his bedclothes, which were also white, were of wool; for linen had not yet reached those parts. He was never observed to relieve himself, or to have intercourse, or to be drunk. He used to avoid laughter.
>
> (Diogenes Laertius viii.19, in Robinson 1968: 62; cf 67)

And death itself? Pythagoras seems to have believed in transmigration of souls: with Plato we shall see how this teaching is transformed so that death, at least for the philosopher, is the longed for release of the soul from its prisonhouse of the body.

Gender and truth

Now, in many respects Parmenides is different from Pythagoras, yet their similarities are significant. Both of them agreed about the overwhelming importance of the soul over against the body; both of them construed the soul in terms of rationality and eternal truth, the path of 'what is'; and both relegated the body and the changing material world to the realm of 'what is not', the way of opinion on which ordinary mortals tread their weary way. Consider, for example, the famous Pythagorean table of opposites:

limit and absence of limit
odd and even
one and many
right and left
male and female
rest and motion
straight and curved
light and dark
good and bad
square and oblong

(Aristotle *Metaphysics* i.5.986.a23)

Robinson (1968: 119) argues that Parmenides' poem, with its insistence on the unity and changelessness of being, is an attack on Pythagorean dualism. But can Robinson's account be correct? Parmenides has the goddess tell him that having taught him the way of truth, she will also teach him about the way of opinion, even though it does not represent the real; and when she does so, it is precisely motion, change and the many that she describes. It is as though the goddess in Parmenides' poem had put a vertical line through Pythagoras' table of opposites, taken all the items in the left column as characteristic of being and truth, and relegated all the items in the right column to the erring way of opinion. All that is missing is that soul and body should be added to the left and right columns respectively.

The table of opposites brings out explicitly Pythagoras' ideas of gender, which are partly camouflaged in Parmenides by his ventriloquism of the goddess. In Pythagoras' table the female is linked with the many, with motion, with the dark and bad and oblong, and – even though it is not included in the table – with the body and the material. These are all the things which, for Parmenides, signify the way of opinion and 'what is not'. The male, by contrast, is linked with the one, with the straight and light and good, and by implication with rationality and the gods. That Pythagoras denigrated women and perhaps feared them was standardly taken as part of his teaching. 'Being asked, once, when a man ought to approach a woman, he replied, "When you want to lose what strength you have"' (Diogenes Laertius viii.19, in Robinson 1968: 62).

Nevertheless, Pythagoras looked to the cultivation of rationality, and in particular to mathematics to separate the soul from the senses. Its kinship with the divine would be fostered by freedom from the body. Reason (*logos*) for the Pythagoreans seems to have been closely linked to number, which they held characterized the world order as a whole. The world order as number was investigated, for example, in the mathematics of musical harmony, and perhaps even in terms of the just rule of a city and the distribution of its material resources (if Socrates is expressing a Pythagorean attitude in Plato *Gorgias* 507e). The point is that turning to rationality is, for them, turning away from the body, gender and the material world to the changeless world of the soul, the divine and immortality. With Pythagoras the former are part of the right-hand side of the table of opposites. With Parmenides they are dismissed altogether, as the 'way of opinion', fit only for mortals who wander in delusion.

It is clear, however, that, whatever Parmenides may say, ordinary experience is experience of the many, of change: indeed even Parmenides could not arrive at the house of the goddess except by starting from the world of change. As Adriana Cavarero, in her telling exposition of Parmenides' poem, points out, Parmenides can only arrive at his eternal 'truth' by rejecting and denying his own history, annihilating the very world he came from, and his own birth and bodily life (1995: 38). It is obvious, however, that this heroic thinker, whatever his denials, still does actually live in the physical world: he eats and sleeps and leaves his socks lying around. Unless someone were there to pick them up, and to prepare his food, he could not pretend for long that the world of appearance was unreal. Thus in order to maintain his philosophical position that denies the physical, he must simultaneously have someone – traditionally women/slaves – to do his physical work. Yet at the same time, he must ignore their contribution or erase it from his consciousness. In Parmenides' *Prologue* we have seen this happening: the maidens are necessary to bring him to the house of the goddess and are forthwith forgotten. Though he could not have thought his truth without them, they disappear entirely from that truth. As Cavarero says,

> It almost seems as though women (excluded from the realm of thought both in reality and because of the 'unthinkability' of their gender) become the sacrificial food for the journey toward the realm of philosophy that will exclude them. In other words, it almost seems as though philosophy was attempting to leave a residual trace of the matricide committed at the outset.
>
> (Cavarero 1995: 39)

It is a matricide, a denial not only of the goddess but also of natality, gender, and the body.

For it is indeed death which occupies the pivotal point in Parmenides' poem: his concern is with perishing. How could true being perish? How could that which is changeless pass away? If the philosopher could really define true being as the changeless, and then live in that dwelling place of being, he would have escaped death and become immortal. For this he will give up the whole world of life and growth and experience; indeed he will redefine the ceaseless growth and change and transformations characteristic of the living world as signifying 'not-being', a negative portrayal under the sign of nothingness, the unthinkable, death. The reversal in Parmenides thought echoes the reversal in the Homeric writings, in which death, especially the death of young men in battle, was presented as preserving beauty forever, and guaranteeing the immortality of fame.

In Parmenides, however, it is not the warrior but the heroic thinker who is most highly esteemed, the thinker who in his thought can relegate death to that which is not, even if in the process he must relegate all of ordinary life, all experience of birth and growth and the flourishing of the world to the realm of non-being. But is it worth it? Who stands to benefit from this sort of thinking, and who must bear the cost? Elite men, men who have women and/or slaves to serve them, will be the ones who can indulge in Parmenidian philosophizing, while women and/or slaves support their physical needs. But women bear the cost also in a less immediate way. For if true being is changeless and eternal, then bodies, gendered bodies, are to be disregarded by the (male) one who knows. Such disregard, however, means that what in fact is happening is that implicitly it is the thinker who is deemed to be normatively human. Anything else is different, deviant: according to the Pythagorean table, 'opposite'.

Beauty and mechanism

The devaluation of the body and the valorization of a rationality that counted strict logic more important than actual experience went along with a change in what would count as beautiful. As we have seen, in the *Iliad* beauty was paradigmatically the beauty of a young, fragile body, preserved forever in that body's early heroic death. Sappho praised beauty – the beauty of a particular beloved person – as that which was of the highest value. But the philosophers after Parmenides who separated soul or mind from body in the manner of Pythagoras rejected the idea that the body is beautiful. The body is mortal, corrupt. In Empedocles' teaching, a person is thought of as a divine spirit exiled in the world as a punishment for wrong doing, 'a fugitive from the gods and a wanderer'.

> For thrice ten thousand seasons he wanders, far from the blessed gods, being born throughout that period in all kinds of mortal shapes, exchanging one painful path of life for another. For the mighty ether drives him into the sea, the sea spews him forth upon the dry land, earth casts him into the rays of the burning sun, and the sun casts him into eddies of ether. One receives him from the other, and all hate him.
>
> (31B115; trans. Robinson 1968: 152)

Apart from the emphasis on reincarnation there are similarities both to Odysseus and to the biblical story of Cain, hated and driven out by all. But in Empedocles, it is the body itself that is the vehicle of the punishment. Indeed the embodiment *is* the punishment. Bodies are not celebrated for their beauty or particularity; birth is exile to

a joyless place, where Murder and Vengeance dwell, and swarms of other Fates
– wasting Diseases, Putrefactions and Fluxes – roam in darkness over the
meadow of Doom.

(31B121; trans. Robinson 1968: 153)

Though in other passages Empedocles contrasts Beauty and Ugliness in a system
of opposites, the human body is not for him a locus of Beauty but of punishment.

If the body is no longer deemed beautiful, beauty is gradually taken to be a
property of mind. Empedocles' writings do not specify this; indeed he has little to
say about the immortal spirit that suffers the reincarnations. His contemporary,
Anaxagoras, however, has much more to say about the mind, which he considers
to be different from the body. Although Anaxagoras believed that all physical
bodies are composites of all the kinds of things there are, this was not true of the
mind.

Other things have a share of everything, but mind is infinite and self-ruled
and not mixed with anything, but is alone by itself. . . . For it is the finest of
all things and the purest, and it has all knowledge concerning all things and
the greatest power; and over everything that has soul, large or small, mind
rules.

(59B12; trans. Robinson 1968: 181)

Does Anaxagoras mean that there is only one mind, ruling over all living things?
If so, what is the relationship of individual embodied minds to this one mind? The
answer to these questions are not clear (cf Taylor 1997: 218–19); but whatever
the case, it is the mind that is 'finest and purest'. If anything can be said to be
beautiful, it is mind and the eternal truths that it knows.

By the time Democritus considered the matter late in the fifth century BCE, the
linkage between beauty and the mind was explicit. Bodies might be good looking,
but unless the mind was active such good looks were of little account.

Beauty of body is merely animal unless intelligence is present.

(68B105; trans. Robinson 1968: 230)

The value of the soul over the body, and the distinction between them, is shared
with his precursors even though Democritus parted company with them in
declaring that there is no such thing as immortality. The soul does not exist after
the body dies; and it is therefore misguided to be troubled by notions of an after-
life. Even the gods, though they are long-lived, are not immortal according to
Democritus (Taylor 1997: 235). It is a strange full circle: the earlier thinkers
rejected the beauty of the body and emphasized the mind *because* the former is
mortal and corruptible. With Democritus the value of mind over body remains *in
spite of* the mortality of both, and even of the gods.

Whatever the differences in their cosmological systems, philosophers after Pythagoras who separated mind from body invariably valued the former and its activities over the latter. For some of them, like Parmenides, there is no discussion of what happens to the mind after death. Others, like Democritus and the later atomists, explicitly denied immortality, even though they accepted the hierarchy of mind and body. The efforts of the presocratic philosophers can be seen as attempts to find a way out of the changing world of birth, death and bodiliness to a realm of eternal truth. Eternity, as surely as violence, was linked with a denial of natality. It was Plato who recognized the tensions; and it is to his thought that I now turn.

Chapter 10

How to give birth like a man

> No, you must keep up your spirits and say that it is only my body that you are burying, and you can bury it as you please, in whatever way you think is most proper . . . [Socrates] talked to [his wife and children] and gave them directions about carrying out his wishes. Then he told the women and children to go away, and came back himself to join us,
>
> (*Phaedo* 116a–b)[1]

Thus Socrates dies. His final hours are spent discoursing with his male friends on the true life of the soul, which death will release from the prison house of his body. His wife and the other women of the household are given orders and then sent away, lest they disturb Socrates' tranquillity with their weeping and wailing (117e). The scenes of Socrates' last hours have engraved themselves deeply upon western culture. Second only to the death of Jesus, the death of Socrates has perhaps done more to shape the genealogy of death in the west than any other single event.

Plato's representation of the teachings of Socrates on life and death, truth and opinion, mind and body, male and female did not emerge out of thin air. Influential as his books are, they draw much from the presocratics: from Parmenides on the 'way of truth', of logic rather than the senses; from Pythagoras' system of opposites; from Empedocles' idea of this world as a place of exile; from Anaxagoras' exaltation of the life of the mind, of philosophy as immortality. Less overtly, but no less significantly, we find Plato's determined suppression of myth and poetry, of the feminine, and of the goddess: all of these are seen as contrary to true wisdom. We find Plato mimicking Parmenides' strategy of putting his own teaching into the mouth of a female: in the case of Plato, that of Diotima, a wise religious woman. In fact, Plato goes further, taking to himself (or at least to Socrates)[2] the functions of birth and reproduction, as we shall see. Yet we also find in Plato sustained philosophical attention to beauty, the first in western culture. Though not without its tensions – to some of which Plato himself drew attention – his work placed beauty at the heart of the western philosophical agenda for 1,500 years. Moreover Plato employed strategies which called his own thinking, including his thinking about gender, violence and eternity, into question.

In this chapter I shall focus on Plato's gendered representation of death. This will involve, first, an account of what Plato says about death itself. Second, I will look at the role of women in death ritual in traditional Greek society, how Plato transposed the social role of women into a discussion of manliness and control, and banned poets whose descriptions of death might undermine such manliness. The third part will discuss how Socrates took to himself (and to men) the function of midwifery and reproduction; and the chapter will conclude with a discussion of the deadly effect of mathematics on Plato's epistemology. In the following chapter I will continue to discuss Plato, showing how his account of beauty is invested in death, but also how he himself questioned that investment, destabilized his own categories, and suggested possibilities of thinking otherwise. Plato's positioning of himself in relation to violence and eternity is alive to tension and complexity, and open to negotiation even within his own work.

Hemlock, exile and the polypods

Plato's most famous representation of death is the death of Socrates in the *Phaedo*.[3] Socrates' death was a violent death, execution by hemlock poison in prison. Although in the dialogue the death seems peaceful, death by hemlock was actually 'an agony not at all like the cessation of warmth Plato describes easing its way up Socrates' limbs,' and Plato and his readers knew it (Woodruff 1992: 86). The reason for his execution was his conviction upon charges of impiety and corrupting the youth. In the *Apology* Plato presents these charges as utterly misguided, indeed as an indication that those who decided Socrates' fate cared more for themselves than for the exercise of justice. Socrates has the high moral ground. He is much more concerned about truth than about preserving his life; indeed he virtually courts the death sentence in his speech to the court. He says,

> In battle it is often obvious that you could escape being killed by giving up your arms and throwing yourself upon the mercy of your pursuers, and in every kind of danger there are plenty of devices for avoiding death if you are unscrupulous enough to stick at nothing. But I suggest, gentlemen, that the difficulty is not so much to escape death; the real difficulty is to escape doing wrong, which is far more fleet of foot.
>
> (*Apology* 39a)

Although he is old and slow, he has managed to escape wrong; whereas those who have convicted him, youthful though they may be, are in its clutches. 'When I leave this court I shall go away condemned by you to death, but they [his accusers] will go away convicted by truth herself of depravity and wickedness' (39b). Socrates rebukes them for their injustice, and denounces a political system that relies on violence rather than on truth: 'If you expect to stop denunciation of your wrong way of life by putting people to death, there is something amiss with your reasoning' (39d).

What, then, is this death which Socrates accepts? In the *Apology* he says,

> Death is one of two things. Either it is annihilation, and the dead have no consciousness of anything, or, as we are told, it is really a change – a migration of the soul from this place to another.
>
> (40c)

These were the opinions of Presocratic thinkers: the first had been held by Democritus; the second by Empedocles and Anaxagoras. If the first is true, Socrates says, then death is gain, because it is like the deep dreamless sleep that even a king hopes for every night. But if the second is true, then death will give Socrates the opportunity of meeting and conversing with the heroes of old: Hesiod and Homer and Odysseus and Ajax. 'I am willing to die ten times over if this account is true,' says Socrates (41a).

In the *Phaedo* Plato has Socrates defend the second of the two options. Death is the separation of the soul from the body. The body has been a prison for the soul just as the Athenian gaol was a prison for Socrates' body. Socrates' argument depends on Parmenides' account of truth as unchanging and eternal. The soul, he says, is naturally akin to truth.

> The soul is most like that which is divine, immortal, intelligible, uniform, indissoluble, and ever self-consistent and invariable, whereas body is most like that which is human, mortal, multiform, unintelligible, dissoluble, and never self-consistent.
>
> (*Phaedo* 80b)

This being the case, the body, that is to say bodily senses, are least likely to be able to provide knowledge of truth. The bodily senses have access to the changing things of the world, and are therefore fitted only to what Parmenides had called the 'way of opinion'. Therefore when inquiry is made through 'the instrumentality of the body', the soul gets bewildered: 'it is drawn away by the body into the realm of the variable, and loses its way and becomes confused and dizzy, as though it were fuddled' (79c). Absolute beauty, absolute goodness, absolute truth can never be discerned in this way. They can be found only by a soul that is not contaminated by the body or the efforts of the senses.

> When it [the soul] investigates by itself, it passes into the realm of the pure and everlasting and immortal and changeless, and being of a kindred nature, when it is once independent and free from interference, consorts with it always and strays no longer, but remains, in that realm of the absolute, constant and invariable through contact with beings of a similar nature. And this condition of the soul we call wisdom.
>
> (79d)

Now, wisdom is what the philosopher seeks: Socrates emphasizes that the word 'philosophy' means 'love of wisdom'. But if attaining wisdom requires the separation of the soul from the body with its distractions and hindrances, then the true philosopher will, already in this life, discipline himself[4] as much as possible to purify himself from the constraints of the body. And since death is the completion of that process, the ultimate separation of the soul from the body, the true philosopher does not fear death but rather looks forward to it as the culmination of his efforts. 'True philosophers make dying their profession' (67e). It would therefore be ridiculous for a philosopher to try to escape from death when it presents itself. Socrates says,

> We are in fact convinced that if we are ever to have pure knowledge of anything, we must get rid of the body and contemplate things by themselves with the soul by itself. . . . If no pure knowledge is possible in the company of the body, then either it is totally impossible to acquire knowledge, or it is possible only after death, because it is only then that the soul will be separate and independent of the body. It seems that so long as we are alive, we shall continue closest to knowledge if we avoid as much as we can all contact and association with the body, except when they are absolutely necessary, and instead of allowing ourselves to become infected with its nature, purify ourselves from it until God himself gives us deliverance.
>
> (66e–67a)

Plato thus combines Pythagoras' distinction between the soul and the body with Parmenides' way of truth and way of opinion. Not only is there absolute truth, unattainable by the senses or by ordinary experience, as Parmenides and Anaxagoras had taught, but it can be reached only after death. Whereas they had denied mortality by asserting the changelessness of true being, Plato celebrates death as the way to true life of the soul. He thus carries even further a denial of ordinary experience and a reversal of its usual import: physical birth is now birth into a prison-house; death is liberation.

It can of course be objected that in other, probably later, dialogues Plato has a much more complicated understanding of the human person than this simple hierarchical dualism: in the *Phaedrus*, for example, the 'myth of the charioteer' develops a tripartite idea of the self (*Phaedrus* 246a): I shall return to this in the next chapter. It has even been argued that all Socrates' talk of immortality and an other-worldly realm of ideas can be dismissed from Plato's real meaning in the *Phaedo*, which should be read as an account of the persecution of philosophy rather than as offering a view of the nature of the human person, at least in the obvious sense that emerges from a first reading (Strauss 1952; cf Zuckert 1996: ch. 4). Be that as it may, it can hardly be doubted that Socrates' teaching on death just before he drinks the hemlock has had an enormous impact on the western conception of death as separation of body and soul, and thus also on the idea of the human person as a soul lodged, in this life, in a mortal body.

In the *Phaedo* Socrates argues that our souls must have existed before our birth, and been acquainted with the absolute realities of beauty and goodness; so that our learning of them in this life is a rediscovery of our own former knowledge (76e). This is also the theme of the *Meno*, in which Socrates argues that learning is really recollection of what was known in former life (*Meno* 81c, 86a–b): 'if the truth about reality is always in our soul, the soul must be immortal'. Now, why would the soul ever have left its place of knowledge of true reality to be born into the shackles of a body? Socrates does not use the vocabulary of exile, but for those who read Plato after Empedocles, that notion was ready to hand. Plato can be read as developing Empedocles' idea of this earthly life as the soul's exile from its true home in the realm of being, sent to live in this mortal body as a punishment for sins.

This interpretation is strengthened by a reading of the 'myth of the cave' in the *Republic*.

> Picture men dwelling in a sort of subterranean cavern with a long entrance open to the light on its entire width. Conceive them as having their legs and necks fettered from childhood, so that they remain in the same spot, able to look forward only, and prevented by the fetters from turning their heads. Picture further the light from a fire burning higher up and at a distance behind them, and between the fire and the prisoners and above them a road along which a low wall has been built, as the exhibitors of puppet shows have partitions before the men themselves, above which they show the puppets.
>
> (*Republic* vii. 514a–b)

The prisoners see the shadows of the puppets, cast by the flicker of the fire; they also hear echoes of the sounds made behind the parapet; but they cannot turn their heads and so cannot see one another nor the puppets themselves. For all they know, the echoes and the dance of shadows is the whole world. Indeed they become quite adept at predicting sequences, precedences, and the like, and give honour to those who can do it best.

Socrates' listener objects that this is 'a strange image' that he presents, and 'strange prisoners'. Socrates responds impatiently, 'like to us', and presses on with his portrayal. But in what way is it 'like to us'? Although Plato's topic in the *Republic* is the parallel between justice in the city and justice in the soul, one way of interpreting the allegory is to see the cave as the material world and the physical body in which we are shackled. The cave/world is both womb and tomb. Our bondage in our bodies means that what we take to be knowledge is no better than a dance of shadows and a play of echoes.

Such an interpretation is strengthened as Socrates proceeds. In his parable, one of the prisoners is released from his fetters, turned around, and taken from his place of captivity up into the world lit by sunlight and filled with the things of which he had previously seen only shadowy representations. At first he is dazzled, but gradually he becomes accustomed to the light and would not for all the world go back to be bound again in the darkness of the cave. Socrates asks,

> do you think . . . that he would envy and emulate those who were honoured by these prisoners and lorded it among them, or that he would feel with Homer and greatly prefer while living on earth to be serf of another, a landless man, and endure anything rather than opine with them and live that life?
>
> (516d)

The reference is to Homer's Achilles, lamenting his existence in Hades where he had been made king of the dead. The allusion increases the resonance of the cave with the tomb. Our normal life is the cave, the place of death; true life is possible only when we are released from the shackles of our mortal life. With consummate skill, Plato uses Homer to make his point even while effecting a complete reversal of the Homeric stance. This earthly life, which Homer celebrates, is for Plato the shadowy cave. True life can be enjoyed only when one is released from its shackles.

Socrates next asks what would happen if such a person, who has now seen truth and reality, were to re-enter the cave in an attempt to release those who are still imprisoned in it. He would again be blind, this time because of the darkness; and the prisoners in the cave would mock him for his incapacity to join in their evaluations and predictions of the dance of shadows:

> Would he not provoke laughter, and would it not be said of him that he returned from his journey aloft with his eyes ruined and that it was not worth while even to attempt the ascent? And if it were possible to lay hands on the man who tried to release them and lead them up, would they not kill him?
>
> (517a)

It is easy to read this passage through the lens of later Christian Platonism, as a description of what happened to prophets and martyrs and even to Christ himself. Even reading it in the more appropriate context of the pre-Socratic thinkers, the Empedoclean idea of exile is never far away, especially when this allegory is coupled with the Platonic idea that knowledge is recollection. The soul in the cave of the body is wandering from its true home and longs to escape to the light.

However, some qualifications must be added. When Socrates draws out the implications of his analogy of the cave in the *Republic*, he does so not in terms of death but of conversion. In the *Republic* the theme is, after all, how to ensure justice in the state; it is about the politics of this world, and not (overtly at least) about death. Socrates discusses the education of the part of the soul concerned with thought, and says,

> this part of such a soul, if it had been hammered from childhood, and had thus been struck free of the leaden weights, so to speak, of our birth and

becoming, which attaching themselves to it by food and similar pleasures and gluttonies turn downward the vision of the soul – if, I say, freed from these, it had suffered a conversion toward the things that are real and true, that same faculty of the same man would have been most keen in its vision of the higher things, just as it is for the things toward which it is now turned.

(519 b)

Such a 'converted' person, Socrates argues, would be most unwilling to take on the duties of presiding over a state, and yet would have the most competence to do so. Nevertheless, although the concern is for conversion, echoes of exile can be heard; and birth is still a 'leaden weight'.

These echoes reverberate when the allegory of the cave is set alongside Plato's comments on reincarnation, especially as found in the *Phaedo* and the *Timaeus*. It will be recalled that in the *Phaedo* Socrates had claimed that the philosopher, who all his life had prepared for death by detaching himself as much as possible from the demands and desires of the body, would at last be freed to look upon truth and goodness, and converse with others of like mind. But what of those who do not live the philosophical life, those who are attached to their bodies and do not seek to purify themselves from it? What happens when they die? Socrates suggests that such souls wander about as ghosts in graveyards 'until at last, through craving for the corporeal, which unceasingly pursues them, they are imprisoned once more in a body' (*Phaedo* 81d). The body in which they now find themselves will be suited to the sort of character they have developed. Those who have been gluttonous or selfish may find themselves in the form of a donkey; those who have been lawless and violent become wolves and hawks and kites. Decent but unphilosophical people 'will probably pass into some other kind of social and disciplined creature like bees, wasps, and ants, or even back into the human race again' (82b).

The teaching of reincarnation also forms part of the cosmological scheme depicted in the *Timaeus*. Here Plato says that the first to be created were men, whose souls were actually inhabitants each of his own star (41e). If they lived well, they returned at death to dwell on their star. But if they did not, then they must expect, as punishment, to be reincarnated as women.

> Of the men who came into the world, those who were cowards or led unrighteous lives may with reason be supposed to have changed into the nature of woman in the second generation.
>
> (91a; cf 41b)

Even worse is to come. A man (now in the body of a woman) can persist in evil, and 'continually be changed into some brute who resembled him in the evil nature which he had acquired' (41c) until, having passed into the lowest state, the reversal at last begins. It should be noted that in this passage (41a–e) all souls are male, even those temporarily enduring the punishment of inhabiting women's bodies. The same teaching is repeated at the end of the dialogue, with elaborations. The unrighteous, as noted, are reborn as women.

> But the race of birds was created out of innocent, light-minded men . . . they grew feathers instead of hair. The race of wild pedestrian animals, again came from those who had no philosophy in any of their thoughts. . . . In consequence of these habits of theirs they had their front legs and their heads resting upon the earth to which they were drawn by natural affinity, and the crowns of their heads were elongated and of all sorts of shapes, into which the courses of the soul were crushed by reason of disuse. And this was the reason why they were created quadrupeds and polypods.
>
> (91e)

How seriously and literally this is meant to be taken is of course open to question. But even if it were meant as allegory, or in a light-hearted way – and in the *Timaeus* there is nothing to indicate that it *should* be so taken – the allegory or joke would still depend on devaluing women in comparison with men, and on the division between body and soul prominent in many of Plato's dialogues.

Women, death and manliness

Before Socrates drinks the hemlock, the women and children are dismissed. Socrates has already taken a bath, giving as his reason: 'I prefer to have a bath before drinking the poison, rather than give the women the trouble of washing me when I am dead' (*Phaedo* 115a). And when he drained the cup, and all his friends broke down in tears, Socrates admonished them:

> Really, my friends, what a way to behave! Why, that was my main reason for sending away the women, to prevent this sort of disturbance, because I am told that one should make one's end in a tranquil frame of mind. Calm yourselves and try to be brave.
>
> (117d–e)

Socrates distances himself as far as possible from anything 'womanly'. He does not want women to touch his body, even after he has died: his choice to have a bath could be interpreted less as a wish to save women trouble than as his distaste at the thought of their touch. And what of his dismissal of them? Is it out of consideration for them? Or is it rather that if he is going to keep up his welcoming attitude toward death then he must at all costs not allow any expression of feeling that might confront him with the reality of death and thus threaten to undermine his resolve?

In fifth-century Athens, as in much of ancient Greece, women were associated with birth and death rituals. It was women's task to wash and lay out the corpse, and perhaps place herbs or even jewellery on it, ready for friends to come to the house to pay their respects. Although male members of the household mourned, the intense ritual lamentation, including tearing the hair and perhaps even laceration, was the provence of women. The process of death and the corpse itself were considered to be polluting. So, for that matter, was childbirth, which few women could avoid. Some scholars argue that 'since women could not escape the pollution of giving birth, as men could, they were presumably better suited to deal with the pollution of death' (Shapiro 1991: 635) and thus had placed upon them the task of washing and preparing the corpse. Karen Stears, however, argues that the importance of women for the correct conduct of death ritual also had a positive value for them. It meant that women could use it to enhance their status; and could use their subsequent visits to the tomb as an occasion for other sorts of visits which would not otherwise be socially sanctioned (Stears 1998: 124). Either way, women had a particularly close association with death, birth and the functions of the body.

Plato, characteristically, transposes this social theme into a philosophical key of considerable subtlety. Pivotal for his thinking, though often left implicit, is the distinction between manliness on the one hand and womanliness or effeminacy on the other. In Plato's presentation, it is characteristic of womanly souls to give way to grief, but characteristic of manly souls to exercise restraint, control and courage in the face of death. Plato considers it natural for a woman to weep and wail. That is what womanly souls can be expected to do, just as a hen can be expected to cackle or a cow to moo. But for a man to lament in the same way shows that he is effeminate; and this is shameful. This is not to say that men should never weep at all in the face of death. The prison officer who comes, in the *Phaedo*, to instruct Socrates and say goodbye to him just before the poison is administered, praises Socrates for his goodness and bravery, and bursts into tears as he leaves. Rather than castigate him, Socrates says,

> What a charming person! All the time I have been here he has visited me, and sometimes had discussions with me, and shown me the greatest kindness – and how generous of him now to shed tears for me at parting.
>
> (*Phaedo* 116d)

Yet when his friends break down and cry, Socrates reprimands them for their womanish behaviour. The difference seems to be one of control. When the prison officer begins to weep, he leaves the room. Apollodorus and Socrates' other companions, however, stay with him. Does their 'storm of passionate weeping' endanger his self-control, the composure and self-mastery that proves his manliness, in a way that the prison officer's weeping does not? Might Socrates himself be threatened with effeminacy?

This suggestion gains plausibility from Plato's remarks on grief and manly control in his discussion of why poets should be banned from his ideal Republic. Plato recognizes that the poets – Homer, and the tragedians – portray intense emotions: love, fear and grief. Those who go to the theatre to hear such poetry naturally respond to the work that so strongly affects them.

> When we hear Homer or some of the other makers of tragedy imitating one of the heroes who is in grief, and is delivering a long tirade in his lamentations or chanting and beating his breast, [we] feel pleasure, and abandon ourselves and accompany the representation with sympathy and eagerness.
>
> (*Republic* iii.605d)

Yet this behaviour of lamentation and sorrow in the theatre is behaviour that Plato says we would 'be ashamed of' and 'abominate' in real life. It is womanly, not manly.

> But when in our lives some affliction comes to us, you are also aware that we plume ourselves . . . on our ability to remain calm and endure, in the belief that this is the conduct of a man, and what we were praising in the theatre was that of a woman.
>
> (605d)

This is not to say that the actors were women – in Athens all actors were male – but rather that they represent men who behave, in their grieving, in a womanish fashion. Plato asserts that such loss of control should never be extolled or encouraged. If we 'feed fat' the emotion of pity or grief while watching the suffering of someone else on stage, it will not be 'easy to restrain it in our own sufferings'. So the part of our soul 'that has hungered for tears and a good cry and satisfaction' is pandered to by poets who present us with tragedy; but the net result is a weakening of manly self-mastery.

Indeed men must be careful never to imitate women, nor should men play any female roles in drama. Men are expected always to be 'manly', and should be taught such manliness from an early age. Socrates says,

> We will not then allow our charges, whom we expect to prove good men, being men, to play the parts of women and imitate a woman young or old or wrangling with her husband, defying heaven, loudly boasting, fortunate in her own conceit, or involved in misfortune and possessed by grief and lamentation – still less a woman that is sick, in love, or in labour . . . Nor may they imitate slaves.
>
> (*Republic* iii.395d–e)

Everything that a young man is taught should work together to enable him to fight valiantly in warfare and to meet death bravely. Plato is invested in the role of warfare in the state and the necessity for men to engage in violence. If the tragedians undermine that capacity for violence, they should be banished.

Just the same is true in relation to music. Only such music should be permitted as is compatible with warfare and manly occupations. Both rhythm and harmony should lend itself to martial pursuits. Modes of music like the Lydian or the Ionian that were associated with dirges and conviviality respectively (and thus with women) are banished.

> But leave us that mode [the Dorian] that would fittingly imitate the utterances and the accents of a brave man who is engaged in warfare or in any enforced business, and who, when he has failed, either meeting wounds or death or having fallen into some other mishap, in all these conditions confronts fortune with steadfast endurance and repels her strokes.
>
> (*Republic* iii.399a–b)

Manly self-mastery must be constantly drilled into young men in their education, so that they become good soldiers and learn not to fear death.[5]

It is important to emphasize that Plato's banning of some musical modes and of poetry from his ideal republic is connected with his gendered understanding of death.[6] This is evident in Book iii of the *Republic*. Socrates cites again the passage from the *Iliad* in which Achilles laments his death. Passages like this, he says, should be prohibited, especially for those who are to be warriors. The reason he gives is that if men who are going to fight hear such accounts of the underworld, it will sap their courage and willingness to die for their city. No longer will they be fearless in battle and 'prefer death to defeat and slavery' (386b). Rather, they will dread death and do all they can to avoid it; thus they will make poor soldiers. Socrates goes even further: he argues that all poetry to do with what happens after death should be banned for the same reason.

> Then we must further taboo in these matters the entire vocabulary of terror and fear, Cocytus named of lamentation loud, abhorred Styx, the flood of deadly hate, the people of the infernal pit and of the charnel house, and all other terms of this type, whose very names send a shudder through all the hearers every year.
>
> (387c)

A good man is never to entertain the impression that death is a terrible thing, either for the one who dies or for the one who loses a friend, son, or brother through death. Rather, a good man is emotionally self-sufficient and controlled, and accordingly makes 'the least lament and bears it most moderately' when someone he loves dies. And Socrates concludes this part of the discussion with another specifically gendered remark:

> Then we should be right in doing away with the lamentations of men of note and in attributing them to women, and not to the most worthy of them either,

and to inferior men, in order that those whom we say we are breeding for the guardianship of the land may disdain to act like these.

(388a)

As Socrates himself points out, this is a very different attitude to death and loss than is found in the *Iliad*, in which heroes are portrayed in excesses of grief at the deaths of their friends, wailing and rolling in dung and smearing themselves with ashes, simultaneously lamenting their loss and celebrating their immortal glory. Such behaviour Socrates considers wholly inappropriate for men; it is womanly. But as Elizabeth Spelman points out, although Plato's overt attack here is on poets, this banning of lamentation also serves to marginalize women. As she says,

> Given the central role women in classical Athens played in funeral rites as mourners, and vivid Socratic castigations of weeping and lamenting as womanish behaviour, attempts in the *Republic* to mute grief appear to be aimed at minimising forms of typically feminine behaviour. The virtual de-griefing of the polis thus is a kind of de-feminizing of it.
>
> (Spelman 1997: 31)

Men must learn self-control. Poets who compromise such control are to have no place.

But the banning of poets from Plato's ideal republic on the grounds that they promote womanish behaviour in relation to death is only one of the ways in which gendered death shapes the *Republic*. Arlene Saxonhouse (1994), in a closely observed article, shows how death is present from first to last as a guiding theme of the dialogue. The whole discussion of justice, which is its main topic, is introduced in relation to death: the conversation begins when Cephalus, an old man, expresses concern lest he depart to 'that other world' without paying his just dues either to the gods or to other people (3316). The *Republic* also ends with death; this time with the 'Myth of Er', the hero who returned from death to tell what the world beyond is like (614b–621d). And all along the way, death plays a crucial role. Gyges, the shepherd in the service of the king of Lydia, found the ring that made him invisible on the finger of a corpse: it is his story that compels Socrates to rethink justice not only for the individual but for the city (359d). Above all, death is the undercurrent in all the discussion of war and what makes a good warrior. Political activity is activity that crucially concerns war with other cities: as Pericles had said in his funeral oration, it is those citizens who die in battle for their city who are to be truly honoured as citizens. Even the myth of the cave, as we saw, conflates the imagery of the womb and the tomb, so that what might have been deemed the (female) source of life is instead a deathly prison chamber from which escape is urgently required.

Saxonhouse points out that in the *Republic*, as in Plato's dialogues more generally, the philosopher is shown to be useless at politics. A philosopher's nature is to seek truth and pursue the good wherever it may lead, even if that would be to undermine a political structure or to question the rationale for war. A politician, by contrast, must not indulge in such potentially damaging speculations but must wholly give himself up to the needs of the community. Thus a philosopher who is required to be involved in politics is as disorientated and as violated in his true nature as a man who has lived for a while in the sunshine and is then forced to go back and live in the cave. For a philosopher to be politically effective, his nature has to be changed.

This situation is parallel, Saxonhouse argues, to Plato's treatment of the question whether women can become guardians: they can, but only by a radical change in their nature, whereby they are turned away from generation and nurture to warfare and death (1994: 82). Skills traditionally linked with women, such as birth and nourishing, have no place in warfare; if women are to be warriors, their training must be a training in masculinity. Plato's comments have led some scholars to ponder whether Plato could be considered the first feminist, or at least a proto feminist (Vlastos, 1994; Okin 1979). It must be noted, however, that although in the *Republic* Plato toys with the idea of female guardians, by the time he writes the *Laws* no mention is made of it. Even in the *Republic*, the norm remains masculine, violent, even if it might be possible for some women to reconstruct themselves according to that masculine standard (Smith 1994). Some people happen to have 'manly souls in female bodies', as Spelman has put it (1988: 32), and where, unusually, this is the case, they should not be debarred from governing only because of the sex of their bodies. Moreover all of this is compatible with – indeed dependent upon – a large population of 'natural' slaves, both male and female: the idea that Plato was toying with equality is hardly credible.

The philosopher gives birth

The linkage of gender, death and violence is again apparent in Plato's *Theaetetus*, where he rejects actual experience of birth and death, and appropriates to the philosopher 'true' birthing in a way reminiscent of Parmenides. Even more overtly than in the *Republic*, Socrates in the *Theaetetus* contrasts the life of the philosopher with the life of the man of affairs. From the point of view of the latter, 'the world has the laugh of the philosopher, partly because he seems arrogant, partly because of his helpless ignorance in matters of daily life' (175b). Socrates says that a philosopher takes no interest in political factions or meetings, is not in the slightest concerned with questions of a person's pedigree or ancestry, and is useless even in practical matters of daily life, 'because it is really only his body that sojourns in his city, while his thought, disdaining all such things as worthless, takes wings . . . ' (174e). He tells the story of Thales who was so intent in his study of the stars that he fell into a well at his feet: the maidservants laughed at him as the common people will laugh at any philosopher's ineptitude in practical this-worldly matters. But the whole thing is reversed when the philosopher 'drags' the man of affairs 'upward to a height' at which he may be challenged about justice, and 'the whole question of human happiness and misery'.

In all this field, when that small, shrewd, legal mind has to render an account, then the situation is reversed. Now it is he who is dizzy from hanging at such an unaccustomed height and looking down from mid-air. Lost and dismayed and stammering, he will be laughed at, not by maidservants or the uneducated – they will not see what is happening – but by everyone whose breeding has been the antithesis of a slave's.

(*Theateteus* 175d)

The underlying theme is the same as that of the myth of the cave: contrary to appearances and the 'way of opinion', true life of the mind is not that of the body. 'Nothing is more like the divine' than one who pursues wisdom; 'all other forms of seeming power and intelligence in the rulers of society are as mean and vulgar as the mechanic's skill' (176c).

Moreover, the *Theaetetus*, like the *Republic*, is a dialogue set into a framework of violence. The setting for the dialogue is the meeting of two of Theaetetus' friends, Euclides and Terpsion, with Euclides bearing the news that Theaetetus has just been carried off the field of battle 'only just alive'. They comment on his bravery in the face of death: in other words, they are representing a man who has learned to conduct himself in the manly way that Socrates advocates in the *Phaedo* and the *Republic*. From this point the dialogue proceeds. At its end there is another reminder of violent death. The dialogue concludes with Socrates saying, 'Now I must go to the portico of the King-Archon to meet the indictment which Meletus has drawn up against me' (210d): it is of course the indictment which will lead to Socrates' execution. Thus both Socrates and Theaetetus, the main characters of the dialogue, are set in a framework that deliberately reminds us of their violent deaths, deaths which reveal their courage and manliness.[7]

And yet the central metaphor of the *Theaetetus* is a female metaphor: Socrates casts himself as a midwife who assists at the birth of philosophical ideas. The metaphor is repeated at crucial points of the dialogue. Socrates says that he is the son of a midwife, and that he himself practices 'the same art', enabling others to give birth even though he does not bear fruit himself. 'But the delivery is heaven's work and mine', Socrates says (150d). 'My art of midwifery is in general like theirs [i.e. women midwives]; the only difference is that my patients are men, not women, and my concern is not with the body but with the soul that is in travail of birth' (150b).

The difference is hardly trivial. Socrates is at pains to show that the midwifery he practices, on the souls of men rather than on the bodies of women, is much the superior of the two. He describes the tasks of midwives, and continues: 'All this, then, lies within the midwife's province, but her performance falls short of mine' (150a). He concerns himself, for instance, with 'phantom births', ideas that present themselves as true but are not: this, he says, is a more difficult skill than any midwife has to practice. Again, he says,

In yet another way those who seek my company have the same experience as a woman with a child; they suffer the pains of labour and, by night and day,

are full of distress far greater than a woman's, and my art has power to bring
on these pains or to allay them.

(151a)

Thus not only does Socrates do more skilful work than any midwife, but his
patients also have to labour more intensively. The philosopher is paralleled with
the female, but what the philosopher does trumps every time anything that a
woman could do. Philosophers are the true life-givers, soaring above ordinary
experience in the realm most like the divine.

It is in the context of Socrates' appropriation of reproduction and midwifery
that I believe we can best understand the role of Diotima in the *Symposium*. The
Symposium is Plato's representation of a series of speeches in praise of the god of
Love, given by men at the end of a dinner party. Socrates gives the last speech;
but rather than speak in his own voice he recounts (in a manner reminiscent of
Parmenides) what he has been taught about love by a woman, Diotima, a prophetess whose teaching he claims to admire.

There has been much discussion among philosophers as to why the figure
of Diotima is introduced: I suggest that careful attention to context gives important clues. In the first place, a close look at what Diotima is made to say in the
Symposium reveals a similar dualistic preoccupation with death and the life of the
mind as we find in the *Theaetetus*, the *Phaedo* and the *Republic*, together with a
similar denigration of actual birth, bodies and women. However, one of the main
differences is that in the *Theaetetus* Socrates claims the superiority of philosophical
over physical fecundity in his own voice, whereas in the *Symposium* this claim is
made in the voice of Diotima. Why?

This question brings us to the way Diotima is framed in the dialogue itself. It
should not be overlooked that 'Diotima's' speech at the dinner party was not
spoken by her: Diotima was not on the guest list. The speech is Plato's account of
Socrates' account of what Diotima said. Yet even that gives a much more direct
impression than is warranted. As Plato constructs the dialogue, he (Plato) indicates
that Diotima's speech is reported through a long sequence of Chinese whispers.
Plato says that he is reporting what Aristodemus who had been at the dinner
party told Apollodorus, about an event that had occurred while the latter was
still an infant. Appolodorus then told the story to Glaucon, Plato's brother, who
presumably told it to Plato. So the train of transmission is represented as Diotima
– Socrates – Aristodemus – Apollodorus – Glaucon – Plato (Halperin 1994: 46).
Moreover there is said to be a considerable lapse of time between Aristodemus'
hearing of Socrates' speech and his recounting it to Apollodorus; Socrates says that
Diotima taught him these lessons 'once upon a time' (201d). To cap it all, the main
reporter (Aristodemus) insists that he had a considerable hangover when he heard
the speech. It is hard to imagine how Plato could have signalled more clearly that
Diotima is functioning in the dialogue for his own purposes. He is thorough to the
point of buffoonery in showing that he is not reporting actual speech.

But that leaves open the question of what his purposes might have been. Why put the speech which scholars generally think most represents Plato's own view (cf Ferrari 1992) into the mouth of a woman? Here a third aspect of context should be remembered. Parmenides, it will be recalled, represented his teaching as coming from the goddess; he put his words into her mouth even while actual goddess worship was losing ground. Plato, we know, was much impressed with Parmenides, having written a dialogue in which he represented Parmenides as the hero.[8] It must at least be a serious possibility that Plato is taking over and modifying Parmenides' rhetorical device of putting 'truth' into the mouth of a female divinity, just as he took over and modified some of Parmenides' central metaphysical ideas.

I suggest that what is happening in the *Symposium* is only slightly different from what we have observed in the *Theaetetus* where Socrates arrogates a female role for himself and for philosophy as he personifies it. In this case he simply projects such a teaching on to a 'prophetess'. This can best be seen from the teaching itself, which like that of the *Theaetetus*, is far more closely intertwined with issues of birth and death than is usually recognized. Plato represents a discussion between Socrates and Diotima which is shot through with anxiety about death and the prospect of immortality. At the outset Diotima insists that Love (*Eros*) is 'halfway between mortal and immortal', 'a very powerful spirit . . . halfway between god and man' (202d–e). But only a little further on, she says that since Love is love of what is lovely, and wisdom is the loveliest of all things, 'Love is a lover of wisdom' (204b), that is, a philosopher. So a philosopher is a powerful spirit (like the priestess Diotima), already half-way to immortality, just as Plato had taught in the *Phaedo* in which the philosopher looks forward to death as a fulfilment.

Even at this early stage in the discussion Plato already slips in a negatively valenced comment on the female, a positively valenced comment on Love/ philosophy as manly, and a hint that concern with death lies at the bottom of the whole discussion. Eros, Diotima says, is the son of Resource, who is full of wisdom and energy and gallantry, and a poor beggar woman called Need, who is devoid of all wisdom and resource, not at all to be admired. Eros himself, as their son,

> is neither mortal nor immortal, for in the space of a day he will be now, when all goes well with him, alive and blooming, and now dying, to be born again by virtue of his father's nature, while what he gains will always ebb away as fast.
>
> (203e)

The male sexual imagery of arousal and orgasm as 'death', with its excitement and anxiety, is here personified and then transferred to the philosopher who, as Lover of wisdom, is also always between the immortals who already possess wisdom and the ignorant who do not seek it (see Irigaray 1993: 23–4; Rosen 1987).

The nature of Eros, Plato has Diotima say, is a drive for propagation, both of body and of soul.

> And why all this longing for propagation? Because this is the one deathless and eternal element in our mortality. And since we have argued that the lover longs for the good to be his own forever, it follows that we are bound to long for immortality as well as for the good – which is to say that Love [or the philosopher] is a longing for immortality.
>
> (206e)

'Diotima' teaches that 'the mortal does all it can to put on immortality' (207d), and does so primarily by breeding, ensuring that young people will perpetuate their elders. But it is not only through breeding that people seek immortality, but also, she says (as if she had Homeric writings in mind) through glory and fame: they will endure great hardship and danger 'to win eternal mention in the deathless roll of fame' (208c). By far the best way, however, rises above all of this, to fecundity of the spirit, the same fecundity that Socrates extolled in the *Theaetetus*.

> Those whose procreancy is of the body turn to woman as the object of their love, and raise a family, in the blessed hope that by doing so they will keep their memory green, 'through time and through eternity'. But those whose procreancy is of the spirit rather than of the flesh . . . conceive and bear the things of the spirit.
>
> (209a)

Here as elsewhere in Platonic writings, women are mentioned not as subjects in their own right but as enabling men to achieve their aims. Men of spirit, however, rise even above the use of women, and procreate otherwise, to eternity.[9]

Here begins the famous 'ascent'. The philosopher falls in love with a beautiful (male) body, and from there passes to all lovely bodies, and then to loveliness itself.

> And thus, by scanning beauty's wide horizon, he will be saved from a slavish and illiberal devotion to the individual loveliness of a single boy, a single man, or a single institution. And turning his eyes toward the open sea of beauty, he will find in such contemplation the seed of the most fruitful discourse and the loftiest thought, and reap a golden harvest of philosophy.
>
> (210d)

I shall come later to discuss the conception of beauty at work here. For now what I wish to emphasize is that all this is undertaken for the sake of immortality, a theme repeated with great frequency in 'Diotima's' speech.[10] The two philosopher friends – both male – conceive, produce, and rear their offspring of wisdom, she says, and their bond will be closer than those who raise their children together 'because they have created something lovelier and less mortal than human seed' (209c): again, the language of giving birth is appropriated for men in a project to fend off mortality. Moreover, once the philosopher has a glimpse of the eternal that is 'subsisting of itself and by itself in an eternal oneness' then he will never again be seduced by flesh and blood or the bodies of 'lads just ripening to manhood' (211b–d). Rather,

> he shall be called the friend of god, and if ever it is given to man to put on immortality, it shall be given to him.
>
> (212a)

Thus, as in the *Theaetetus*, men (at least men who are philosophers) can do what women do, and can do it better. They can reproduce, not merely of the flesh but of the spirit, and in so doing make a bid to overcome the mortality to which they were consigned by their birth from a woman.

Nevertheless, although Diotima as she appears in the *Symposium* is a construction of the masculinist imaginary of Plato, and puts forward an account of reality and knowledge which is consistent with his teaching in other dialogues, feminists have not been entirely wrong to see her as a destabilizing voice. I suggest however that this is not an indication that Diotima was a historical figure after all, but rather (as with Penelope in the *Odyssey*) a glimmer of hastily repressed recognition within the masculinst imaginary that there is a different reality, a way of thinking otherwise. This alterity is sometimes represented for Plato, as for Homer, by the feminine, a feminine that is, however, in tension with his linkage of the female with death and with his overriding misogyny. In the next chapter, I shall discuss Diotima again in relation to Plato's account of beauty, and show how even while she is inscribed in a masculinist symbolic and used for Plato's ventriloquism, it is not quite possible for Plato to evade the recognition that there is also a linkage between life, beauty and the female which undercuts his presentation of deathly knowledge and manly violence. Indeed, I shall argue that by the time Plato wrote the *Phaedrus* he was beginning to take very seriously indeed the female voice, and the living beauty which she represents.

Plato and mathematics: deadly knowledge

In order to appreciate Plato's account of beauty in Diotima's speech, however, it is helpful first to take a detour through a topic which at first glance seems to have nothing to do with beauty: namely mathematics and its (changing) role in Plato's theory of knowledge. This theory has, of course, a vast literature (e.g. Vlastos 1970; Heineman 1997); my purpose is not to survey it. Rather I wish to show how some aspects of Plato's theory of knowledge are much more closely aligned with preoccupation with death than is usually acknowledged. But if this is the case, then Plato's dictum that philosophers live with one foot in the grave may be true in a sense quite different from what Plato meant in the *Phaedo*.

Plato placed a very high importance on mathematics, not merely for its utilitarian value but as central to his epistemology. Although I will argue that he subsequently developed a less rigid stance which abandoned the idea that mathematics is central to epistemology and was more accepting of the finitude and fragility of human life, in the early and middle dialogues Plato sets out an epistemology in which mathematics has a very important place. In the *Republic*, Socrates argues that the potential philosopher-kings must undergo rigorous mathematical training, including arithmetic, geometry, stereometry, astronomy and harmonies. This mathematical phase of their preparation is envisaged to take ten years; only upon successful completion of it are they ready to proceed to dialectics (*Republic* vii.522d–532a). Presumably since Plato considered mathematics so important for his ideal republic, he would also have given it significant space in the Academy which he founded (Mueller 1992: 170–5).

The question, however, is why. What was so valuable about mathematics that it was allowed to take up so huge a chunk of life? This Socrates is at pains to spell out in the *Republic*. Time after time Glaucon, his interlocutor, assumes that each branch of mathematics as Socrates introduces them will serve a utilitarian purpose: geometry will enable formation of an army in battle; astronomy will be serviceable for understanding the seasons and their courses for agriculture, navigation, and the conduct of war. Time after time Socrates insists that such utilitarian goals are shallow. They are no better than one would expect of cave-dwellers arguing about how best to predict the dance of shadows. If one were appealing to such a benighted multitude, then it might be right to fear that they would condemn anything nonutilitarian as a waste of time. However, those who realize the true nature of the soul, and seek absolute reality and true wisdom – in other words, only the philosopher, the one who has escaped the cave – will understand Socrates' words and will see that utility is not the ultimate goal. 'But those who . . . have had no inkling of it [i.e. of this capacity of the soul for truth] will naturally think them all moonshine. For they can see no other benefit from such pursuits worth mentioning' (*Republic* vii.527e).

By repeating the same pattern of argument several times Plato underlines the message: learning mathematics is primarily about development of the soul. When Socrates suggests astronomy as one of the necessary branches of mathematics, Glaucon eagerly agrees, saying that instead of 'vulgar utilitarian commendation of astronomy' he will praise it because 'this study certainly compels the soul to look upward and leads it away from things here to those higher things' (529a). But Socrates will have none of this: Glaucon has again completely missed the point.

> For apparently if anyone with back-thrown head should learn something by staring at decorations on a ceiling, you would regard him as contemplating them with the higher reason and not with the eyes. . . . But if anyone tries to learn about the things of sense, whether gaping up or blinking down, I would

> never say . . . that his soul looks up, but down, even though he study floating on his back on sea or land.
>
> (529b–c)

The important thing, always, is the soul. But how does Plato believe that mathematics helps the soul? The short answer is that mathematics trains the soul away from the sensible world, the 'cave' of ordinary experience, and teaches it to look to the intelligible world, the world of 'true reality' removed from this passing show.

That short answer needs some elaboration, however; and when we look at it more closely it is startling to find that once again it is primarily *generation*, this world of birth and life, that Socrates repeatedly singles out as inimical to the 'contemplation of true being' (525a). Arithmetic is useful for the soldier, he says, because it enables him to marshal his troops; but for a philosopher it is important 'because he must rise out of the region of generation and lay hold on essence' (525b), specifically the essence of unity, the one. Again, he says that the study of calculation should be imposed on all those who are to become rulers, and they should become proficient at it

> until they attain to contemplation of the nature of number, by pure thought, not for the purpose of buying or selling, as if they were preparing to be merchants or hucksters, but for the uses of war and for facilitating the conversion of the soul itself from the world of generation to essence and truth.
>
> (525c)

And when it comes to geometry Socrates reemphasizes the point. Its study is a study of what is 'eternally existent', 'and not of a something which at some time comes into being and passes away' (527b).

What leaps off the page is the entanglement of mathematics with eternity and with violent death. The soldier learns mathematics to enable him to conduct his warfare: numbers are a help to him in the infliction of death. And the philosopher seeks truth as an escape from the world of generation – and implicitly from reproduction, embodiment and women. The whole point of mathematics for the philosopher is to 'rise above' the world of ordinary experience, to come out of the cave.[11] Mathematics is presented by Socrates in the *Republic* as the intellectual discipline that will bring about the turn from birth and life and this world to soldiery, death-dealing and other-worldly 'truth': it is the conversion required for any philosopher or ruler.

Binary oppositions and the quest for control

It might seem that this is a rather inflated burden to impose upon mathematics: how could the study of number have such a major effect? In the *Republic* the effect of mathematics is presented as coming about because it sets the mind free of sensible things, the shadows of the cave, and releases it to the intelligible world: mathematics thus is the perfect discipline for the philosopher looking forward to death, as presented in the *Phaedo*. But in the *Protagoras*, which is usually taken as an early dialogue (Kraut 1992a: 5), Plato has already presented another aspect of the importance of number for the philosopher. What he stressed in that dialogue was binary opposition and its place in logical thinking. Martha Nussbaum (1986) has given a telling interpretation of Plato's use of number in the *Protagoras*. I shall draw upon her work to make more explicit than she does the connection of Plato's use of number theory with death and gender.

Nussbaum discusses the *Protagoras* within the broader context of the tension between *tuché* and *techné*. *Tuché* is sometimes translated 'luck' or 'fate': it is the seeming arbitrariness of what happens to people. As the concept was developed among Greek thinkers, *techné*, came to mean the development of foresight and resource rather than 'blind dependence on what happens'

> *Techné*, then, is a deliberate application of human intelligence to some part of the world, yielding some control over *tuché*; it is concerned with the management of need and with prediction and control concerning future contingencies.
>
> (Nussbaum 1986: 95)

As Nussbaum presents it (in contrast with Irwin 1977), both Socrates and Protagoras agree in the dialogue about the need for *techné*, for some form of practical reasoning that will deliver us as much as possible from being at the mercy of whatever happens. Their disagreement is about the nature and extent of practical reason, and how *techné* will affect human nature. Protagoras wants to stay as close as possible to ordinary experience, and holds that the most important education is education in virtue, so that people will develop the inner resources to deal with whatever happens to them. He therefore argues for the teachability of virtue, and presents himself as a teacher of it (*Protagoras* 328a). Socrates, challenging Protagoras' claim that virtue can be taught, looks for an altogether stricter practical reason, guided by binary oppositions and quantification, to try to bring the contingencies of human life under control. Without *techné* we are at the mercy of death.

Socrates begins his questioning of Protagoras by getting him to explain virtue in terms of number: is virtue one or is it multiple? Protagoras replies that 'virtue is one' and all these characteristics are aspects of it, like mouth, nose, eyes and ears are part of a single face but not reducible one to another. Socrates, however, presses Protagoras to agree that justice and holiness resemble one another; indeed 'that justice is either the same thing as holiness or very like it' (331b). But Protagoras registers disquiet about it. He says,

> I don't think it is quite so simple, Socrates. I can't really admit that justice is holy and holiness just; I think there is some difference there. However

. . . what does it matter? If you like, let us assume that justice is holy and holiness just.

(331c)

But Socrates will have none of this 'does it matter' and 'if you like'. Either it is or it isn't. From this point on Socrates begins a relentless process of setting up binary oppositions and forcing Protagoras to choose between them or at least to acknowledge their nature: foolish behaviour is the opposite of temperate, the fair is the opposite of foul, and so on. 'In short . . . to everything that admits of a contrary there is one contrary and no more' (332). Time after time Protagoras protests, shows his unease, agrees only with reluctance and indicates that he thinks things are more complicated.

The dialogue can be read as a triumph of strict logical reasoning embodied by Socrates over the vague insistence on complexity by a self-important Sophist. But it can also be read in quite a different way, as Socrates using binary logic as a club with which to bludgeon more nuanced thought into a single formulation, like an intellectual bully boy. He asks questions which Protagoras considers complex, but when Protagoras tries to respond Socrates demands that he make his answers short. When Protagoras objects to the rules of argument that Socrates wishes to impose, Socrates tries to leave, like a spoiled child. His companions implore him to stay, and to treat the exchange as a discussion between friends of good will, not as a dispute between rivals and enemies (337b): they recognize that the adversarial method that Socrates is adopting as unhelpful.

Soon, however, Socrates is up to his old tricks. He manoeuvres Protagoras into a series of choices between contraries which end up by reducing the good to pleasure and the bad to pain. Therefore what is good and bad, for individuals or for social policy, can be ascertained on a utilitarian calculus. Socrates sums up: 'since our salvation in life has turned out to lie in the correct choice of pleasure and pain – more or less, greater or smaller, nearer or more distant – is it not in the first place a question of measurement, consisting as it does in a consideration of relative excess, defect, or equality?' (357b). Virtue, then, turns out to rest on *techné*, a science of measurement.

As Nussbaum points out, there are clear advantages to a reduction of ethics and social policy to quantification. Things that seem different in kind turn out to be measurable against one another after all.

> The science presupposes agreement on the scale and units of measure; this achieved, many other things fall into place. . . . For if we set ourselves to gauge, in each situation, the quantity of a single value and to maximize that, we eliminate uncertainty about what is to count as good activity. Choosing what to do becomes a straightforward matter of selecting the most efficient instrumental means to maximization, not the far messier matter of asking what actions are good for their own sake. And measurement, being precise, will

also deliver a definite verdict about the instrumental alternatives, by a clear public procedure that anyone can use.

(1986: 108–9)

Thus knowledge of the good turns out to be a *techné*, a branch of mathematics, in which the skills of measurement and quantification, not the skills of poetry or rhetoric or the imitation of good or heroic people are the essential skills.

Now, it is plain that this is quite a different account of the importance of mathematics than Plato gives in the *Republic*. There, mathematics was praised because it enabled its practitioner to rise above the world of ordinary experience, whereas here it is used to bring ordinary experience into order and to make utilitarian assessments of it. In each case it is mathematics that gives true knowledge, knowledge of the good. In the *Protagoras*, however, 'the good' is cast as the good *life*, which in turn is described as the life of most pleasure and least pain, not at the mercy of everything that comes along; while in the *Republic* such a hedonistic notion of the good is utterly scorned.[12] Although the style of reasoning is similar across these dialogues, in terms of the substance of the argument the Socrates of the *Protagoras* is very different indeed from the Socrates of other dialogues.

The mathematics of eternity

So what was Plato doing? Scholarly opinion advances several possibilities (Penner 1992); what is important for my purposes, however, is not to takes sides on the question, but rather to show how, no matter which way mathematics is taken – that is, whether as calculus of pleasure and pain or as a means of rising to the intelligible world – the investment in mathematics is once again connected with death.

If, in the first place, we read the *Protagoras* as an effort to find 'salvation . . . in the art of measurement' (356e), controlling by quantitative science those things that would otherwise seem to just happen at random, then knowledge and ignorance turn out to be true and false calculation, respectively. This reading helps to make sense of Socrates' final argument in the dialogue, where he contends that no one does wrong knowingly but only out of ignorance (358ff). On the face of it this seems like an absurd claim. But if we were to define good and bad in terms of pleasure and pain, each of which is quantifiable, then choices of action become choices of amounts or quantities, and it would become unreasonable to suppose that we would knowingly choose the lesser *quantity* of qualitatively commensurable pleasure. As Nussbaum explains, *akrasia* (weakness of the will) is taken, ordinarily, as what happens when we fail to act rationally: we know something is bad but do it anyway, overcome by desire or passion. Socrates, in arguing against the possibility that we could do wrong knowingly is showing what is involved if rationality is *techné*, mathematical. We will only do wrong if we miscalculate: evil is a result of ignorance. But is such a calculating machine still human? What has happened to desire and passion? If pleasure and pain are the sole measure of good and evil, and knowledge is reduced to calculating their quantity, then we may well have developed a *techné* of control, but we will hardly any longer be what we have hitherto known as human. 'In our anxiety to control and grasp the uncontrolled by *techné*, we may all too easily become distant from the lives that we originally wished to control' (1986: 260).

If we get what we want, will we want what we get? If knowledge is turned into calculation, and goodness is a question of quantity, then both knowledge and goodness have become lifeless. Here is the connection with death; and it is deeply ironic. The reason for reducing knowledge to calculation is to escape from the mercy of *tuché*, the threat of death and harm. But the means of escape is one that effectively kills our humanness, makes us into calculators, turns our messy and conflicting living passions into so many quanta of pleasure or pain. It is like committing suicide because we so desperately fear dying, rendering ourselves lifeless because we are so threatened by the fragility of life.

It is possible that Plato intended this as irony, meant us to see that Socrates, whom he represents in the *Protagoras* as a young man in a hurry, was advocating a position that undermines human life in its clever efforts to save it. Or it is possible that Plato came to see only later that this reduction will not do. Certainly by the time he wrote the *Phaedo* and the *Republic* his account of mathematics and its importance for the philosopher was very different, as we have seen. But was it any better? Or is it just as much invested in death?

Tuché had after all not gone away; and neither has Plato's concern with it. The individual, like the state, must have some means of dealing with events; and it would be a poor social and political policy that did not do what it could to predict and prevent disaster. So *techné* cannot just be dismissed as dehumanising. There must be ways of using 'science' that will foster human life, whether individual or social. And yet we have seen that when Glaucon, Socrates' interlocutor in the *Republic*, interprets Socrates' emphasis on the various branches of mathematical science in utilitarian terms, Socrates insists that he has missed the point. The reason for the focus on mathematics is not to be able to calculate policy for society or strategy for warfare but to raise the soul away from this whole domain to a contemplation of the intelligible, the One. And though the philosopher must take his turn at governing, Plato presents him as one who, having lived in daylight, is forced to return to the cave and make social policies about the dance of shadows.

It is always important to notice how Plato sets the stage for the discussion that takes place in his dialogues. In the very first sentence of the *Republic* we find Socrates returning from paying 'his devotions to the goddess' (327a), and the games and celebrations he and his friends intend to watch are to be in her honour. At the end of the *Republic* Socrates recounts the 'myth of Er', in which the goddesses decree the fate of souls who have died, and philosophers hope to receive their reward 'as the victors in the games go about to gather in theirs' (621c). Now, it is of course true that religion, including rituals, sacrifice, and festivals were very much a part of Greek life in the fifth century, and in those terms Socrates' attentions to the goddess are not unusual (Morgan 1992; Burkert 1985). I suggest, however, that there is more to it than a gesture to convention: conventional religion, after all, receives a searing examination in the pages of the *Republic*.[13]

Who is this goddess to whom Socrates pays his devotions? Scholars are generally agreed that her name is Bendis, and that she is a Thracian goddess, recently imported to Athens. She is akin to Artemis, the huntress, and is a goddess who it is hoped will bring victory in war. Such victory is sorely needed. If, as is usually assumed, Plato sets the dialogue in the year 421, it is during the relatively brief Peace of Nicias, an interlude in the Peloponnesian War (431–404).[14] Now, this war was one that Athens ultimately lost; and it was the end of Athenian supremacy and from Athens' point of view a disaster. If Bendis was invoked to help them win the war, she was a spectacular failure, and by the time the *Republic* was written and read, everyone knew it.

The dialogue was composed about 370, fifty years after the events it describes. By that time the war had been lost and Athens was in decline. Moreover many of the dialogue's central characters had met a violent death. Socrates had been executed, as had Polemarchus and Niceratus. Plato's own family had led a faction which murdered others for power and property. What price justice in the state? Anyone reading this dialogue would read it in the knowledge that the characters who are here presented solemnly discussing justice and the philosophical life would soon be killing each other. Not only would this colour any reading of Plato's account of justice, but also his emphasis on the *techné* of the philosopher: arguably only Socrates had the *techné* that enabled him to meet his death with equanimity. The others should have learned it from him before it was too late, but they did not do so. The juxtaposition of the dramatic date and the date of composition reveals, therefore, an undercurrent of a failed goddess, a *techné* that succeeds for Socrates but which the others did not learn in time, and an overarching context of violent death.

The atmosphere of death is reinforced by the second scene of the *Republic*, the house of Polemarchus and his aged father Cephalus, who, like Socrates, has finished sacrificing to the goddess. Socrates talks with him about old age and death. Cephalus is anxious. 'For let me tell you, Socrates, that when a man begins to realize that he is going to die, he is filled with apprehensions and concern about matters that before did not occur to him' (330d), in particular penalties that perhaps must be paid in the world to come for wrongs done in this life. Cephalus proposes to use his wealth as far as possible to clear any debts to people or to the gods so that his 'ledger of life' may be in credit when he reaches the other world: it is this idea of paying everyone their due as the essence of justice that gets the main discussion of justice in the *Republic* underway. Thus once again the undercurrents of the dialogue reveal a preoccupation with death.

Socrates professes himself impressed with Cephalus' experience of life and his preparations for death. Indeed it could itself be seen as a *techné*, a skill or science or calculation regarding sex, sacrifice and money. But in the main body of the dialogue Socrates presses for a much more rigorous *techné*, one befitting a philosopher. This is no longer the *techné* of the *Protagoras* with its utilitarian calculus. Rather, the way of dealing with *tuché* in the *Republic* is not by trying to manage the world so as to prevent disaster: that may be appropriate for the statesman or the soldier, but by the time the *Republic* is written their efforts to prevent the disaster of the Peloponnesian War have already been shown to be ineffectual. The only way, the only *techné* for the philosopher to avoid *tuché* is to make himself invulnerable to it, to rise above it so that it does not concern him. The mathematics of the philosopher are not utilitarian calculations; they are the mathematics of eternity. The body, its appetites and passions, are strongly disciplined. Death itself is welcomed rather than feared. It is eternal wisdom, not this world or anything in it that the philosopher longs for. Moreover, it is for men only, indifferent to women and the earth and ordinary experience, including the ordinary experience of birth and death, whether someone else's or one's own. The assimilation of human excellence to what is unchanging and immortal, as in the *Phaedo*, the *Republic* and 'Diotima's' speech in the *Symposium*, is a detachment of human excellence from life, a fixation on a world other than this world. It is a way of making oneself invulnerable to death. But the price of doing so is renouncing life, giving birth like a man only to those things that belong to eternity.

But Plato was not content with this. In fact, it was his engagement with beauty that propelled him to a drastic rethinking of his position. In the next chapter I turn therefore to Plato's accounts of beauty, beginning by revisiting Diotima's speech in the *Symposium*.

Chapter 11

The open sea of beauty

> And now . . . I want to talk about some lessons I was given, once upon a time, by a Mantinean woman called Diotima – a woman who was deeply versed in this and many other fields of knowledge. It was she who brought about a ten years' postponement of the great plague of Athens on the occasion of a certain sacrifice, and it was she who taught me the philosophy of Love.
>
> (*Symposium* 201d)

In the elaborate literary staging which Plato uses to present the figure of Diotima in Socrates' speech in praise of Love in the *Symposium*, he represents her as a unique and awe-inspiring priestess. She is an intermediary to the divine, a woman who by her sacrificial intervention was able to keep the plague at bay. Plato is giving a clear signal that what she says about love and about beauty is to be taken very seriously. And so it has been. Diotima's speech in the *Symposium* has been treated as synonymous with Plato's understanding of beauty, and foundational for what has come to be known as the 'Great Theory of Beauty' which informed western thinking for 1,500 years (Tatarkiewicz 1972: 165).

Now, for all that Diotima's speech cannot be treated as the literal utterance of a Mantinean woman of the fifth century, it can hardly be accidental that in one of the most important places where he addresses the issue, Plato places his views on beauty into the mouth of a woman. Diotima is indeed a pivotal figure, though not in quite the way that some feminists have claimed. What I want to show in this chapter is that Plato uses the figure of Diotima in much the same way as Parmenides used the figure of the goddess. I will argue that just as Parmenides' work is illuminated by considering it in relation to ancient goddess religion, so Plato's use of Diotima takes on an altogether different perspective if we think of it in relation to Sappho. Plato puts his own words into Diotima's mouth in such a way that beauty is removed from the world of ordinary experience and particular embodied love into an immortal realm, beyond gender and death. Plato uses Diotima to vanquish Sappho.

But Plato is a thinker who continually scrutinizes his own thought; and I shall argue that there are indications, especially in the *Phaedrus*, that he came to believe that his rejection of Sappho's understanding of beauty was misguided. Later in the chapter I shall discuss an alternative view, presented by Plato himself, which reconsiders beauty and presents embodied particularity in a different light. I shall use Derrida's famous deconstruction of Plato's *pharmakon*, not quite in the way that Derrida might have intended, to show the presence and absence of women in Plato's understanding of beauty, and their linkage with violence and death.

Beauty's number

It is useful to begin by asking, where do Plato's views on beauty originate? In books discussing the history of aesthetics, Plato's theory of beauty regularly stands at the beginning, as though it is the fountainhead of thought about beauty in the west (Beardsley 1966; Cooper 1997). But Plato owed much to the Pythagoreans. He followed them, for example, in his understanding of the soul as imprisoned in the body. He also took from them a good deal of their account of beauty, which for them was connected with number and proportion. The paradigm case for the Pythagoreans was music: the discovery is attributed to Pythagoras that there is a mathematical relation between the length of a plucked string and the sound that is produced.[1] The mathematical basis of musical intervals was then generalized by them to apply to other art forms. Sextus Empiricus, who system-atized ancient Pythagorean teaching in the early third century CE, said that they taught that

> There exists in sculpture, and likewise in painting, a certain proportion whereby unvarying resemblance is preserved. And, to speak generally, every art is a system composed of perceptions, and system is a number. Hence it is a sound saying that 'all things are like unto numbers' – that is, like unto the reason that judges and is akin to the numbers which compose all things. Such is the doctrine of the Pythagoreans.
>
> (Sextus Empiricus 1961: I.110)

Pythagoreans also held that harmony was directly related to war. Harmony was believed to reconcile hostile elements within a city, and to turn the hostility outward upon an external enemy instead. Thus Plato in the *Republic*, taking over Pythagorean theory, emphasized harmony as essential for the good of the soul and for its larger image, the state, if soul and state are to be at peace within themselves rather than in conflict. The same harmony, in fact, was held to be reflected in the cosmos itself. Theon of Smyrna wrote:

> The Pythagoreans, whom Plato follows in many respects, call music the harmonization of the opposites, the unification of disparate things and the conciliation of warring elements. For they claim that not only rhythms and melody but in fact the whole system [of the world] depends on music, whose object is unity and harmony. God harmonizes warring elements and this in

fact is his greatest aim in music and the art of medicine, namely that he reconciles things that are hostile.

(Quoted in Tatarkiewicz 1970: I.87–8)

Since beauty (which is central to the cosmic order) is based on harmony, and harmony is based on number, it is clear that for the Pythagoreans mathematics is at the heart of the universe; and the mathematical intellect or soul can grasp its inner principles. 'In mathematics, therefore, the soul lives as it were a life of its own, and participates, as far as possible for it while it is in the body, in the divine nature' (Robinson 1968: 68). We have already seen how Plato, at least in his early writing, seems to have taken over this view of the importance of mathematics: the point here is that it was applied to aesthetic theory as well. Thus Pythagorean theory, mediated and modified by Plato, 'laid the foundation of European aesthetics' (Bredin and Santoro-Brienza 2000: 23).

However, Plato had available to him an alternative account of beauty, which we have already encountered. It was as different from the Pythagoreans as it is possible to be. That account was to be found in the tradition of lyric poetry epitomized by Sappho. Sappho, it will be recalled, thought that 'the most beautiful thing on the dark earth . . . is what you love' (du Bois 1996: 80): the individual, embodied beauty of a particular woman, 'the bright radiance of her changing face'. Sappho never talks about numbers, never mentions mathematics; indeed it is hard to imagine how it could fit into her idea of beauty. Nor, as we have seen, does she express interest in other worlds, or in any general system of cosmology. Her concern is with the particular beauty of her beloved.

Now, Sappho's poems were well known in Plato's Athens. Plato was certainly aware of her: he mentions her in the *Phaedrus* (235c), a dialogue which, significantly, also turns on the question of the love of particular beautiful bodies, as does Diotima's speech in the *Symposium*: I shall discuss it later in this chapter. In modern studies of Plato, however, although there are countless studies of the influence upon him of presocratic philosophers, the fact of his acquaintance with Sappho is hardly noted. Plato does not mention Sappho in the *Symposium*, and it is of course impossible to prove my conjecture that he had her in mind as he wrote Diotima's speech. Yet I suggest that when we consider Diotima's speech in the *Symposium* in the light of Sappho's poems, Plato's account of beauty takes on interesting new dimensions. I want to show how Diotima's speech can be read as a calculated rejection by Plato of Sappho's celebration of beauty and love, in favour of a Pythagorean account of beauty that establishes its connection with death; and how his reversal in the *Phaedrus* can be read as at least a partial reinstatement of a Sapphic view.

Eternal beauty

The conversation between Socrates and Diotima, as Plato represents it, begins with the story of Eros, and the way in which Eros is involved in the attraction of the lover to the beloved. As Diotima points out, it is beauty that attracts erotic attraction. The emphasis on Eros, on the appeal of beautiful bodies, continues a theme that has dominated the whole of the *Symposium*, whose previous speakers have praised Eros and the delights of bodily love. Like Sappho, they have focused on the beauty and desirability of the beloved: on particular, embodied beauty. But although Diotima similarly begins with a particular body, she quickly slips in a few comments that suggest a different tone: she deftly connects beauty with harmony, immortality and the divine. She says,

> there's a divinity in human propagation, an immortal something in the midst of man's mortality which is incompatible with any kind of discord. And ugliness is at odds with the divine, while beauty is in perfect harmony.
>
> (*Symposium* 206d)

With this comment Diotima implicitly introduces Pythagorean concepts based on mathematics and on the separation of soul and body into the discussion in a way that generates tension with a Sapphic notion of beauty's location in a particular embodied beloved person. Moreover, in her reference to the 'immortal something in the midst of man's mortality' Diotima signals the connection for Plato of beauty and death. Every 'mortal creature', Diotima tells Socrates, is possessed of a 'passion for immortality'. However, this passion cannot be granted in a literal sense. A mortal 'cannot, like the divine, be still the same throughout eternity' (208a). What a mortal creature can do, however, with the help of beauty which arouses its attraction, is to reproduce itself, bringing about the new life that will take its place when the old one dies: 'this . . . is how the body and all else that is temporal partakes of the eternal: there is no other way' (208b). Beauty is therefore of fundamental importance to the continuation of the living world. Without it no newness could enter the world. There would be only death.

As I showed in the previous chapter, however, Plato presents Diotima as moving quickly from bodily reproduction to 'those whose procreancy is of the spirit rather than of the flesh' (209a). Not only things of the body but also the more important things of the spirit depend upon beauty to attract us to them. Unless wisdom were beautiful we would not be drawn to it. The philosopher, the lover of wisdom, is thus above all the one who finds wisdom beautiful, attractive. And only those whose characters have been formed to respond to beauty will ever become wise. To some extent at least, this formation (or 'initiation' as Diotima calls it (210a)) can be a deliberate undertaking. Now, it is interesting that in the *Symposium* that undertaking begins not with a course in mathematics, as the Pythagoreans would have advocated, and as Plato also had it in the *Republic*, but with the love of particular beautiful bodies. Diotima seems to be beginning from Sappho's position. She says,

> the candidate for this initiation cannot, if his efforts are to be rewarded, begin too early to devote himself to the beauties of the body. First of all . . . he will

fall in love with the beauty of one individual body, so that his passion may give life to noble discourse.

(210a)

The attraction is erotic, focused on an individual body's beauty.

Although this starting point appears similar to Sappho, it is nevertheless subtly different. In Sappho, the most beautiful is that which is loved: the love inspires the recognition of beauty. In Plato just the reverse takes place: it is beauty that generates erotic attraction which is then encouraged to develop into friendship with its 'noble discourse'. But if the beauty is the cause of the friendship (rather than the friendship enabling the recognition of beauty) then the next step quickly follows, and it is a step that moves decisively away from Sappho and towards Pythagoras:

> Next he must consider how nearly related the beauty of any one body is to the beauty of any other, when he will see that if he is to devote himself to loveliness of form it will be absurd to deny that the beauty of each and every body is the same. Having reached this point, he must set himself to be the lover of every lovely body, and bring his passion for the one into due proportion by deeming it of little or no importance.
>
> (210b)

Whereas Sappho founds beauty upon love – 'Anactoria far away' is not replaceable by some other beautiful woman – Plato founds love upon beauty, and thus must hold that beautiful bodies are interchangeable. For all that Diotima's speech seems to be like Sappho in starting with a particular body, in fact Diotima reverses Sappho's position, and gives a fundamentally different account of beauty. Bodies are commensurable, interchangeable. Particular embodied individuals are ultimately not important.

In Plato's move from the physical to the spiritual, he has Diotima step by step remove the account of beauty from anything to do with a beloved individual.

> Next he [the lover of beauty/wisdom] must grasp that the beauties of the body are as nothing to the beauties of the soul, so that wherever he meets with spiritual loveliness, even in the husk of an unlovely body, he will find it beautiful enough to fall in love with and to cherish. . . . And when he discovers how nearly every kind of beauty is akin to every other he will conclude that the beauty of the body is not, after all, of great moment.
>
> (210c)

If beauty is ultimately a question of harmony and proportion – of number, as the Pythagoreans have it – then equal harmony, equal number, must mean equal beauty. And since perfect proportion can never actually be realized (it is easy to conceptualize a perfect circle but impossible to draw one), the beauty of the mind is of greater moment than the beauty of the body. Ultimately, this beauty of mind and of mental things leads to 'the beautiful itself', universal beauty.

> Starting from individual beauties, the quest for the universal beauty must find him ever mounting the heavenly ladder, stepping from rung to rung – that is, from one to two, and from two to *every* lovely body, from bodily beauty to the beauty of institutions, from institutions to learning, and from learning in general to the special lore that pertains to nothing but the beautiful itself – until at last he comes to know what beauty is.
>
> (211c)

Particular bodies, particular persons, are in the end just rungs of a ladder, to be trodden upon in the philosopher's spiritual quest. And with every step of the ladder the climber moves further away from Sappho's emphasis on love for the individual; further also from ordinary embodied experience of this beautiful world.

What does Plato mean by 'the beautiful itself'? Plato holds that the changing beauties of bodies and things in the physical world, for all their differences, share something which appears in them all. This is their participation in absolute Beauty, the Form or Idea of Beauty, which can be grasped only by the mind, not seen with the eyes (*Phaedo* 65). A person who thinks of beauty only in physical terms, to be seen with the eyes, Plato dismisses as a 'lover of spectacles' not a lover of wisdom (*Republic* v.476a). The true lover of wisdom understands that there is absolute Beauty, just as there is absolute Truth and absolute Justice (*Phaedo* 75, 78; *Phaedrus* 250b; *Republic* v.479a); and it is by participation in this transcendental Beauty that individual things are beautiful. They partake of Beauty itself. In the *Symposium* Diotima describes the 'final revelation' that comes to the one who has climbed the ladder rung by rung and comes at last to gaze upon 'the open sea of beauty':

> And now . . . there bursts upon him that wondrous vision which is the very soul of the beauty he has toiled so long for. It is an everlasting loveliness which neither comes nor goes, which neither flowers nor fades, for such beauty is the same on every hand, the same then as now, here as there, this way as that way, the same to every worshipper as it is to every other.
>
> (210e–211a)

Plato has moved decisively away from Sappho; and, via the Pythagorean idea of beauty as mathematical, he has arrived at an account of eternal Beauty that is reminiscent of Parmenides' One. It is permanent, unchanging and deathless. Indeed the vision of this Beauty is the immortality available to mortal men – those few choice philosophers who undertake the odyssey of heroic ascent. Diotima continues,

Nor will his vision of the beautiful take the form of a face, or of hands, or of anything that is of the flesh. It will be neither words, nor knowledge, nor a something that exists in something else, such as a living creature, or the earth, or the heavens, or anything that is – but subsisting of itself and by itself in an eternal oneness, while every lovely thing partakes of it in such sort that, however much the parts may wax and wane, it will be neither more nor less, but still the same inviolable whole.

(211a–b)

And so we are back again with the preoccupation with death, and the wish to escape it into some bodiless and unchanging immortality. The 'radiant face' and the 'way of walking' of Sappho's Anactoria are displaced in favour of an 'eternal oneness' available only to the (male) philosopher, and achieved by stepping on actual bodies like so many rungs of a ladder. Though Plato begins from a position that looks similar to that of Sappho, and though he places his teaching into the mouth of a woman, he ends up with a doctrine not far from that of Parmenides' changeless 'way of Truth', applied specifically to Beauty. Even his use of a woman's voice to present the teaching is similar. The concern with death and immortality displaces beauty to an immortal, changeless realm, a realm not of this world. Women and lesser men are limited to the mortal realm and to physical procreation and death. But the philosopher can 'gaze on beauty's very self – unsullied, unalloyed and freed from the mortal taint that haunts the frailer loveliness of flesh and blood' (211e).

If we pause for a moment to look ahead, we can begin to see how christendom's appropriation of Platonism in late antiquity and the Middle Ages used this ladder of ascent to Beauty (or a beatific vision) as a favourite trope. For Plato, Beauty is one, eternal. Moreover, Beauty is coextensive with Goodness and Truth: 'the good and the beautiful are the same' (*Symposium* 201c; see also *Republic* vii.517c). Christian thinkers developed this as their understanding of God, absolute Being, in whom Truth, Goodness and Beauty were united in an Eternal One. The spiritual life was the life that, by mortification (literally 'putting to death') of the flesh, aspired to the beatific vision, the vision of God. They held that Diotima's speech in the *Symposium* had pointed to it; and that pagan philosophers had dimly discerned the truth that would be revealed in Christ. And christendom, like Socrates in the *Phaedo*, believed that the ultimate vision would come only after death, which for the Christian as for the philosopher is the goal: the best life is the life lived 'with one foot in the grave'. In the meantime, with the beauty of this world displaced to a heavenly realm, this present life is constituted by death and violence, the warring absence of harmony.

There is more than one step between Plato and christendom, of course; and it is all too easy to distort Plato's texts by reading them through the lenses of later appropriations. Moreover, there were many contrary voices, much nuancing which we will explore in due course. But we can already see that in the genealogy of death, the speech of Diotima in the *Symposium* which removes beauty from a

Sapphic insistence on the particular beloved to a realm characterized by mathe-matical commensurability and immortality is a step of utmost gravity for the western symbolic.

'Anything worth living for'

Even in Plato however there is more than one side to the story. Although there is much in his dialogues that circles around issues of mortality, beauty for Plato is also about this life. Indeed beauty is what makes life worth living. 'If man's life is ever worth the living,' says Diotima, 'it is when he has attained this vision of the very soul of beauty' (*Symposium* 211d). Although in the *Phaedo* (as in later Christian appropriations) the fullness of this vision was reserved for beyond the grave, it is this present life to which Diotima is referring when she says that the one who sees 'the heavenly beauty face to face' is the one whose life is not 'unenviable'. A life given to beauty, a life in love with beauty, is the best life, the life worth living.

Such a life, in Plato, is a life that is well educated. Because beauty, truth and goodness are coextensive, the pursuit of beauty is also the pursuit of truth and goodness: 'the love of truth and the love of beauty feed upon one another, and . . . the aim of education is to produce a love of beauty' (Bredin and Santoro-Brienza 2000: 32; see *Republic* iii). Seen from this side of the Enlightenment, in which science with its pursuit of true beliefs and utilitarian outcomes dominates society and education, it is almost impossible to grasp how centrally important beauty was for Plato, or his passionate interest in it, an interest mirrored by the importance of beauty and art in Greek culture. Beauty is *tó kalón*, the fair, but also the good and right and noble; and without beauty there is ugliness of every sort, moral as well as aesthetic. Thus whereas in the *Symposium* the 'open sea of beauty' is connected with immortality, in the *Republic* Plato argues that the development of love for beauty is crucial for the education of the future rulers of the ideal state. We have already noted his reservations about particular aesthetic expressions: poetry, music and drama must always foster 'manliness'. Nevertheless the impor-tance of beauty in his thought cannot be overstated.

What makes something beautiful? When he explores this question in the *Phaedo*, Plato has Socrates begin by 'assuming the existence of absolute beauty and goodness and magnitude and all the rest of them' (100b) – that is, the ultimate forms or ideas. This having been granted, Socrates then says that 'whatever else is beautiful apart from absolute beauty is beautiful because it partakes of that absolute beauty and for no other reason' (100c). He disregards explanations to do with colour, shape, or other such properties, and insists 'that it is by beauty that beautiful things are beautiful'. Plato holds that absolute or ultimate beauty is reflected in beautiful things, since they are what they are by participating in that absolute or universal beauty. Beautiful things are copies, reflections of the form of absolute beauty.

Now, in one sense this explanation mystifies more than it clarifies. It does not, for example, offer any criteria whereby we could discriminate between ugly and beautiful things. But what it does make clear is that for Plato beauty is a way of describing the absolute character of reality. Beauty is not a chance characteristic or feature of an otherwise dull world. Neither is it merely a subjective preference. Rather, beauty is central to the way things are. To be is to be beautiful, or at least in some sense to participate in beauty; and ugliness is a deviation, falling away from the standard of beauty. It is to be deplored and worked against as seriously as wickedness or untruth; the three are in fact closely linked in Plato's thought. Since in Plato's metaphysics all that exists does so by participation in the forms, and Beauty, with Truth and Goodness, is the absolute form, it follows that the beauty that we can perceive is an imitation or reflection of eternal beauty. From a post-Enlightenment perspective dominated by an economics of utility and in which beauty (or even aesthetic pleasure) is an optional extra, it is scarcely possible to imagine the shift in worldview that is necessary to grasp the significance of beauty for Plato (see Halliwell 2002). His accounts of it are interwoven with a gendered preoccupation with death and violence with which, I shall argue, it is in tension and from which it needs to be disentangled. But his commitment to beauty is absolute.

Mimesis

If Plato had so strong a commitment to beauty, then why did he give artists such a hard time? I have already discussed his insistence that poets like Homer should be banished from the ideal Republic, and his similar strictures on other forms of art, notably music and drama. Was Plato perhaps less committed to beauty in his other writings than we would expect from the *Symposium*? I suggest that the opposite is the case. It was precisely because Plato put so high a valuation on beauty that he felt that true beauty could not be represented by the things that normally attract us with their emotional or erotic power: poetry, tragic drama, music, human (especially female) bodies. Although there are tensions in Plato's thinking, which will emerge later in this chapter, the tensions are not to do with any ambivalence on his part about his absolute commitment to beauty.

To see where the difficulties arise for Plato it is necessary to get to grips with his theory of mimesis. According to Platonic thinking, art is mimetic: it imitates nature, and produces only images or semblances. This is easy to understand in relation to representational painting or sculpture, which, no matter how realistic, can at best produce a good likeness of a person or thing, not the person themselves. Similarly, drama can stage a compelling enactment of an event, but even a great performance is still a performance, not the original event. For Plato the same holds true of all art: it is mimetic, a copy (more or less accurate) of the things or events of the world.

Art takes over the grand primary works from the hands of nature, already formed, and then models and fashions the more insignificant, and this is the very reason why we call them artificial.

(*Laws* 889d)

Speaking of the things and events of the natural world as causes, Plato then continues:

Art, the subsequent late-born product of these causes, herself as perishable as her creators, has since given birth to certain toys with no real substance in them, simulacra as shadowy as the arts themselves, such as those which spring from painting, music, and the other fellow crafts.

(*Laws* 889d)

But even that 'natural' world is a copy. In Platonic metaphysics, nature itself is mimetic. The natural things of the physical world are, according to Plato, copies of eternal metaphysical Ideas or Forms, and it is these which are the true reality, eternal, changeless and immaterial. Hence works of art – even very good works of art – are copies of copies. Now, no copy is ever a perfect representation of the original: error and distortion inevitably creep in. So the more times something is copied, the more error there will be: copies of copies are further and further removed from the original. Since works of art are copies of copies, they end up being falsifications of the very reality which they purport to represent. Imitation of this sort is 'the third remove from the truth' (*Republic* x.602c). And it gets worse. Some arts, such as painting or drama, deliberately rely on optical or auditory illusions: scene painting, for example, uses perspective to make a flat surface appear to have depth.

And so scene painting in its exploitation of this weakness of our nature falls nothing short of witchcraft, and so do jugglery and many other such contrivances.

(602d)[2]

In his discussion of this, Plato uses the metaphor of mating (a metaphor that comes very easily to him) to represent what happens in art. The product of mimetic art (the painting or poem or song) appeals to a part of our minds, but it is a part that is confused, 'remote from our intelligence' (603b). When the work of art and the muddled mind mate or cohabit, only confusion will result. 'Mimetic art . . . is an inferior thing cohabiting with an inferior and engendering inferior offspring' (603b). This can lead only to faction and strife, and corrupts both the individual and the state.

What occurs, in fact, is a third level of mimesis. Not only does nature copy the Forms, and art copy nature, but we who receive the art in turn copy it. We see a dramatic representation of a hero, for example, and take it as a model which we try to imitate in our lives (Murray 1992: 39–42). We thus fashion ourselves by copying copies of copies, removing ourselves ever further from true reality. It is this that makes art so dangerous for Plato. The beauty that is to be found in art (as also in one degree less in the physical world) is a distortion and distraction from truth and goodness; and copying it removes us ever further from the perfect original. Therefore an ideal society which educated its youth to be attuned to the Ideas or Forms of true reality would banish artists (*Republic* iii and x). Sometimes Plato seems to be referring only to those artists or those works that offer models which he considers harmful: models that inspire cowardice, for example, as we have seen. But sometimes he cuts deeper. It is the very idea of models, models of whatever kind, that is bad, simply because models are not the original, and remove our desire from the original upon which our attention should be fixed.

Much has been written about Plato's attitude to poets; but I would suggest that the central point here is actually not so much a point about poetry as a point about beauty. Beauty, whether natural or artistic, draws us towards itself. It is pleasurable, attractive. That which we are drawn towards inspires us to copy it, or try to become like it: the teacher from whom a pupil will learn most is not the one who merely tells the pupil what to do, but the one who is an inspiring example for the pupil to copy. Now, if poetry or painting or drama is beautiful, its attraction and the pleasure this affords can trap a person who is drawn by art into its satisfactions and delights, so that the one who gets involved in art never presses onwards to the Forms themselves, the Ideas of Truth and Goodness.

When Plato writes in the *Republic* and the *Laws* about the pernicious effects of poetry or music and the need to banish artists from the ideal Republic, his reasons are thus utterly different from the utilitarian considerations that give rise to the ugliness of modernity. Art and beauty must be treated with enormous caution not because beauty is trivial or insignificant (let alone because it is uneconomic) but because of its enormous power. Contrary to contemporary Philistinism which dismisses beauty as irrelevant to the political and economic conduct of life and would be perplexed at the very idea of shaping the character in relation to standards of beauty and aesthetic sensibility, Plato held that art and the pleasures of beauty are so strong a force in the formation of character that they must be looked upon as a grave danger. If given way to, they could cause the person drawn to them to rest in imitations, copies of copies, rather than turn to the source and origin of truth. Moreover in so doing they would stir the passions and emotions in inappropriate ways, offering sensory gratification rather than intellectual advancement, and forming characters that sought pleasurable indulgence rather than the good of the state.

Or so Plato argues in some parts of the *Republic*. But of course we have already seen that for Plato things were much more complicated. Even in the *Republic* he argues for wholesome art, specifically encouraging imitation. He says, for example, that wise craftsmen should be sought out,

> craftsmen who by the happy gift of nature are capable of following the trail of true beauty and grace, that our young men . . . may receive benefit from all

things about them, whence the influence that emanates from works of beauty may waft itself to eye or ear like a breeze that brings from wholesome places health, and so from earliest childhood insensibly guide them to likeness, to friendship, to harmony with beautiful reason.

(*Republic* iii. 401c–d)

The soul would become 'beautiful and good' be learning to value beautiful and good things, while finding the ugly and the evil distasteful. Moreover we have noted that in the *Symposium* it is precisely the attraction exerted by beauty – indeed by beautiful *bodies* – that draws the lover of beauty to climb from the particular to the general, until they come to gaze upon 'the open sea of beauty' and see the Forms themselves. In both the *Republic* and the *Symposium* the attractive power of beauty is the great educative force that draws the soul upwards. Mimesis, the imitation of beauty, is never content with the imperfections of copies but moves through them rung by rung until perfection is attained.

Although Plato's warning about art and artists in the *Republic* thus seems in some ways opposite to Diotima's presentation of the ladder of ascent in the *Symposium*, or even his comments on the role of beauty in education in the *Republic*, one of the central underlying assumptions (an assumption that places both books at an angle to modernity) is the same. Beauty is powerful. Indeed, beauty is the most powerful force for the construction of character, whether of an individual or society, because beauty is attractive, and that which we find attractive we try in various ways to imitate. Plato's complicated attitude to beauty and the arts rests upon this fact of mimesis. On the one hand, beautiful things are at best copies of true reality, and as such are inevitably distortions of it. Yet provided that the perceiver does not rest content with the copy, what better way could there be to come to the knowledge of true beauty than by studying and imitating its best copies? In the *Republic* Plato is worried about the negative possibilities of mimesis; in the *Symposium* he presents its positive potential. But in both it is the drawing power of beauty, its virtual irresistibility, that grounds the whole discussion and that generates the ambivalence. Plato, however, never rests content. In the next part I shall offer a reading of the *Phaedrus* which presents yet a third possibility, and with it a (partial) return to Sappho.

'False, false the tale'

It is not only in relation to beauty that Plato's views are in internal tension. In the previous chapter I discussed Plato's two responses to *tuché*, trying to master death and misfortune either by social programming based on utilitarian calculus or by rising above vulnerability to death and risk. Both of these, like both aspects of Plato's discussions of beauty, have been repeated in countless ways in the history of the west. Yet it is arguable that in each case Plato himself saw the inadequacy of both these responses, and tried to overcome them. It is important not to lose sight of the fact that Plato wrote dialogues, with varying points of view represented, not treatises in a single authorial voice. As Leo Strauss has argued, 'Plato's work consists of many dialogues because it imitates the manyness, the variety, the heterogeneity of being . . . Each dialogue deals with one part; it reveals the truth about that part. But the truth about a part is a partial truth, a half truth' (Strauss 1964: 61–2). Not only do the dialogues take up different issues (even if Strauss's claim that they 'reveal the truth' about that issue may be somewhat optimistic), but sometimes later dialogues return to an issue which had been considered in an earlier work, and come to quite different conclusions.

Most interesting of all is yet a third case, which occurs in the *Phaedrus* when Plato presents two contrasting arguments in the same dialogue, the second a deliberate refutation of the first. Since the first argument is consonant with his views in previous dialogues, its recantation signals a significant turn in Plato's thought. Socrates and Phaedrus take a walk outside the town, along a river to a place where it was said that Boreas had seized and raped a young girl, Orithyia. They sit down under a tree and Phaedrus reads to Socrates a speech written by his friend Lysias. These details of setting should begin to raise questions regarding what is about to happen. Moreover, such questions are heightened at the beginning of Socrates' response, when Socrates expresses discomfort with what he is about to say because he seems to remember something else, something from Sappho. Sappho? What is Sappho doing here? What is Plato signalling by invoking her name?

At first it is impossible to tell. The dialogue proceeds recognizably enough. Phaedrus' speech is in praise of the love of an older man for a young boy. Socrates challenges his argument and expands it on the familiar grounds that the pursuit of a young boy by an older man will lead to evil consequences, because the embodied and particular nature of such love means that the lover will be filled with passion, not with reason; so he will be looking for his own pleasure, not the good of the lad. Disinterested love, however, where the lover is 'one possessed of reason and not in love' (241c) will save the beloved from the problems that are bound to arise if instead of reason the passions are in control. Although he does not do so here, one can easily imagine Socrates going on in the same vein as he does in the *Symposium*, in which the aim of this love, so far from yielding to the 'madness' of passion, is to rise to the contemplation of the eternal and unchanging forms. It is the intellect and its search for wisdom that is to be cultivated: only a mad, drunk man (Alcibiades in the *Symposium*) praises erotic passion as good in itself. In like manner Socrates in the *Phaedrus* 'attacks erotic passion as a form of degrading madness, and characterizes the passions as mere urges for bodily replenishment, with no role to play in our understanding of the good' (Nussbaum 1986: 201).

Then suddenly everything changes. Socrates says that he has heard a voice, a reprimand for an 'offence to heaven', and he knows that his speech is wrong (242c). He quotes the poet Stesichorus, who had been struck blind because of the falsity of his verse, and thereupon wrote a recantation beginning, 'false, false the tale . . . ' He says that his first theory was 'terrible', a sin. Thereupon Socrates makes another speech, in direct opposition to the first. He recognizes, in this second speech, that things are very much more complicated than his earlier position allowed. Madness, for instance, is not the simple opposite of reason: madness can be prophetic ecstasy, poetic inspiration, 'a gift of the gods, fraught with the highest bliss' (245c). But if that is so, then by implication reason, which has hitherto in the dialogue been presented as the binary opposite of madness, is also more complicated than had been granted. Wisdom may well consist, not in a detachment of the mind from the passions and their madness, but in an integration of passion (or some form of it) into reason.

The recognition that madness and reason must be reevaluated leads Socrates immediately to reconsider 'the nature of soul, divine and human, its experiences, and its activities' (245c), and this reconsideration changes his whole approach to death and immortality. The first thing he establishes is that the soul is immortal because it moves itself; 'soul is not born and does not die' (246a). Thus far it is characterized similarly to the *Phaedo* and the *Republic*, as immortal and separable from the body, though it is noteworthy that its immortality is not said to be because of its goodness or its wisdom, but simply because it moves itself. But this is where the similarity ends. The soul is now represented as far more complex than anything Plato has indicated before; moreover that complexity is discussed not by argument or dialogue but by a complicated story based on an equally complicated analogy. Plato is indicating in very large letters that his previous account (in the *Phaedo*, for example) of a unified soul inhabiting a body until it is released from it by death will just not do.

The analogy he uses is a curious one. Socrates says, 'Let it [the soul] be likened to the union of powers in a team of winged steeds and their winged charioteer' (246a): this analogy holds both for the gods and for humans. In the case of the gods, however, all three parts – the two winged horses and the charioteer – are good; but with other souls this is not the case. One of the horses is good and noble, but the other is not.

> He that is on the more honourable side is upright and clean limbed, carrying his neck high, with something of a hooked nose; in colour he is white, with black eyes; a lover of glory, but with temperance and modesty; one that consorts with genuine renown, and needs no whip, being driven by the word of command alone. The other is crooked of frame, a massive jumble of a creature, with short neck, snub nose, black skin, and gray eyes; hot-blooded, consorting with wantonness and vainglory; shaggy of ear, deaf, and hard to control with whip and goad.
>
> (253d–e)

This makes the 'task of our charioteer . . . difficult and troublesome' (246b).[3] The purpose of the wings is to carry the chariot of the soul into the divine realm, 'and more than any other bodily part it shares in the divine nature, which is fair, wise, and good, and possessed of all other such excellences' (246e). The gods, led by

Zeus, drive their winged teams around the heavens and do their work of ordering the universe. But other souls have a harder time of it, because of their unruly steeds; and although they may try to follow in the train of the gods, they fall into mishaps and confusion, and 'trample and tread upon one another' (248b).

> Thus confusion ensues, and conflict and grievous sweat. Whereupon, with their charioteers powerless, many are lamed, and many have their wings all broken, and for all their toiling they are balked, every one, of the full vision of being, and departing therefrom, they feed upon the food of semblance.
>
> (248b)

Since they are now unable to pasture in the 'meadow of Truth' which nourished their wings, these souls fall, wingless to earth, to be incarnated in various forms of life: a philosopher, a statesman, a trader, an athlete, and so on. It will take ten thousand years, and many incarnations, for the soul to regain its wings. But there is one exception. The soul 'who has sought after wisdom unfeignedly, or has conjoined his passion for a loved one with that seeking' will find its wings growing sooner. The philosopher is the one who, by fostering his remembrance of divine and unchanging truth, recovers his wings. 'Standing aside from the busy doings of mankind, and drawing nigh to the divine, he is rebuked by the multitude as being out of his wits, for they know not that he is possessed by a deity' (249d).

From this presentation of the analogy we might think that the charioteer represents the rational mind, and the two horses the spirited and the appetitive parts of the soul. This sort of tripartite division of the soul had already been mooted in the *Republic* (iv.441a). However, the analogy of the winged charioteer and his winged horses is unique to the *Phaedrus*; indeed the use of analogy, poetry and myth takes a central place in the *Phaedrus* and undermines any notion of a clear division between poetry and philosophy. Moreover, it seems to be the spirited part – the white horse – which exercises control for the good over the charioteer himself.

> Now when the driver beholds the person of the beloved, and causes a sensation of warmth to suffuse his whole soul, he begins to experience a tickling or pricking of desire, and the obedient steed, constrained now as always by modesty, refrains from leaping on the beloved.
>
> (254a)

There follows an account of a violent struggle in the soul, with the dark, shaggy, disobedient horse 'shamelessly' pulling at the bit while the good horse 'in shame and horror drenches the whole soul with sweat' (254c) and assists the driver in his resistance to passion.

Plato is often read as a champion of soul–body dualism, and we have seen that in the *Phaedo* this is indeed what he teaches. The struggle in the *Phaedo* is between the soul, which is rational, and the body, which is beset with passions and desires.

But in the *Phaedrus*, although Socrates still asserts a division between body and soul, that division is not equivalent to the reason–passion divide. Reason and passion are both now *within* the soul. The struggle is not a struggle between soul and body but between 'parts' of the soul. Moreover, it is not the body or even the wanton horse that feels the 'tickling or pricking of desire', but the driver himself. If the driver is meant to represent rationality – and in much of what Socrates says this is a natural interpretation – then desire and rationality are no longer separable, whether as two distinct parts of the soul or as soul and body. Rationality has taken desire into itself; desire is not irrational.

This must not be overstated: it is certainly not the case that desire is to be acted upon without further ado. The driver, much assisted by the obedient horse, refuses the compulsion of passion as pictured in the wanton horse, 'jerks back the bit . . . with an even stronger pull, bespatters his railing tongue and his jaws with blood, and forcing him down on his legs and haunches delivers him over to anguish' (254e). It is a picture of violent mastery. And yet the mastery is not for the eradication of passion but for appropriate rather than inappropriate expression of it. This is a world away from the *Phaedo*, where the soul of the philosopher tries to extinguish the passions of the body, tries to live with one foot in the grave. Instead, here we find that passion itself, passion for a particular embodied individual, is good so long as it is properly controlled; indeed is a means of joining lover and beloved in the philosophical life. The restraint forced upon the wanton horse does not mean that the lover abandons his beloved, but 'follows after the beloved with reverence and awe' (254e), seeking opportunities to be near him, rendering him every possible service, and befriending him until the beloved loves him in return.

Two outcomes are now possible, the first better than the second, but both of them good. If both partners exercise self-control, then they will resist physical consummation of their passion.

> If the victory be won by the higher elements of mind guiding them into the ordered rule of the philosophical life, their days on earth will be blessed with happiness and concord, for the power of evil in the soul has been subjected, and the power of goodness liberated; they have won self-mastery and inward peace. And when life is over, with burden shed and wings recovered they stand victorious . . . nor can any nobler prize be secured whether by the wisdom that is of man or by the madness that is of god.
>
> (256b)

It may be, however, that such self-control cannot always be achieved, and from time to time 'the wanton horses in their two souls will catch them off their guard' (256c). But even if they yield, all is not lost.

> When death comes they quit the body wingless indeed, yet eager to be winged, and therefore they carry off no mean reward for their lovers' madness, for it

is ordained that all such as have taken the first steps on the celestial highway shall no more return to the dark pathways beneath the earth, but shall walk together in a life of shining bliss, and be furnished in due time with like plumage the one to the other, *because of their love*.

(256d–e; emphasis mine)

It is not because of their rationality or even their self-mastery that this good result becomes theirs but because of their love: love of particular embodied individuals for one another. We are much nearer to Sappho here than we were in the *Symposium*.

If we compare this result of the divine madness with the *techné* of the *Protagoras* or even of the *Republic* or the *Symposium*, the contrast is vast. Here we have love of a particular, fragile person, a person who is vulnerable to misfortune, a person who will die. The good life here does not consist of any *techné* of making oneself invulnerable to such love, whether through utilitarian calculus or through rising above the particular and sensible to the unchanging, intelligible world, the open sea of beauty. Rather, it is precisely the passion of love as seen in the eyes of one another that causes their wings to be quickened into growth: as Sappho had said, the most beautiful thing is what one loves. Moreover although all this is presented as though it were a matter of the soul and its 'parts', it is obvious that the body is not separable from what is going on. There is far more soul–body integration here than in the earlier dialogues where the body is represented as the enemy or prison house of the soul. The body, here, is involved in the passion which is not a curse but a gift of the gods. It renders the lover vulnerable to *tuché*; but without such vulnerability to fragile particular beauty, the wings would never grow.

All this means that death, also, must now be reconsidered. Some of the familiar themes remain. Immortality in the pure vision of Truth and Beauty remains the goal; and this earth is characterized as the opposite of that blissful realm. The sequences of reincarnation for punishment and purification are also repeated here. Moreover it is the philosopher's life that will most quickly rise to wisdom and escape these earthly bonds, in particular 'that prison house which now we are encompassed withal, and call a body, fast bound therein as an oyster in its shell' (250c). It would hardly seem that much has changed.

And yet everything is different, destabilized by the admission of love. That love is *eros*, passionate desire for a fragile particular person. Although it is not reducible to physical sex, sexual attraction plays an indispensable part: it is the bodily sight of the beloved's beauty that, in the terms of the myth, stimulates the wings to grow.

> For by reason of the stream of beauty entering in through his eyes there comes a warmth, whereby his soul's plumage is fostered, and with that warmth the roots of the wings are melted, which for long had been so hardened and closed up that nothing could grow; then as the nourishment is poured in, the stumps

of the wing swells and hastens to grow from the root over the whole substance of the soul.

(251b)

The wings, to be sure, are part of the myth; but the myth only gets its purchase if there is actual sexual attraction to another's body. So although in one breath Socrates continues to call the body a prison house, in the next breath he subverts that negative comment by a recognition that without the body's beauty and desire the wings of the soul will never grow and wisdom will not be attained. This is a long way from the *Phaedo* in which only death would set the soul free. Here life and love are celebrated.

To some extent this was foreshadowed in the *Symposium*, where it was indeed the admiration of a beautiful body that led to the recognition of beauty in general and ultimately to the invisible and changeless immortal Beauty. Once again, however, that teaching is both affirmed and subverted. Socrates portrays the lover and the beloved lying together, touching, kissing – and talking philosophy! That talk, rather than sexual intercourse, is the ideal consummation of their embrace: to that extent the *Phaedrus* is like the *Symposium*. However, there is no suggestion in the *Phaedrus* that this passionate love for a particular person should be transcended or overcome. Although Socrates' ideal is self-control, it is self-control *within* a passionate relationship, not a *techné* that makes the philosopher invulnerable to such a passion. The individual, not the ideal form, is the object of love. Indeed, Socrates portrays the lovers (even those who have given way to their passion) as still loving one another after death: they shall 'walk together in a life of shining bliss' (256e). Rather than supersede such particular passion for some abstract or ideal form, it is precisely the particular embodied beloved who is the locus of bliss, not only in this life but even in the next.

So for all that Socrates characterizes this world as the opposite of the life after death, in the *Phaedrus* he offers the possibility of a very different evaluation from that of earlier dialogues. Embodied life, and this earth where it is lived, is the place where the wings of the soul can grow. Bodies and their passions and desires are beautiful and wholesome. Ordinary experience, the sensory, vulnerable experience of passionate love is the means to wisdom; wisdom does not come by rejection of the ordinary in favour of an abstract intelligible realm. Socrates' ideal lovers talk philosophy, but they do so while embracing and kissing, and there is no suggestion in the *Phaedrus* that the kissing stops when the philosophy starts. There is no rush toward death, or denigration of life. Death will come; but it is accepted rather than longed for as the only possible route to wisdom. It can hardly be merely incidental that at the beginning of this dialogue Socrates has invoked 'the fair Sappho' (235c): it was she who had taught that wisdom and beauty are to be found in the love of the particular beloved, and she who had scorned as lust the abstractions and violence that others had proffered as beauty.

Pharmakon, Pharmakos, Pharmakis: the gender of wings

Sappho's beloved, however, was a woman. In Socrates account, even in the *Phaedrus*, it is taken for granted that all the participants are male. If the *Phaedrus* destabilizes a good deal of Plato's earlier teaching, does it destabilize his gender assumptions or does it leave his misogyny intact? Martha Nussbaum, in her brilliant account of the *Phaedrus*, uses inclusive language, substituting 'person' or 'human being' for the usual 'man', or using vocabulary that circumvents gender identification. But what warrant is there in the text for such inclusiveness?

At first sight it might seem that the very fact that Nussbaum is able to use inclusive language without grating against the text shows that Plato has not deliberately foreclosed the possibility. Indeed, when he begins the myth of the charioteer he makes a point of saying that the souls of *all* living beings, and all the gods too, are like the two winged horses and their winged charioteer. It is only when the soul has lost its wings that it 'sinks down until it can fasten on something solid, and settling there takes to itself an earthly body' (246c). But when Socrates enumerates the nine types of human into which the wingless soul falls, he does so by listing professions occupied by men: king, warrior, man of business, athlete, farmer and so on. Women are nowhere visible. Moreover the growth of wings is presented as developed by male homoeroticism. There is no space here for women: to introduce the female would, it seems, be a wing too far. Socrates recants his earlier rejection of madness and passion, and radically changes his account of self-control away from the *techné* that strives for invulnerability to a self-mastery within a relationship of desire. With that, also, is a whole new theory of beauty and its relation to particular embodiment. But there is no indication that he ever recants the misogyny of his previous writings, or even is conscious of it as such.

This being so, is his perspective on death really altered as much as I have suggested above? After all, as we have seen, gender and death have been regularly correlated in his thought, and indeed in the thought of others before him. To explore this question, I propose to reconsider Derrida's famous account of the *pharmakon*, but to take it in a rather different direction from that taken by him.

Derrida concentrates on a part towards the end of the *Phaedrus*, where Plato represents Socrates and Phaedrus discussing the relative merits of speech and writing. This was a natural question for the dialogue, since it had been a written discourse on love, read out by Phaedrus, which had given rise first to Socrates' speech asserting that a non-lover is a better friend than a lover, and then to Socrates' speech of recantation which included the myth of the charioteer and the wings of the soul. In his discussion, Derrida refers to many of Plato's dialogues, but curiously he never refers to the discussion of love or the myth of the charioteer. Indeed it is striking that he pays little attention to the dramatic setting, or to the rest of the dialogue's content. Rather, he lifts this particular theme from the *Phaedrus* as though it could stand outside it, linked instead to strands similarly plucked from other dialogues (cf Zuckert 1996: 224). While I find Derrida's analysis indispensable, I wish to show that it can be both deepened and challenged if set in the context of the rest of the dialogue, and that doing so exposes the tensions and affinities, in Derrida's work as well as in Plato's, between gender and death. Derrida suggests that Socrates becomes the sacrifice or even scapegoat that enables Plato to write: Plato writes Socrates' speeches only after Socrates himself has been killed. What I propose is that there is also a far deeper and more hidden sacrifice/scapegoat, namely the female, both human and divine. It is only by erasure of the woman/goddess that Plato's philosophy, even in this later phase, can proceed. And it is everywhere interlaced with death.

The Myth of Theuth

Just as Socrates had explored the relation between reason and passion in his recantation by telling the myth of the charioteer, so he now offers another myth, the myth of Theuth, as a basis for thinking about speech and writing. Theuth was the god who invented 'number, calculation, geometry and astronomy' – all the aspects of mathematics Socrates had been discussing in the *Republic* – 'and above all writing' (274d). Theuth went to 'the king of the whole country' whose name was Thamus or Ammon, and offered him all these *techné* that he had invented. The most important, according to Theuth, was writing: 'There, O king, is a branch of learning that will make the people of Egypt wiser and improve their memories; my discovery provides a recipe for memory and wisdom' (274e). The king, however, disagreed: he judged that harm would come to those who employ this *techné*, which he describes as Theuth's 'offspring'.

> If men learn this, it will implant forgetfulness in their souls; they will cease to exercise memory because they rely on that which is written, calling things to remembrance no longer from within themselves, but by means of external marks. What you have discovered is a recipe not for memory but for reminder. And it is no true wisdom that you offer your disciples, but only its semblance.
> (275a–b)

Once people can write, they will see no reason to carry in their heads what they can carry in their notebooks. And if their notebooks are filled with notes, they will consider themselves wise and learned, even if they have not thought through the implications of all the notes they have taken, have not become wise.

Now, the word which is translated 'recipe' in the speeches of both Theuth and the king is '*pharmakon*'. But as Derrida points out, *pharmakon* in Greek has more than one meaning. It can mean drug or medicine, a recipe for healing. But it can also mean 'poison'. In the *Phaedo*, for example, the hemlock that Socrates is required to drink is referred to as a *pharmakon*. So the myth of Theuth presents us with the recipe (*pharmakon*) of writing. But which is it – remedy or poison? In the dialogue it seems that Socrates sides with the king: writing is poison. As he goes on to explain to young Phaedrus, written words are like paintings. They look as though they were alive, but they are not. Writing is dead. It is mechanical, while seeming to have life. Words 'seem to talk to you as though they were intelligent, but if you ask them anything about what they say, from a desire to be instructed, they go on telling you just the same thing forever' (275d). Moreover they are unable to exercise any control over who reads them, or how. They get into the hands of the wrong people, or are misinterpreted and cannot defend themselves. When writing 'is ill-trusted and unfairly abused it always needs its parent to come to its help, being unable to defend or help itself' (275e). Without life themselves, writings also bring the death of wisdom to those who rely on them.

> Books, the dead and rigid knowledge shut up in *biblia*, piles of histories, nomenclatures, recipes and formulas learned by heart, all this is as foreign to living knowledge and dialectics as the *pharmakon* is to medical science.
>
> (Derrida 1993: 73)

But how foreign is that, really? Certainly medical science has as its aim to cure and not to kill. Poisoning is not meant to be part of it. And yet a drug that may cure in small doses may kill in large doses, or may help one patient and harm another. And the doctor has available the means of death as well as of life. The patient is dependent on the doctor's knowledge and integrity, not on the absence of the poison from the doctor's pharmacy.

Thus although it at first seems as though it would be possible to make a sharp division between medicine and poison, speech and writing, in practice things are much less neat. The ambivalences and resonances are already there in Greek. As Derrida admits, sometimes 'remedy' is a good translation of *pharmakon*. The point is that irrespective of whether the word is rendered 'remedy' or 'poison, 'recipe' or 'medicine', the ambiguities that are present in the original are lost once a specific translation is given. Think for example of the *Phaedo* where Socrates drinks the hemlock. It is intended to kill him, and it does; it seems entirely accurate to translate *pharmakon* as 'poison'. And yet as we have seen, Socrates says that a true philosopher does not fear death, but looks forward to it as a release from the prison house of the body. If that is the case, what sort of *pharmakon* is the hemlock? Is it poison? Or is it a cure? The answer, surely, is that it is undecidably both. The system of binary oppositions, *either* remedy *or* cure, is too rigid to cope with the ambiguities. It destabilizes them, just as the ambiguities of love in the myth of the charioteer destabilizes the binaries of the body and soul, death and life; as we shall see, speech and writing are similarly ambiguous.[4]

In the myth of Theuth, Derrida points out, the king tries to master the ambiguity of *pharmakon*, placing it in a clearcut opposition of harmful/helpful, which is part of a whole system of binary oppositions: 'good and evil, inside and outside, true and false, essence and appearance' (Derrida 1993: 103). The whole Pythagorean table of opposites comes to mind, including male and female, and body and soul, though Derrida does not mention these. If speech and writing can be placed into the same scheme of oppositions, it will make for a tidy universe. And indeed there are times when it seems clear that Plato goes in this direction, seeing the world, including speech and writing, in terms of oppositions. In such a system, the opposites are external to one another; each one represents alterity for the other in a binary structure of logic and value, as we have seen in relation to Pythagoras. As Derrida puts it, 'Plato thinks of writing, and tries to comprehend it, to dominate it, on the basis of *opposition* as such'. But this has an important precondition.

> In order for these contrary values (good/evil, true/false, essence/appearance, inside/outside, etc.) to be in opposition, each of the terms must be simply *external* to the other, which means that one of these oppositions (the opposition between inside and outside) must already be accredited as the matrix of all possible opposition.
>
> (1993: 103)

So for opposition to get started as the foundation of a system of thought, it first has to be assumed. The reasoning cannot avoid arguing in a circle, even while trying to set up the linear chain by which thought is to be bound.

Already in the *Phaedrus* the circularity becomes evident. King Thoth has just pronounced on the externality and thus inferiority of writing as contrasted with speech which is internal, from the heart, and Socrates has apparently endorsed this judgement, when Socrates says to Phaedrus,

> But now tell me, is there another sort of discourse, that is brother to written speech, but of unquestioned legitimacy? . . . The sort that goes together with knowledge, and is written on the soul of the learner, that can defend itself, and knows to whom it should speak and to whom it should say nothing.
>
> (276a)

Phaedrus is enthusiastic, and responds in words that Socrates commends:

> You mean no dead discourse, but the living speech, the original of which the written discourse may fairly be called a kind of image.
>
> (Ibid.)

Speech and writing, like remedy and poison, are life and death. But if the writing is on the soul, then it is remedy and life, not poison and death. And yet it is not speech. The system of opposites begins to unravel. Thus Derrida's analysis of the ambiguity of writing generates the same sorts of undecidability as does *pharmakon*. It is also parallel to the ambiguities of love in the myth of the charioteer. All of these render the inside/outside dichotomy dysfunctional, and with it the binary opposites of body/soul, life/death, and the rest.

But the question returns: what about gender? According to Derrida's reasoning, the 'clear-cut oppositions' that Plato elsewhere tries to control, are undone by the ambiguities of *pharmakon*, writing, love. Yet when Derrida lists the oppositions he does not include male/female, even though that also had been part of Pythagoras' list. Only once in his extended discussion does Derrida acknowledge that 'nothing is said of the mother'; and immediately adds, 'but this will not be held against us', and suggests that the mother can perhaps be dimly discerned as a faint upside down picture 'at the back of the garden' of Adonis (1993: 143). But what is this garden? And what persuades Derrida that his lack of attention to the mother/female will not be held against 'us'? Against whom? Derrida? Plato? What implicit identifications does this 'us' betoken?

Derrida's deconstructive strategies need to be carried further. He has shown how, with the admission of living writing, writing on the heart, Plato's argument for the superiority of speech over writing depends on the very thing it denies. I suggest that we need to take another step. I suggest that the female, who is virtually erased in both Plato's and Derrida's accounts, is actually necessary for their arguments to get any purchase.

One of the prominent metaphors in Socrates' discussions after the presentation of the myth of Theuth is that of legitimate offspring. Socrates says that discourse which is 'written in the soul of the learner' is 'of unquestioned legitimacy', much better than its bastard brother of written speech (276a). Again, he says that discourses on 'justice and honour and goodness' are 'veritably written in the soul of the listener, and that such discourses as these ought to be accounted a man's own legitimate children – a title to be applied primarily to such as originate within the man himself, and secondarily to such of their sons and brothers as have grown up aright in the souls of other men' (278a–b). What is going on here, surely, is another instance of the theme of masculine appropriation of reproduction that we have already encountered in the *Theaetetus* and the *Symposium*, with actual women and physical birth even less in evidence than they were in those dialogues. This is reinforced by Socrates' analogy of the farmer, who would not plant his seeds 'in a garden of Adonis' but 'in suitable soil' (276b): – not, therefore (contrary to Derrida), in a garden where we might find the shadow of a mother. Socrates continues,

> The dialectician selects a soul of the right type, and in it he plants and sows his words founded on knowledge . . . words which instead of remaining barren contain a seed whence new words grow up in new characters, whereby the seed is vouchsafed immortality, and its possessor the fullest measure of blessedness that man can attain unto.
>
> (277a)

The garden of Adonis – heterosexual love – would produce short-lived offspring, children who are mortal and are therefore born to die. This is equivalent to 'barrenness'. By contrast, philosophical emissions produce words that grow up into immortality.

It is a breath-taking reversal, parallel to reversals we have already found in

Parmenides. Bodily, sexual reproduction is 'barren'; words are fecund. Words in the wrong place produce bastards, but 'written in the soul of the listener' produce 'a man's own legitimate children'. Not only are women unnecessary for this all-male reproduction; they are actually a hindrance to it, precisely because of their link with death. Here again we find Plato characterizing bodily birth not as a necessary condition for life but only as a prerequisite for death, while the masculine word produces immortality. The link between gender and death/immortality is blatant. Socrates/Plato never seems to have pondered the fact that they themselves presumably did not arrive in this world because people talked philosophy; they never consider the philosophical implications of human natality. To read the *Phaedrus* one would think that the world would be just as good or even better if there were no women. Women are almost entirely absent from the dialogue; and virtually invisible also in Derrida's discussion. While Derrida makes much of the connection between writing and death, he is silent about the linkage of death with women.

There is, however, the 'garden of Adonis', the hint in Plato and in Derrida that all is not as it seems. If Derridean deconstructive strategy has taught us anything, it has taught us to look in the margins, the chinks, the seemingly inconsequential asides, for it is here, if anywhere, that the repressed returns. I shall argue that it is precisely the shadow of the woman in the garden of Adonis, tucked into a metaphor in Plato and a marginal remark in Derrida, that offers an opening that would enable a reversal of the deadly writing of philosophical misogyny.

But that is to anticipate. To allow the repressed to reveal itself it is, as usual, necessary to go by the longer road of association, which Derrida also partly traces. The ambiguity of *pharmakon*, shifting between remedy and poison, is paralleled by the ambiguity of the name of its practitioner, the *pharmakeus*, a magician, sorcerer, or even poisoner. The *pharmakeus* is the one who knows the properties of the *pharmakon*, the one who can use it to accomplish his purposes for good or ill. Now, the place in Plato's writings where we find the *pharmakeus* most prominently is in 'Diotima's' speech in the *Symposium*, where she characterizes Eros.[5] As we saw in an earlier part of this chapter, Eros is there described as the offspring of Resource and Need: he is neither immortal nor mortal but is 'at once desirous and full of wisdom, a lifelong seeker after truth, an adept in sorcery, enchantment, and seduction' (203d). In short, Eros is a *pharmakeus*. He can administer medicine or poison, life or death. His undecidability is parallel to the undecidability of passion and of writing in the *Phaedrus*.

As Derrida points out, however, this is not a picture only of an abstraction personified as Eros.

> Behind the portrait of Eros, one cannot fail to recognise the features of Socrates, as though Diotima, in looking at him, were proposing to Socrates the portrait of Socrates.
>
> (1993: 117)

Like Eros, Socrates is not rich nor beautiful or delicate but spends his time philosophizing: 'Socrates in the dialogues of Plato often has the face of a *pharmakeus*' (ibid.). Does the philosopher become the sorcerer, the poisoned man the poisoner? Here are yet more complexities and reversals in Platonic writing not often considered in contemporary analytic accounts of Plato's philosophy. Socrates is not only the midwife of the *Theaetetus* assisting at the birth of knowledge; he is also the *pharmakeus* who has affected Alcibiades like the venom of a poisonous snake (*Symposium* 215b, 218a), the gadfly who stings the Athenians with his poison/medicine until they slap him away with a *pharmakon* of their own (*Apology* 30e–31a).

The sorcery of the Socratic pharmacy, Derrida points out, is directly reliant upon fear of death: 'the fear of death is what gives all witchcraft, all occult medicine, a hold. The *pharmakeus* is banking on that fear' (1993: 120). Socrates tries to administer a remedy that frees people from that fear, the remedy of dialectics, whereby its practitioners follow after wisdom and immortality and are no longer concerned about bodily death, or indeed birth. But there is a price which Socrates must pay for his mastery of life and death as a *pharmakeus*: it is his 'on the condition that Socrates overtly renounce its benefits: knowledge as power, passion, pleasure. On the condition, in a word, that he consent to die. The death of the body, at least . . . ' (Derrida 1993: 120). The *pharmakeus* must take his own medicine; the gadfly must be poisoned.

It is time to take a step backwards and consider again the wider picture: what is Plato doing here? Whatever the actual historical events surrounding the life and death of Socrates in fifth-century Athens, it is clear in the first place that Plato is not simply reporting what happened. He is writing a series of complex literary-philosophical works in which it suits his purpose to use Socrates as a central figure. By the time he writes the *Phaedrus* he has established an intricate web of ironies. Most to the fore is the one just now discussed, in which Socrates the *pharmakeus* must drink the *pharmakon*, which kills him and (in the terms of his philosophy) gives him life. But the imagery of the *pharmakon* is sited in the dialogue in which speech is privileged over writing: there is the obvious irony of Plato writing a dialogue in which he attacks writing, and, as Derrida demonstrates, actually reveals its priority over speech while purporting to do the opposite. Moreover, this written text is associated with death; yet it is only through this writing that Plato keeps the spirit of Socrates, the philosophical quest, alive, even while death was the penalty imposed on Socrates for his philosophizing.

Derrida uncovers yet another layer here, frequent in Plato's dialogues and well illustrated in the *Phaedrus*, and that is the image of Socrates as father, but a father who must die in order for the son to come into his own. The *pharmakeus* becomes *pharmakos*; the family scene becomes patricide. The word *pharmakeus* was also written *pharmakos*: both meant 'magician, sorcerer, poisoner'. *Pharmakos* also meant 'scapegoat'; one who was sacrificed as an atonement for others. As Derrida reads the situation, informed by psychoanalytic perspectives, it is the father who must die, who is indeed killed off by the sons; but having been thus killed he is venerated as divine, immortal. Again in all this the female – the mother, the daughters, the goddess – is invisible while the sons work out their preoccupation with death. Or is she? Is she invisible, or is it just that the men choose to look the other way? I shall argue that although the men refuse to acknowledge her, she is actually never out of sight. In fact, neither the family scene, the *pharmakos*, nor philosophy can take place without her: she is both repressed and necessary, but to acknowledge her would turn the patricide, and the western philosophy upon which it is based, inside out.

I begin with the ritual as it was practised in Plato's Greece. Ritual involving a *pharmakos* or scapegoat was widespread in ancient civilizations from the Hittites to the Romans.[6] In Greece it took place at the Thargelia, a festival of Apollo celebrating the first fruits at the beginning of harvest. Usually it involved choosing some repulsive or ugly person, who might first be feasted on fine foods, and then was whipped with figsprays all over his body but especially on his genitals, and driven out of town or killed. The individual was called the 'offscouring', and the procedure was seen as catharsis, purification. Thargelia, the day when the first harvest is brought in, was the day when the city must first be cleaned, 'as a receptacle is cleansed to take in and store the new wealth or "life", *bios*, which comes from the crops' (Burkert 1979: 65). The city defined itself and its purity by driving out of its boundaries someone designated as impure.

René Girard emphasizes, however, that the *pharmakos*, like the *pharmakon*, is ambiguous, undecidable. He is seen as ugly and evil, yet it is upon him that the purity and health of the city depends.

> On the one hand he is a woebegone figure, an object of scorn who is also weighed down with guilt; a butt for all sorts of gibes, insults, and of course, outbursts of violence. On the other hand, we find him surrounded by a quasi-religious aura of veneration; he has become a sort of cult object. . . . The victim draws to itself all the violence . . . and through its own death transforms this baneful violence into beneficial violence, into harmony and abundance.
> (1972: 95)

Girard is referring specifically to Sophocles' portrayal of Oedipus as the polluted one who must be expelled; but the discussion is strikingly applicable to Plato's portrayal of Socrates. Socrates is himself the *pharmakos*, the one who must be purged for the purity of the city. Not only was the hemlock that he drank both medicine and poison; the same was true of himself. He thus becomes, like Eros, undecidably mortal and immortal, the executed criminal and the cult figure, the scapegoat and the sorcerer. Plato is at pains to remind his readers of Socrates' snub nose, his physical ugliness. Just to underline the message, we are informed that Socrates' birthday fell on the feast day of Thargelia, the day of the *pharmakos*.

Thus in Plato's representation of Socrates, philosophy is implicitly founded upon an expulsion, violence and ritual killing, whether Plato was conscious of it or not. Moreover the killing is the killing of the father so that the son can take his place.

Plato can write only after Socrates has died; only then can he make him say whatever he likes.

> In effect, the father's death opens the reign of violence. In choosing violence – and that is what it is all about from the beginning – and violence against the father, the son – or patricidal writing – cannot fail to expose himself, too.
> (Derrida 1993: 146)

The ambiguities of the *Phaedrus*, Socrates' recantation of his harsh words about madness and passion, the consequent rethinking of reason, the body, speech, writing, and death can be taken as Plato's own attempt at undoing in advance the system of binary oppositions which have plagued western philosophy, and which have had such baneful consequences for gender. Yet these very ambiguities rely on a violent gesture, repeated indefinitely, of expulsion, death and the refusal to recognize women. In the end it is the dialogue itself, and the whole of Plato's writings absorbed with death and immortality, that becomes the undecidable *pharmakon*, the medicine and the poison of the western symbolic.

Pharmakis: the shadow in the garden/tent

The question can no longer be avoided: where is the mother? Socrates insists that just as the sensible farmer sows his seed only in suitable soil, so a philosopher will 'use his pen to sow words' only upon a soul of the right type, one who will be a faithful son to him (*Phaedrus* 276c, 277a). These seeds, *spermatoi*, are as ambiguous as the *pharmakon* and the writing, moving undecidably between life and death: 'that *pharmakon* which can *equally well* serve the seed of life and the seed of death, childbirth and abortion' which Socrates as midwife professes to have at his disposal (Derrida 1993: 153; cf *Theaetetus* 149c–d). But all the seeds/*spermatoi* in the world will produce no new birth unless there is a mother. Invisible as she is, she must be in the background somewhere. And there are indeed several hints of women's absent presence in the *Phaedrus*.

First, as we have noted, Derrida has suggested that she is a shadowy figure lurking in the foliage in the garden of Adonis, that garden which the sensible farmer rejects in favour of more suitable soil (*Phaedrus* 276b). But who is Adonis, that women should be lurking in his garden? Adonis, in ancient mythology, was a young god, a consort of the Goddess of vegetation. In Greece this Goddess was celebrated by Sappho (no less!) as Aphrodite, the goddess of love and beauty: in other cultures she was called Tammuz or Astarte/Asheroth, and we will meet her again. Adonis' death was sometimes said to be due to being gored by a boar, sometimes an effect of his making love to the goddess: in either case it is hard not to read the myth as a castration or a 'little death', and the resurrection as renewed sexual energy. It was held that after the lament of women with the goddess, Adonis was raised to life again, transformed. The rituals involved included the sowing of seeds or 'gardens' in shards which were later discarded, seeds that would never come to maturity. Walter Burkert describes the festival of Adonis in fifth-century Athens as 'an unofficial ceremony, spontaneously performed by women, and viewed with suspicion by the dominant male', and having an 'emotional atmosphere of perfumes, seduction, wailing and despair' that provided a space of release from the everyday oppression of Greek women (Burkert 1979: 107; cf Detienne 1977).

So in the rituals of the garden of Adonis there was opportunity for women to identify with the goddess, and to share with the goddess power over male sexuality. Small wonder that the 'dominant males' felt threatened; and small wonder that Socrates counsels against sowing seeds in the garden of Adonis which these women control. Once again Socrates claims reproduction for the male philosopher; and once again women and the goddess are consigned to oblivion. But it is not because they are not there. It is rather that the writing on the soul that is philosophy is premised on their exclusion. And although we find none of this explicitly acknowledged in the text of either Plato or Derrida, neither of them can avoid a tell-tale comment about Adonis that gives a hint of the repressed woman. In fact, although it is Socrates who is presented as the *pharmakos*, it would be more accurate to see the real scapegoat as the woman/goddess: the female is the one who bears the impurity and bodiliness of the philosopher so that by her exclusion he can soar to immortality on the wings of the soul. Instead of the *pharmakos* is the *pharmakis*, the female scapegoat, sorcerer, witch, goddess.

There is, in fact, another hint in Plato's text, a second place where the absent woman appears only to be quickly suppressed; and on this occasion there is not only violence but also a direct link to the *pharmakis*. I noted that very near the beginning of the dialogue, Plato represents Phaedrus and Socrates walking together beside the river in the countryside. It is hot, and they sit down together in the shade of a plane tree to rest and talk. As Rosen says,

> The location is marked by grace, purity, and clarity; as Socrates says, it is a good place for maidens to play (but not perhaps for Bacchic maidens). Light and shade, heat and coolness, reclining humans and a flowing stream, feminine nature and masculine logos: the setting takes on the character of a harmony of opposites.
>
> (Rosen 1988: 85)

But if this is such an idyllic place, why should there be a problem for Bacchic maidens? The reason can be found in the conversation between Socrates and Phaedrus as they walked along. Phaedrus comments that this is the very place where Boreas, the west wind, seized and raped a maiden named Orithyia when she was playing with her friend Pharmacia: Socrates helps tell the story, but quickly dismisses it as something in which he has no interest. So yet again we meet the ambiguity of Plato's pharmacy, this time in the virginal figure of Pharmacia, at once the innocent playmate and the occasion for rape. And it is in this space, this place of a women's violent annihilation, that Socrates and Phaedrus settle down to develop their philosophy.

A third glimpse of women is a glimpse of Sappho herself, whom, as I have noted, Socrates invoked when he confessed that his initial theory had been wrong. He then presented an account of beauty and the love of vulnerable, embodied individuals which is much closer to Sappho's position than is that which he had earlier put into the mouth of Diotima. It is the woman Sappho that causes him to reconsider his whole position, and to develop a theory of beauty, love and the human soul which accepts and celebrates people as they actually are, celebrating this life rather than merely looking towards death. And yet when he has done so, he does not acknowledge Sappho, does not admit women. Once again, women are erased. But women are there, in the margins, waiting to emerge again with beauty and love, and with the celebration of life as newness enters into the world.

Chapter 12

The fault lines of flourishing

Arete [excellence], you whom the mortal race wins by much toil,
the fairest prey in life,
for the beauty of your form, maiden,
it is an enviable lot in Hellas both to die
and to endure toils violent and unceasing . . .
Because of the gracious beauty of your form the nursling
[Hermias] of Atarneus forsook the sun's rays.
Therefore the Muses will exalt him, famous in song for
his deeds and immortal.

(Aristotle, in O'Brien 1992: 20–1)

It may not be great poetry, but it spoke of genuine tragedy. Aristotle was devastated. Hermias, ruler of Atarneus had been executed by crucifixion. Like Aristotle, Hermias had been a student of Plato, and when he came to power in Atarneus he welcomed to it some of his former fellow students, including Aristotle who married his daughter.[1] Atarneus, however, was a point of strategic importance between Macedonia and the Persian Empire. In 341 BCE Hermias was caught by the Persians carrying on a correspondence with their rival, King Philip of Macedon. Hermias was tortured in an effort to extract secrets from him; and when he refused to talk he was crucified.

Aristotle's poem in honour of his father-in-law combines familiar themes: excellence, heroism, beauty, death and immortality. Gender assumptions, also, are implicit: Arete is personified as the beautiful maiden for whom the manly hero is willing to die. All these themes are by now familiar from Homer and the tragedians, and from Plato, who had been Aristotle's teacher for twenty years. How was it, then, that whereas Plato had wanted to banish the poets from his ideal Republic, Aristotle admired them?

Aristotle has been much discussed in terms of his contrast with Plato. Not only does he honour the poets and tragedians whom Plato banned. He also focuses his interest on this life and the concerns of this world, rather than the concerns of some other world of ideal forms. For Aristotle, the good life is the life of flourishing, flourishing here on earth, not in some supposed heaven. His *Ethics* and *Politics* are written in order to discuss what will count as flourishing and what will best facilitate it. Aristotle can therefore appear highly congenial to those who are looking for alternatives to the preoccupation with death and other worlds that so strongly marks the trajectory of western philosophy.

Yet feminists have been ambivalent about Aristotle. His view of gender was, if anything, even more misogynist than Plato's, as we shall see. Some feminists believe that this can be bracketed out; and that the rest of his philosophy illuminates contemporary concerns. I shall argue, however, that while his emphasis on flourishing does indeed mark a significant shift in the genealogy of death, his characterization of the life supremely worth living is premised on slavery and the oppression of women, on dominance and privilege, and thus ultimately on violence. Flourishing is only for the few: the many exist to make it possible. As we examine Aristotle's philosophy, from his *Poetics* to his *Politics*, we will find that time after time there comes a point at which masculinist privilege asserts itself in a manner which, if not preoccupied with death, is contemptuous of the lives of all but the privileged few, and reinscribes necrophilia at a deeper level. The task of this chapter is to explore these fault lines in Aristotle's concept of flourishing; to find in it resources for an alternative imaginary while avoiding the reinscriptions of violence.

Who was Aristotle?

Aristotle was born in 384 BCE. His father was the court physician to Amyntus III of Macedon: Aristotle and Philip (later King Philip) of Macedon may have been boyhood companions (O'Brien 1992: 19). Aristotle was sent from Macedon to Athens when he was about fourteen, to study in Plato's Academy, and stayed there for twenty years. Although he came to disagree with many of Plato's ideas, Aristotle's writings can often be read as conversations with Plato, even when Plato's name is not mentioned. In 347 Plato chose his nephew Speusippus to succeed him as head of the Academy, passing over Aristotle: it was at this time that Aristotle went to live in Assos, a city of Hermias' Atarneus.

Having spent twenty years in Plato's Academy, Aristotle was well acquainted with Plato's negative attitude to Homer and the tragedians. Yet in the poem he wrote for Hermias he used Homeric terms to venerate him. Moreover, by the time Aristotle wrote that poem he was back in Macedon at the invitation of Philip, as tutor to the young Alexander, and was engaged in instilling in the young boy the veneration for Achilles that, as we saw in chapter 5, was to inspire Alexander all his life. When Alexander became king and embarked on his military expeditions, Aristotle returned to Athens, where he stayed until about a year before he died in 323.

It would hardly be possible to have so profound a teacher as Plato, or so illustrious a pupil as Alexander, without being strongly influenced by both of them. Although scholars regularly consider the effect of Aristotle on Alexander, they rarely ponder the implications for Aristotle's thought of teaching the boy who would rule the world, or, more broadly, the effects of having been so deeply involved as Aristotle was in the Macedonian court. By contrast, commentators standardly discuss the influence (or lack of it) of Plato on Aristotle, comparing their theories of knowledge and reality in ways that have direct implications for a genealogy of death. For instance, it is often held that whereas in his early writings Aristotle echoed Plato's soul–body dualism and belief in personal immortality, in his later work he moved away from that view to a this-worldly holism and emphasis on flourishing (Nussbaum 1986; Rist 1989). On the other hand, Alisdair MacIntyre argues that when Aristotle returned to Athens after Alexander set forth to conquer the world, Aristotle came to accept, with modifications, Plato's views of what counts as human excellence, rather than the Homeric–Alexandrian ideals of glory, fame and power, in reaction to his former pupil's conduct (MacIntyre 1988: 88–90).

Although the arguments about the influence of Plato on Aristotle seem to oppose one another, they actually have more in common than at first appears. They assume that the core of each man's thought is his ontology (theory of what is real) and his epistemology (theory of knowledge). Politics and poetry receive attention by Plato scholars because of their significance in the *Republic*, but for Aristotle they are often left to the end. Gender is rarely discussed; certainly not in ways that illuminate his whole philosophical project.[2] A moment's reflection, however, suggests that Aristotle's political situation and his political philosophy may have had an impact on the rest of his thought, and that his writings on poetry are far more central than their cursory treatment by many modern scholars would suggest. In both of these gender is crucial as I shall show.

To begin with politics: Aristotle was closely involved with the Macedonian Court all his life. He was the son of the court physician; as a young man he married the daughter of a man executed for his affiliation with King Philip; as a teacher he was appointed to educate the heir apparent. Yet he also lived for long periods in Athens. Now, all of this was at a time of growing tension between Athens and Macedonia. After Athens' defeat in the Peloponnesian War, Athens made a remarkable recovery in the early fourth century, even regaining something of her imperial status. But her attempts at rebuilding an empire made her increasingly unpopular among Greek cities and islands, and her attention was consumed by skirmishes and wars to try to consolidate and extend her mastery. At the same time, Philip of Macedon had his own designs on Athens and her empire. There was war between them in the 340s and again in the 330s: each time, Athens was defeated, and was increasingly and grudgingly subservient to Alexander. In the last year of Alexander's life Athens rebelled and was defeated again: this time a Macedonian ruler (tyrant) was imposed. Aristotle, for all that he spent many years in Athens, was always identified with the court of Athens' greatest enemy. He was a *metic*, a resident alien. He could not own property in the city and was not a citizen; he could not have a voice in the *polis*. The *Lyceum* that he founded to teach his students was in rented buildings outside the city. When Athens was defeated in 323 there was such strong anti-Macedonian feeling that Aristotle was forced to leave. Aristotelian scholars typically dismiss this historical background, and assert that 'contemporary political events and social changes . . . left few marks on his political and moral philosophy' (McKeon 1941: xv): certainly nothing like the influence of Plato.

I am not so sure. How if, instead of assuming the centrality of Plato's influence and the negligible effects of Aristotle's ambiguous political situation, we were to start from the other end, thinking through his perspectives on violence, death and beauty from a gendered reading of his poetics? This is not meant to be a claim about the order in which Aristotle's books were written, a question I happily leave to specialists. It is, however, to apply again the feminist principle that there is no such thing as unsituated knowledge; the political and cultural context inevitably affects the thought of its subjects even while they in turn – if they are thinkers of Aristotle's stature – also have an impact upon it.

'A mutilated male'

Aristotle's ideas about women are notorious. Like other Greek thinkers since Pythagoras, he saw the female as passive and imperfect as contrasted with the active male who is the norm. In his book on *The Generation of Animals*, Aristotle says that 'the woman is as it were an impotent male'. In Aristotle's opinion one ought to think of 'the female character as being a sort of natural deficiency'.

> The female is, as it were, a mutilated male, and the catamenia (i.e. female secretion) are semen, only not pure; for there is only one thing they have not in them, the principle of soul.
>
> (1912: I.728a–737a)

It is this 'principle of soul' that is the distinguishing feature of men, which they pass on in their semen, thus causing new life to develop. Women, by contrast, are passive, and supply only the matter, not the form or soul of the developing foetus.[3] In the *Politics* when Aristotle discusses the right age for marriage, he says that women ought not to be too young when they begin to bear children, because if they are, they will have an unfortunate tendency to bear females.

The idea that the male is superior to the female and is her natural ruler is applied in the *Politics*, where Aristotle begins his discussion of the state with a discussion of the family.

> It is clear that the rule of the soul over the body, and of the mind and the rational element over the passionate, is natural and expedient . . . the male is by nature superior and the female inferior; and the one rules, and the other is ruled.
>
> (1254b)[4]

The male is the natural ruler not only of his children but also of his wife. While children grow up, and their father's rule over them comes to an end, 'the relation of the male to the female is of this kind, but there the inequality is permanent' (1254b). Aristotle emphasizes that this is not a matter of social convention or preference, but is inscribed in nature. 'For although there may be exceptions to the order of nature, the male is by nature fitter for command than the female' (1259b): here is another example of the naturalization I discussed in chapter 3.

However, it is not only over his wife and children that the male exercises his command. Every family also has slaves as part of its basic constitution (1253b). The slave is property, 'a living possession' whose function is like that of a domesticated animal, 'for both with their bodies minister to the needs of life' (1254b) – the master's life, that is. Such ministry is essential, because 'no man can live well, or indeed live at all, unless he be provided with necessaries' (1253b). As we shall see later in this chapter, Aristotle's central focus was on what it is to 'live well', to flourish. From the outset we have an indication that such flourishing will be the prerogative of the privileged few, men who will be enabled to live well by the ministry of their wives and their slaves.

Aristotle asserts that just as it is natural for the male to rule over the female, so there are some human beings (presumably both male and female) who are slaves 'by nature'. A slave is a person 'who is by nature not his own but another man's' (1254a). Arguing explicitly against those who say that slavery is unjust, Aristotle says that the duality between ruler and ruled (slave, wife, etc.) 'originates in the constitution of the universe'.

> For that some should rule and others be ruled is a thing not only necessary, but expedient; from the hour of their birth, some are marked out for subjection, others for rule.
>
> (1254a)

There is a problem with this, however: Aristotle cannot help but recognize that, as the tragedians insisted, many slaves are slaves simply because they have been conquered and captured in war. They might have been rulers of households in their own cities, or queens, like Hecuba or Andromache. In what sense could such captives – of whom there were many in fourth-century Athens – be 'natural' slaves? Aristotle concedes that there is a difference between people who are slaves by nature and those who are enslaved through war, and is clearly uncomfortable about the latter. In a later passage of the *Politics* where he is considering good statesmanship, he says that statesmen ought not to 'study war with a view to the enslavement of those who do not deserve to be enslaved'; and above all they should ensure that they themselves do not become slaves (1333b). It is an implicit admission that *anyone* could become a slave. In what sense, then, could there be 'natural' slaves and 'natural' rulers? Aristotle sees the inconsistency. And yet his idea of the best life requires that those who live it must be served, and will acquire the necessary slaves through 'hunting or war'. Thus the masters may be among 'those who are in a position which places them above toil' because they 'have stewards who attend to their households while they occupy themselves with philosophy or with politics' (1255b).

Aristotle insists that men should rule their households well. They should not be harsh or cruel, either to their wives or their slaves, but rather should teach them their duties and form their characters. Women and slaves have moral virtues as surely as do men. For slaves, to be sure, these are rather attenuated: 'a slave is useful for the wants of life, and therefore he will obviously require only so much virtue as will prevent him from failing in his duty through cowardice or lack of self-control' (1260a). A wife, on the other hand, should have the same moral virtues as her husband; only he should have the virtue in a 'manly' way and she in a 'womanly' way. For example, 'the courage of a man is shown in commanding, of a woman in obeying' (1260a).

'And this', says Aristotle, 'holds of all other virtues' (1260a). But quite *how* it holds, or how Aristotle is able to decide what the complementary virtues are for free men and women, let alone how these are 'natural', he leaves unexplained. As with slavery, so with gender: what it comes down to is that Aristotle inscribes as 'natural' those social institutions that maintain privilege. The arguments and evidence that he brings to bear are so full of holes that a logician of his stature would have seen through them at once, unless he had strong non-rational motives for retaining his conclusion. And so, of course, he had.

Feminists have often pointed out the fallacies and injustices of Aristotle's views on women and slaves (see Spelman 1988; Bar On 1994; Freeland 1998). Some feminists, however, have argued that in spite of his misogyny and his acceptance of slavery, Aristotle's central philosophical insights, his ethics and ontology and epistemology, still have much to recommend themselves. His comments on gender and on slavery can be separated off from his other work. The former can be discarded; the latter retained. Linda Hirshman (1998), for example, argues that excising Aristotle's misogyny clears the way for a reading of his works that generates valuable insights for jurisprudence; and Martha Nussbaum wants to recuperate Aristotle to help surmount limitations of contemporary liberalism (1998).

Could his misogyny be stripped away while the rest of his thought was left intact? The argument is sometimes offered that Aristotle was a man of his time and reflected the common assumption of his society, in which slavery and the subordination of women were taken for granted: we should not expect him to have modern, progressive, enlightened views. This argument, however, will not do. Aristotle was a profound thinker who challenged the assumptions of his society on many issues; nevertheless he left intact precisely those assumptions which facilitated his own privilege. Moreover, Aristotle was 'one of the greatest researchers in the history of biology,' making observations and classifications of minute detail; yet he thought, for example, that men have more teeth than women and that a mirror turns red when a menstruating woman looks into it. Nussbaum admits 'that Aristotle said stupid things without looking, despite his evident genius

for looking;' 'a starfish elicited from him a greater wonder and attention than
the body of the sort of creature with whom he lived, made love and bore children'
(Nussbaum 1998: 250). He can hardly be excused just on the grounds that he was
a man of his time.

Nevertheless, Nussbaum believes that Aristotle's own methodology, if properly
applied, would have led him to better conclusions. She holds that in spite of the
stupid and oppressive things Aristotle says about women and slaves, these things
can be stripped away and the rest of his philosophy retained to give important
insights into social and political life. As she puts it, 'we may proceed to appropriate
other elements of his thought without fear that they are logically interdependent
with his political and biological misogyny' (250).

I am not so sure. As I shall show in the rest of this chapter, Aristotle's
explorations in areas of thought, from tragedy to ontology, initially offer promise
of great insight; but when we follow through on that promise it is fatally undermined precisely by his misogyny and his assumption of privilege. I am not claiming
that this is true of every aspect of his work: I shall not discuss his logic, for example,
or his catalogue of political constitutions, or his ideas on the nature of the stars.[5]
But in those areas of his thought that are of greatest importance for a genealogy
of death, a fault line opens up. He praises poetry, for example, and unlike Plato
he welcomes the work of Homer and the tragedians; but then he effectively
eliminates just those tragedies which show the oppression of women and the cruel
consequences of war. He insists on this life, not some other life beyond the grave,
as important; but then he propounds a life of contemplation, like that of the
immortal gods, as the highest form of human life – a life possible only for privileged
males. He advocates flourishing, fullness of life; but the flourishing he envisages
will be at the price of the lives and deaths of lesser mortals. It is this fault line in
his thinking, and its implications for the genealogy of death in western culture,
that I wish to open up. I begin with an examination of his ideas of beauty and its
relation to tragedy.

Beauty domesticated?

Homer, for Aristotle, is the 'poet of poets' (*Poetics* 1448b); 'he excels the rest in
every respect' (1451a; 1458a) and is the model and example for poets (1460a).
If the young Alexander of Macedon thought the *Iliad* the greatest of all books, and
tried to model himself upon Achilles, he would have been encouraged by his
teacher. The banning of Homer from the education of young men, as Plato
advocated in the *Republic*, was not Aristotle's way. Rather, he looked to Homer,
and after him to the tragedians, for models to imitate.

The poets, according to Aristotle, fashion something beautiful (1447a): the
Greek word *kalon*, often translated 'good', also carried 'beauty' in its meaning. It
is precisely this beauty that inspires imitation; and Aristotle wrote his *Poetics* to
try to understand it. What exactly is beautiful about tragedy? It seems at some level
perverse to call a tragedy beautiful, let alone worthy of imitation; yet all who are

moved by the work of the great tragedians, as Aristotle clearly was, also recognize the appropriateness of 'beauty' as a descriptive term for their work. The story is told that Aristotle was once asked why he should think so much about the meaning of beauty. 'This is the question of a blind person,' he replied shortly (Bredin and Santoro-Brienza 2000: 33).

Yet Aristotle did not write very much about the nature of beauty itself (though, as we shall see, he wrote a good deal about art). Not for him the soaring vision of beauty and the good that Plato offers in the *Republic* or the *Phaedrus*, let alone the climb to the contemplation of the 'open sea of beauty' of the *Symposium*. Rather, Aristotle in his writings on art, measures and categorizes and sets things into tidy patterns. As we have seen, Plato regularly uses dialogue form, and his writings self-consciously use literary techniques of dramatic placement, myth and story. We might legitimately wonder whether Plato, for all his attacks on poetry, is after all also among the poets. But no one would ask that of Aristotle. His writings are presented in severe prose in which literary artifice is at a minimum. He sets out his categorizations and explanations in as few words as possible, without myth or story or the supposed presence of interlocuters.

It is sometimes speculated that Aristotle's writings as we have them were akin to lecture notes, and that this accounts for their spare style; such dialogues as he wrote have been lost (cf Ross 1930: 9). But it is not only in literary style that Aristotle differs from Plato. His whole approach is different. Aristotle's method is to divide a subject up into categories, to make lists and classifications and taxonomies, and draw up rules and structures which he partly finds in his subject matter and partly imposes upon it. In his books on logic and reasoning he draws up lists of kinds of argument, classes of reasoning, types of fallacies, and the like. His biological writings are concerned with how animals should be classified, what the categories of likeness and differentia should be; in the course of his discussion he mentions at least five hundred different animals. His political writings collect up varieties of constitutions of different states and draw up categories of political structure and organization. Even in his ethical writings there are lists of feelings, virtues and vices, which are organized into schemes and systems; his doctrine of the mean (that is, that the virtuous action is the action falling between two extremes) is perhaps the most famous. If one comes to Aristotle, not as a logician or ethicist or historian of science considering only one aspect of his extant work, but rather reading him in the round, one of the first and overwhelming impressions is of a man with a compulsion to intellectual tidiness. Everything is listed; the lists are organized into categories; the world is structured into manageability.

Moreover, and most importantly, it is *this* world that is thus examined and categorized. When Aristotle looks for overarching categories, whether for a taxonomy of animal species or for the types of political structure, his categories are generalizations drawn from considering examples in this world, not efforts to discern an ideal, eternal, non-material form, whether of a crustacean or of a state. This whole approach, its style, its content and its aim, is far removed from anything to be found in Plato. Whereas Plato represented this world as dance of shadows in the cave of our material existence, Aristotle lists, categorizes and explains the 'shadows', with the clear implication that this is the world we actually have, and it is better to understand it and learn to live in it than to speculate about some other. This will obviously have a bearing on Aristotle's understanding of death; but for the moment let us return to his account of poetry and its beauty.

Aristotle accepts the idea current in Greek aesthetic thought that beauty has to do with harmony and proportion, to which a person can respond: 'to be beautiful, a living creature, and every whole made up of parts, must not only present a certain order in its arrangement of parts, but also be of a certain definite magnitude' (1450b). If a thing is either minute or vast, its parts or its unity are impossible to grasp. And if this is the case for other forms of beauty, it is especially true for drama.

> Just in the same way, then, as a beautiful whole made up of parts, or a beautiful living creature, must be of some size, but a size to be taken in by the eye, so a story or Plot must be of some length, but of a length to be taken in by the memory.
>
> (1451a)

As a rough guide for the appropriate length of a drama Aristotle suggests the length necessary to show the hero passing from happiness to misery or vice versa.

We are in a different thought world from that of Plato. Plato's account of what would make life truly worth living was to gaze upon the open sea of beauty. This is of course beyond ordinary perception: in Plato, that is part of the point. The soul must be stretched, expanded, made great so that it can at last perceive Beauty itself. Aristotle, by contrast, weighs and measures and classifies, subjecting even beauty to an analysis of size and the arrangement of parts. This is not the wild wonder of beauty, but beauty tamed: not so much displaced as domesticated. Compared with Plato's grand vision, Aristotle's discussion may seem crass, even blasphemous.

But is it? What interests Aristotle is the response of the beholder: how can one learn to respond to art or beauty? In particular, what are the necessary features of poetry or tragedy that enable such response? Aristotle has little to say about beauty in general; he is concerned with the specific, practical task of showing how good tragedy elicits ethical and aesthetic response and thereby brings the viewer pleasure and moral profit. Aristotle is not talking about some ultimate reach of the soul; rather, he is concerned with the ways in which the dramas his readers might watch during an ordinary evening in Athens bring about the pleasure of moral learning.[6]

Central to this learning is *mimesis*, imitation or representation. In Plato, as we saw, it was *mimesis* that makes art suspect because, as a copy, it is to some extent false. Aristotle is not bothered about that. What he is concerned about, particularly with reference to tragedy, is that the drama should imitate action and life, should represent happiness and misery and the slide from one to the other. It should do this in a way that elicits intellectual and emotional engagement from the viewer, who, by that engagement, is morally enriched. As he puts it,

> A tragedy, then, is the imitation of an action that is serious and also, as having magnitude, complete in itself; in language with pleasurable accessories, each kind brought in separately in the parts of the work; in a dramatic, not a narrative form; with incidents arousing pity and fear, wherewith to accomplish its catharsis of such emotions.
>
> (1449b)

So, for example, in Sophocles' *Oedipus the King*, which was one of Aristotle's favourite plays, the drama represents the story of Oedipus, the wise and successful king who, by insisting on probing into an unknown past, discovers truths about himself that lead him to complete wretchedness. The captivating language and presentation of the play draws the viewer into pleasurable engagement, even as we are also horrified at what happens. It could happen to any of us: not precisely these things, of course – not many of us are likely to discover that we have killed our fathers and married our mothers. But any of us could discover things we had not known about ourselves or those close to us which would turn our world upside down. Watching Oedipus, we feel pity and fear; and our moral horizon is expanded. If the beauty of tragedy as Aristotle presents it does not have the wild affinity that Plato suggests in the *Symposium*, neither does it have anything to do with the merely pretty. It carries with it a charge of horror and compassion which, as we engage with it, leaves us changed, our moral insight purified.[7]

The mimesis or imitation that is involved in the beauty of tragedy is, broadly speaking, of two kinds. On the one hand there is the imitation inherent in the drama itself: the plot represents a sequence of actions, and the actors represent or 'imitate' the characters who do those actions. Aristotle has much to say about plot and character and how they should be fashioned in good tragedy. On the other hand there is the 'imitation' or mimetic effect upon the audience as they identify themselves with a character like Oedipus or Electra, or pattern themselves on them as Alexander did on Achilles. Again, this is not imitation in any carbon copy sense. It is rather a question of taking someone as a model and trying to be like them; or, conversely, being horrified at a character or action and therefore taking great care not to fall into the same pattern. It is this moral learning which Aristotle sees as the aim of tragedy, and which beautiful tragedy is able to achieve, because everyone is a mimic and everyone loves to learn.

> Imitation is natural to man from childhood, one of his advantages over the lower animals being this, that he is the most imitative creature in the world, and learns at first by imitation. And it is natural for all to delight in works of imitation. . . . The explanation is to be found in a further fact: to be learning something is the greatest of pleasures not only to the philosopher but also to the rest of mankind, however small their capacity for it.
>
> (1448b)

We delight in imitation: we enjoy seeing how a painting or a poem imitates reality because in doing so we are 'at one and the same time learning – gathering the meaning of things' (ibid.). And this is not mere abstract learning: indeed according to Aristotle learning proceeds most naturally by imitation, appropriating to ourselves and our own action the 'meaning of things' that we gain from the work of art. It engages and integrates our reason and our emotions, so that our response purifies and expands our moral insight and we learn to become better. According to Aristotle, this is the way that moral character is shaped. Without beauty and receptive mimetic response we would be morally unformed. Aristotle can be read as insisting, just as much as Plato, on the centrality of beauty and its intrinsic connection with goodness; but he brings it right down to situations of daily experience. It is not hard to imagine Aristotle teaching Alexander or his students in the Lyceum: not trying to get them to gaze upon the open sea of beauty, but to look at paintings and sculptures and attend theatrical productions. It is in the situations of life which they depict that moral character will be shaped or it will not be shaped at all.

Now, if moral character is formed by imitation then it is of the first importance that the models for imitation should be selected with great care. When the young men under Aristotle's tutelage watched the dramas on the Athenian stage, with all the slaughter and violence and death that they portrayed, which characters and actions should they choose as models? It will be recalled that one of the reasons Plato wanted to banish Homer and the tragedians was that he thought they offered bad models to copy, partly because they would undermine their viewers' manliness and readiness to go to war. Aristotle in the *Poetics* takes a different view: he sets out the criteria for good tragedy, for models worthy of attention. 'First and foremost they (the characters) shall be good' (1454a): as good as ordinary people or a bit better. If they are perfect, they will be too good to be true and will not serve as models because ordinary people cannot hope to become faultless. On the other hand, if they are bad, they are not appropriate models at all.

> There remains, then, the intermediate kind of personage, a man not pre-eminently virtuous and just, whose misfortune, however, is brought upon him not by vice or depravity but by some error of judgement.
>
> (1453a)

Again, Oedipus is an obvious example. As Aristotle insists elsewhere, a human being is neither a beast nor a god but something in between; therefore a model for human flourishing will similarly have to have an 'intermediate' sort of character. Although for Aristotle the norm is a privileged male, he does concede that in tragedies goodness can be portrayed by any of the characters, 'even in a woman or a slave, though the one is perhaps an inferior, and the other a wholly worthless being' (1454a). In the context, this seems to be no more than a passing comment; but it serves as an early warning of Aristotle's assumptions about gender and status which will reveal the fault line in his treatment of tragedy.

In addition to being good, the dramatic character should be appropriate, portraying on stage the sorts of action that would be expected: for example a king should behave with dignity, a woman should not be manly, and so on. Related to these are Aristotle's criteria of realism and consistency. The attention of the audience should not be deflected by incongruity; rather, by watching someone sufficiently like themselves they form the mimetic identification with the character and thus are able to experience the horror and compassion that broadens moral insight (Halliwell 1992).

Now, what does all this come to? Suppose that Aristotle's students came to his Lyceum the day after watching a tragedy at the theatre: what sorts of discussion would Aristotle hope to have? If he had recommended that they should go and see a play that met all his criteria, which of the tragedies would he have selected? And what sorts of moral insight might the students have gained?

Since Aristotle emphasizes that the best tragedies focus on a single character and that the plot depicts misfortune that comes upon that character by their own error or misjudgement, then tragedies in which the suffering is due to external circumstances like war or social oppression would be left out. Only tragedies that fix attention on a good and decent hero who makes a tragic mistake will be selected. *Oedipus the King* is one of his favourites, but plays like *The Persians* or *The Trojan Woman*, which depict the cruelty of war and the suffering it inflicts on foreigners and women do not fit his description. Neither does *Iphigenia in Aulis*, which shows the sacrifice of a young woman because of the greed for power of men, nor do plays that show how masculine oppression can distort a woman's character so that she in turn becomes evil and vengeful, like *Medea*, or Euripides' *Electra*. These are plays in which the tragedy results neither from bad choices of the central character nor from the gods, but from the cruelty and violence of others.

Precisely because of this, these are the plays which called Athenians to account. They show the evils of Athens' policies of war and oppression, reveal the degradation that cruelty and violence perpetuate, and portray the utter folly of revenge and the cycles of violence that it breeds. These, however, are not topics that ever arise in Aristotle's *Poetics*. He never concerns himself with political hypocrisy or with the ways in which war, revenge and violence take a particularly harsh toll on women, slaves, asylum seekers, or other disadvantaged groups. As Angela Curran points out, Aristotle's ideal 'tragic protagonist is a wealthy, powerful man, someone with room for significant action and choice' (1998: 299). Such a protagonist would, to be sure, be the sort of person with whom Aristotle's students at the Lyceum could readily identify: they were privileged males with their lives before them. But the point is that if the young men of Aristotle's Lyceum went to see plays that met his criteria, their attention would be riveted on an individual; there would be no place for political learning. Yet these young men were also, presumably, citizens of the *polis*, men who were (or would soon be) making decisions about the social and political policies that Athens should adopt. How should Athens respond to the rise to power of Macedonia? Should Athens go to war? How should the old animosity with Sparta be dealt with? It does not seem that Aristotle's discussion of tragedy would give them any help. The plays Aristotle delights in are not plays that show how the social structure is the source of misfortune (e.g. *Andromache*), how patriarchy undermines and distorts women's characters (e.g. *Medea*), how war devastates lives (e.g. *Persians*, *Women of Troy*). The pity and fear – or, better, horror and compassion – that Aristotle sees as the product of good tragedy is focused not on victims but on heroes. His students are not urged to try to understand or identify with those who bear the brunt of the social and political decisions they will be making as citizens of Athens. Their attention is deflected from such considerations and focused entirely upon themselves as they mimetically identify with the hero protagonist.

Aristotle is often taken as much more receptive than was Plato to poetry and drama. If Aristotle's criteria of good tragedy are observed, however, then anything politically disruptive or challenging the social or political conscience is effectively sidelined. Plato wanted to censor poetry, and not allow drama that might lead young men to question the value of war or refuse to go out and kill. Aristotle is much more subtle. He gives no hint of wanting to impose censorship; he simply holds up a set of standards that marginalizes tragedies with a political message and turns the attention instead to the heroic individual. It is, arguably, a far more effective ploy than an outright ban: the censor will be internal and unconscious; and violence and its gender assumptions will remain unchallenged.

If the audience of Aristotle's favourite tragedies would not be prompted to political learning, what other sort of learning could be expected? Might it be the case that even if there were no serious political learning, there could still be significant individual moral illumination? Many scholars answer in the affirmative. According to Martha Nussbaum, for example, the pity and fear that the viewer of a tragic hero feels, enables genuine moral lessons that clarify their attitudes and responses to the things life may require them to face in their own lives. 'These emotions can be genuine sources of understanding, showing the spectator possibilities that there are for good people' (Nussbaum 1992: 281). Similarly, Stephen Halliwell argues that according to Aristotle, 'tragedy does not just confirm us in pre-existing comprehension of the world: it provides us with imaginative opportunities to test, refine, extend and perhaps even question the ideas and values on which such comprehension rests' (1992: 253). We have seen in the previous chapters that this is certainly true of the works of the tragedians themselves. But to what extent would it be true of those tragedies which conformed to Aristotle's ideals?

Aristotle sometimes acknowledges the significance of what is often called 'moral luck': events that happen seemingly by chance or at random that have a big impact on the character's happiness or moral endeavour (Williams 1976; Nagel 1979). Bad moral luck is not the central factor of a hero's tragic downfall, however; rather, it gets a purchase through a frailty or mistake that the hero makes, a fault (but not a depravity) of the hero's character. It was Oedipus' bad luck that the man he met and killed at a crossroads was his own father; but unless he had insisted, against all advice, that he would get to the bottom of the mystery with which he was confronted he might have lived with Jocasta happily forever after. Thus a spectator of Aristotle's ideal tragedies would have been reminded of the role of luck and its combination with human frailty and fallibility, and might have been led to ponder the vulnerability of human life. In his *Nichomachean Ethics* Aristotle quotes the saying of Solon which the tragedians had made their own: 'count no one happy until he is dead' (I.ix.1100a). Even a good and happy life can meet with wretchedness before it ends if bad moral luck and a flaw of personality combine to bring about a tragic downfall; alternatively a stroke of good moral luck can bring happiness to someone who is wretched, as happens in another of Aristotle's favourite plays, *Iphigenia in Taurus*.

Even if the moral illumination Aristotle could expect for his students would involve their recognition of their own vulnerability, and might have prompted them to think about their flaws and frailties, it would not involve thinking about the immense destructiveness suffered by victims of war or oppression through no fault of their own. Nor, as already emphasized, would it challenge the futile cycles of revenge masquerading as justice. Nor would they question their assumptions of gender and privilege. As Cynthia Freeland says, in Aristotle's terms 'tragedy ought to depict only certain people, certain circumstances, certain outcomes – those in accord with Aristotle's moral views' (1992: 122). They will be individualistic, offering mimetic identification with a hero whose life consequences do not disturb political or social structures. In the perspective of Berthold Brecht as discussed by Angela Curran, Aristotelian catharsis does not provide moral education about the real sources of human suffering – war, violence, cruelty, hypocrisy. Rather, 'the pleasure provided by a catharsis of pity and fear gives a kind of emotional closure, preventing the viewer from critically reflecting on the ways in which oppressive social structures make for needless suffering and misfortune' (Curran 1998: 298). War, slavery and revenge are topics which fill the pages of the tragedians, but one would never know it from reading Aristotle's *Poetics*.

On how to live

Aristotle has very little to say about war in any of his writings. In his *Politics* he argues briefly that warlike pursuits, although honourable 'are not the supreme end of all things, but only means' (1325a). He spends much more effort on thinking about how internal revolution can be avoided. In the light of the way in which Athens was caught up in the hostility between Alexander and Persia, and the impact of this conflict on Aristotle's personal life, it is a strange silence.

Not only is there little about killing in Aristotle; there is little about death. Overtly at least, Aristotle seems far less preoccupied with death than was Plato. His concern was much more focused on how to live than on death. Unlike Plato, Aristotle did not produce sustained writing on the topic of death and immortality.[8] When Aristotle does speak of death, he treats it in biological rather than metaphysical terms: death is just the event that ends life, whether for plants, animals, or people (King 2001). It is a different thought world from Plato. On the face of it, it would seem that Aristotle makes a sharp break with the preoccupation with death and violence which has marked the genealogy up to this point. I shall show, however, that the reality is again much more subtle. Just as Aristotle initially appears much more welcoming of poetry than does Plato but turns out to introduce an internal censorship that would be far more effective than an outright ban, so also, I shall argue, Aristotle's turn away from discussion of death actually reinstates necrophilia at a deeper level.

Nevertheless, there is in Aristotle a clear focus on life and how to live: how to make the most of the actual lives humans have. Aristotle regularly takes his bearings from what people say and think, from the ordinary language and conventions of his time. Thus for example in his analysis of happiness he observes that 'we call neither ox nor horse nor any of the other animals happy', neither a child, nor those who have died: what does this tell us about how the concept of happiness should be understood (*Nichomachean Ethics* I.ix.1100a)? This is not to say that he accepts the opinions of others without argument: much of the *Metaphysics*, for instance, is taken up with refutations of the views of previous philosophers. But whereas he often disagrees with the conclusions others have reached, especially those who count themselves experts, he seldom rejects ordinary language or ways of speaking as the basis from which he begins his classifications and analyses. We do not find in Aristotle the contrast between the way of truth and the way of opinion, the wise man and the unwashed multitude that is central to Parmenides and many other presocratic philosophers. Nor do we find the distinction between experience, as the way of the ordinary person, and the superior reasoning of the philosopher. Aristotle takes for granted, to be sure, that the philosopher will be a privileged male, not a woman or a slave, and also that the philosopher does have a role to play: the masses may well be ignorant and in need of education or even domination. But the problem is not with convention, experience, or ordinary language.[9]

Martha Nussbaum argues that Aristotle's approach is deeply rooted in a commitment to human community and what is involved in living in it. It is impossible to live together without respect for the language and common experience of the members of the community. Ethical, political and religious conventions are part of human community, part of a shared world. In Aristotle's practice wisdom does not emerge by way of a solitary philosopher arising in a chariot to the goddess, away from the world of mortals and their opinions; neither does it result, as in many Socratic dialogues, from showing that those who claim expertise in medicine, generalship, or some other profession don't know what they are talking about. Rather, understanding arises from attention to ordinary human language and experience. Although Aristotle may agree with Plato with regard to certain key doctrines, his approach to the method of philosophy is radically different.

This difference of approach is of considerable significance for a genealogy of death. In the first place, as I have said, Aristotle was not interested in speculating about other worlds, whether of an after-life in Hades or Heaven, or of some world of Platonic Forms or ideals, which in Aristotle's view would not increase our understanding of *this* world with which we are concerned. This is not to say that Aristotle offers a proof against immortality. Indeed, as we shall see later, he seems to have accepted conventional ideas about the gods and perhaps an after-life; but he makes it clear that such doctrines, like the doctrine of the Forms, do not get us much further in understanding this life and this world. It is a very long way from Plato's *Phaedo* in which the true philosopher lives with one foot in the grave, and makes dying his profession. Aristotle rather makes *living* his profession, and concentrates on what makes for flourishing in this life.

When Aristotle does speak of death, his comments are so different from Plato's that if we are thinking in a loosely Platonic framework they come as a jolt. One passage occurs in the *Nichomachean Ethics* where Aristotle is considering what constitutes human happiness, and remembers the saying attributed to Solon, that no one should be counted happy until he is dead (*Nichomachean Ethics* I.x.100a). Aristotle first comments on the uncertainties of life; but he quickly proceeds to consider other possibilities:

> is it also the case that a man *is* happy when he is *dead*? Or is this not quite absurd, especially for us who say that happiness is an activity?

There is no discussion of life after death. Nor is the possibility held out for a philosopher to gain release from his body for an incorporeal encounter with Truth, Beauty and Goodness, as anticipated in Plato's *Phaedo*. Aristotle simply asserts flatly that it is 'absurd' to attribute any activity to the dead. Death *means* the cessation of activity, and hence also of feelings, sensations and thoughts. Aristotle does not dwell on it; he just takes it as obvious.

Instead, he goes on to consider the question in a different way. Can good or evil affect a person retrospectively, so that a person who has had a fulfilled life and a peaceful death could nevertheless be affected by what happens to their descendants? They would not know about it; but then, good and evil do happen to those who are alive but unaware of what is happening: Aristotle mentions 'honours and dishonours and the good or bad fortunes of children and in general of descendants'. A person may never know that her life's work eventually brought about a better world, or, conversely, that it was completely ignored; but it is not unreasonable to say that these results are good and evil, respectively, for the person concerned (cf Pitcher 1993: 163–8; Feinburg 1993: 181–90). Aristotle therefore allows that there is a sense in which retrospective happiness or wretchedness can be attributed to those who have died, but having granted this, he turns away from it as from a distraction of his real concern: namely, what constitutes happiness for the *living*. There is no sense in which Aristotle uses the fact of death, let alone any prospect of immortality, as a fulcrum from which to judge human ethics or happiness. The idea of postmortem rewards or punishments is completely alien to his thinking. In a passage in the *Nichomachean Ethics* where he is analysing what it means to wish for something, he says, by way of example, that 'there may be a wish even for impossibles, e.g. for immortality' (III.ii.1111b). His whole focus is on life, on virtue and flourishing, which are considered in themselves and for their own sake, not for any implications they might have for a future state.

When Aristotle analyses these virtues, as usual making lists and categories (cf Ross 1930: 203), there is a further occasion when he comments on death; and in this instance he shows the strong influence of Homer on his thinking. First of the virtues, he says, is courage. What is courage? It is the ability to stand ones ground in the face of fear or danger, the 'terrible things' that can happen.

> Now death is the most terrible of all things, for it is the end, and nothing is thought to be any longer either good or bad for the dead.
>
> *(Nichomachean Ethics* III.vi.115a)

Yet courage is not facing just any death bravely: death at sea or death from disease do not count, or at most count only by extension. Only the 'noblest' deaths are those where the virtue of courage comes into its own.

> Now such deaths are those in battle; for these take place in the greatest and noblest danger. And these are correspondingly honoured in city-states and at the courts of monarchs. Properly, then, he will be called brave who is fearless in face of a noble death, and of all emergencies that involve death; and the emergencies of war are in the highest degree of this kind.
>
> (Ibid.)

We are back with the *Iliad.* The glorious death in battle, celebrated 'in city-states and at the courts of monarchs' is the death that is justly praised and shows the highest virtue. This does not make death welcome; it is 'the most terrible of all things'. Moreover it is terrible precisely because 'it is the end'. This, indeed, is why courage in the face of death is the supreme virtue.

Again the contrast with the *Phaedo* is striking. There, Socrates faces death with equanimity because it is the gateway to what he most desires and for which he has been preparing all his life. The point of Plato's teaching is that death is *not* terrible, neither is it the end. Aristotle does not discuss that position or argue against it in any way; he just assumes that the opposite is obvious. It is interesting to speculate on *why* he never discusses Plato's presentation of death and immortality, especially since, as I noted earlier, he seems at one time to have held somewhat similar views. In any case, Aristotle's few mentions of death have much more in common with that of the Homeric writings, especially the *Iliad,* and with the behaviour of Alexander, than with Plato in whose Academy he spent twenty years, more resonance with violence than with eternity. If we take it that Alexander learned at least some of his values and attitudes through Aristotle, the Homeric conception of courage and the noble death which he taught resonated with the noise of siege canons and battle cries and the weeping of slaves across vast tracts of the ancient world.

The soul

Although Aristotle never discusses Plato's views on death and immortality, Aristotle does write about immortality in the *De Anima*; and some scholars have linked this to his discussion of contemplation in Book X of the *Nichomachean Ethics*. The aim of the *De Anima* is to 'grasp and understand, first [the soul's] essential nature and secondly its properties' (I.i.402a). When Aristotle writes of the soul, however, he is not writing about a substance or quality that sets human beings off against other living things. Rather, all living things are 'besouled': better, 'soul' can be understood as the principle of life of all animate things. Again, Aristotle sees things in terms of a hierarchy, with each higher element containing all that went before and adding to it. Thus, plants have a 'nutritive' soul, the power of self-nutrition which enables them to live. Animals, in their different grades, have not only this capacity for nutrition, but also sensation and local motion: they have a sensitive soul. Humans, moreover, have a capacity to think: the rational soul that this betokens is not a separate *part* of the soul but rather a higher power of soul which includes the nutritive and sensitive, yet goes beyond these capacities to include calculation, imagination and thought (cf King 2001). Whereas Platonic thinking often seems to set the divine and the human mind together over against all other animate and inanimate things, including the human body, Aristotle is more inclined to see earthly things as a continuum reaching from the simplest plants to human persons: the gods are alone on the other side of a divide, and they alone are the 'living immortals' (cf Bodéüs 2000).

Then Aristotle says things that destabilize this picture. He writes that mind is not the soul, but 'an independent substance implanted within the soul' that is 'incapable of being destroyed' (I.iv.408b). The mind is 'impassable'. The body and its organs are the vehicle of the mind, necessary for it to function. 'That is why, when this vehicle decays, memory and love cease; they were activities, not of mind, but of the composite which has perished; mind is, no doubt, something more divine and impassable' (ibid.). In this comment, mind is set together with the immortal gods and contrasted with the body in tones that are after all reminiscent of Plato's *Phaedo*.

This is even further complicated when Aristotle says,

> Mind is not at one time knowing and at another not. When mind is set free from its present conditions it appears as just what it is and nothing more: this alone is immortal and eternal.
>
> (III.v.429b)

Here it seems that mind exists both before and after the living person who thinks and acts, but not as an individual, or as having memory and thought. To ask after the personal identity of this mind, that is, to ask whether this is the mind of Socrates or of Alcibiades or of Diotima would be to confuse categories. And yet in some sense this eternal and impassable mind is continuously knowing, though clearly not (in this passage) in the sense of personal consciousness.

The obvious question, then, is, what does this mind know? There are other places in Aristotle's writings in which he discusses the notion of an eternal and impassable mind, especially *Metaphysics* Book XII; but this is not the mind of a human person but of the Unmoved Mover of the universe. Aristotle here argues that the motion of the universe is eternal; and therefore there must be a prime mover, itself unmoved, that keeps it all going. The way in which it does this is not by force, by pushing the world around, but rather by attraction; it is an object of desire and thus draws the spheres of the heavens into movement around it.

> The first mover, then, exists of necessity; and insofar as it exists by necessity, its mode of being is good, and it is in this sense a first principle. . . . The final cause, then, produces motion as being loved.
>
> (*Metaphysics* XII.vii.1072b)

This unmoved mover, whom Aristotle considers to be divine, is an unceasingly thinking mind, since thought is the most divine of all activities. But what does it think about? Surely the divine mind would only think of good things, indeed of the best: 'it thinks of that which is most divine and precious' (XII.ix.1074a). The obvious conclusion, which Aristotle immediately draws, is that the unmoved mover thinks of itself, contemplates itself through all eternity. He says,

> Therefore it must be of itself that the divine thought thinks (since it is the most excellent of things), and its thinking is a thinking on thinking . . . so throughout eternity is the thought which has *itself* for its object.
>
> (Ibid.)[10]

There is, therefore, in Aristotle's thought, an eternal mind that is in some sense the first principle of the universe; and he identifies it with God. Beginning from the assertion that by our own experience we know contemplation to be the pleasantest and best activity, Aristotle continues,

> If, then, God is always in that good state in which we sometimes are, this compels our wonder. . . . We say therefore that God is a living being, eternal, most good, so that life and duration continuous and eternal belong to God; for this *is* God.
>
> (XXII.vii.1072b)

We must be careful not to equate 'God' in Aristotle's conception to the God of christendom: Aristotle's God, here, is not a creator of the universe, neither is God providentially involved in the world or in human affairs: indeed God does not even know about them (cf Ross 1930: 179–86). Nevertheless, Aristotle invokes the divine as immortal, as in the best state, as compelling our wonder, and as the unifying and organizing power of the cosmos.

It seems, then, that contemplation is an activity common to the divine and to humans, even though for us it can only be fleeting. The mind that thinks in us, that is 'implanted' in us, is related to the divine mind, even though it is immortal and we are not (Rist 1989: 31).

Contemplation of immortality

Or are we? In the *Nichomachean Ethics* X Aristotle writes in a way that casts doubt on the portrayal of him as concerned exclusively with this world and life within it, and dismissive of immortality. As in the *Metaphysics* he takes contemplation as the highest human activity, most productive of happiness (*eudaimonia* – flourishing) and akin to the divine.

> Whether it be itself also divine or only the most divine element in us, the activity of this in accordance with its proper virtue will be perfect happiness . . . this activity is contemplative.
>
> (*Nichomachean Ethics* X.vii.1177a)

It is self-sufficient (though it requires leisure and adequate provision of material necessities) and it is loved for its own sake. Aristotle acknowledges that such a life of blessed contemplation seems beyond human reach:

> But such a life would be too high for man; for it is not in so far as he is man that he will live so, but in so far as something divine is present in him; and by so much as this is superior to our composite nature is its activity superior to that which is the exercise of the other kind of virtue. If reason is divine, then, in comparison with man, the life according to it is divine in comparison with human life.
>
> (1177b)

From this we might have expected Aristotle to veer away from contemplation as an ideal for human life. He is, after all, supremely a thinker who places things neatly into categories arranged in hierarchies where each thing must be understood in its proper place; and he repeatedly insists that people are neither beasts nor gods. Our place in the scheme of things, and hence our function, will therefore be unique to ourselves as rational mortals. Suprisingly, however, in this passage Aristotle draws a different conclusion. Immediately following from what I just quoted, he says,

> But we must not follow those who advise us, being men, to think of human things, and, being mortal, of mortal things, but must, so far as we can, make ourselves immortal, and strain every nerve to live in accordance with the best thing in us. . . . And that which is proper to each thing is best and most

pleasant for each thing; for man, therefore, the life according to reason is best and pleasantest, since reason more than anything else *is* man.

(Ibid.)

Thus for all Aristotle's emphasis on this world and this life, in passages like these his ideal is immortality. In this life the nearest we come to immortality is the life of reason, or more particularly, the life of contemplation. Reason in this sense is self-sufficient, detached, unchanging and divine. It is mastery: to know is to dominate (*De Anima* 429a). Aristotle never supposes that we can achieve this ideal; he quickly remembers our bodily needs, our weakness of will, our finitude. Nevertheless, read in this way (as he regularly is, by commentators from Ross (1930) to MacIntyre (1988)) Aristotle in these passages presents an ideal for humanity – or at least for privileged males – that once again 'strains every nerve' to make ourselves immortal. Whether or not he believed that immortality was an actual possibility after death (and mostly it seems he did not) immortality remains the focus of the ideal life.

This is so in spite of the fact that the bulk of Aristotle's work is on the phenomena of this world, on the physics, biology, politics and psychology that he could observe and classify. The difference is so striking that the discussion of contemplation, especially linked to immortality as an ideal, could be thought to be an anomaly. Martha Nussbaum argues in fact, that 'there is incompatibility here, not just difference of emphasis' (1986: 375), and thinks that it is likely that the passage in which these comments occur, *Nichomachean Ethics* X.vi–viii, were inserted by someone else into Aristotle's work, perhaps extracted from some of Aristotle's earlier writings (377), when he was much more under the influence of Plato. They might even be a forgery, she suggests. Whatever the case, Nussbaum argues that these chapters on immortality as an ideal of reason 'represent a line of thought that Aristotle elsewhere vigorously attacks' (377).

I am, however, not persuaded by Nussbaum's rejection of the ideal of immortality and contemplation as uncharacteristic of Aristotle. Although it is true that his focus is primarily on this world and on flourishing within it, his persistent strategy, as we have seen, is to arrange and classify things by what he perceives as their essence, and thus to arrange them in hierarchies. It would be congruent with his normal procedure, therefore, to see reason or mind as the essence of the human, and to place the divine in the hierarchy of living beings above the human. That human beings should strive toward a god-like existence, which is immortal, is thus unsurprising in his system, even though he repeatedly emphazises that we are *not* gods. And if we do so strive, it will be with that which Aristotle sees to be most god-like in us, our capacity for contemplation. Though it is arguable that Aristotle held that we would never attain that for which we strive, would never become divine or even immortal, this is not incompatible with immortality as the ideal to which we should 'strain every nerve'.

Moreover, whereas Nussbaum asserts that *Nichomachean Ethics* X.vi–viii where this ideal of immortality is discussed, is at variance with Aristotle's other writings,

I doubt whether this is so. As is clear in the *De Anima* and the *Metaphysics*, Aristotle regularly presented the whole spectrum of a hierarchy, whether of soul or of substance, and placed the rational and the divine at the top. That he should do so again in the *Ethics* is therefore consistent with his pattern, not an anomaly. Émile Bréhier, arguing this point, makes specific reference to the passage in question, and says,

> Just as in his theory of substance Aristotle first defined substance as a general notion, including in its extension a multitude of different substances, and then passed from this general notion to that of an individual substance, God, who is pre-eminently substance, so in his ethics he passes by a very similar rhythm from the general notion of virtue, considered as the common term of human virtues, ethical and intellectual, to a virtue which is pre-eminently virtue, a virtue transcending human virtues, a divine virtue, which is the faculty of intellectual contemplation (X.vi–viii) . . . It is, therefore, the life of what is truly divine in man, the only life which men may share with the gods.
>
> (Bréhier 1963: I.227)

As Bréhier understands Aristotle, there is no major discrepancy in his thought, which forms a systematic whole, with the final chapter of the *Nichomachean Ethics* as its crown.

The fault line

Rather than arbitrate between the views of Nussbaum and Bréhier, I suggest that we can discern in relation to the question of immortality the same sort of pattern that was discussed above in relation to tragedy. Just as Aristotle seemed to have a much more open and tolerant view of tragedy than did Plato, so also he seems to offer a world view that is not preoccupied with death but rather concerns itself with human flourishing. Yet closer investigation shows that only certain sorts of tragedy are deemed good, namely those which turn away from external violence and war, and focus instead on an individual hero. Similarly, in Aristotle's view not just any sort of flourishing will do. What counts as flourishing is above all the sort of life whose focus is contemplation. It is a life that rises above worries about daily living, and does not concern itself with evil social structures and their oppressive consequences. Rather, it is a life shared with the gods. Its ideal is god-like immortality.

There is thus a fault line running through Aristotle that resonates through the western cultural symbolic's genealogy of death. On the one hand he can be read, as Nussbaum does, as turning away from the focus on death which had taken up the attention of earlier thinkers. What is important is how to live, how to flourish. Death is the event that terminates life, and receives appropriate attention as a reality that must be faced; but death is not what gives meaning to life and it is not a goal. Reading Aristotle on this side of the fault line, it is possible to use his writings as a resource for an alternative imaginary, an imaginary that takes natality rather than mortality as central, that pursues life and what makes for flourishing, not death, as the locus of meaning.

Yet reading Aristotle on this side of the fault line quickly comes up against barriers. The sort of flourishing that Aristotle talks about is available only to the privileged few: relatively wealthy males living in a situation where choices are open to them. In *Nichomachean Ethics* III, for example, where Aristotle is defining and cataloguing the virtues, he emphasizes such things as temperance as contrasted with self-indulgence, liberality with money rather than meanness, appropriate pride and ambition rather than false humility: these are the sorts of ethical issues which arise only for the privileged. Those who are hungry and poor do not have to struggle with vices of self-indulgence; the slaves of Athens would not have room for pride. Yet Aristotle writes as though he is propounding universals; as though his ethical ideals and definitions are universally true. Even when he writes about justice, his discussion concerns itself with justice between equally privileged males, citizens of the *polis*: the justice of a husband to wife, or father to children, or master to slaves is justice only in an analogous sense, 'for there can be no injustice in the unqualified sense towards things that are one's own', like 'chattel' or children (*Nichomachean Ethics* V.vi.1134b). The question of whether a social system might itself be unjust could never arise if one began from Aristotle's assumptions. To the extent that Aristotle's focus is on this life, it is on this life as experienced by privileged males like himself.

Even then, as we have seen, ultimately Aristotle moves to the other side of the fault line. The ultimate good, even for the privileged male, is contemplation with its ideal of immortality. The male mind considers itself god-like, above ordinary earthly life. We should not forget that Aristotle's comments on contemplation and immortality as the ideal of human life are a very small part of a large body of writing, most of which is firmly centred on this world and its workings. Yet repeatedly he indicates that it is the goal, the *telos* of all the rest. It is not surprising that, read on this side of the fault line, Aristotle's emphasis on contemplation could be taken as having close affinities with Plato's goal of immortality.

As we shall see in subsequent chapters, writers in late antiquity such as Porphyry and Plotinus tried to interpret Aristotle's work as compatible with Plato, distorting both of them in the process. Aristotle's passages on reason and contemplation as the highest good for humanity, and the striving through reason for immortality, are the parts of his work most easily made to fit a Platonic world view. Once this Platonism was taken up (and again reshaped) by christendom, moreover, the desire for godliness and immortality became even more emphatic. Most of the writings of Aristotle were lost to the Latin west until the twelfth and thirteenth centuries, except for parts of his works on logic, translated by Boethius who was again sympathetic to Platonism. So also were many of the Muslim scholars, through whose commentaries and translations Aristotle eventually became available to the west (Peters 1968). Thus by the time Albert the Great and Thomas Aquinas made a point of taking up Aristotle into Christian philosophy, it was an Aristotle thoroughly saturated with Augustinian Platonism. The scholasticism against which humanists of the Renaissance protested, though regularly identified with Aristotelianism, was also therefore mixed with doctrines derived from Platonic and Christian sources, not least in relation to death and immortality (Schmitt 1983).

It is obviously unacceptable to read Aristotle as though he were nearly a scholastic philosopher, living before christendom. Nevertheless, as Aristotle was transmitted and taken up, 'contaminated' with Christian Platonism as it might have been, one of the effects on the western symbolic was a reinforcement of the ideal of reason as self-sufficient, masculine, immutable and god-like. Ultimately it is by contemplation that men come near the divine; it is the mind that is immortal. In the genealogy of the western symbolic of death, Aristotle was appropriated (whatever he himself might have thought of it) for a focus on immortality through contemplation. This world and its violence, its wars and its oppressions, could be forgotten as the philosopher soared above it to eternity.

Meanwhile, Rome had conquered the world.

Part III

Eternal Rome?

Introduction

Rising up forty metres from the ground, Trajan's Column presides over the ruins of ancient Rome's Imperial Forums. Even today it is a magnificent sight. Its entire surface is covered with a continuous sculpted frieze that spirals from bottom to top. There are more than 2,500 human figures in the carving, many of them mounted on warhorses, modelled in a series of exquisitely detailed scenes of a Roman military campaign. The figures are about two-thirds life size, and are engaged in all sorts of activities: holding council, engaged in battle, collecting food, bringing in a spy, capturing slaves and, at the top, celebrating a great martial victory. The Emperor Trajan is always depicted as a calm, heroic, commanding presence, ensuring that all is done well. Above the frieze, topping the column, is a huge bronze statue. Today it is a statue of St Peter, but originally it was Trajan himself, the victorious Emperor under whose direction the Roman Empire reached its greatest extent.

Trajan was Emperor from 98–117 CE, and was arguably one of the greatest rulers in the history of Rome (Grant 1979: 236–8; Hornblower and Spawforth 1998: 739–42). By the time he came to power Rome had passed through the troubled period of civil war following the collapse of the Republic, and the Empire had been enormously enlarged. Its slaves, taxes and tribute money brought prosperity to Rome and paid for its huge army, which in Trajan's time was enlarged to thirty legions (about 180,000 men) besides large numbers of auxiliaries (Anderson 1987: 89–106). The Column itself was erected to commemorate Trajan's victory over the Dacian kingdom beyond the Danube. The vast wealth brought to Rome's treasury from this conquest paid for large-scale public works including the Column; and the scenes of its sculpted frieze are a continuous narrative of the Dacian War (Janson 1969: 144–6; Rossi 1971; Lepper and Frere 1988).

Citizens of Imperial Rome might have felt enormous pride and security looking at Trajan's Column. That pride would only have increased if they had entered it and climbed the spiral stairs – 185 steps cut in marble – to emerge on to the viewing platform. From there, the splendour of the city would be spread out before them. On either side were the Latin and Greek Libraries, symbols of Roman culture. Immediately in front of the column was the Ulpian Basilica, its gilded bronze roof tiles blazing. Just beyond was Trajan's Forum, and then the Forums of

Caesar, Nerva and Augustus: these were busy markets and financial centres. The ancient Roman Forum filled with temples, monuments and markets was only a little further away. The Colosseum, which could accommodate audiences of 50,000 people, could also be seen: Trajan had celebrated his victory over the Dacians by spectacles in the Colosseum involving 10,000 gladiators and 11,000 wild animals.

Yet the Column, this huge symbol of military triumph and proud imperialism, was also a tomb. The base of the Column was a burial chamber for Trajan's ashes. Descending the spiral steps inside the celebration of Imperial Progress, the visitor must come back to earth and to the reality that all men, even Roman Emperors, are mortal. Trajan's Column is simultaneously a recognition and a denial of his own mortality. Like a Homeric epic in stone it immortalizes his glorious deeds; yet it holds his last remains like any ordinary grave.

The genealogy of death in the Roman Empire is superbly symbolized by this Column. It is a masculinist preoccupation with mortality: it celebrates the infliction of death while holding the ashes of the man who led the slaughter. The thousands of human figures are virtually all depictions of male warriors, the victors and the vanquished: the only women are slaves who have been captured by Roman might and are led in triumphal procession. The phallic symbolism of the Column is obvious. So is its celebration of violence.

Moreover, in the exquisitely detailed carvings of the Column there is also apparent a particular understanding of beauty, an aesthetic representation of lavish expenditure of money and time. Sculpture by the time of Trajan had taken up a narrative form; the spirals of the Column can be read as though they were a scroll, on which is inscribed a story in figures rather than in words (Wheeler 1964: 175–8). The intricacy and beauty of the carving is made to proclaim the central message of the invincibility of the Emperor and hence of the Empire which he epitomizes. Beauty, creativity, was pressed into the celebration of violent imperialism.

The century inaugurated by the rule of Trajan is often taken as the height of the Roman Empire: Edward Gibbon called it 'the golden age', the 'period in the history of the world during which the condition of the human race was most happy and prosperous' (Gibbon 1960: 1). For the upper classes in Rome and her vast Empire there is much to be said in favour of Gibbon's observation. There was political stability and economic prosperity, as money and material flowed into Rome from the territories she had conquered (Bauckham 1991: 58–76). Rome itself was a city of grandeur and opulence, its buildings and public works proclaiming its place as head of the Empire and setting a standard both for public buildings and private residences that was emulated across the Empire (Griffin 1991; Huskinson 2000a). For the elite there was a high standard of learning, with deep roots in Greek culture. Along with literacy, the arts flourished. Life was comfortable. Even for those on the edges of Empire, from Africa to Britain, it is arguable that 'the Roman Empire offered more than it demanded', at least in terms of its material and cultural contributions to the quality of life (Branigan 1991: 95).

There were certainly those, like the Jews, who revolted against Roman rule, and Christians who were persecuted by it. Yet many Jews, among them the philosopher Philo, and Josephus the historian, made their peace with Rome and prospered (Goodman 1991; Williams 2000); and Christians were able to grow in numbers, prosperity and influence until early in the fourth century they were poised to take their place as the religion of the Empire (Brown 1987; 1971; Clark 1991).

Reflection on Trajan's Column, however, shows that such flourishing was at best the prerogative not of the 'human race' but of the upper-class Roman citizen. As if in enactment of Aristotle, flourishing did not include slaves, or the vast underclass who supported the prosperity of the wealthy. It included women only if they were wives or daughters of privileged men, and then only if the men chose to treat them well. It was built on military conquest and sustained by oppression; and its favourite entertainment was gladiatorial spectacles of violent killing in the Colosseum and the amphitheatres that were built in many of the Empire's chief cities. It was preoccupied with death.

From earliest times Rome was premised on violence and grew up under the sign of Mars, the God of War. According to its founding myth, it was Mars who raped a Vestal Virgin (custodian of the shrine of Vesta, goddess of the hearth), in consequence of which she bore twins, Romulus and Remus. The king ordered the twins to be disposed of, but they were rescued and suckled by a she-wolf and grew up to be valiant men. Romulus founded Rome, killed his brother for transgressing its boundaries, and procured wives for the men of his new city by stealing women from the Sabines (a neighbouring tribe) before turning into a god. Whatever credence the Romans gave to this story, it is a founding myth that valorizes gendered violence and lends support to those who see war as the chief business of Rome.

The Roman Empire was based on the army, and thus premised upon the willingness of ordinary men to kill and to die. From the time of the unification of Italy at the beginning of the third century BCE until the collapse of the western empire with the sack of Rome in 455 CE, Roman soldiers marched across North Africa and Western Europe. About one quarter of all male citizens were, in ordinary times, involved with the army, most of them as soldiers and the rest in trades that directly serviced the military. Length of service varied, but for extended periods of the Empire a standard period of service was twenty-five years in the professional army. During the Republican period this figure was higher. It has been estimated that 30–60 per cent of male citizens between 225 and 223 BCE were serving in the army or were veterans (Hopkins 1978: 31–6). Thus military culture was central to Roman values and to its whole way of life and death (Anderson 1987; Watson 1987; Webster 1998). Romans were expected to be proud of their fatherland; and to be proud of Rome was to be proud of the army.

Pride was not the only reason for maintaining a military culture. There were also important economic considerations. Roman citizens were exempt from direct taxation, as also was the agricultural land of the Italian peninsula. Moreover those who lived in Rome were supplied with free corn, and at least for some periods, also with oil and pork (Finley 1973: 40, 170–1; Grant 1979: 212–13): this practice was intended to help the poor, though it was applied without means testing and many wealthy people also benefited (much to the disgust of moralists). But the wealthy expected other sorts of benefits as well: the taxation, tribute and booty appropriated from the conquered peoples fed the coffers of Rome to the further enrichment of the wealthy. Leading citizens showed their greatness by undertaking vast building projects and public works, or by mounting lavish games or spectacles in the Circus or, later, the Colosseum. All this had to be paid for, as, of course, did the army itself. It was therefore necessary to maintain an army sufficient to enlarge the Empire and to keep the territories thus subjected to Roman rule properly pacified so that the tribute and taxation of the provinces kept up a steady financial flow to Rome. It was of course far more efficient if the provinces could be brought to pay their taxes 'voluntarily': to become puppet kingdoms under a *Pax Romana*. In that way they would contribute not only to Roman coffers but to the Roman army as well, sending cohorts of their own young men to the frontiers of the Empire, and receiving financial benefit in their turn. The economic stability of the Roman Empire was thus entangled with its military culture and its implicit commitment to violence.

The tribute exacted from conquered territories was not only financial but also human. The economy of Rome and of Italy more generally (as well as of other cities of the Roman Empire) was built upon the slave trade. Slaves were necessary for Italian agriculture; and in the cities they were used for everything from the most menial domestic tasks to positions of influence such as educators and doctors. Keith Bradley has estimated that at the end of the first century BCE slaves represented 33–40 per cent of the population of the Roman heartland (Bradley 1994: 30). Some of the slave population was maintained by breeding: the children of slaves were the property (and sometimes the offspring) of their mother's master. Nevertheless continual external replenishment was necessary. Bradley has calculated that 'from about 65 BC to about 30 BC 100,000 new slaves were needed each year in Italy and that from about 50 BC to AD 150 more than 500,000 new slaves were needed every year for the empire as a whole' (32).[1] The main source of new slaves was conquest. When a city or area was taken, mass enslavement followed; and although not all of the slaves necessarily went to Rome, very large numbers did; 'the connection between warfare and slavery at Rome was never broken' (33). This is not to say that all slaves were treated with violence. After all, since they were a major source of labour it would be in the interests of their owners to treat them at least as well as cattle. Moreover the practice of manumission was widespread. Nevertheless most slaves were never set free; and 'the abuse of slaves was undeniably a permanent feature of the slavery system in the Roman heartland' (Bradley 1998: 81). In addition to slaves intended for labour, there was also a huge demand for captives and prisoners for games and spectacles, not to mention the wild beasts which Roman citizens loved to watch fighting gladiators or each other. I shall say more about these spectacles in a later chapter. The point here is twofold: military violence was necessary to keep up the steady supply of slaves, captives and wild animals; and the domestic economy, built upon such military booty, reproduced violence on the homefront.

There was a further reason for the continuation and expansion of the military culture which had to do with the expectations of the army itself. From the time of the Republic, veterans upon demobilization were customarily given a grant of land – an 'allotment' – and came to expect and even demand it. Agricultural land near Rome and in the Italian heartland quickly became unavailable, partly because the very wealthy owned vast estates (Finley 1973: 80–1). It therefore became customary for veterans to receive land grants in the provinces: land was appropriated in Spain, Gaul, North Africa, and even Britain for villas for retired Roman military personnel. Slaves were used to work the land; sometimes captives were retained by senior army personnel precisely for this purpose rather than being sold in the markets or transported to Rome. All this meant that the army had to be large and powerful enough over centuries to keep extending its control and ensuring the pacification of subjected territories, so that land and slaves, as well as tribute and tax money, would continue to be supplied. Indeed it has been argued that the eventual collapse of the Roman Empire in the west came about when this economic situation could no longer be sustained: the army could not be further enlarged because of the escalating costs in money and land; and once the army declined the whole system moved inexorably to collapse (Finley 1973: 176).[2] For the duration of the Roman Empire the military and its wars and violence were 'part of the fabric of society, on a par with earthquakes, droughts, destructive storms and slavery' (Hornblower and Spawforth 1996: 1619).

The Roman story stretches over centuries and across enormous territory; the preoccupation with death is neither static nor uniform. In this part I shall trace some of the contours of that preoccupation, showing differences from the Greek and Hellenistic world examined in the last part, and also shifts that took place from the late Republic to the high imperial era, and finally to the early signs of the fracture of the western empire in the third century CE. Lucretius' anxiety to dismiss the fear of death as a bogeyman to frighten children gives place to Cicero's emphasis on the 'manly man', a construction of gender well suited to a society dependent upon military valour. The *Pax Augusta*, while representing itself as a golden age, was built on violence and slavery; its monuments exalt violence while its poets subvert its pretensions. But what is a man of integrity to do if he is in a position of influence in a despotic regime? The example of Seneca shows a shift to individualism and a stoic attitude to death as release from intolerable situations. Yet at the same time, the gladiatorial displays and spectacles of death were escalating right across the Empire; and although, as I shall argue, these spectacles were not an aberration but an accurate symbol of Roman preoccupation with gendered death, they also offered a context of radical dissent, as shown by the pagan and Christian martyrs. In the final chapter of this part I shall discuss Plotinus' resolute turn to a world beyond death as the Empire began to crumble around him, a world whose eternal beauty is reflected in the eyes of iconic portraits and the light from beyond in Byzantine windows or glittering mosaics. I shall leave to the next volume a fuller discussion of necrophilia in early Christianity, even though it falls both chronologically and geographically within the Roman Empire. As in the previous part, I have chosen topics and vignettes that particularly illuminate the shifting symbolic interweavings of violence, gender and beauty: I have made no attempt to write a political or cultural history of the Roman world.

It is a commonplace that, as Michael Grant puts it, 'we ourselves, whether we like it or not, are Rome's heirs' (Grant 1979: 1). The influence of Rome is so pervasive that we hardly notice it: indeed it has formed the identity of western culture. 'The majority of Europeans [and North Americans] still live by some form of Roman law. Many speak a dialect of Latin. We write in the letters of the Roman alphabet' (Edwards 1999a: 18). Though Christianity was sometimes in tension with Rome, it was also shaped by Rome; the christendom that structured the west symbolically as well as geographically and politically is unthinkable without its Roman formation. The renaissance is so named to indicate the rebirth of the culture of classical antiquity, and gained its impetus from a rediscovery of Greek and Roman texts (Cronin 1967; Hale 2000); the enlightenment of the eighteenth century was a deliberate attempt to construct secular modernity after the pattern of pagan Rome (Gay 1977). Behind Shakespeare is Seneca; behind Milton is Vergil; behind Locke and Hume is Cicero. The architecture of public buildings in Europe and North America is modelled on classical styles, and virtually every aspect of western culture from rhetoric to music and from sculpture to philosophy rests on a classical foundation (Jenkyns 1992; Vance 1997; Edwards 1999b). Indeed for centuries education itself was equated with a grounding in Latin language and literature: the writings of Rome literally shaped the thinking of educated people in the western world (Newsome 1961; Stray 1992; Marchand 1996), and a privileged young man's education was regularly completed with a 'Grand Tour' (Black 1997). So pervasive is the conscious and unconscious shaping of our thoughts by Roman influence that Sigmund Freud found Rome an appropriate analogy for the human mind and a model for understanding psychoanalysis (Freud 1985: 257–8).

Perhaps nowhere is the influence of Rome greater than in the political structures of modernity. The classical ideals of humanism, liberty and democracy were rediscovered and reformulated during the renaissance and became the rhetoric and sometimes the reality of European states and their offshoots (Skinner 1978). The French Revolution looked back to the Roman Republic, taking for its hero Brutus who assassinated Julius Caesar rather than submit to tyranny; similarly the United States of America modelled itself on Republican Rome, drawing up its constitution and political structures in conscious imitation, even taking the Roman eagle as its national symbol (Vance 1989; Richard 1994). Often, however, it was not the Republic but the Empire that was the paradigm. Napoleon modelled himself on Caesar Augustus and his empire on that of Rome; he even set up the Vendôme column in Paris as a celebration of his triumph in deliberate echo of Trajan: when Napoleon was defeated Nelson's column was duly erected in Trafalgar Square (Huet 1999). British animosity to Napoleon was of course intertwined with Britain's own burgeoning empire, for which again the Roman Empire provided the model (Lucas 1912; Betts 1971; James 1994). Young British men, educated in Latin language and literature, went to every corner of the world to paint the map red: British activity in India in particular was often thought of in direct parallel to the Roman Empire (Bryce 1914; Metcalf 1994; Majeed 1999). Even now, whatever the actual motivation for war and conquest, even when it is quite blatantly conducted for purposes of political and economic dominance, the rhetoric of freedom, democracy and the spread of civilized values is still used to justify military violence in western modernity.

> In a thousand different ways, the Romans are permanently and indestruc- tibly woven into the fabric of our own existences. They lived through many events and developments which resembled, prefigured and caused what has happened, is happening, and may happen in the future to our own communities and our own selves.
>
> (Grant 1979: 1)

This being so, how does the Roman assumption of military dominance and its preoccupation with violent death impact upon the western symbolic and its genealogy of death? Although many aspects of the influence of Rome have been extensively studied, little attention has been paid to Roman attitudes to the links between death, violence and gender, let alone to their enduring effects in western thought and action. How is beauty displaced or appropriated to serve the ends of violence? Above all, how can we discern the hitherto 'silent voices' in Roman society (of the conquered, or of minorities within the mainstream culture such as women and children)' (Huskinson 2000a: 2), voices of dissent who characterize death, life and beauty otherwise? These are the questions that set the framework for this part.

Chapter 13

Anxiety about nothing(ness)

Lucretius and the fear of death

O Julius Caesar, thou art mighty yet!
Thy spirit walks abroad, and turns our swords
In our own proper entrails.
(Shakespeare *Julius Caesar* V iii; 1980: 856)

Thus speaks Shakespeare's Brutus upon finding the body of Cassius; he quickly joins Cassius in suicide rather than be taken by an army avenging the assassination of Julius Caesar. In Shakespeare as in the writings of Cicero, Brutus is depicted as honourable, choosing to kill Caesar not out of personal motives of spite or desire for power or wealth but because he believed that only by Caesar's death could the ancient values of the Republic be restored. The assassination of Caesar is presented as the violent culmination of a period of intense anxiety; the intention of his murderers was peace, order and the restoration of freedom.

But it was not to be. Caesar's army led by Mark Antony and Lepidus, together with his chosen heir Octavian defeated the forces of Brutus and Cassius; and in 31 BCE Octavian (now called Caesar Augustus) became sole ruler of the Roman Empire. From that point on, emperors were in effect dictators, even though some, especially Augustus, made a great show of respect for the Senate and of attempting to restore the morals and values of the Republic.

It was prudent for him to do so. Romans of the first century BCE were proud of the Republic and what it stood for. They had devised a system of government whereby their rulers were elected by the citizens and accountable to them in a complex hierarchy of senior offices of state. There were checks and balances so that no one could become too powerful; and a well-developed code of law. And yet even during the centuries that this democratic system was gaining ground, rival violent structures were growing up that would undermine the much vaunted peaceable values of the Republic. There was huge economic disparity between the elite and the large underclass upon which it rested. Moreover the whole society was dependent upon slaves, often procured as prisoners of war or through piracy or brigandage. Above all, Roman society was a vast military complex, which conquered and maintained an empire by means of continuous war, and which naturalized violence in the thinking and the activity of Romans in all ranks of society. These structures of violence were in increasing tension with the ostensible values and the system of government of the Republic, so that by the first century BCE it was becoming apparent that radical change was essential.

In this chapter I shall discuss one response to the enormous anxiety generated by this escalating tension, that of the philosopher-poet Lucretius who argued that anxiety about death was as pointless and unnecessary as children's fear of the dark. But what darkness did Lucretius himself fear? I shall argue that his account of the fear of death as anxiety about nothing(ness) betrays deep and unresolved worries; and that these worries were tangled with anxieties about gender and female sexuality. Lucretius' book *On the Nature of Things* is too often discussed without reference to its political context; but I suggest that the anxiety it bespeaks and its situation in a genealogy of death are more easily understood when set against the background of its time.

A world disordered

Lucretius was born in 94 BCE. It was the beginning of a troubled time, during which the fabric of the Roman order was unravelling; the troubles would culminate with the assassination of Julius Caesar and the end of the Republic. During Lucretius' youth Rome was engaged simultaneously in civil and in foreign war, both of which shocked Roman society with their unprecedented brutality. Moreover the generals of these wars, Sulla and Cinna respectively, were bitter political rivals who engaged in reprisals and 'by far the bloodiest civilian massacres that Rome had ever experienced' (Grant 1979: 159). The various components of Republican government, instead of acting as checks and balances, became implacably opposed to one another so that government was effectively at a stalemate.

The situation was made all the more difficult by the social turbulence relating to land distribution. Roman and Italian farmers were required for prolonged military service; and much land was appropriated in their absence by the elite, and worked by war captives and slaves. Returning veterans, however, demanded land; but although efforts were made towards land reform they were blocked by vested interests. The result was that if a general was perceived to have their welfare at heart, soldiers and veterans would give to him (rather than to Rome itself) their personal loyalty. Rome was convulsed by a series of military crises such as the conspiracy of Cataline in 63 BCE, and the demands of Pompey and his army, returning to Rome in 62 after a major victory over Mithradates. The situation would eventually be resolved by one man assuming total power: first Julius Caesar and then Augustus. During Lucretius' lifetime, however, this was still in the future. Powerful men were jockeying for position, and the settled comfortable life of the elite in the middle and late Republic was under severe threat.

To compound the problems, starting in 73 BCE a slave revolt broke out. There had been slave wars before, including two in Sicily in the previous century; but this revolt began in Capua and over the next two years affected much of the Italian peninsula and threatened Rome itself. It was led by Spartacus, a slave-gladiator; and at its height may have involved as many as 70,000 rebels. The revolt was eventually put down, though with considerable difficulty. Crassus, the victorious general, was utterly ruthless. 'Six thousand captives were crucified along the Via Appia from Capua to Rome' (Bradley 1998: 98). Although the insurrection was over, the fact that it occurred and the brutality with which it ended was a permanent lesson to slaves and masters alike: everyone knew that it could happen again and that once it started, slaves would have nothing to gain by restraint. Roman citizens were not safe in their beds. In such a setting, it is hardly surprising that fear and anxiety should grip the minds of many, as it did that of Lucretius.

Lucretius' On the Nature of The Universe (1951), completed in about 55 BCE, has at its centre the anxiety of death. In order to deal with that anxiety, Lucretius drew upon and developed the teachings of Epicurus, a Greek philosopher who lived in Athens in the fourth century BCE. In modern times the sentiments most likely to be associated with Epicurus are expressed in the words, 'Let us eat, drink and be merry, for tomorrow we may die': even the term 'Epicurean' connotes an abandonment to bodily pleasures. But this misrepresents Epicurus. It was not he, but his enemies, who treated his philosophy as though it were unbridled hedonism. Epicurus himself said something very different.

> What constitutes an agreeable life is not drinking, possessing women, or eating at sumptuous tables; it is rather sober thought which discovers the causes of all desire and all aversion and which drives away opinions that disturb souls.
>
> (Cited in Bréhier 1965: 71)

The most pleasurable context for Epicurus, and the one which best facilitated such 'sober thought' was the context of friendship. Even by the standards of antiquity, Epicurus gave friendship a very high significance (Rist 1972: 127); he was known for his choice of a quiet retired life in his house and garden in Athens, where he and his friends conversed together.

Among the things which most 'disturb souls', in Epicurus' view, is the fear of death. His physical philosophy, which was a variant of the atomism of Democritus, was intended to alleviate that disturbance: if we really understood the composition of the universe we would see that death is no cause for dread. It is this idea that Lucretius took up as a way to resolve his own anxieties. He thought it so wonderful that he called Epicurus a god: 'a god indeed . . . who by his art rescued life from such a stormy sea, so black a night, and steered it into such a calm and sun-lit haven' (Lucretius 1951: 171). Whereas Epicurus had also discussed pleasure, friendship and logic, Lucretius' whole focus is on death – the death of the individual, the death of a civilization or a city through warfare or plague, even the death of the world as we know it – and it is to cope with that anxiety that he appropriates such aspects of Epicurus' teaching as are useful to him (Clay 1983; Segal 1990).

Anxiety pervades his poem. Lucretius is ostensibly writing to promote peace and calm; and yet his poem contains horrific scenes of violence, death, dying and the decomposition of corpses. His 'diatribe against the fear of death' (Wallach 1976) offers a rational explanation intended to remove such fear; but the vividness of his writing ensures that at an emotional level those fears are at least as likely to be raised as to be resolved. From a psychoanalytic perspective his philosophical activity could be interpreted as anything but an expression of tranquillity: as I shall argue, it reads more like repression of unbearable dread. The necrophilia that lurks in Lucretius' rationality is a significant step in the gendered genealogy of death in the western symbolic.

To see this, it is first necessary to examine what Lucretius offers as a rational explanation. Lucretius accepts a materialist account of the origin and nature of the world. The ultimate constituents of reality are tiny atoms or seeds, impenetrable and indestructible, in motion through infinite space: 'empty space extends without limit in every direction and . . . seeds innumerable in number are rushing on countless courses through an unfathomable universe under the impulse of perpetual motion' (1951: 91). These atoms collide with one another; and in the process of time such collisions result in the formation of bodies: first the heavenly bodies and then the earth and all that it contains, including human beings.

> Our world has been made by nature through the spontaneous and casual collision and the multifarious, accidental, random and purposeless congregation and coalescence of atoms whose suddenly formed combinations could serve on each occasion as the starting-point of substantial fabrics – earth and sea and sky and the races of living creatures.
>
> (91)

The objects and creatures that are formed in this way have the potential for growth and development as atoms are attracted each to their own kind. This is 'the natal season of the world, the birthday of sea and lands and the uprising of the sun' until everything 'is brought to its utmost limit of growth' (93).

It cannot remain there, however. Once it has reached its peak, it begins an inexorable decline. As for an individual, so for the world itself, 'the strength and vigour of maturity is gradually broken, and age slides down the path of decay' (93).

> It is natural, therefore, that everything should perish when it is thinned out by the ebbing of matter and succumbs to blows from without. . . . In this way the ramparts of the great world also will be breached and collapse in crumbling ruin about us. Already it is far past its prime . . .
>
> (94)

and Lucretius gives as evidence for this his observation that huge beasts are no longer brought forth from the earth, nor the abundance of food that could once be gathered. Even farming, he says, is much more difficult than it used to be!

There are two main points to Lucretius' resolutely materialist account of the world. The first is that the gods have nothing to do with it. The universe was not created by the gods, and they do not intervene in it: 'nature . . . runs the universe by herself without the aid of the gods' (92). Neither should the world itself be thought of as divine or as having a soul: 'in fact, the earth is and always has been an insentient being' (79). Lucretius in no way denies the existence of the gods. On the contrary, he takes them for granted. It is just that they have nothing whatever to do with the world and its inhabitants.

> For it is essential to the very nature of deity that it should enjoy immortal existence in utter tranquillity, aloof and detached from our affairs. It is free from all pain and peril, strong in its own resources, exempt from any need of us, indifferent to our merits and immune from anger.
>
> (79)

This picture of divinity owes more to Aristotle's idea of the Unmoved Mover than to the Homeric pantheon. Elsewhere, Lucretius seems to accept the Olympic gods (they have bodies (56), they live contentedly in cloudless habitations in the sky (96)); but the idea that they are in any way involved in the world and its workings is 'sheer nonsense' (176).

The second main point and indeed the focus of his whole poem, is that we, too, are composed of atoms. Like anything else, therefore, we too will die; but that death is only the dissolution of the particles out of which we are made in the first place. The universe is in constant conflict between generation and destruction.

> The war of the elements that has raged throughout eternity continues on equal terms. Now here, now there, the forces of life are victorious and in turn vanquished. With the voice of mourning mingles the cry that infants raise when their eyes open on the sunlit world. Never has day given place to night or night to dawn that has not heard, blent with these infant wailings, the lamentation that attends on death and sombre obsequies.
>
> (77)

From the moment of fertilization, the embryo which will become a new human being grows by accretion of atoms. Our bodies are simply a particular configuration of atoms.

The same is also true, Lucretius holds, of our mind or spirit: 'it is of very fine texture and composed of exceptionally minute particles' (101). The mind or spirit is not some other form or substance that could pre-exist the body, as some of Plato's dialogues teach; neither could it continue after the death of the body. Rather, the somewhat coarser atoms that compose the body contain the flimsier atoms of the mind or spirit, which grows and develops with the growth of the body (116). But once the body dies, the spirit can no longer be contained, just as a broken vessel no longer contains liquid, which runs out and dissipates in all directions.

Spirit is similarly dispelled and vanishes far more speedily and is sooner dissolved into its component atoms once it has been let loose from the human frame. When the body, which served as a vessel for it, is by some means broken and attenuated by loss of blood from the veins, so as to be no longer able to contain it, how can you suppose that it can be contained by any kind of air, which must be far more tenuous than our bodily frame?

(109)

The spirit is unable to hold itself together without the containing structure of the body. Once it leaks out of the body, it 'scatters into the air' (108) and is no more. But conversely, the body also depended on the spirit. Like a vessel whose contents are drained away, a body whose spirit has escaped collapses into itself and in turn disintegrates 'in a foul stench'.

That explains why the body is transformed and collapses so utterly into decay: its inmost foundations are sapped by the effusion of the spirit through the limbs and through all the body's winding channels and chinks.

(113)

Death is nothing to us

As far as Lucretius is concerned, this is wonderful news. It means that after death there is no more existence; hence there is nothing to fear, no matter what happens.

So, when we shall be no more – when the union of body and spirit that engenders us has been disrupted – to us, who shall then be nothing, nothing by any hazard will happen any more at all. Nothing will have power to stir our senses, not though earth be fused with sea and sea with sky.

(121)

It is like a very deep sleep 'prolonged to eternity'. No-one in a deep sleep is upset about what is going on in the world or even what is happening to themselves.

Death, therefore, must be regarded, so far as we are concerned, as having much less existence than sleep. . . . For death is followed by a far greater dispersal of the seething mass of matter: once that icy breach in life has intervened, there is no more waking.

(124)

Time after time Lucretius insists on the point that if death is understood as extinction then there is no need to distress ourselves about it. He points out that we are not troubled by the fact that before we were born aeons passed in which we did not exist: why then should we be troubled that we will not exist for the ages of the future (125)? He draws his reader's attention to the uncertainties of life – maybe living longer would only bring suffering or ill fortune – and to the inevitability of death. Even if one could stave off death for awhile, 'the time of not-being will be no less for him who made an end of life with yesterday's daylight than for him who perished many a moon and many a year before' (129). So why struggle? Why be afraid? Nothing is gained by it.

Best of all, however, is that there is no need to fear Hell. Once Lucretius has seen that we are composed of atoms and that we cannot survive physical death, then he reports that although he still saw the habitations of the gods, 'nowhere do I see the halls of Hell' (96). It is freedom from this prospect which calls forth his strongest emotional response: 'at this I am seized with a divine delight, and a shuddering awe' (96). Indeed it is the fear of Hell above all others with which he wants to contend, and that provides his motivation for writing his book:

> In so doing I shall drive out neck and crop that fear of Hell which blasts the life of man from its very foundations, sullying everything with the blackness of death and leaving no pleasure pure and unalloyed.
>
> (97)

Lucretius acknowledges that many people deny this fear; but he argues that such denial is not to be believed. Repeatedly he returns to his theme that fear of Hell or of torment after death is 'groundless terror' even though 'there really are mortals oppressed by unfounded fear of the gods and trembling at the impending doom that may fall upon any of them' (126). By receiving his good news, this fear can be resolved.

> If the future holds travail and anguish in store, the self must be in existence, when that time comes, in order to experience it. But from this fate we are redeemed by death, which denies existence to the self that might have suffered these tribulations. Rest assured, therefore, that we have nothing to fear in death. One who no longer is cannot suffer, or differ in any way from one who has never been born, when once this mortal life has been usurped by death the immortal.
>
> (122)

Lucretius thus presents his teaching as liberation. The one who follows it will be released from fear of death, because once it is properly grasped that death is extinction then such fears will be dissipated as surely as the spirit itself is dissipated like a cloud of smoke when the body no longer contains it.

So, at least, he would have his readers believe. But is he convincing? Would his readers – even supposing that they accepted Lucretius' physics and agreed that death is extinction – have stopped dreading death? The question is all the more insistent because of the vivid presentations of death in Lucretius' poem: the process of dying and the dissolution of the corpse, the brutality of killing (especially in war), the horrors of the plague. Lucretius' accounts are so lurid that unless a reader is utterly convinced by his argument, their anxieties are at least as likely to be heightened as to be alleviated. Although there is no independent evidence, it would seem from his descriptions that he is writing from traumatic personal experience that has left deep scars.

Whose anxiety?

Can the tension between Lucretius' rejection of the fear of death and his anxiety at its manifestations be resolved? An interesting attempt has been advanced by Charles Segal in his book *Lucretius on Death and Anxiety* (1990). Segal suggests that Lucretius should be read as a therapist *avant la lettré*. Like any therapist, Lucretius is aware that deep anxieties cannot be resolved merely by rational argument. Even if the argument is entirely convincing, all it achieves is to make the patient feel foolish or guilty for their anxieties and thus repress them further. What is needed instead is to bring the anxieties out into the open, to articulate and examine them in all their most threatening detail. Only when this is done is it possible to let go of the fears and to find a healthy way forward. So Lucretius stays 'awake through the quiet of the night, studying how by choice of words and the poet's art I can display before your mind a clear light by which you can gaze into the heart of hidden things' (1951: 31). He deliberately describes in vivid detail the most gruesome forms of death and dying, so that the deepest fears are brought to consciousness rather than allowed to fester unresolved. Lucretius recognizes that many of the things we do, including grasping for wealth, property and mastery, are displaced efforts to overcome the threat of death. Thus, Segal argues,

> Lucretius invites us to read both life and the poem in a way that leads up to death as the climactic experience and the ultimate fear facing humankind. . . . By seeing how the smaller fears grow out of the fear of death, like branches from a central trunk, we gradually liberate our entire life from fear and from the violence, folly, and suffering that fear generates.
>
> (1990: 237)

By facing up to the reality of death and to the unconscious fears surrounding it we can be free to live a full and rich life, liberated from 'this dread and darkness of the mind' (Lucretius 1951: 31).

Segal's insightful reading of Lucretius brings to the fore significant dimensions of his thought, especially in relation to the ways in which greed, violence and war can be understood as displacement of an unconscious dread of death. It is not only religion, sacrifices to the gods, which Lucretius sees as attempts to ward off death: such rituals are at least out in the open and their motivations are acknowledged. Much more damaging, he says, is the 'greed and blind lust for power' which men engage in, in a displaced attempt at mastery: 'These running sores of life are fed in no small measure by the fear of death' (98). Ignominy and poverty are linked in the mind with misery and death; and therefore

> from such a fate men revolt in groundless terror and long to escape far, far away. So in their greed of gain they amass a fortune out of civil bloodshed: piling wealth on wealth, they heap carnage on carnage.
>
> (98)

Thus violence and warfare, with all the suffering and death they entail, are generated by unconscious dread: the irony is that the fear of death itself causes death. Lucretius takes this to its bitter extreme:

> Often from fear of death mortals are gripped by such a hate of living and looking on the light that with anguished hearts they do themselves to death.
>
> (98)

This is not the courageous suicide of the manly man who chooses active killing (though it be killing of himself) rather than passive dying; it is rather the despairing action of a desperately fearful person who 'forgets that this very fear is the fountainhead of their troubles' (98).

Surely by now our suspicions should be raised. Is it really the case that people 'often' commit suicide out of fear of death? With the possible exception of people suffering from severe psychic disorder (for whom therefore the careful rational argument of Lucretius' book would hardly be helpful) this claim seems as implausible for late antiquity as it does for the present, and there is no evidence to support it. Suicide was acceptable and even admired in certain circumstances, as I shall discuss later, but hardly as an escape from fear of death.[1] Lucretius sees clearly the violent social effects of unresolved fear of death; but by pushing it as far as he does, we may begin to wonder whether he himself is free from the obsession.

> As children in blank darkness tremble and start at everything, so we in broad daylight are oppressed at times by fears as baseless as those horrors which children imagine coming upon them in the dark.
>
> (98)

Is Lucretius the therapist? Or is he in fact the patient?

The questions gain strength when we reconsider Lucretius' emphasis on the fear of Hell, which he insists underlies much of the fear of death. When we look at actual beliefs about death in the late Republic, and at the rituals involved in funerals and mourning, they do not bear out Lucretius' claim. There was little belief in hell as a place of torment, such as we find in later christendom. As we shall see in more detail later, funeral rituals were more concerned to honour the deceased in relation to the continuing living community than to emphasize any post-mortem fate. Scholars are clear that 'the Romans were not sure of survival after death, and the dead played no central role within organized religious belief'

(Walker 1985: 13; cf Veyne 1987: 219). Once a year the Romans had a 'feast of the dead' in which they commemorated deceased loved ones and left offerings of food on their graves; but as Paul Veyne comments, 'they no more believed that the dead ate these offerings than we believe that the dead admire or smell the flowers that we place on their graves' (Veyne 1987: 220).

It is true that the common people probably took beliefs about after-life and the efficacy of ritual somewhat more literally than did the cultivated classes. In the second century CE Lucian wrote a series of essays in which he mocked their credulity: here is part of his dialogue between Charon (lord of the underworld), and his helper Hermes. Charon begins by expressing surprise at some common burial rituals:

CHARON: Why, they are putting flowers on the stones, and pouring costly essences upon them! . . . Look: there is a splendid banquet laid out, and they are . . . pouring wine and mead . . . What does it all mean?

HERMES: What satisfaction it affords to their friends in Hades, I am unable to say. But the idea is that the shades come up and get as close as they can, and feed upon the savoury steam of the meat and drink the mead in the trench.

CHARON: Eat and drink when their skulls are dry bones? Oh, fools and block-heads! You little know how we arrange matters, and what a gulf is set betwixt the living and the dead!

                          (Lucian, cited in Davies 1999: 132, slightly adapted)

Even in such sharp ridicule, however, there is no suggestion of any intense fear of Hell or Hades on the part of common people, let alone those of Lucian's own social class. The evidence simply does not bear out Lucretius' claim when he insists that central to the fear of death is the fear of Hell. Whose fears, really, was he expressing? Perhaps his own?

By contrast, what people really did fear, then as always, was the possibility of long or intense suffering: not death so much as the process of dying. For this fear Lucretius' philosophy supplies no effective remedy. The assurance that death is extinction is at best a reassurance that the suffering will end, but it hardly eliminates anxiety at its prospect. In fact, Lucretius' vivid portrayal of the process of dying is at least as likely to heighten that anxiety as to alleviate it. He describes in detail the physical misery and mental disorientation of terminal illness, and the lurid symptoms of imminent death (1951: 110–13). It is hard to see how this could serve as a therapeutic articulation of unconscious fears: for most people these fears are not unconscious; and even if they were, Lucretius offers nothing that will resolve them. Since they cannot be dismissed as groundless, detailed rehearsal of them is unlikely to be therapeutic.

The other common dread of death is the fear of extinction, and with it the sense of the impending multiple loss that death brings. The dying person may well grieve that she or he will not see their children growing up, will never know what happens to the world or to the things and people in it for whom they care. Here again Lucretius' remedies fail to help. He insists that once one is dead, one is dead forever, so there is no point struggling to postpone it. This, however, will carry little comfort to someone who longs to see a child grow up or a friend surmount a problem. Moreover the 'reassurance' that death is complete annihilation is unlikely to help someone for whom annihilation is precisely what they dread. The therapy – if such is what is intended – does not heal, and Lucretius might have been expected to realize it.

Instead, Lucretius piles detail upon detail in scenes of death and carnage. Besides his stage-by-stage account of the process of dying, he also gives a lurid description of death in warfare: the blood, the toes still twitching on a foot that has been hacked off, the madness and the agony of killing and dying (1951: 115–18). Lucretius ends his book with a graphic account of the plague, and again gives descriptions of the symptoms of the suffering and death of its victims detailed enough to give any reader nightmares. He believes that such plague results from an imbalance in the atmosphere: humans can do nothing to prevent it, and it could strike at any time. Again, the account is more likely to generate alarm than to defuse it. And there the book ends.

I suggest, therefore, that if Lucretius did think that he was bringing fears to consciousness in order to face them and deal with them, his efforts are not completely successful. In fact, his book reads more as though his own half-conscious fears keep coming to the surface, fears for which his philosophy of death as extinction provides at best only a partial remedy.

They must not wriggle

Now, how is this anxiety and its expression to be understood? The violent context of first-century BCE Rome, I have suggested, offers a partial explanation: anxiety was an entirely justified response when the fabric of society was crumbling. But there is a further aspect of Lucretius' thought that bears on his anxiety about death. Scholars have not interested themselves in questions of gender; but I suggest that when gender issues are raised then the idea of unconscious fears can be seen in a different light. Moreover, it also becomes clear how Lucretius' anxieties are critical in the continuing genealogy of death.

It is, as usual, the throw-away remarks which indicate the underlying attitude. Early in his book, where Lucretius first makes reference to Epicurus, he speaks of him as one who refused to be crushed by superstition, fables, or thunder and lightning. 'Rather, they quickened his manhood so that he, first of all men, longed to smash the constraining locks of nature's doors' (1951: 29). But what would cause Lucretius to think that the awakening of virility leads immediately to a desire for violence, for 'smashing nature's doors'? 'Nature' is of course conventionally female, and regularly so in Lucretius: she is 'the creatress and perfectress' (93). What unacknowledged violent fantasies are at work here?

Suspicions are intensified when we consider what Lucretius says in his chapter on reproduction. For this, he grants that sex is necessary; but Lucretius describes it as warfare, 'fighting at close quarters' (163). He warns his reader never to get caught up in a 'grand passion', since this is likely to cause more unhappiness than pleasure. Sexual longing is like insanity, and its physical expression is 'goaded by an underlying impulse to hurt' the one who gives rise to the desire (164). Really? Why – and for whom – might this be so? Is this fantasy of sexuality as violence unique to Lucretius, or is it more widespread in Roman society? And how does it connect with his philosophy of death?

Lucretius' description of sexual activity is as graphic and detailed as is his account of dying. He represents it as 'raging fever', as utter frustration only briefly interrupted by moments of rapture, and all too likely to lead to a life of sloth, bitterness and regret. While this is what the men – poor, self-deluded creatures – are feeling, the women, in the meantime, are as likely as not to be scheming, unsightly, foul-smelling traps (166–7). There is nothing here about love, tenderness, or friendship between people who care for one another. After a lengthy misogynist account of passionate liaisons, Lucretius does eventually settle down to a more matter of fact statement of marital sex. This, however, is singularly lacking in passion. Above all 'wives have no need of lascivious movements'; women are not to 'wriggle' (170). Reproduction, not enjoyment, is what sex within marriage is about.

The woman is to be passive, while the man is active. In sexuality as elsewhere, violent fantasies prevail. The active man is the one who kills rather than the one who is defeated; he fights; his impulse is to hurt. Whether or not this is an accurate description of Roman masculinity especially as expressed in private life may be open to question. What is clear, however, is that such an ideology cannot but lead to a fear of death – the ultimate passivity – that is the undoing of the manliest of men. If Lucretius is right in his linkage of ideas, then masculine activities, especially masculine sexuality, will be linked with violence; he is astute in his insight that greed, cruelty and war may then often be displaced fears of death. But for Lucretius, the fear of death as a threat to virility is linked to a fear of women. That linkage remained unexamined in his writing, repressed as the fears of death are repressed for others. In the genealogy of death, that repression, and indeed that linkage of women with death while the manly man was linked with violence and war, would have lasting consequences. It is time to look more closely at the Roman construction of gender which made those links seem natural.

Chapter 14

'If we wish to be men': Roman constructions of gender

'If we wish to be men . . .'

In Cicero's famous *Tusculan Disputations*, written in 44 BCE, Cicero argues that the very word 'virtue' is derived from the word for 'man' (*vir*). Thus 'if we wish to be men' it is necessary to pursue '*virtus*': the word is usually translated into English as 'virtue' or 'manliness' or even 'courage' (Cicero 1971: 74–6; cf Skinner 1978: 87). The truly 'manly man' is the man who has come to possess *virtus*, whose chief characteristic is active control or power, as we shall see in a moment.

Cicero was born in 106 BCE, and was a contemporary of Lucretius, whom he outlived. Like Lucretius, therefore, he lived through the turbulent period of social and political unrest of the first half of the century. But whereas there is no record of Lucretius ever being personally involved in politics, Cicero was in the thick of it from the start. He rose through the political hierarchy until he achieved the highest office, that of consul, in 63; but it was to be a mixed blessing. On Cicero's personal responsibility five men accused of conspiracy were executed without trial; and although Cicero always protested that he had acted to save Rome, the legality and morality of his hasty violence were open to challenge and made him some permanent enemies.

Cicero was a conservative at heart, wanting to save the Republic; but time after time he compromised in the prolonged and convoluted struggle between Pompey and Julius Caesar. Although in the end he sided against Caesar in the Civil War, he was willing to accept pardon from Caesar and to participate again in the Senate. Given his record of vacillation, it is not surprising that Cicero was left out of the conspiracy to murder Caesar. Nevertheless, Cicero was publicly delighted at Caesar's assassination, and hoped for a reinstatement of the Republic. When the army of Mark Antony and Octavian (later Augustus) defeated the forces led by the assassins Brutus and Cassius, Cicero was condemned even though he had made overtures to Octavian, misjudging his intentions. He tried to escape by sea; but he was caught and died in 43 BCE (Everitt 2001).

Cicero was a gifted orator and rhetoritician; and his speeches and writings were enormously influential. For Cicero, the greatness of the Republic could be summed up in the idea of manliness: his writings frequently revert to the themes of manliness and virtue. Cicero was much more concerned to promote manliness than to develop an internally consistent philosophical system as Lucretius did, and was happy to draw on a range of writings that were actually in tension with one another to make his case. Epicureanism, Stoicism, Neopythagoreanism and Neoplatonism jostled with one another in the Hellenistic and Roman period. Cicero used all of them when they suited his purpose, just as he sided (at least in appearance) now with one political faction and then another.

It is obvious that for Cicero manliness is not innate, not an automatic characteristic of someone who happens to be anatomically male. In this he reflects Latin usage. There are in Latin two nouns which are both translated as 'man': *vir* and *homo*. *Homo* is usually used as a generic term or in contexts that belittle or demean; *vir* is used for aristocratic men, or to give praise. Although there are exceptions, 'the *vir* is of higher status than the *homo* and it is the *vir* with whom we should identify the ideal man' (Alston 1998: 206). But if a man is not automatically to be called *vir*, if the ideal manliness is something he must strive for, it is nevertheless the case that it is men who strive for manliness. Unless one had the right anatomical equipment, one could hardly aspire to the ideal of manliness.[1]

How, then, is manliness to be achieved? What are its characteristics? As Cicero presents it, the truly manly man is the man who is 'safe, secure, inconquerable, impregnable: a man whose fears are not just insignificant but non-existent' (1971: 74). He is a man who is completely self-sufficient. 'A man who lacks the absolute certainty that everything depends on himself and himself alone is in no condition to hold his head high' (75). A manly man is an autonomous man, one whose liberty is not threatened: a slave would not be a *vir*; nor would a man who was financially or legally in someone else's power. Cicero's political compromises that made him dependent upon Caesar, seen in this light, humiliatingly undermine his manliness.

Putting the idea the other way around, a *vir* was a man of power, *potestas*. He could wield *potestas* himself: over slaves, over lower classes, and over his household. Roman private life rested on the *pater potestas*, the father whose power over his own household was absolute. A Roman man's paternal authority extended even over his adult sons: if he chose to, he could have them beaten, though this might be seen as outrageous. Moreover, whatever a man's social status, and whether or not anyone else referred to him as a *vir* rather than a *homo*, his wife could be expected to do so: in her eyes he must be seen as a man of honour. His title as *vir* was a reflection of his patriarchal power over his household, and was always backed by the possibility of legitimate use of violence.

Even though Cicero was executed, his ideas about manliness were shared by Augustus. In Augustus' view the emperor was to be regarded as the *vir* with the greatest *potestas*. Thus in 2 BC Augustus declared himself father of the country, *pater patria* of the Empire: it was a move that connoted fatherly concern for all its citizens, but also ultimate authority over them. But if the emperor was indubitably *vir*, the status of the soldier was more ambiguous. In battle he had power over others, the power to kill; yet he was always under the power of his commanding officer to whom he owed unquestioning obedience. Throughout the Republic, the virtue of courage was strongly associated with the life of the soldier: 'militarism, masculinity and morality are inseparable in Roman thought' (Braund 2002: 83). Gradually, however, as the imperial army was increasingly recruited from poorer elements of society and from the conquered provinces, soldiers were not seen as *vir*; they were rustics rather than the ideal of civilized masculinity (Alston 1998: 211). Nevertheless the ideal continued to place power, *potestas*, as central to manliness.

The opposite of manliness in the Roman thought reflected by Cicero was *mollitia*, effeminacy. Cicero in his speeches often accused his enemies of effeminacy, behaving like a woman: it was an accusation intended to belittle or humiliate. But what did 'behaving like a woman' entail? Fundamentally, it meant the opposite of having active power, the power of manliness, and having instead to submit oneself to another. At its root is a conception of gender and sex roles which we have already seen in Lucretius: the male is the active, dominant partner and the female is passive and submissive. When men engaged in homosexual relations, male slaves could be used to gratify their masters; but for a free man to accept a 'passive' role – to submit to anal penetration – was considered shameful. When Cicero accused an opponent of effeminacy, he regularly linked the ideas of the feminine, the servile, and the sexually passive: Such a person could not be a *vir*, a manly man worthy of respect (Edwards 1993: 68–78).

This is not to say that Cicero was necessarily accusing his enemy of actual homosexual behaviour. Rather, with penetrative sex thought of as 'stabbing', being penetrated could be a metaphor for many kinds of passive or servile behaviour that might be far removed from actual sex; indeed even men who were notoriously sexually involved with women might be called effeminate if they allowed themselves to become emotionally 'enslaved', or if they manifested behaviour that was not regarded as showing manly courage and independence. The manliness Cicero looked back to was that which displayed Republican values. At the end of his life, with the Republic in tatters, he grieved that 'the real Rome has gone forever' (Cicero 1971: 135). Sophisticated and educated men of the upper classes behaved and dressed in ways which were now considered elegant but which men like Cicero regarded as effeminate. Thus, for example, Plutarch attributes to Cicero perplexity about Julius Caesar. On the one hand, he believed that

> he could detect in everything that Caesar planned or undertook in politics a purpose that was aiming at absolute power. 'On the other hand,' he said, 'when I notice how carefully arranged his hair is and when I watch him adjusting the parting with one finger, I cannot imagine that this man could conceive of such a wicked thing as to destroy the Roman constitution.'
>
> (Plutarch 1972: 247)

How could such an effeminate man have the manliness, the power, to become an effective leader of a revolution? For Cicero, these were not compatible. Events were to prove him wrong.

Now, this contrast of *vir* and *mollitia*, the manly and the effeminate, has a direct bearing on the genealogy of death. To penetrate, to stab, whether with the penis or the sword, was the act of a man. To be penetrated was womanly. Putting it another way, to kill was manly; to die was womanly; unless of course one died fighting, stabbing in return. It was shameful in war to die with one's back to the enemy; on the other hand to be a courageous warrior was manly indeed. Cicero himself did not like the military; but on his own terms it was far more manly to inflict death than to suffer it. To be manly meant to be powerful, in control, not subject to penetration or required to submit.

Manliness and suicide

The shift in the genealogy of death comes out clearly in the way in which suicide came to be understood. Suicide was nothing new, of course. We have seen how the Greek tragedians presented suicide as an awful but understandable response to impossible circumstances: Sophocles' Jocasta hangs herself when she discovers that Oedipus is both her husband and her son; Ajax falls on his sword when he finds that he has dishonoured himself by slaughtering a herd of cattle in a fit of madness. It is impossible to say whether the actual frequency of suicide was higher in the late Republic and the Empire than it had been in fifth- to fourth-century Athens, or whether it was simply given higher prominence. What is significant is its construction: suicide comes to be seen as a manner of death which enabled a person to retain virtue – manly control and autonomy – as they took the violently active role in their own death rather than passively submitting to events. Thus in Rome, suicide – especially suicide using a sword (as contrasted with drowning or hanging) – could be the most manly of all acts, the active contempt of death.

In the writings of Cicero this construction of suicide is prominent. As we have seen, Cicero emphasized autonomous power as central to manly virtue. But Cicero was perfectly well aware that not everything is actually in anyone's control. Not even the most powerful man can escape pain, disease and death; fate or bad luck can bring the highest man low. Cicero has a twofold response, derived from a mixture of ideas from Epicurean and Stoic philosophies. First, he argues that the truly manly man can retain his power no matter what happens, because the greatest power he has is over his own passions and feelings. Thus whatever he has to face, he will never feel fear. Even if he is tortured on the rack (Cicero refers to torture often enough to prompt questions) he will be tranquil and even happy.

> Happiness . . . will not tremble, however much it is tortured. Clinging stead-fastly to its integrity, its self-control and above all its courage, with all the strength of character and endurance that the word implies, happiness will not flinch even when the countenance of the executioner is revealed. While

the virtues, one and all, move fearlessly onwards to suffer the torments of the rack, happiness . . . will scorn to linger behind.

(1971: 95)

Cicero proceeds to consider a range of disasters that could happen to anyone: poverty, loss of fame and glory, exile, blindness or deafness. None of these, he says, can disturb the tranquillity of the man whose passions are firmly under his own control.

Then Cicero asks what would happen if 'all these afflictions are simultaneously heaped on one and the same individual'; moreover 'that they are greatly prolonged, and inflict agonies' beyond what anyone could be expected to endure.

In that case, why, for God's sake, should we continue to suffer? After all, there is a haven close at hand. I refer to the eternal refuge of death – where nothing is felt any longer.

(114)

Suicide may be the best and most courageous way to deal with intolerable physical pain or sorrow. If a situation is unendurable, then 'whatever assaults fortune may launch against you, if you are unable to face them, there is nothing to prevent you from running away' (115). Such 'running away' is not the cowardly act that it might seem. On the contrary, it is the assertion of ultimate autonomy. Though one cannot always avoid disaster, a truly manly man stays in control because he retains the ultimate weapon. He can always commit suicide. In this way he rejects womanly passivity and exercises violent control even over his own death. Though he dies, he is the one who stabs, the one who penetrates.

Suicide as political resistance

The evils of which Cicero wrote were not abstract. He himself had been exiled, had lost wealth and property, and had been in public disgrace in the tumultuous period preceding the Civil War. Though he was reinstated, he had plenty of reason not to suppose that all this was behind him or that he himself would never have to make the ultimate choice. Indeed one could argue that he had already made that choice several times, and not in a way that reflected well upon his own standards of manliness: he had chosen to compromise rather than to accept death as the price of resistance. Moreover his letters to his friend Atticus during his period of exile and loss of honour are full of complaints, anger and vituperation; they are not exactly models of a man whose passions are fully under control.

In spite of this (or maybe because of it) Cicero continued to think about manliness and suicide as political resistance. After all, he might again be called upon to make the choice (as indeed he was, and tried to run away). In whatever way Cicero's own behaviour should be interpreted, his writings are very clear. Choosing to die rather than to betray ones principles was not passive acceptance;

it was actively taking violence into ones own hands. No despot could deprive a manly man of this last courageous exercise of freedom. In the *Tusculan Disputations* immediately after Cicero has made the point discussed above that for a true *vir* 'everything depends on himself and himself alone', he gives an example:

> When Philip of Macedon sent a letter to the Spartans threatening to prevent them from acting in the way they wished to, they wrote back and asked if he proposed also to prevent them from dying!
>
> (75)

In Cicero's eyes this was cause for great admiration.

Cicero's most important presentation of suicide as a manly form of political resistance is in his pamphlet on Cato. Cato the Younger was a contemporary of Cicero, and was embroiled in the turbulence of Julius Caesar consolidating his power, an effort on Caesar's part which eventually brought him into conflict with his old ally Pompey. Cato sided with Pompey in a conspiracy against Caesar. The conspiracy was defeated. Whether out of magnanimity or political strategy, Caesar offered to pardon Cato. But Cato spurned the pardon and committed suicide instead.

By those who opposed the absolutism of Caesar, Cato was held up as a martyr for old Roman constitutionalism and the virtues of the Republic. As Cicero presents him, Cato is a model of true manliness, who keeps his destiny in his own control and reserves for himself the right to die by his own hand. Caesar was furious at this representation of Cato, with its implication that it was Cato rather than Caesar who was the more manly man. He wrote a hostile reply in a pamphlet called *Anticato*. In his anger, however, he overplayed his hand and readers reacted in just the opposite way to what he intended. Cato became more famous than ever; and more to the point for our purposes, the idea of suicide as a manly form of political resistance gained ground.

Cicero compares Cato's suicide to Socrates' death in Athens in 399 BCE. Just as Socrates had chosen prison even though he was offered a way of escape, and just as he had drunk the hemlock cheerfully without being forced to do so, so also Cato had chosen to die rather than to accept life on Caesar's terms. In both cases death was preferable to betraying their principles. Cato could have accepted Caesar's pardon just as Socrates could have made his escape, but in both cases this would be a retreat from the Republican virtues by which they had lived. It would be more courageous, more manly, to hold true to those virtues and remain in control of their death than to passively submit to the conditions of life laid down by a tyrant. Thus, as Ramsey MacMullen puts it, 'Cato was made the equal of Socrates. Together they had sanctified suicide, and schoolboys could recite set pieces on "Cato and the Contempt of Death"'(1967: 5).

In fact, Cicero's representation of Socrates is one-sided, to say the least. Although Socrates in Plato's *Phaedo* argues that death is to be welcomed rather than feared, because the soul has thereby been released from the body which had impeded its search for truth, he does not see this as an argument for suicide. Quite the contrary. Socrates argues that suicide is wrong. He refers to an 'allegory', as he calls it, 'that we men are put in a sort of guard post, from which one must not release oneself or run away' (*Phaedo* 62b): it is the old argument that represents suicide as an act of desertion or cowardice rather than facing duty and danger like a man. Moreover, Socrates argues that 'the gods are our keepers, and we men are one of their possessions'; the gods therefore would be angry and punish us if we destroyed ourselves before they gave permission. In consequence 'we must not put an end to ourselves until God sends some compulsion like the one which we are facing now' (62c).

In Cicero's view, Cato did indeed face a 'compulsion' very similar to that of Socrates. True, he was not imprisoned nor was he about to be executed; but the integrity of his virtue was threatened just as Socrates' had been. Their motives therefore were the same. If the motive for suicide was not fear or retreat from duty but rather retention of dignity and autonomy in an impossible situation, then it was acceptable and even laudable, the most manly act available. At the time of Cato this view, emphasizing motive, was not yet as prevalent as it would become in later Stoic teaching; Cicero's celebration of it in his pamphlet helped to bring it to the fore (MacMullen 1967: 4–5).

Of course the question of the legitimacy of suicide depends partly on the conception of death. Is it extinction, as Lucretius believed? Or is there some form of immortality, as Socrates had taught in the *Phaedo*? In the first book of the *Tusculan Disputations* Cicero leaves the question open. The case that death is not to be feared, he insists, can be made either way.

> For if the last day brings not extinction but change of place, what could be more desirable? But if it utterly destroys and does away with us, what better than to fall asleep in the midst of the toils of life and closing our eyes to sleep an everlasting sleep?
>
> (1985: 87)

Sometimes Cicero seems to take for granted that death is indeed the end of all sensation, an 'everlasting sleep'. Sometimes, however, he holds that death is the release of the soul into some better world of truth and beauty, much as Socrates taught in the *Phaedo*.

Thus, for example, in *The Dream of Scipio*, which was to have enormous influence through the Middle Ages, Cicero thinks of an after-life in terms of eternal reward, far better than earthly fame or glory which at best could last only for a few generations (itself a marked shift from a view of immortality as the fame accorded to a hero by an epic poem or even a monument).

> Rest assured that it is only your body that is mortal; your true self is nothing of the kind. For the man you outwardly appear to be is not yourself at all. Your real self is not that corporeal, palpable shape, but the spirit inside. *Understand*

that you are god. You have a god's capacity of aliveness and sensation and memory and foresight; a god's power to rule and govern and direct the body that is your servant, in the same way as God himself, who reigns over us, directs the entire universe. And this rule exercised by eternal God is mirrored in the dominance of your frail body by your immortal soul.

(1971: 353)

In provenance the assertion is a confident mixture of Platonism and Stoicism; but in the hands of Cicero it is turned into a statement of manliness. In life and in death a *vir* is very much like a god.

'Steel's what they crave'

What about women? If men aspire to manliness, active power and autonomy, what should women strive for? What virtues are womanly? At a linguistic level the question is of course badly formed: *vir*tues are characteristic of *vir*, of men, not of women. But that does not mean that there were no qualities for which women were particularly praised, no constructions of female gender.

Those who wrote about women, and hence those who provide the literary sources for the construction of femininity, were men. As Alison Sharrock has observed,

It is very difficult to come to a sense of Roman constructions of femininity that do not tell us more about masculine attitudes to the Other (female, slave, foreigner) than they do about real Roman women, but since the lives of real Roman women will have been partly shaped by these masculine attitudes, such a sense is still useful.

(2002: 96)

It is useful above all as a way of seeing what Roman men thought they themselves were *not* (but what women should be). It is hardly surprising, in the light of the Greek scholarship in which many Roman writers were saturated, that to a con-siderable extent Roman literary representations of womanhood set women as opposite and inferior to men: one need only recall Pythagoras' table of opposites, or Aristotle's description of women as misbegotten males. But as Roman thought developed the concept of *vir* for manliness, so also there were, I suggest, devel-opments in the (masculine) construction of womanhood. As the manly man held power and autonomy, the womanly woman was submissive and obedient. As he was active, she was passive. And above all, as he penetrated, she was penetrated.

Now, given that men's self-representation as active regularly assimilated the penis to the sword, how would this affect the representation of women? We find an important clue in the notoriously misogynist sixth Satire of Juvenal, written in the first century CE. In this Satire Juvenal viciously mocks women who lust after gladiators. He picks out for attack 'Eppia', whom he describes as a 'senator's wife' who 'eloped with her fancy swordsman' to Egypt, abandoning husband, children and country. But what, he wonders, could she see in the man?

> Deformities marred his features – a helmet-scar, a great wen on his nose, an unpleasant discharge from one constantly weeping eye. What of it? *He was a gladiator*. That makes anyone an Adonis; that was what she chose over children, country, sister, and husband: steel's what they crave.
>
> (Juvenal *Satires* VI; 1998: 38)

Like much of the rest of this thoroughly nasty satire, Juvenal's coarse mockery barely hides his fear of women: their voracious sexuality, their power over men, their meddling in matters like poetry or rhetoric that 'are men's concern' (48), their complete lack of conscience. Even allowing for the fact that the genre of satire permitted crude lampooning, and that in his other satires Juvenal attacks men (homosexuals and foreigners, but also powerful men and courtiers), there is little to redeem the virulent hatred and fear of women, especially of women's sexuality. And one of the worst forms women's sexuality takes, in Juvenal's opinion, is infatuation with gladiators.

After all, the whole point of gladiatorial spectacles was to watch men (and wild animals) thrusting, stabbing, penetrating or resisting penetration. This was of course most obvious when the fighting was done with swords: even 'the word *gladius* – sword – was vulgarly used to mean penis' (Hopkins 1983: 22). The thrust and counterthrust of a swordfight, ending with the fatal penetration of one of the contestants, carried a heavy erotic charge. Other forms of fighting in the arena could be assimilated to this model of penetration, especially the goring or mauling by tusks, horns or claws: wild boars were often used in the arena, as were bulls, elephants, and large cats such as lions, tigers and leopards. Keith Hopkins gives examples that further identify gladiators with sexual penetration: a gladiatorial helmet shaped like a penis; a stone relief depicting a gladiator fighting a huge penis; and, puzzlingly, a bronze figurine of a gladiator trying to fend off with his sword a wild beast that grows out of his own penis (1983: 22). To please the people – to be really entertaining – sex and violence were conjoined in the spectacles of the amphitheatre. Women were regularly among the spectators. And Juvenal is anxious lest women find all this penetration rather *too* entertaining, and actually fall in love with the gladiator.

Juvenal was not alone in that anxiety. Given the social construction of gender along the axis of penetrating and being penetrated (Walters 1997), it could be expected that Roman men, voyeuristic themselves, worried that women who came to watch the spectacles might find the gladiators sexually stimulating. If to be a woman is to be one who submits willingly to penetration, then was there not a risk that women would be inordinately attracted to gladiators, masters of penetration? The trained gladiator inevitably became an object of psycho-sexual fascination: for all that he might be a slave or a barbarian and thus outside the domain of *vir*, he was a model of manliness in his courageous willingness to fight and in his physical prowess.

Moreover, such attraction as women might feel (or be feared by men to feel) would be further compounded by the custom (to us bizarre) for a new bride to have her hair parted with a sword dipped in the blood of a dead gladiator. A contemporary writer offered several interpretations:

> just as the spear had been conjoined with the body of the gladiator, so should she be with her husband; or . . . because it was a sign that she might give birth to brave men; or because by the rights of marriage a wife is subject to the commands of her husband.
>
> (Cited in Hopkins 1983: 22, n31)

Whatever the correct interpretation, if these were the ideas and fantasies surrounding gender and violence, it is not surprising that men would worry about women's responses to gladiators.

The worry was taken seriously at the highest level. The Roman historian Suetonius makes a point of listing among the reforms which Caesar Augustus introduced when he came to power that he banned women from watching athletic contests. And 'whereas men and women had hitherto always sat together, Augustus confined women to the back rows even at gladiatorial shows': they were less likely to get out of hand if they were kept at a great distance (Suetonius II.44; 1979: 80). It is of course debatable to what extent women of Rome's 'good' families actually did fraternize with gladiators or whether such laws pander to male paranoia. Nevertheless, given the construction of gender and its complicated patterns of association with violence and death, it becomes easy to see how such paranoia could arise.

Even more worrying were women who actually wanted to be gladiators themselves. Rather than submitting to being penetrated, they wanted to penetrate, to become 'men'. They took up a sword: did they think they would also grow a penis? Again, Juvenal's mockery is scathing:

> what modesty is there in some helmeted hoyden, a renegade from her sex, who adores male violence. . . . Hark how she snorts at each practice thrust, bowed down by the weight of her helmet; see the big coarse puttees wrapped round her ample hams – then wait for the laugh, when she lays her weapons aside and squats on the potty!
>
> (*Sat.* VI; 1998: 42)

It is unlikely that there actually were many female gladiators, though there were some: Suetonius includes in his negative assessment of the Emperor Domitian the comment that he 'presented many extravagant entertainments in the Colosseum . . . gladiatorial shows in which women as well as men took part' (XII.4; 1979: 301). But the very thought of female gladiators generated anxiety. At the time of Septimus Severus (193–211 CE) there was a gladiatorial contest in which women competed 'so fiercely that jokes about their conduct were also directed at other very prominent women'. This was too much; such threats to gender identity could not be tolerated. 'Because of that it was no longer permitted for any woman, whatever her origin, to fight in a gladiatorial contest' (Dio 1987: 76.16.1). Women who could penetrate would destabilize too many boundaries. If a gladiator functioned for the Roman psyche as a model of manliness, what were they to make of a female gladiator? And how could a female gladiator be an exemplar of manly virtue?

I shall return in a moment to the anxieties raised by such transgressions of gender boundaries and its implications for a genealogy of death. But it is important to remember that the vast majority of the victims of spectacles of death were not trained gladiators but captives or criminals, including political criminals (like Christians). In these groups there were large numbers of women as well as men; and the manner in which they were made to fight was calculated to heighten the erotic charge. They were stripped naked; they might be tied to a stake or even to an animal with their genitals exposed to wild beasts. There are many illustrations of such spectacles in imperial painting and sculpture. A terracotta from Roman North Africa, for example, shows a naked female victim tied to a bull, with a leopard attacking her breasts. The spectacles of such gendered violence were enormously popular; and raise disturbing questions which I shall return to in chapter 18. What sort of people would enjoy watching these defenceless victims? Who would find it attractive enough to actually want to make, own, or display a 'work of art' like this terracotta? What fantasies of gender and death are being enacted and reinforced by such scenes?[2]

Sometimes things went too far even for Roman tastes. The Christians Perpetua and Felicitas and their male companions were offered to a variety of beasts – a bear, a wild boar, a mad heifer and a leopard – finally assisted by a young gladiator. Perpetua had a nursing infant when she was arrested; Felicitas was heavily pregnant and gave birth in prison. When they were stripped and brought into the arena, 'the people were horrified, beholding in the one a tender girl, in the other a woman fresh from child-birth, with milk dripping from her breasts' (Musarillo 1972: xx). If their condition was intended to titillate, it seems to have had the opposite effect. The spectators were sympathetic and demanded that the women be given clothes: this done, the show continued until all the Christians in the arena had been killed.[3]

The threat posed to (male) Roman identity by women who transgressed gender roles went very deep; and the issue of female gladiators raised that threat inescapably. As is the nature of popular entertainments, spectacles of death both reflected gender assumptions and inculcated them more deeply. As Jonathan Walters argues,

> The pattern that emerges is of a social pyramid. At the apex are the small class of *viri*, true men, adult Roman citizens in good standing, the impenetrable penetrators. Just below them are sets of people – freeborn male youths and

respectable women – who are potentially penetrable because they are not, or not yet, men, but who are defined (because of their family connections with respectable Roman men) as inviolable, and therefore under the protection of the law. Below them, on the lowest slopes of the pyramid, are those, whether male or female, who are . . . sexually penetrable.

(1997: 41)

These latter would include male and female slaves who might be bought specifically for sexual purposes, non-citizens, courtesans and prostitutes. Thus 'a sexual protocol that proclaims itself to be about gender-appropriate behaviour turns out to be part of a wider pattern of social status, where the violability or inviolability of the body is a privileged marker of such status' (ibid.). In such a context women who desired gladiators, or worst of all women who wanted to be gladiators, were not just harmless eccentrics. By their transgression of sexual roles they posed a threat to the social pyramid itself.

Important as this is in relation to gender construction, I suggest that it is equally important for the genealogy of death. The nature of the anxieties raised by female gladiators reveal a shift from Greek configurations of death to something distinctly Roman: the centrality of active violence. I have already argued that this was a significant component of a revised understanding of suicide: the man who commits suicide retains power and autonomy and is not penetrated by anyone else. I now suggest that the idea of manly mastery of death goes well beyond this construction of suicide to a much more fundamental symbolic of violence and gender.

As we have seen in previous chapters, in Greek thought women were metonymically linked with death, whether as the beautiful Helen of Troy who 'caused' the Trojan War, or the seductive and treacherous creatures of the sea in the *Odyssey*, or the passive, misbegotten male of Plato and Aristotle who could reproduce only mortal bodies, not immortal, god-like souls. The male hero conquered woman/death: he defeated Troy, or tricked the Sirens, or refused the reproduction of the body in order to gaze upon immortal truth.

In Roman thought in the late Republic and the Empire, the passive–active distinction is retained as a demarcation of gender. There is, however, a transposition of this distinction into a key of violence. The truly manly male was god-like in his active power, above all in his power to kill, and to kill by penetration. This power to kill, and to master by killing, so defined manliness that defeat was total disgrace; hence death was scorned, taken as preferable to the degradation of being mastered. The gladiator and the soldier were the most overt exemplars of the equation of manliness with the power to kill. Above all, the Emperor, in whose hands rested the ultimate power to kill by virtue of his command of both the army and the spectacles, was seen as god-like. Not infrequently the Emperor was actually deified. Thus for the Romans the active–passive distinction became the killing–dying distinction. It is manly to kill, womanly to die, slavish to be defeated. Men also die, of course. But a man's death is not womanly if it is not passively accepted. In contexts of violence such as military or gladiatorial battles, men were supremely active even though – indeed partly *because* – they might be killed. To embrace death actively while fighting to inflict death on others was the very opposite of effeminacy; it was the icon of manliness. There is of course a strong continuity with the Greek celebration of the beauty of youthful death; but there is also a difference: the active infliction of death has become central. Warfare abroad, suicide rather than submission, and the entertainment provided by the spectacles of death in the amphitheatres are the violent standards against which gender and death are constructed in the Roman Empire.

Real women and masculine fantasies

To what extent did actual women in the Roman Empire conform to the construction of women projected by masculinist fears and fantasies? An apparent contradiction presents itself: women were as always defined by their role as mothers, in other words as those who brought forth and nurtured new life; yet women were also defined as penetrable, where penetration was linked with violent death. Thus even though there is obviously no possibility of motherhood without sex, there is a tension between the idea of women as mothers and women as sexual beings. How was this tension resolved in practice?

One part of the solution came by a division of labour. Among the upper classes (and presumably also among the respectable people of modest station who accepted the standards of the aristocracy) girls were brought up to expect to be mothers, but also to expect that their sexual relations with their husbands would be limited to what was required for procreation. These women took on the burden of motherhood; slaves and concubines took on the burden of sexuality, and could be used or discarded by men at their pleasure. Husbands, therefore, were not to be 'uxorious'; that is, they were not to go to their wives for sexual satisfaction but only for reproduction. Wives, in their turn, were not to manifest sexual desire: Plutarch in 'Advice on Marriage' in his famous essays on morality written in the first century CE argued that (respectable) women should not be taught about love, and should not object to their husbands' use of slaves or concubines for sexual satisfaction (Plutarch 1927).

To what extent did this teaching reflect reality? It is certainly true that men commonly used slaves and concubines; but were their wives content to forego sexual pleasure? Aline Rousselle has argued that, given the perils of pregnancy and childbirth and the social ostracism attached to sexual pleasure, women would be only too pleased not to have frequent sexual relations. Girls would be brought up strictly, and married from the age of twelve or earlier; they were taught to be 'oblivious of their bodies to the point of ignoring the possibility of pleasure'.

> The constraints on their behaviour were so fully internalized, so bound up with their sense of their own value, that in my view few women were attracted by pleasure.
>
> (Rousselle 1992: 323)

While the manly man was expected to be virile, the ideal wife was to be submissive but not passionate, just as Lucretius had said.

Reality was doubtless more complicated, especially after the Augustan reforms of the first century which strongly encouraged large families. Even at the highest level the example set for women of the Empire was hardly one that signalled abstinence: Vipsania Agrippina bore nine children to Germanicus; and the wife of the emperor Marcus Aurelius had thirteen. Women therefore had to cope with mixed messages. On the one hand, passionate sexual desire was a cause for male anxiety; yet on the other hand women were encouraged to bear children for the empire. Women – wives – were thus situated ambivalently between life and death. As submissive and penetrated, they were, symbolically, in the place of passivity and death; yet by that very submission they were the bringers of new life.

Some thinkers tackled the problem head on. The Stoic philosopher Musonius Rufus, who wrote in the second half of the first century CE, went so far as to argue that women should be virile just as men are. Like men, women are to be virtuous; and the virtues of a good woman are no different in kind from those of a good man. Girls and boys should be educated in the virtues from the beginning. The best way to do this is for them to study philosophy, of which women are as capable as men.

> When these qualities [of virtue] have been developed, both men and women will inevitably be sensible, and the well-educated person, whether male or female, must be able to endure hardship, accustomed not to fear death, and accustomed not to be humbled by any disaster, for this is how one can become manly.
>
> (Quoted in Lefkowitz and Fant 1992: 75)

Moreover this manliness is above all to be fostered in women so that they are courageous, especially when it comes to defending themselves against rape, or protecting their young. Even hens and other birds do as much: shall women be inferior?

> The best sort of woman must be manly and cleanse herself of cowardice, so that she will not be overcome by suffering or by fear. If she cannot, how can she be chaste, if someone can compel her to endure disgrace by threatening her or torturing her? . . . How can it be that women do not need courage? That they are capable of taking up weapons, we know from the race of Amazons who fought many nations in battle.
>
> (Ibid.)

Musonius' idea that women should be virile was shared to some extent by Galen and other medical writers of the time (Rouselle 1992: 328). It completely overturns the idea that men must be active and women must be passive. What is most instructive is that it does so by attributing to women the power of the sword: like men, they have the power to fight and to kill. As radical as is Musonius' reconfiguration of gender, in this respect he retains the Roman understanding of manliness: to be a *vir*, to be virile, is to be able to inflict violent death. It is just that in his view women can do it as well as men. But to what extent was the idea of the virile woman accepted in Roman society?

The writings of Tacitus can be read as though he is confirming Musonius' theory that women can be powerful – but that this is deeply to be regretted. In the *Annals* three strong women are discussed, each of them alleged to be cruel murderesses and construed as a threat to the Empire. The first is Livia, wife of Augustus, a 'feminine bully' who 'had the aged Augustus firmly under her control' (1996: 33–4). Tacitus does nothing to dispel the 'rumour' that Livia had schemed and murdered in order to ensure that her son Tiberius would succeed Augustus as emperor: he suggests that she may even have killed Augustus. The second powerful woman whom Tacitus discusses at some length is Messalina, who became the wife of Claudius, emperor from 41 to 54 CE. She is presented as an utterly shameless adulteress, carrying out assassinations and involved in political intrigue against her husband. At last he ordered her execution. When she realized that death was inevitable she attempted to commit suicide like a man. 'Terrified, she took a dagger and put it to her throat and then her breast – but could not do it. And so the officer ran her through' (1996: 250). Tacitus has only contempt for this woman who usurped masculine power until it came to the real test and then she showed herself weak as a woman after all. The third woman he discusses is the worst of all, Agrippina the mother of Nero. She schemed and murdered to get her son to the throne, using her sexuality when it could buy favours. She then attempted to rule through him (he was only a teenager), even offering her body to him: 'her training in abomination was complete' (313). Her 'violence, inflamed by all the passions of ill-gotten tyranny' (285) is presented as utterly destructive until at last Nero broke free from her control and had her murdered.

I have no evidence that Tacitus had actually read Musonius Rufus or that he was deliberately commenting on his assessment of women. Yet if Tacitus' representation of these three women is taken in the context of Musonius' teaching, what emerges is the message that powerful women are a disaster. Women can indeed become manly, taking to themselves control over the lives and deaths of others; but when they do, no good comes of it. This message is all the stronger in the light of two further considerations. First, although all three women were unquestionably ruthless, they can each be presented in more positive terms than Tacitus chooses to use: Livia as an important co-ruler with the aging Augustus; Messalina as a helper to the sometimes feeble Claudius; and Agrippina as keeping the teenage Nero in check: it was only after her execution that his violent self-indulgence knew no bounds (Barrett 1996). Second, ruthless as these women were, their actions pale beside the violence of their husbands and sons; yet Tacitus accepts the cruelty and aggression of the men more readily than that of the women. What could not be tolerated was for a woman to take charge of national affairs in 'a rigorous, almost masculine despotism' as Tacitus says of Agrippina. Her qualities of courage, ambition and leadership, qualities which would have been praiseworthy in a man, he presents as utterly perverted (1996: 255). 'The assertive woman became identified as an immoral virago' (Arthur 1987: 102; see also McNamara 1987: 110). It is not without significance for the construction of gender and death in western culture that subsequent writers from Gibbon (1960) in the eighteenth century to Robert Graves' (1953) popularization in the twentieth have shown far less hesitation in accepting Tacitus' negative representation of women in the *Annals* than his accounts of central male figures.

In contrast to these wicked viragos who appropriated masculine roles, there are also stories of ideal women of the Roman (mythical) past, stories which every schoolchild would learn and which were part of national consciousness. One of the most famous is that of Lucretia, retold by Livy in his narrative of the early history of Rome (Livy I: 57–9; 2002: 100–3). Lucretia was the wife of a nobleman. She was left at home, as were other women, while their husbands were away on a military campaign. One evening, the worse for drink, the men argued about the relative merits of their wives; and decided to settle the quarrel by riding home and surprising the women. Some of the women were caught indulging themselves or being lazy; but Lucretia and her slaves were at their spinning. Obviously she was the ideal wife.

The story does not end there, however. Lucretia's goodness excited the lust of one of the noblemen, Prince Tarquin, and a few days later he returned and raped her, though she did all she could to resist. When he left, Lucretia summoned her husband and her father, told them the whole story, and then took a dagger and killed herself. The incident became the symbol of how royalty would overstep proper limits, and thus part of the ideology of a republican rather than a monarchical system of government. It also inscribed into the very heart of that ideology a symbol of what a woman should be: industrious and conscientious in running her husband's household, completely faithful and submissive to him alone. When Tarquin's rape violated Lucretia's fidelity to her husband she died in token of the chastity of her intention. She was an ideal woman – and a dead one: 'A dead woman became a political symbol' (Dixon 2001: 47).

Lucretia, in other words, had shown the proper extent of female virility. She was active and intelligent and managed her husband's household while he was away. She became a model for Roman women who would be industrious and perhaps well-educated and wealthy in their own right. All this was entirely respectable in the Roman Empire, so long as she was appropriately subservient to her husband. Moreover, it was also proper for a woman to show courage, even to the extent of committing suicide. Though active penetration with a sword or dagger was a manly act, women were praised for it if it was in faithful honour to their husbands. Lucretia was the model; she was emulated by actual women such as Cato's daughter after her husband Brutus was defeated in the war following the assassination of Julius Caesar.

The subordination of women, even courageous and educated women, to their husbands was thus a standard part of Roman ideology even if it was to some extent challenged by writers like Musonius Rufus. And intertwined with the construction of gender along the axis of penetrator–penetrated was a construction of killing and death, manliness and femininity. To be a man was, symbolically and often in fact, to be in the place of violence. In the next chapter I shall discuss how this gendered violence was appropriated by the Empire, and how beauty was bent to serve its purposes.

Chapter 15

Valour and gender in the *Pax Augusta*

> While Caesar is guardian of the state, neither civil war nor civil madness will drive away our peace, nor will anger beat out its swords and set city against unhappy city.
>
> (Horace *Ode* iv.15; 1997: 130)

So wrote Horace, celebrating in poem after poem the achievements of Augustus, his emperor and patron. Horace, like many of his contemporaries, was deeply impressed with Caesar Augustus. Augustus, earlier known as Octavian, was the nephew and heir of Julius Caesar, and gradually emerged as the leader, with Mark Antony, of the the forces that defeated his assassins. With Antony away in Egypt, Augustus steadily consolidated his position in Rome, and in 31 BCE at the Battle of Actium Augustus defeated Antony, incorporated Egypt into the Empire, and became in fact if not in theory sole ruler of the Roman Empire.

After the turmoil and slaughter of the preceding period, many Romans were relieved at the peace which his authority brought to Rome and the Italian heartlands. The peace was achieved by silencing all rivals, making them compliant to his will, or, if that was impossible, eliminating them by exile or execution. Augustus purged the Senate of possible dissidents and arrogated to himself supreme power by side-lining the elected Senate and curtailing the power of other officials or ensuring their subordination. Augustus always paid lip service to the ideal of the Republic and insisted that his goal was to relinquish supreme power. In practice, however, he consolidated power in his own person and effectively made himself absolute ruler over Rome itself and also over the Empire. He ensured his popularity with the people of Rome by providing food and water supplies and putting on splendid entertainments as well as effective administration. He introduced moral reforms and encouraged family life. He patronized literature and the arts; and his building programme made Rome an architectural glory so that it became known as *urbs et orbis*, the city and the world. 'Through his buildings Augustus became part of the geography of Rome' (Hope 2000: 77), and by having his image in public places, on coins, and in inscriptions he ensured that the people were reminded at every turn how much they owed to him.

What I wish to suggest in this chapter is that those achievements are closely intertwined with the ideology of gender and violence which I discussed in chapter 14. The Empire, and its alleged peace and prosperity, in fact rested on the military: the ideology of manliness was appropriated for the Empire. So also was the ideal of womanhood and respectability. Moreover art and beauty were taken over by the state and made to glorify violence. None of these things were new; all were developments of trends whose roots reach into the Republic and back to classical Athens. Yet I shall show in this chapter how under Augustus these strands of gendered violence and the appropriation of beauty were consolidated in the genealogy of death. In the next chapter I shall turn to voices of dissent who tried to resist and to celebrate life.

Pax Augusta?

Augustus assumed absolute power. Even those who saw through what he was doing and objected to his destruction of the Republic could not help but admire his tactics. Tacitus, writing some years later, described the strategies Augustus used to suppress dissent and to gain control, strategies that ranged from bribery and seduction to brute force.

> He seduced the army with bonuses, and his cheap food policy was successful bait for civilians. Indeed he attracted everybody's good will by the enjoyable gift of peace. Then, he gradually pushed ahead and absorbed the functions of the senate, the officials, and even the law. Opposition did not exist. War or judicial murder had disposed of all men of spirit. Upper-class survivors found that slavish obedience was the way to succeed, both politically and financially.
>
> (*Annals* 1.2; 1996: 32)

The tax and produce of the provinces flowed into Rome and made the life of 'upper-class survivors' even more comfortable. The elite of Rome could afford a lavish lifestyle of conspicuous consumption, provided that they did not question their consciences too closely about the loss of Republican freedoms or the price that conquered peoples had to pay for the comfort of Roman citizens.

Romans of the Augustan era saw themselves as civilized, and saw the people of the territories they conquered as barbarian. Romans considered themselves superior. They had the best political system, the highest culture, the noblest morality. They certainly had the wealth and power to impose their views. If the people they conquered had the wisdom to submit with good grace and accept Rome's terms, they could become provinces or territories of the Empire as Greece and North Africa had long been. Such provinces had considerable autonomy as long as they paid their taxes and remained loyal client states of Rome. On the other hand, any territory that rebelled or resisted could expect that Rome would use all necessary means to bring it into compliance, including massive all-engulfing force. Thus Augustan Rome was the single superpower and the self-appointed policeman of the world of late antiquity. From their own perspective Romans were bringing civilization to that world and raising its material and moral standards. As Horace saw it, Augustus was the greatest blessing that could have been given by the gods:

> A greater blessing than Caesar, the fates and kindly gods have never given to the earth, and never will give though Time should return to the Age of Gold.
>
> (*Ode* iv.2; 1997: 114)

But what did it look like from the perspective of those who were conquered?

The answer varied. When Augustus took power, Rome already controlled a vast empire; under his rule that empire was extended so greatly that it could make a plausible claim to rule the whole world. After the Battle of Actium and the defeat of Antony, Rome annexed Egypt with her enormous wealth, the resources of which helped to fund Augustus' continuing foreign campaigns. Although Rome and the Italian heartlands were at peace, Augustus' armies were fighting for new territory through much of his time as emperor: indeed his popularity at home was in part dependent on continuing victory on the frontiers.

Horace was one of several Augustan poets who sought to 'immortalize his virtues': in an *Ode* he celebrates the delight with which all the territories greet Augustus, adoring him as a god (*Ode* iv.14; 1997: 129–30).[1] Not only had Augustus conquered all these territories but he ruled them in such a way that provided they were amenable to Rome's demands, especially in taxes, they retained relative independence and enjoyed peace, stability and perhaps greater prosperity than they had known before. The *Pax Augusta* became the *Pax Romana* (Hardwick 2000: 337–50). It was intended to last forever: eternal Rome. As Aelius Aristides said in his *Address to Rome*,

> Extensive and sizeable as the Empire is, perfect policing does much more than territorial boundaries to make it great. . . . Like a well-swept and fenced-in front yard . . . the whole world speaks in unison, more distinctly than a chorus; and so well does it harmonize under this director-in-chief that it joins in praying this Empire may last for all time.
>
> (Quoted in Hardwick 2000: 349)

Such words would be music to the ears of those who sought to further Roman imperialism: many of them liked to think (and doubtless sincerely believed) that Roman rule was benevolent. Roman jurisdiction ensured peace and stability of government, economic growth and trade, and the development of culture and education and a civilized and often more prosperous way of life. Augustus pushed forward the construction of the network of roads for which Rome is still famous; and undertook massive building programmes not only in Rome but also in other cities of the Empire. Although there is an element of obvious propaganda in the assertion that Roman domination was entirely benevolent, it can hardly be doubted that not only Rome itself but also the provinces and territories of the empire benefited in many ways (Branigan 1991; Nutton 1978), though clearly the benefits would vary across different parts of the Empire.

There are obvious parallels between this 'Romanization', as it came to be called, and the globalization of culture, economics, and ideology of subsequent imperialist superpowers such as Britain in the nineteenth century or the USA in the twenty-first. In each case, some nations or peoples eagerly embrace the cultural system of the superpower and are glad to shelter under its military and political umbrella, while others are more reluctant, and still others have the system imposed on them by brute force. Moreover as recent scholarship has emphasized, considerable nuance is necessary: neither the dominant cultural system nor the peoples on whom it is imposed (or who align themselves to it voluntarily) are homogeneous. Various forms of hybridity, some of them highly creative, result (Garnsey 1978; Barrett 1997; Mattingly 1997). Moreover, those who are the chief beneficiaries of the system are most likely to have their views promulgated: dissenters face various forms of silencing ranging from ridicule to persecution.

I shall consider dissent and its cost more fully in the following chapters; noting here only that Roman historians themselves saw that more than one evaluation of the *Pax Augusta* was possible. Tacitus, for example, tried to give a balanced view. On the one hand, he says, there were those who held that Augustus' arrogation of power and his expansion of the Empire were necessary for the peace and overall good of Rome and the Empire, and that 'force had been sparingly used – merely to preserve peace for the majority' (*Annals* I.9; 1996: 38). And then Tacitus says simply, 'The opposite view went like this'; and proceeds to explain Augustus' policies not in terms of the needs of the empire but as sheer lust for power, a lust that drove him to impose his own will ever more strongly, even to the point of having himself venerated as a god. 'There had certainly been peace', says Tacitus, 'but it was a bloodstained peace' (ibid.). Tacitus does not need to say which of the two points of view he finds more compelling.

Modern historians have often disagreed with Tacitus, and have taken the *Pax Augusta* as the apex of Roman civilization, from which western culture derives some of its most significant values. Particularly from the Enlightenment onwards, Latin classics formed the basis of European education: it was therefore perhaps inevitable that modern imperialism – Prussian, Napoleonic, British and American – should use the Roman Empire as a deliberate and conscious model (Koch 1961: 67f; Vance 1989; James 1994: 99; 184f; 1997: 151f). The influence went the other way, too. It has been shown that great modern historians of the Roman Empire such as Mommsen in Germany in the nineteenth century and Haverfield in Britain in the first quarter of the twentieth accepted the ideology of benevolent imperialism prominent in Germany and Britain respectively and read it back into their studies of the Roman Empire (Haverfield 1923; Mommsen 1996; Freeman 1997).

My purpose is not to enter the scholarly debates surrounding these issues,[2] neither do I wish to deny that western culture derives many of its values from

Augustan Rome. On the contrary, it is central to my thesis that the symbolic of western modernity, its ideology and its practice, is deeply rooted in classical antiquity. This being granted, it is all the more important to investigate the central ingredients of the ideology that underpinned the *Pax Augusta*, especially in relation to violence and death, gender, and beauty, a constellation of ideas without which the *Pax Augusta* is unthinkable.

Dulce et decorum est pro patria mori

> Sweet – [beautiful] – it is and honourable to die for one's native land.
>
> (Horace *Odes* iii.2; 1997: 78)

The *Pax Augusta*, for all its reforms and its imposition of peace and its cultivation of learning, was founded on violence, killing, and preoccupation with death, sometimes repressed and sometimes bubbling in blood to the surface. In the famous lines of this *Ode*, Horace was expressing a sentiment crucial to the ideology of the Augustan empire.

In 29 BCE when Augustus came to Rome as supreme ruler, he signified the coming of peace by closing the gates of the temple of Janus, the god who presided over military operations. The symbolism proclaimed that Rome was at peace. The reality, however, was quite different. The military was almost constantly active, subduing vast areas such as Northern Spain, the Alps and central Asia Minor: the size of the empire doubled through the military operations conducted by Augustus, and was portrayed on a map by his trusted friend Agrippa as encompassing the whole world. Eternal Rome was intended to be unbounded in either time or space. And that pre-eminence rested squarely on the army.

There have been modern historians who have argued that all Rome's wars were 'accidental' or 'defensive': Rome was provoked by her neighbours and, to avert threat to herself, had to use military force. In one sense this is true. If Rome saw herself as the appropriate and legitimate ruler of the whole world, then any resistance to that hegemony would be a threat and its suppression would be in defence of her complete dominance. And it is clear that at least some of the time Rome did see herself that way. Polybius, writing of the Roman conquest of Greece in the second century BCE states matter-of-factly that

> the supremacy of the Romans did not come about . . . without the victors knowing what they were doing. On the contrary, since the Romans deliberately chose to school themselves in such great enterprises, it is quite natural that they should not only have boldly embarked upon their pursuit of universal domination, but that they should actually have achieved their purpose.
>
> (I.63; 1979: 109)

If it is taken for granted that Roman domination is the natural state of affairs, then any alternative will be a threat and all force used to maintain or extend domination can be called defensive.

Of course in *this* sense, every schoolyard bully is acting only in self-defence to preserve his dominance. If on the other hand 'defence' is used in its more normal sense of preserving Rome or her provinces from aggression or attack, then the wars of the Empire under Augustus and the vast extension of its territory could hardly be called defensive. The unwillingness of people beyond the Rhine or the Danube, half way around the known world, to be controlled by Rome could not be said to constitute a clear and present danger to Rome or its empire. Rather, Augustus' personal glory and *auctoritas* were enhanced by frequent victorious wars, especially when these wars were far away and could be presented to the Romans as having a just cause, with the honour and security of Rome at stake, and in any case as bringing civilization and all the benefits of Rome to the conquered peoples as soon as they submitted.[3]

The army was central to the Augustan empire. Augustus' reforms set the size of the army at twenty-eight legions, approximately 150,000 men, matched by about the same number of auxiliaries: the difference was that legionaries had to be Roman citizens while auxiliaries did not and were often conscripts from the provinces. The usual length of service was sixteen years, extended to twenty years in 6 CE, with a further five years in a veteran corps (Anderson 1987). The experience of the army and its assumptions of violence and killing were therefore formative of a large percentage of citizens, and its ideology permeated the so-called 'peace' of the Augustan era.

Roman soldiers were expected to be victorious or to die in the attempt: Rome was contemptuous of soldiers who were taken prisoner or who failed to achieve the goals of a battle. The Roman biographer Suetonius recounts the expectations Augustus had of his army and the means he used to achieve them, including the notorious practice of decimation. 'If a cohort broke in battle, Augustus ordered the survivors to draw lots, then executed every tenth man, and fed the remainder on barley bread instead of the customary wheat ration' (II.24; 1979: 66).

To achieve the discipline and hardness necessary to inflict or suffer death, the violence of the amphitheatre was useful. It taught people to endure or even enjoy the sight of brutality, blood and death. Those who were to enter the army could not afford to be squeamish: 'exposure to the blood and death of humans in the arena was considered a positive acculturation for citizens of this warrior nation' (Kyle 1998: 43). Gladiatorial combats could act as a 'demonstration of the power to overcome death' (Wiedemann 1992: 35), just as the army was to overcome death by victory in battle. The combats of the amphitheatre were thus a valuable aspect of military culture, training for killing and becoming inured to violence. K. Welch (1994) has argued that the spread of amphitheatres around the Roman world in the late Republic and the Augustan era was linked on the one hand to military training throughout the empire, and on the other to the interests and pleasures of veterans: having spent their lives in the service of death, violence had become essential to their entertainment. I shall return in chapter 18 to these spectacles of death; but it is already apparent that within the supposed civilization and peace of Augustus strands of violence were deeply interwoven.

Moreover, as I argued in the previous chapter, these strands were part of the symbolic of gender. To be a man was to have the power to penetrate, with the penis or the sword; thus to be a man was actively to inflict violence rather than passively to suffer it. Virtue, manliness, was expressed through military might, if necessary giving up one's life to extend or maintain the empire, *pro patria mori*. The beauty of the courageous death of young men in battle was praised in Rome as it had been in Greece. Vergil's *Aeneid*, for example, was as we saw in chapter 6 a transposition into a Roman context of some of the key themes and features of the Homeric writings, central to which was the idea of immortality conferred by glorious death in warfare. That theme was perfectly suited to the ideology of the Augustan military machine.

Vergil traced the descent of Rome – and in particular of Augustus himself – from the Trojan heroes through book after gruesome book of battle and slaughter in stories which today's reader may find as tedious and objectionable as their parallels in the *Iliad*. Eli Sagan has pointed out that

> For long stretches of the book [Sagan is referring to the *Iliad*; but the same applies to the *Aeneid*] – in fact, for most of the book – "nothing happens". Nothing, that is, except human beings killing each other. If one lacks a keen interest in this particular brand of homicide, the reading promptly becomes tedious.
>
> (1979: 6)

Yet for the Greek or Roman reader of these epics, these scenes of blood and battle were obviously anything but tedious. Violence and killing were precisely the means by which the beauty of manly heroism was depicted. In whatever way we choose to understand the emphasis on death in the epics that stand at the foundations of western culture, we must begin from the premise that Greek and Roman readers found the violence fascinating, and, as in the quotation from Horace with which this part began, death in battle was 'sweet and honourable'.

However, although the theme of the beauty of death in battle runs through both Greek and Roman literature, a major shift of emphasis takes place between the two. As we saw in chapter 5, the Homeric heroes are represented as achieving glorious immortality through their deaths, an immortality conferred by the poet's song. For the Romans, by contrast, the beauty is to die 'for one's native land'. It is not a question of brave individuals performing memorable feats, but rather of rank upon rank of disciplined soldiers carefully trained to obey orders even in the face of death. And the death of the soldier is *pro patria*, literally 'for the fatherland'. It is Rome itself, eternal Rome, whose glory and immortality are celebrated, not the immortality of the individual soldier.

The contrast should not be over-stated. Although the Homeric writings celebrate the dashing bravado of individual heroes, the city states of Greece from the fifth century to the rule of Alexander had armies comprised of the hoplite phalanx: heavy infantrymen in close-packed formation. The Spartans in particular were noted for their organization and disciplined chain of command. Although brave individuals were honoured in epic verse, the actual success of Greek armies rested on the steady obedience of troops, unnamed and unsung, fighting as a unit (Ferrill 1985). Nevertheless the recruitment and training and above all the sheer scale of the Roman army placed a new emphasis on *patria*, the fatherland. It was this, rather than the individual soldier, who was glorified; or rather, the glory of the individual was for the greater glory of Rome.

Augustus introduced reforms of morals and family law which reinforced the connections between masculinity, violence and the empire. In 2 BCE he chose to have a new title conferred on himself, *pater patriae*, father of the fatherland. In chapter 14 I discussed the paternal authority of any father over his wife, children and household; he was *pater potestas*. Augustus, by calling himself *pater patriae*, could be seen as taking to himself as much benevolent care for the fatherland and its people as any father would have for his family. Yet at the same time he was with this title asserting his absolute right to the submission of every member of the empire.

As *pater patriae*, Augustus could claim it to be his duty to guard the moral purity of women, encourage their industry, and cultivate manliness and military prowess in men. He therefore made it his business to revise old laws or enact new ones that 'dealt, among other matters, with extravagance, adultery, unchastity, bribery, and the encouragement of marriage' (Suetonius II.34; 1979: 73). Suetonius, describing these laws, admits that 'his marriage law being more rigorously framed than the others, he found himself unable to make it effective because of an open revolt against several of its clauses' (ibid.). Augustus' own daughter Julia was banished for her adulterous affairs; according to ancient historians Augustus' rage at Julia for flouting his authority in this matter was unappeasable (Dio 1987: 199; Suetonius 1979: 89), though he himself was notorious for his womanizing and in particular for his fondness for deflowering little girls.

Central to Augustus' reforms was the importance he attached to reproduction. Men and women were encouraged to marry and bear children not for reasons of abstract morality or personal fulfilment but to thwart death and achieve immortality – the immortality of eternal Rome. Dio Cassius gives a telling account of an incident illustrating the connections between gender, empire and the genealogy of death. Dio makes liberal use of his own imagination in his history, especially in the speeches he places in the mouths of his main characters; but whether the words were his or Augustus', the constellation of attitudes is revelatory of the ideology of empire. According to Dio, Augustus assembled in the Forum the knights of the equestrian order and divided them into two groups, the married and the unmarried. The former group received his lavish praise. They were, he said, the manly men, true *viri*, like those who had made Rome great and able to rule the world.

We should remember this and take consolation for what is mortal in our nature through a perpetual succession of generations, who will take up the torch like runners in a race. In this way we can with one another's help achieve immortality.

(1987: 224)

Only with a steady supply of children will Rome be able to sustain her hegemony in space and time.

> How excellent, and how imperative it is, if cities and peoples are to exist, and if you are to rule others and the rest of the world is to obey you, that there should be a flourishing race of ours; such a race as will in time of peace till the soil, sail the seas, practise the arts and pursue handicrafts, and in time of war protect what we hold with an ardour which is all the greater because of the ties of blood, and which will bring forth others to take the places of those who fall.

(225)

The unmarried, by contrast, he cannot even address as men (*viri*): they are guilty of murder by not begetting children, of sacrilege to the ancestors and the gods, and above all of treason because they are 'guilty of destroying the state by disobeying its laws, and of betraying your country by making her barren and childless' (226) so that there will not be enough men to fight for Rome and the empire. It is the duty of every citizen to marry and have children, children who in turn would be willing to die for their fatherland and thus by their own mortality ensure the continuance of eternal Rome.

It was a constellation of ideas that was replicated in subsequent empires of the western world, steeped as they were in classical civilization. British boys in the nineteenth century learned *dulce et decorum* in the public schools where Latin was deemed the foundation of an educated outlook on life. In Thomas Arnold's Rugby, for example, and the public schools that modelled themselves upon it, study of the classics was central to the curriculum and took up much the greatest part of the time. It was intended to inculcate 'manliness', the good learning which was to give rise to a 'muscular Christianity' (Newsome 1961; Chandos 1984; Wee 1994). The products of these schools, their minds full of the history and literature of antiquity, became educators, missionaries, entrepreneurs, soldiers and civil servants, and married women trained to be respectable upholders of the sanctity of motherhood and the family. These men and women went out to colour the map red, creating an empire even larger than that of Rome and in many respects modelled upon it.[4] The will to violence and the ideology of sacrifice in warfare, not for one's own immortal glory but for the sake of one's country, *pro patria*, became part of the structure of the western symbolic. It was and remains central to the genealogy of death in western culture. And its roots are in the heart of the *Pax Augusta*.

Funerals and funeral rites

Although the glory that was achieved was not that of personal heroism, fallen soldiers did sometimes receive public recognition. Proper funeral rites were of great importance to the Romans; and their pomp and circumstance would reflect class divisions (Davies 1999: 147–8). At the top was the Emperor, who was deemed commander-in-chief of the entire military complex: the Emperor's funeral was therefore a military event, and, far from being nameless, he might be deified after his death, as were Julius Caesar and Augustus. Ordinary soldiers received no such honours, of course, yet their funerals replicated (on increasingly modest scale) the funeral of the Emperor. Soldiers were required to belong to a burial club which used money deducted from their pay to ensure proper observance of rites including a funeral feast and perhaps the erection of a monument which might give the soldier's name and birthplace, age, rank and unit. Sometimes the monuments also had an effigy of the soldier as if on parade; while 'cavalrymen are depicted riding over the prostrate foe, usually a naked, cowering, hairy barbarian' (Webster 1998: 280). A monument would commemorate a specific individual; but the point of the effigy is not so much about the fame or activity of the deceased as about the unvanquished army of which he was a part.

A similar emphasis pervaded the funerals of great citizens. The deceased's body would be carried to the forum and made to sit upright on the rostra as though he were alive. An actor who resembled the deceased would put on his wax death mask and accompany the bier, along with a procession of his 'ancestors', each represented by their death masks called *imagines*.

> For who would not be moved by the sight of the images of men renowned for their excellence, all together in one place, portrayed as if still alive and breathing? What finer spectacle could there be than this? . . . Since the renown of these noble men and their reputation for excellence is constantly being called to mind, the fame of men who have done great deeds is immortal, and the glory of those who have faithfully served the fatherland becomes well known to the people and handed down as a model to future generations. The most important thing, however, is that young men are inspired to endure or suffer anything on behalf of the common good.
>
> (Polybius, in Shelton 1988: 99)

Eulogies would be pronounced, probably by a close relative; and then the ancestor masks would be taken home again and placed in a position of honour, so that every visitor to the house would be reminded of the importance of the family and its ancestors to Roman history (MacMullen 1967: 7–8; Davies 1999: 142–4). The transition in the understanding of death is evident. Polybius does not omit to mention the glory and immortal fame of the men who have done great deeds; but the most important thing is not their perpetual remembrance but the inspiration of youth to serve their country. The grief of survivors was acknowledged; and the excellence of the deceased was emphasized; yet the focus was 'not so much their own separate post-mortem fate as their continuing responsibilities for and membership of their living families and societies' (Davies 1999: 145).

There are thousands of funeral monuments and tomb inscriptions scattered across the former Roman Empire, many of them for civilian men and women. Yet even these non-military commemorations typically situate the deceased within an on-going family connection or trade, or address passers-by to connect them with the virtue of the deceased. A second-century BCE epitaph of a woman named Claudia illustrates the point:

> Stranger, my message is short: stop and read it.
> This is the unlovely tomb of a lovely woman.
> Her parents gave her the name Claudia.
> She loved her husband with her heart.
> She bore two sons, one of whom she left on earth, the other beneath it.
> She had a pleasant way of talking and walking.
> She looked after the house and worked wool.
> I have said my piece. Go your way.
>
> (Cited in Dixon 2001: 117)

Moreover the motifs on Roman funerary art of the period regularly emphasize the gender of the deceased and indicate that they were models of decorum for their gender. Women would be represented with the beauty of Venus, or as ideal wives: partner to her husband but submissive to him. Men's manliness would be portrayed in battle or hunt scenes. In the case of prominent families the most important aspect of the commemoration would be their place in and service of their fatherland. All deaths ultimately were recuperated to point back to the glory of Rome: 'the life of the Empire was celebrated; the death of the Empire was denied' (Davies 1999: 145).

Imperial beauty

The Augustan Golden Age was glorious not only for the extent and prosperity of its empire but also for its beauty and creativity. Suetonius records that Augustus did so much to improve the appearance of Rome 'that he could justifiably boast, "I found Rome built of bricks; I leave her clothed in marble"' (II:28; 1979: 69). Augustus encouraged learning, and fostered the arts and literature so that his era was seen to be a cultural high point of Roman history: Vergil, Horace, Ovid and Livy are only four of the greatest writers who flourished under his reign. But as with morals, gender and even death, creativity was expected to serve the glory of Rome. Augustus appropriated beauty to imperial ideology, or, where this proved impossible, made the artist pay the price, as we shall see in the next chapter. Thus beauty itself was bent to the service of power, and made to give a glorious face to violence and death. Some examples will make this broad claim clear.

I have already discussed various aspects of Vergil's *Aeneid* in connection with Homer. Here I want to draw attention to the way in which this book, a model of Latin prose from its first appearance and throughout the subsequent history of western Europe, in fact served the ideology of empire. In Vergil's *Aeneid* Augustus himself is portrayed as having descended from the gods, and as ruling Rome at their bidding. According to a prevalent reading of the *Aeneid* the whole history of the Trojan War, indeed the whole history of civilization, led to the consolidation of power finally effected by Augustus. In the eighth book of the *Aeneid* an ancient Golden Age is recalled. It is natural to read the work as suggesting that the Augustan Golden Age is a reinstatement of that era, bringing more peace and prosperity than ever before.

In book eight, also, Vergil describes the great shield of Aeneas, presented to him by Venus just as Achilles was given his shield by Thetis before his battle with Hector at the walls of Troy. Aeneas' shield, however, is a prophecy of the 'fame and fate of his descendents' (1990: 210). Around the periphery are depicted incidents from the Italian Wars, starting with the wolf who suckled Romulus and Remus, and the rape of the Sabine women, and going on through six scenes significant in the ideology of Roman greatness. But at the very centre of the shield, described in greater detail than the other six scenes put together, is a portrayal of Augustus' victories over Antony and Cleopatra and the Battle of Actium which in effect made Augustus sole ruler of Rome (205–10; cf 333–4).

> Caesar was riding into Rome in triple triumph, paying undying vows to the gods of Italy . . . [Caesar] was seated at the white marble threshold of gleaming white Apollo, inspecting the gifts brought before him by the peoples of the earth and hanging them high on the posts of the doors of the temple, while the defeated nations walked in long procession in all their different costumes and in all their different armour, speaking all the tongues of the earth.
>
> (209)

Small wonder that when Vergil died, having given instructions that the *Aeneid* should be destroyed, Augustus countermanded the order and had the book published. Did it not portray Jupiter himself announcing that he had given Rome 'an empire that will know no end', its boundaries the limits of the world and its fame reaching to the stars (11–12)?

Yet even in Vergil there are undercurrents which destabilize or at least qualify the praise. Was the Golden Age of Augustus really a reinstatement of the ancient Golden Age? Or might it be more accurate to describe it as a travesty of that time when gold signified peace, whereas now it represents luxury, a luxury which Aeneas had been exhorted not to pursue: 'you . . . must have the courage to despise wealth. You must mould yourself to be worthy of the god' (198). Was Augustus worthy? Was Vergil asking? Perhaps he was: his book, although filled with war and violence, is also filled with a knowledge of suffering. The glory of war is heavily qualified; its price is the death or enslavement of the conquered; and also too easily the corruption of the conquerors. In Michael Grant's estimation Vergil

> was a man deeply divided within himself. The benefits Augustus had brought to a war-torn world inspired him with deep gratitude. Yet he also knew better than anyone else that such triumphs, like all the Roman triumphs that have ever been, are built on pain.
>
> (1979: 218)

He also, presumably, was becoming aware of the price of dissent. Augustus, in common with many other would-be rulers of the world, did not take kindly to critics. As we shall see in the next chapter, it could go hard with those whose compliance did not measure up to his demands. But in the case of Vergil, his meticulous control of language and beauty of expression served Augustan ideology. Though Vergil might be aware that triumph is 'built on pain', he is quite clear that the glory of Rome is built on manly violence which he celebrates in book after book of warfare and blood. His consummate skill brings the beauty of his language to the service of the Empire and ultimately to the service of violence and death upon which the Empire rests.

Literature was not the only form of creativity that was brought by Augustus to magnify the Empire. As already indicated, Augustus was proud of his building programme by which he 'clothed Rome in marble'. He made Rome elegant, a worthy capital city of a great empire. He repaired and restored buildings and then ensured, through inscriptions, statues, or other records that the people were aware that it was his generosity that had done these things. He reordered the Roman Forum, enlarging its basilicas and dedicating a temple to his father 'the divine Julius'. The beautification of the city indicated Augustus' own glory and the glory of the Empire.

> Rome provided a potted experience of empire. The people of Rome were presented with a spectacle of empire brought to them courtesy of the emperor: exotic beasts in the arena, defeated prisoners on display, varied tongues and modes of dress on the street, inscriptions and maps listing distant places and peoples, and monuments and sculptures which through their designs, materials, and scale recalled the wealth and extent of the empire.
>
> (Hope 2000: 87)

Pliny the Elder records how Augustus brought an Egyptian obelisk to Rome (XXXVI.70; 1991: 351); it was an example of the way in which the resources of empire, whether as artefacts or as materials (especially marble) were appropriated to beautify Rome.

The buildings and monuments erected by Augustus (or in his honour) in Rome or other prominent cities of the Empire ranged from places of leisure and entertainment, such as baths and theatres, to places of utility, to temples. Often, indeed, these were not rigidly separated: the Forum of Augustus, for example, would serve as a market and a meeting place, but it also contained the Temple of Mars Ultor. Cassius Dio's history of the reign of Augustus repeatedly draws attention to the dedication of magnificent buildings: 'the temple of Apollo on the Palatine hill together with the precinct surrounding it and the libraries' (53.1; 1987: 127); the Temple of Minerva and the Curia Julia with its statue of Victory (51.22; 1987: 82); and the Pantheon, filled with a 'multitude of images . . . the statues of many gods, including those of Mars and Venus' (53.27; 1987: 149).

Perhaps the most telling is the *Ara Pacis*, the Altar of Peace, completed about 9 BCE. It is a richly carved monumental altar, intended to honour Augustus as the bringer of peace. The sculptured reliefs show a procession which includes the imperial family with Augustus, and priests, magistrates and other dignitaries; on the inner walls are sacrificial animals, Vestals and priests. The realism and intimacy with which the sculptor has portrayed his subjects brings them into relationship with the viewer. Each figure is a distinct and recognizable individual, including a small child who pulls at the toga of a man as if asking to be picked up. There are comparatively few women on Roman historical reliefs, but on the *Ara Pacis* women appear along with men, both in the imperial family and among the members of the court. The morality laws of Augustus and his emphasis on reproduction required that women, though placed in the private family realm, would marry and bear children for the good of the state. As Natalie Kampen has pointed out, 'The *Ara Pacis* used family imagery to reinforce that message as well as to emphasize the great family of potential heirs to the throne, heirs who were insurance against the resumption of civil strife' (1991: 226). Both as art and as propaganda the *Ara Pacis* is brilliant. The tranquil beauty of its scenes, exquisitely carved in marble, has led one modern art historian to comment, 'If we would understand the Augustan period – its quiet good manners and its undemonstrative confidence – in a single document, that document is the *Ara Pacis Augustae*' (Wheeler 1964: 165). That is exactly the response that Augustus would have wished. Beauty is appropriated to empire so that the violence upon which it rests is erased.

However, not all those who pursued literature and the arts were willing to bend their creativity to the service of the Empire. In the following chapters I shall turn to alternative voices, voices of dissent and of the possibility of another way; and shall show that in a context of violence, even dissent itself was expressed in death.

Chapter 16

Dissent in Rome

My intention is to tell of bodies changed
To different forms; the gods, who made the changes,
Will help me – or I hope so – with a poem
That runs from the world's beginning to our own days.
(Ovid 1955: 3)

Ovid, writing during the reign of Augustus, presents in the *Metamorphoses* a song of change, of transformation from one thing to another. Ovid is regularly and rightly read as a master of Latin style who, especially in the *Metamorphoses*, brings Greek myths into western literature. There are in the text some 250 narratives of transformation. The gods change shape, or change humans into something else: Daphne becomes a laurel tree; Arachne is turned into a spider; Baucis and Philemon are made into an oak and linden tree, united as they were in life, as a reward for their hospitality to the gods. Not only do the characters in the poem change; the poem itself goes through transformations of style and genre and can be read at many different levels (Feldherr 2002).

One of the ways in which Ovid's works can be read is as a mocking critique of the Augustan Empire and the idea of 'eternal Rome'. Rome, like everything else, will change. It is not eternal after all: the very idea is a joke. Ovid loved to laugh. But as I shall argue in this chapter, many of his laughs have a very serious intent. Ovid pokes fun at the Augustan regime and its propaganda. So at least Augustus took it: in 8 CE he banished Ovid to Tomis on the Black Sea, and he ordered Ovid's books removed from public libraries. Ovid pled for mercy, but he was never allowed to return, either by Augustus or by his successor Tiberius, and died in exile in about 18 CE. The immediate cause of his banishment is uncertain: it may have had something to do with a scandal surrounding Augustus' daughter Julia who was banished at the same time. Whatever the trigger, however, Ovid's mockery of the pious self-presentation of the Augustan regime was too threatening for that regime to tolerate.

How can dissent be expressed in a world where there is a single superpower insisting on its global hegemony and masking its violence in a rhetoric of peace?

In this chapter and the ones that follow I shall discuss various strategies of dissent, strategies whose effectiveness and even possibility depend in part upon the location of the dissenter. Ovid, writing for most of his life from the heart of the Empire, expressed his dissent in mockery.[1] From the edges of empire more direct challenge was possible: in the second part of this chapter I shall discuss the economic critique of Rome presented by the writer of the Biblical book of the Revelation. In the third part I shall return to the centre of Rome and to a slightly later period when the Empire had, if anything, a firmer grip than ever, and consider the ambivalent critique of Tacitus, before turning in the following chapter to Seneca and the Stoics. All these, I shall show, gave voice (more or less muted) to the violence and death of the regime. But what did they have to offer as alternatives to that against which they protested? In the final two chapters of this volume I shall present two more forms of dissent, utterly different from one another, both of which radically challenge the deadly symbolic and material culture of the Roman Empire and who present starkly contrasting alternatives to it. Yet I shall argue that, struggle though they did against the ideology and practice of violence, and in spite of their efforts to bring newness into the world, they were mired in a symbolic of death from which they could not free themselves, and were important stages in the genealogy which transmitted necrophilia to the Middle Ages and modernity.

What Golden Age? Ovid's mockery

Characteristic of Ovid's amusement at the expense of Augustan ideology is his treatment of the theme of the Golden Age. It was a theme of considerable propaganda value to the Augustan regime. In Vergil, as we saw, the Augustan Golden Age is linked to a supposed Golden Age of peace and simplicity in the distant past: the same theme appears in Horace and in other contemporary Latin writers. Ovid sees straight through the pretence. Yes, Rome is golden; but the gold of the present age is the gold of the marketplace. Anything, including high position, love and culture, is available at the right price.

> Golden, truly, is the present age; for gold most honours are sold, by gold love is won. Even you, Homer, even if you come accompanied by the Muses, it'll be *out you go Homer*, if you haven't brought anything.
>
> (*Ars Amatoria* 2.277–80)

Not only is Ovid rude about the 'Golden Age' of Augustus, seeing it in crass economic terms rather than through nostalgic lenses. He is also under no illusions about the source of all this gold that is funding Roman prosperity and commercialism. Where Vergil hinted, Ovid is explicit: 'Before, there was rude simplicity, now Rome is golden, possessing the wealth of the conquered world' (3.113). The wealth of Rome is achieved through conquest and exploitation: Rome is 'golden' only because Rome is violent. The much lauded *Pax Augusta* ensured peace and prosperity; but to whom, and at whose expense? The propaganda of the Augustan regime, like the propaganda of subsequent empire builders and would-be rulers of the world, was that Roman domination brought political stability, civilization and economic benefit to all who came under her control. Ovid does not pretend that he does not enjoy the luxury of Rome's comforts: 'I congratulate myself for having been born now. This age is suited to my tastes' (3.122). However, Ovid will not pretend that such comforts can be had without someone somewhere paying the price for Roman prosperity: in the second part of this chapter I shall discuss the critique of Roman luxury from the perspective of the exploited.

Early in the *Metamorphoses* Ovid gives another rendition of the ancient Golden Age and an implicit comparison to the Augustan era. He describes the creation of the world, and characterizes four ages, each one a decline from the one before, which succeeded one another after creation. The first was the Golden Age. Here, people lived unselfishly together and needed no laws or moral reforms. They were content with what they had and what the earth produced; they did not have ships to bring them goods and luxuries from abroad. They were at peace.

> No trumpets
> Blared out alarums; things like swords and helmets
> Had not been heard of. No one needed soldiers.
> People were unaggressive, and unanxious.
>
> (1955: 6)

Things did not stay perfect, however. The Age of Silver came, in which people and animals had to work the land to produce food, 'groaning and labouring under the heavy yoke'; and then the Age of Bronze, in which people began to become aggressive. Last of all came the Iron Age, in which

> modesty and truth
> And righteousness fled the earth, and in their place
> Came trickery and slyness, plotting, swindling,
> Violence, and the damned desire of having.
>
> (7)

Ships were built to acquire possessions from elsewhere; people burrowed into the earth and 'found the guilt of iron, and gold, more guilty still'.

> And War came forth
> That uses both to fight with; bloody hands
> Brandished the clashing weapons . . .
> Piety lay vanquished,
> And the maiden Justice, last of all immortals,
> Fled from the bloody earth.
>
> (7)

For once, Ovid is not laughing. The *Pax Augusta* was supposedly a new Golden Age, but which of these four ages did it really resemble? Was it without need of laws and law courts? Could it live without ships and imports? And what about aggression, war and weapons? It was these upon which the empire was built. Ovid does not make the comparison explicit, but it is clear that the Augustan age resembles the dreadful Age of Iron much more nearly than the ancient Golden Age. Has Justice then indeed fled from the earth?

It was part of the ideology of the Golden Age that Augustus had brought back the simplicity of life and the high moral values, especially family values, that had supposedly characterized Rome's ancient past. In the *Ars Amatoria* Ovid makes fun of this as well. Augustus' 'simplicity', he implies, is selective. There is nothing simple about the conspicuous consumption characteristic of Rome which Augustus encouraged as his way of bribing the upper classes into compliance with his policies; neither was the boast that he found Rome brick and turned it into marble exactly the boast of a man for whom simplicity was a core value. Yet Ovid points out that Augustus required that the women of his household should spin and weave their own cloth: this was to be an example to the matrons of Rome of the virtues of hard work and simplicity. Augustus' high moral tone about a simple lifestyle was all very well, but the burden of it was carried by others.

As for the modesty and chastity that were intended as part of the Augustan moral reforms, Ovid shows their hypocrisy and double standards. Again, he does not attack them directly or preach sermons of dissent. He laughs. In his *Ars Amatoria* he uses a supposedly rational and serious method of instruction, like a pedantic professor: but what this instructor is teaching is how to select a mistress (rather as one would select a cow – in daylight, where faults can be spotted), how, once selected, she could be acquired on the cheap, how to use Apollo's advice to 'know thyself' to know how best to flatter and seduce, and how to take the best positions in love-making. Now, the places Ovid suggests as best for rendezvous with illicit lovers are the porticoes of the famous marble buildings of Augustan construction, named after members of his family; and as for the advice of Apollo, this was particularly sacred to Augustus because he associated it with his victory over Antony and Cleopatra. As Sara Mack observes in her account of Ovid's wit as a method of dissent, the serious style of Ovid's poem is utterly incongruous with its subject matter.

> Ovid has chosen a topic that is frivolous by anyone's standards, shocking by the standards Augustus was trying to revive in Rome, and he has treated it in a deadpan fashion – soberly and from all angles, as if it were an important philosophical or ethical question, such as the nature and pursuit of virtue.
>
> (1988: 87)

Not only does Ovid disregard Augustus' solemn moral reforms. He reminds the reader of his *Tristia* that Romulus and Remus, the mythological founders of Rome (and according to Vergil distant ancestors of Augustus himself) were begotten by the adultery of Mars and his rape of the Vestal Virgin Ilia. So Rome began with sacrilege, rape and adultery, and Augustus is their beneficiary. His high moral ground is thus pompous pretence. As Alison Sharrock observes, Ovid in the *Ars Amatoria* is setting up sex 'as an alternative to Augustan citizenship'.

> Although the poem poses as denying that it teaches anything against the Augustan adultery laws, at almost every turn its presentation belies its protestation. The didactic poem undermines marriage not so much because Ovid thinks adultery is a good thing, as in order to offer an alternative to Augustan social control.
>
> (2002: 105)

It is scarcely surprising that Augustus was not amused, even if it were true that 'Ovid's intentions were hardly revolutionary' (James 2000: 292), more a matter of laughing at moral and political stuffiness.

Ovid's light-hearted celebration of love and life contrasts sharply with Roman valorization of war, militarism, and an idea of heroism centred on killing and violence. Again, his tactic is parody, not preaching. The serious conventions of Latin elegy make much of the metaphors of warfare and the army. So does Ovid: but in his hands the soldier is a soldier of love, waging Cupid's battles. In the *Amores* he insists,

> Every lover is a soldier; Cupid too commands a camp: . . .
> *Every lover is a soldier*
>
> (*Amores* I.9.1–2)

and continues,

> I too was lazy, born for unhaltered leisure; writing and life in the shade had softened my spirit. Love for a beautiful girl spurred me to action and forced me to earn my keep in the camp of love. Now you can see I am a man of action, waging nocturnal battles. He who would avoid sloth, let him love!
>
> (9.41–6)

Roman might and her mastery of the world was built on the army; and it was essential for the Augustan regime that the army should be accorded the highest respect. And so it is, by Ovid: but it is the army of lovers, soldiering under Cupid's command. Ovid could hardly have been more outrageous.

Another target for Ovid's wit was the triumphal procession, the highest honour available to a military leader. In *Amores* I.2, however, the general is none other than Cupid: love has conquered all. His chariot has been supplied by Mars, the god of war; and it is drawn by Venus's love birds rather than by horses. It was usual that the kings who had been captured should be forced to walk in chains behind the chariot. In Ovid's poem the 'magnificent triumph' of Cupid similarly has a procession of the conquered.

I myself, fresh prize, will just now have received my wound and my captive mind will display its new chains. You'll lead Conscience, hands twisted behind her back, and Shame, and whoever Love's sect includes. All will fear you [Cupid]: stretching their arms towards you the crowd will cry 'hurrah for the triumph!'

(I.11)

The troops who have helped Cupid gain his victory are called Delusion and Passion. All sing in praise of Love; 'War's not the thing'. And so Ovid goes on, matching detail for detail. The parody is all the funnier because it mimics the first chapter of Vergil's *Aeneid* in which Jupiter predicts the *Pax Augusta* where the Madness of war will be bound: Ovid binds Conscience instead, and exalts Madness as the leader of Cupid's battles. Ovid's treatment is witty and outrageous and could hardly have been calculated to soothe the pride or paranoia of Augustus. Just in case he has not made his point sharply enough, Ovid finishes his poem with an explicit mention of Augustus, imploring Cupid to behave just as Caesar would:

Look at Caesar's similar fortunes of war – what he conquers, he protects with his power.

It may be that Ovid was making jokes which he genuinely did not intend as threatening or offensive to Caesar. Certainly he protested his loyalty after he was exiled, and insisted that his banishment was all based on misunderstanding. Some commentators believe that Ovid's humour simply ran away with him. Once he started laughing he couldn't stop; he wrote with 'more wit than wisdom' (James 2000: 292). But it is also possible to read him as expressing dissent.

Such a reading is particularly compelling in the case of his book the *Heroides*. In this volume Ovid presents a series of letters which he places in the mouth – or on the pen – of women, mostly women who have appeared in Greek myth but in a minor or marginal way: Penelope writes to the absent Odysseus/Ulysses; Medea writes to Jason; Dido writes to Aeneas. In each case Ovid has the woman write to the man she loves, a man whose actions have left her in a desperate situation. The men, often, are men who are heroes according to received ideology. But what price manly heroism, Ovid seems to be suggesting, if this is how heroes treat women? Ovid's letters in the *Heroides* are reminiscent of the plays of Euripides, succinctly and thoughtfully presenting what military exploits, travel adventure and heroic violence look like from the perspective of the women who are victims or onlookers. Now, it cannot be forgotten that these letters are not in fact written by women, but by a man; and it is right to ask as Alison Sharrock does, 'What kind of gendered voice is produced by a male author speaking through a female mask, but completely subsuming his masculine authority into the female writing? . . . How far is Ovid implicated in the exposure and objectification of women and denigrating violence towards them, perpetrated in and by his texts?' (2002: 99). Is this just another case of a man ventriloquizing, as we have seen with Parmenides and the goddess, or

Plato and Diotima? Sharrock argues that Ovid's case is different, and I agree with her. It is hard to read these letters as not expressing an acute challenge to the manly values of military prowess and heroic action that were central to the ideology of Augustan Rome.

Many of Ovid's women could be used as illustration; I shall focus on only one, Briseas, the young woman captured early in the Trojan War and part of Achilles' booty who is then demanded by Agamemnon in the feud with which the *Iliad* opens. In the *Iliad* Briseas is hardly a person; she is simply a pawn in the exchanges between powerful men. Ovid, however, imagines her as a fully developed character with human feelings and fears, writing to Achilles from Agamemnon's tent.

> Not through your fault was I claimed by Agamemnon but
> you failed me by too easily giving me up . . .
> You could not refuse, but you might have eased my pain
> with only a little delay.
> Without a kiss you let me leave you.
>
> (Ovid 1990: 21)

Briseas makes every excuse she can think of for Achilles: he had no choice; he could not have succeeded if he had tried to resist his king.

> Even so, many nights have passed and still you have not
> demanded that I return.
>
> (21)

When Agamemnon tries to effect a reconciliation with Achilles and offers to send Briseas back, Achilles refuses to have her. In the *Iliad* the refusal is presented in terms of Achilles' rage and pride, but Ovid imagines how Briseas must feel. To her it would be a personal rejection. Is it her fault, she cries?

> What act of mine has cheapened me in your eyes?
> Where is your careless love gone to now?
>
> (22)

She is well aware that although she has not slept with Agamemnon, Achilles will quickly have substituted some other girl for her: she can claim no special place in his heart. Nevertheless, she is desperate.

All this is poignant enough. It is made infinitely more so by the fact that Briseas was not just any Trojan woman; she was the wife of one of the Trojan warriors that Achilles and the Greek army had killed, along with three of her brothers. 'Can one fall lower than to love the killer of one's closest kin?' (Mack 1988: 75). The war has utterly destroyed Briseas, both literally and psychologically. Although she tries to retain her dignity there is precious little dignity left as she begs Achilles to take her back on any terms, as his mistress or even as a slave to his wife. She will not be a burden, she promises; and she is good at working with wool – only please, please let her not be left behind when Achilles sails from Troy: she would rather die. It is a devastating representation of the human cost of war, not just in terms of those who are slaughtered but also of those whose lives and characters are shattered beyond dignity and hope. Many of Ovid's writings are humorous, but there is nothing funny about Briseas as Ovid forces his reader to think about who pays the awful cost of the warfare of heroic men.

In the immediate background to much of Ovid's writing and certainly part of the cultural capital of his readership is, as always, the work of Vergil. In Ovid's most famous poem, the *Metamorphoses*, he retells stories of the *Aeneid*. But he tells them in another way. He abbreviates the account of Aeneas' journeys, frequently interrupting them with stories of minor figures from the *Aeneid*. The story of Glaucus and Scylla, for example, continues for many pages in the *Metamorphoses* while the famous visit of Aeneas to Dido that takes up four books of the *Aeneid* is summarized by Ovid in a few lines: Aeneas was driven by wind on to Libya's shore, Dido received him, could not bear his going, and killed herself. 'Herself deceived, she deceived others. And Aeneas left . . . ' (1955: 340–1). And that is that. Each time that someone who was familiar with Vergil's epic would expect a narrative of Aeneas' heroism, Ovid deflects it to yet another vignette of a minor character: the Sibyl, Achaemenides, Picus, Diomedes. In the end the 'main' story of Aeneas and the foundation of Rome is completely overwhelmed by details of characters and incidents which in Vergil's tome are trivial or non-existent. Even the legendary history of Rome has just nicely got underway when after about eighteen lines Ovid interrupts himself to tell the story of a garden nymph – of all things – which goes on for 75 lines, leads to another long digression, and all but displaces Roman history.

What was Ovid doing? Was he trying to do what Vergil had done – write an epic poem about the origins of Rome and filling in details Vergil had omitted? Seen in those terms Ovid's efforts could hardly be seen as successful. But Sara Mack suggests a persuasive alternative. She reads these chapters of the *Metamorphoses* as

> part of a brilliant parody of the whole idea of the heroic. Homer's view of life is only one way of viewing life, Ovid's poem seems to say, offering us another. Vergil's notion of the shape and direction of history, moving inexorably – for better or worse – toward Augustan Rome is only one way, Ovid suggests, of viewing that history.
>
> (1988: 127–8)

In each case, the great heroes of Homer and Vergil are either marginalized, like Aeneas, or behave like something out of slapstick: Nestor leaps into a tree to escape from a wild boar; the hunter Jason tries to kill the boar with his javelin and hits a hunting dog instead; Ancaeus, in a passage full of sexual innuendos, tries to show his superiority and ends up with the boar's tusk in his groin. It is fast-moving farce. Well recited, it would have had an audience doubled over with laughter. 'Everywhere the strategy of the *Metamorphoses* is to take the heroism out of the heroic while professing to write in the heroic mode' (126). And once they had laughed, could Ovid's readers ever take the ideology of Rome and the solemn pomposity of Caesar and the *Pax Augusta* quite as seriously as before? In a context of despotism, where there was little scope for opposition, making a public joke of the regime may have been a most effective method of dissent.

Ovid does not end his poem with jokes, however. In the final book he places a long speech on the lips of Pythagoras, the Presocratic philosopher who had first taught the separation of soul from body and the idea of reincarnation. All things change, says Ovid's Pythagoras:

> Time devours all things
> With envious Age together. The slow gnawing
> Consumes all things, and very, very slowly. . . .
> Nothing, I am convinced, can be the same
> Forever. There was once an Age of Gold,
> Later, an Age of Iron. Every place
> Submits to Fortune's wheel.
>
> (372–3)

Every place? Including Rome? Whatever happened to the idea of 'eternal Rome'? Pythagoras' speech is a rendition in philosophical idiom of the central theme of the *Metamorphoses*: things change. People are changed into trees (Daphne) or cows (Io) or swans (Cygmus) or spiders (Arachne). Gods change too: Jupiter into a bull, Syrinx into reeds. Ovid's Pythagoras makes sure that we know that the same thing happens to cities. 'The eras change', he says; 'nations grow strong or weaken'; and he lists several which have been great: Troy, Athens, Sparta. These 'all flourished once, and now what are they more than names?' (378). In their place has come Rome, superseding all that went before.

> Rome's form is changing
> Growing to greatness, and she will be, some day,
> Head of the boundless world . . .
>
> (378)

Pythagoras does not say that Rome too will decay; that her greatness too will come to an end just as did the pre-eminence of Troy or Athens. He does not have to say it. The message is there for all to see who have paid attention to his speech and its setting within the theme of the *Metamorphoses*.

At the very end of his poem Ovid seems to change his tone. He presents a paean of praise to the emperor, writing of the assassination of Julius Caesar and of the splendid reign of Augustus. Julius Caesar's rule was victorious: Ovid lists his military victories over the Britons, Egypt and North Africa. All this greatness, Ovid says, was

> surpassed only by being father
> Of one yet greater, one who rules the world,

none other than Augustus himself, who has established peace, law and civil justice throughout the world.

> And O gods . . . far be the day,
> Later than our own era, when Augustus
> Shall leave the world he rules, ascend to Heaven,
> there, beyond our presence, hear our prayers!
> (392)

Augustus could hardly have asked for more: it is a fulsome tribute. But what does Ovid mean by it? Is it a bit *too* fulsome after what has gone before, parodying other poets' praise of Caesar as he had parodied their exaltation of heroism or the greatness of the military? Was it like a rendition of 'God save the Queen' or 'God bless America' after a comedy that has made jokes about western pretentions and ideology? Was Ovid covering his tracks, making a self-protective gesture in a regime which was rapidly becoming more repressive? Or did he mean it?

Alas for the Great City

Whatever the case with Ovid, there can be no doubt that the author of the Biblical book of Revelation, written from the perspective of the edges of empire in the late first century, constitutes a fierce attack on Rome and her imperialism. In the Revelation, the target of attack is called 'Babylon the harlot', but it is a commonplace of Biblical scholarship that 'Babylon' is a thin disguise for Rome, 'the great city which has dominion over the kings of the earth' (Revelation 17: 18).

The Revelation was written by a Christian prophet called John, who is in exile on the island of Patmos in the Aegean Sea. It is addressed to 'the seven churches in the province of Asia' (1.4), Christian communities struggling under persecution from a Roman regime which could not tolerate the Christians' refusal to worship the emperor as a god. I shall have more to say about this refusal and its consequences in chapter 18; here my focus is on the nature of John's critique of the Roman Empire especially in relation to imperial economics. John's condemnation is applied directly to Rome; but he also has harsh words to say to those who are seduced by her as by a prostitute, associating with her for the supposed benefits of the *Pax Romana* but actually being corrupted by it.

In a telling analysis, Richard Bauckham (1991) has discussed John's use of the metaphor of the harlot and the economic oppression of Rome upon her possessions. As Bauckham points out, the main point of the metaphor is that 'those who associate with a harlot pay her for the privilege' (55). What is the cost to those who get into bed with Rome? Rome, after all, is no back-street prostitute. She is 'a rich courtesan, whose expensive clothes and jewellery indicate the luxurious lifestyle she maintains at her lovers' expense' (ibid.). The goods that flow into Rome along the roads her armies built and the trade routes that were developed are for her own benefit, like a courtesan's fees.

> To those who associate with her she offers the supposed benefits of the *Pax Romana*, much lauded in the Roman propaganda of this period. Rome offered the Mediterranean world unity, security, stability, the conditions of prosperity. But in John's view these benefits are not what they seem: they are the favours of a prostitute, purchased at a high price. The *Pax Romana* is really a system of economic exploitation of the empire. Rome's subjects give far more to her than she gives to them.
>
> (Bauckham 1991: 55–6)

Moreover, John is acutely aware of the military force that lies behind this economic prosperity: Rome is guilty of the blood 'of all who have been slain upon the earth' (18.24). Only a politics of violence could enforce the economic superiority which Rome enjoys, even if that force is usually exerted well beyond the sight of Roman citizens, at the edges of the Empire, so that the citizens can enjoy the luxuries brought to them by Roman hegemony without having to take into account the suffering inflicted on others so that their lavish lifestyle could be sustained.

John lists twenty-eight types of merchandise which Rome imports from territories she has subdued. The cargo John lists is as follows:

> cargo of gold, silver, jewels and pearls, fine linen, purple, silk and scarlet, all kinds of scented wood, all articles of ivory, all articles of costly wood, bronze, iron and marble, cinnamon, spice, incense, myrrh, frankincense, wine, oil, fine flour and wheat, cattle and sheep, horses and chariots, and slaves, that is, human souls.
>
> (Revelation 17: 12–13)

As Bauckham has shown, every item on this list is instructive; here I shall limit myself to commenting on only a few. In the first century CE, gold and silver were extensively used by wealthy Roman families for such things as dinner services, the ornamentation of their homes and even for shoe buckles. Jewels were worn by women and men (especially in rings) and inlaid into drinking cups and bowls; women also wore pearls to the extent that Pliny the Elder, who remarks on many of the same items as are found on the cargo list, objects to the extravagance of 'luxuries that cost human life' (ix.105; 1991: 135). 'Purple' and the other dyes and textiles were hugely expensive: purple in particular required enormous numbers of shellfish to make the dye, which was therefore exorbitant in price and was used as a deliberate and conspicuous status symbol. The 'scented wood' was citrus from North Africa, and was used for table tops, sometimes with ivory legs: the philosopher Seneca, whom I will discuss in the next chapter, owned a great many of them. They too were enormously expensive because of the length of time needed for a tree to grow large enough for a table to be cut from it in one piece. Marble was much prized for beautifying buildings: we have already seen Augustus' claim to have replaced Rome's brick with marble, and it was used as well for many sorts of ornament including statues and sarcophagi. 'The wealth Rome squanders on luxuries from all over the world was obtained by conquest, plunder and taxation of the provinces. Rome lives well at her subjects' expense' (Bauckham 1991: 78). Last on John's list and epitomizing his whole critique is 'slaves, that is, human souls'. By putting it this way, emphasizing that the slaves are human, John can be read as indicating that in fact *all* the items on his list are acquired at human cost. 'This is more than just a comment on the slave trade. It is a comment on the whole list of cargoes. It suggests the inhuman brutality, the contempt for human life, on which the whole of Rome's prosperity and luxury rests' (79).

Writers from within Rome, such as Pliny the Elder, also objected to these luxuries and to conspicuous consumption, though Pliny's concern was with the moral enfeeblement of citizens rather than the oppression of subject states. Regarding marble, for example, he says that whereas 'Nature' made mountains for her own purposes, men now quarry them for their pleasure.

> Nature is levelled. We carry off materials which were meant as barriers between nations; ships are built to transport the marble. Thus mountain-ranges are carried here and there over the waves. . . . When we hear the prices fetched for these drinking vessels and we see the volume of marble transported by sea or road, let each of us reflect how many people's lives would be happier without these!
>
> (xxxvi.2–3; 1991: 342)

Pliny's objection, from within the heart of the Empire, was to the ways in which Rome's global hegemonic political and economic superpower had brought so many luxuries to Rome that Roman citizens were losing their manliness, and values were distorted. John, writing from exile and as a member of a persecuted group, showed how Rome's opulence was at the price of violence and blood and ever renewed conquest, dominion that was necessary to keep the citizens of the heartland in the style to which they were accustomed.

Pliny calls Romans to a less lavish lifestyle, a call which they largely ignored. He does not, however, challenge the idea of empire itself. John, on the other hand, calls down the judgement of heaven on Rome, predicts her fall and destruction at the hand of God, and in the meantime calls on Christians to be faithful in their witness against her. His call did not go unheeded. Although there were Christians who made their peace with Rome, there were many others who resisted. Some were executed. I shall have more to say about them in chapter 18; but first I shall turn to two more instances of resistance and protest at the heart of Rome, Tacitus the historian in the last part of this chapter, and in the next the ambiguous and towering figure of Seneca the Stoic philosopher.

'They create a desolation and call it peace'

Tacitus writes his history at the end of the first century CE and the beginning of the second. He is explicit in his criticism of tyrannical government. In the case of Tacitus, however, the criticism focuses on abuses of previous emperors, especially Nero and Domitian, which he has survived. The new emperor, Trajan, he avers, has brought an altogether better regime into being. Yet Tacitus too can be read as carefully camouflaged dissent. Although on the face of it he writes as though the tyranny is over, his adverse judgements on previous regimes can be read with an eye to evaluating his own time.

In the book commemorating his father-in-law Agricola, for example, Tacitus begins by lamenting the fact that under Domitian books were burned and professors of philosophy were banished in a bid to silence freedom of expression. He continues,

> We have indeed set up a record of subservience. Rome of old explored the utmost limits of freedom; we have plumbed the depths of slavery, robbed as we are by informers even of the right to exchange ideas in conversation. We should have lost our memories as well as our tongues had it been as easy to forget as to be silent.
>
> (*Agricola* 2; 1970: 52)

But Tacitus is a historian, and a historian's job is not to forget. He makes it his business, therefore, to recall and record what has happened; and his *Annals* and *Histories* can be read as critical histories of the reigns of emperors from Augustus to Trajan. Yet his sometimes harsh criticisms can also be read as oblique commentary on his own time: his readers are implicitly encouraged to question how different, really, is the Roman Empire under Trajan from what it was under previous rulers. In some respects it is clearly much better or Tacitus would not dare to write at all. But his writings are also warnings against abuse of imperial power, abuse which could easily arise again simply at the whim of the emperor.

One of the methods of critique available to historians is to put the criticism of the Empire into the mouth of its opponents, the 'barbarians' whom Rome will conquer. Thus, for example, Cassius Dio has the leader of the Britons, Boudicca, comment about the supposed manliness of the Romans. Roman men, she says, are

> men who are aggressive, dishonest, avaricious and irreligious, if that is we can call them men who take warm water baths, eat exotic meals, drink undiluted wine, smear themselves with oil, recline on soft cushions, and sleep with boys

(who are actually past their prime!). These men are slaves to the lyre player – and not necessarily a good lyre player!

(62.6.4)

Whether Boudicca could actually have known what men were like in Rome or whether they actually behaved in these ways is not the point: Cassius Dio is using her as a mouthpiece to make a critical comment on the degeneracy of Roman manliness as he sees it.

Tacitus uses the same strategy. His book, *Agricola*, is at one level a biography of his father-in-law, who served in Britain during the reign of Domitian. At another level, however, it is a criticism of that reign, and by extension of every reign that is autocratic and diminishes the freedom of its citizens. It is also a criticism of some of the violent policies and practices of empire. Thus Tacitus describes in detail the integrity, moderation, and obedient hard work of Agricola in contrast to the self-indulgence and cruelty of Domitian. But whereas he makes Agricola a model of manly virtue, he puts into the mouth of Calgacus, the leader of the Britons against whom Agricola is campaigning, a speech criticizing Roman imperial policy and practice.

Calgacus is represented as addressing his troops before they join in battle with the Roman forces who have come to enslave them. He begins by emphasizing that the British are free and are fighting to retain that freedom. The Romans, by contrast, although they are supposedly civilized, actually behave like thugs and bullies, greedy and arrogant.

> Pillagers of the world, they have exhausted the land by their indiscriminate plunder, and now they ransack the sea. A rich enemy excites their cupidity; a poor one, their lust for power. East and West alike have failed to satisfy them. They are the only people on earth to whose covetousness both riches and poverty are equally tempting. To robbery, butchery and rapine, they give the lying name of 'government'; they create a desolation and call it peace.
>
> (*Agricola* 30; Tacitus 1970: 80–1)

Now, the historical Calgacus, though he might well have feared for his country and its people, would not have known about Rome's power across the world or how it was expressed. What Tacitus is doing here is using Calgacus as a spokesman for anti-imperialist views that were being expressed in Rome itself, rather than on the edges of empire. The impulse to world-domination which had been part of the rhetoric of empire from the time of Alexander of Macedon was held open to question and exposed as quite the opposite of civilized behaviour (Ogilvie and Richmond 1967: 253–4).

Yet, as Calgacus' speech continues it becomes clear that that so-called civilization and all its luxury is economically dependent upon precisely the continuous expansion of empire: his words bear comparison with those of John in the Revelation.

Our goods and money are consumed by taxation; our land is stripped of its harvest to fill their granaries; our hands and limbs are crippled by building roads through forests and swamps under the lash of our oppressors.

(81)

Worst of all is the slavery. Calgacus says that the Romans rape or seduce the women of the lands they occupy, and send them along with men and children in slavery to Rome. Again it is not clear how much Calgacus could actually have known about Roman slavery; but Tacitus is using him to denounce its evils. Roman society was based on slaves; and as we have seen, Roman economy was dependent upon a steady supply of fresh slaves, at best to work in agriculture or mines or to serve in wealthy households, at worst to provide entertainment for Roman citizens in triumphal processions and spectacles of death. So Calgacus rallies his troops to action:

> Which will you choose – to follow your leader into battle, or to submit to taxation, labour in the mines, and all the other tribulations of slavery? Whether you are to endure these forever or take quick vengeance, this field must decide.

(83)

As Paula James explains, 'the concerns bestowed on Calgacus and the model of oppression he is constructing and opposing represent a Roman-style discomfort with the abuse of power' (James 2000: 283). Tacitus shared that discomfort; indeed he helped to foster it.

The measure of his dissent is limited, however. In the first place, he puts the voice of conscience into the mouth of a barbarian, and moreover a barbarian who is about to be conquered. Now obviously from the perspective of suggesting the moral superiority of the barbarian over the allegedly civilized Romans, this is sound literary strategy. It is however also effective self-protection. If any emperor were to denounce Tacitus as a dissenter to imperial policy, he would be able to say that the dissent comes from a barbarian, not from himself. Tacitus makes a point of saying that the speech he attributes to Calgacus 'is the substance of what he is reported to have said' (79): he leaves room to distance himself from its contents.

In itself such self-protection was probably shrewd common sense. However, Tacitus goes much further, implicitly endorsing Rome's policy by his lavish praise of Agricola as conqueror. Immediately after Calgacus' speech, Tacitus places a parallel speech by Agricola to the Roman troops, urging them to fight courageously 'in the name of imperial Rome's divinely guided greatness' (84). He disparages the Britons as unmanly, cowardly barbarians: there is a sense in which these chapters of his book read less like actual preparation for battle than like speech and counterspeech in a competition at a Roman school of rhetoric. Moreover, although Calgacus' speech can be read as Tacitus' expression of dissent, when it comes to the actual battle Tacitus is clearly on the side of Agricola. The fact that 'the enemy dead were reckoned in thousands' is for him a matter of acclaim, not distress (91). Tacitus has only praise for the aggressive military tactics of Agricola, whom he compares with the Emperor Domitian much to the latter's disadvantage. Even though Tacitus is a beneficiary of the Empire and in many respects assumes the Roman right to dominate, he admires those who struggle against subjugation. Yet on the other hand 'Tacitus' sympathy for Calgacus did not prevent him treating the compulsive militarism of Agricola as the acme of virtuous behaviour for a senatorial Roman' (Goodman 1991: 222–3). It is not violence that Tacitus objects to, nor war, nor killing. Ultimately, he objects to what he sees as Roman degeneracy and effeminacy, and wants a return to the manly virtues of the Republic with all the militarism that that implies.

Already before Tacitus, however, there had been those who came to be disillusioned with those allegedly manly virtues and the violence with which they were implicated. In the next chapter I shall turn to the troubling case of Seneca, Stoic philosopher and advisor to Nero, and consider his position as a practitioner of death.

Chapter 17

Stoical death

Seneca's conscience

In 65 CE Nero the emperor 'invited' his old tutor, Seneca the Stoic philosopher, to commit suicide. Nero was 28, and had been emperor since he was 14. During the early years of his reign he was willing to follow the guidance of Seneca and Burrus, another advisor who worked closely with the philosopher; but he became increasingly self-indulgent and self-willed. He made enemies. As he did so, he became suspicious that they wanted to kill him, and began to see conspiracies everywhere. Not all of the conspiracies were imagined. In 65, a group of senators, officers, and others led by Gaius Piso plotted to assassinate Nero and make Piso emperor. The plot was discovered and its chief perpetrators executed; but Nero's suspicions were now heightened and he accused Seneca, among others, of being involved in the plot.[1]

An officer was sent 'to tell Seneca he must die' (Tacitus 1996: 375). Seneca, 'unperturbed', prepared himself to cut his veins, talking with his friends and trying to 'revive their courage': as Tacitus presents it Seneca's death is a parallel to that of Socrates nearly five centuries earlier. 'I leave you my one remaining possession', he said, 'and my best: the pattern of my life'. And then he cut his arms; but 'Seneca's aged body, lean from austere living, released the blood too slowly'; and to expedite the process Seneca drank hemlock which 'had long been prepared'. To what extent Tacitus' representation of Seneca's death is historically accurate is open to debate; the point is that Seneca is deliberately presented as a Roman Socrates. Tacitus was not alone in this portrayal: there is a famous double herm, showing Socrates and Seneca joined back to back, solidly at one.

It was an identification Seneca would have been proud to own. There were, however, significant differences; and it is by being alert to those differences that we can trace some of the changes in the genealogy of death. The first is immediately evident in Tacitus' representation of the suicide scene. Whereas in the *Phaedo* Plato describes Socrates as coolly sending away the women and children, Seneca's treatment of his wife Paulina is quite the opposite.

> Seneca embraced his wife and, with a tenderness very different from his
> philosophical imperturbability, entreated her to moderate and set a term to

her grief, and take just consolation, in her bereavement, from contemplating his well-spent life.

(Tacitus 1996: 376)

Paulina, however, will not have it. She insists on dying with him. Seneca accedes to her desire in words that indicate his recognition of her equality in courage and freedom: 'We can die with equal fortitude. But yours will be the nobler end.' And so they cut their veins together. Yet it was not to be: Nero gave orders that Paulina's death was to be averted, and Paulina's arms were bandaged to stop the bleeding: she therefore 'lived on for a few years, honourably loyal to her husband's memory' (376). Again, there is no guarantee that Tacitus' account is historically correct; but the very fact that he makes a point of including the tender scene between Seneca and Paulina in a passage otherwise intended as a parallel to the death of Socrates is food for thought. What shifts have occurred in the relationship between gender and death? If suicide is a way of overcoming the passivity and effeminacy of death, and instead meeting death actively with manly courage, what are the implications when a woman freely chooses the same act with equal fortitude?

A second major difference from Socrates is barely hinted at in Tacitus' account but can be seen in detail in Seneca's own writings: Seneca had been preoccupied with suicide for many years, even obsessed by it, in a way that is foreign to Plato's portrayal of Socrates. The hint of this in Tacitus' account is the comment that Seneca had had poison prepared for a long time. In itself, this could be seen as no more than prudence: Seneca lived a life of very high risk under the capricious tyranny of the emperors Caligula and Nero, and the need for poison could have come at any time (Griffin 1976; Rudich 1997: ch.1). It was as well to be ready. Seneca's writings, however, show that he is not just ready for the eventuality, but is constantly thinking about suicide, emphasizing it in relation to the freedom which was for Stoics the special mark of manly virtue. Everything he looks at he sees in terms of the opportunity it offers for death.

In whatever direction you may turn your eyes, there lies the means to end your woes. See you that precipice? Down that is the way to liberty. See you that sea, that river, that well? There sits liberty at the bottom. See you that tree, stunted, blighted and barren? Yet from its branches hangs liberty. See you that throat of yours, your gullet, your heart? They are ways of escape from servitude. Are the ways of egress I show you too toilsome, do you require too much courage and strength? Do you ask what is the highway to liberty? Any vein in your body.

(De Ira 3.15, in Rist 1969: 249)

Trees, rivers, the sea, even the human body are not seen by Seneca as things of beauty but as means of escape: or, better, their beauty in his eyes consists precisely in the fact that they offer the possibility of suicide. In this chilling configuration of beauty and violent death the contempt for death characteristic of Roman ideologies of manliness has become transformed into contempt for life, *contemptus mundi*, which, when united with the sensibilities of christendom, would have a very long run in western consciousness.

The passage is extreme, even by Seneca's standards, and is not representative of Stoic thinking. In modern times Stoicism has come to be identified with emotional rigidity or at least with a strict control of feelings and their expression, no matter what awfulness must be endured. In antiquity, however, Stoicism was a complex philosophical tradition with a significant effect on the genealogy of death, of which Seneca's preoccupation with suicide was only one (extreme) example. Seneca had an enormous effect upon the western cultural heritage.[2] In order to understand his preoccupation with death it is necessary to see him in relation both to the tradition of Stoicism and to the court of Nero and its convoluted politics of power and gender.[3]

Stoicism, nature and the divine

Stoicism, like the other philosophies taken up in imperial Rome, had its origins in Athens. Its first teachers, beginning in the late fourth century BCE, were men like Zeno, Cleanthes and Chrysippus; and their concerns were with questions of the nature of the universe and the place of humans within it, both in terms of the body, regarding which they developed medical theory, and the mind and its rationality, happiness and virtue. They had debts to other philosophical systems – notably Platonism, Aristotelianism and Epicureanism – and disagreements with them, as well as among themselves.

For our purposes, what is especially interesting is the way in which Stoic philosophers developed their idea of the divine and its relation to the universe. Like the Epicureans, the Stoics held to a materialist view of the universe: all things are made of matter in various combinations, and all things obey fixed laws. But whereas Epicureans like Lucretius thought of the gods as separate beings existing in some special realm of perfect bliss without any connection to the events of earth, Stoics thought of the divine differently. All bodies, animate and inanimate, are in some sense alive, held together by a breath or spirit (*pneuma*) which can be thought of as very refined matter (as in Lucretius). But if this is true of the persons and objects that make up the world, it is also true of the universe itself. Just as a living person is a body of coarser atoms totally permeated by a spirit or mind of exceptionally fine matter, so also the material universe is permeated by divine spirit. 'Spirit', here, is not immaterial; rather it is a particularly fine kind of matter, often identified with fire (which the early Stoics held to be the fundamental stuff (*Urstoff*) out of which all matter was ultimately composed). Thus Cicero, in his account of the early Stoics, says that

> Cleanthes, who was [a] pupil of Zeno, says that the universe itself is God, and then goes on to give this name to the mind and spirit which animates the

whole of nature. Finally he finds the supreme godhead in the encircling fire of the upper air, which we call the aether: for this is both the deepest and the highest, surrounding all things in all directions.

(1972: 85)

Cicero is here writing to discredit this idea of God, even though elsewhere in his writings he drew upon Stoic thought for his own purposes. Nevertheless he indicates how, for the Stoics, God and the material universe are not separable: indeed the universe itself, thought of in relation to its life and function, 'is' God. In this sense also God can be thought of as the rationality of the universe, or, put another way, as its fixed laws. Cicero continues,

Chrysippus . . . affirms that the divine power is to be found in reason, and in a mind and consciousness which pervades the whole universe. He says in fact that the universe itself is God, or an emanation of the divine mind. Or again he speaks of the government of the universe as the operation of a rational intelligence and of a universal common nature which embraces all things.

(86)

For the Stoics, it would be a fundamental mistake to think of matter and spirit, the world and God, as opposites. Rather, the world is what it is because it is permeated by divine spirit, just as a person is who she is because the finely textured atoms of spirit permeate the body. (Lucretius had argued for the latter, but not generalized the point to the former.)

Seneca, who adapts Stoic reasoning for his own purposes, conflates the permeation of the world and of the human body by a divine power or presence. In a letter to his friend Lucilius, he writes:

There is no need to raise our hands to heaven; there is no need to implore the temple warden to allow us close to the ear of some graven image, as though this increased our chances of being heard. God is near you, is with you, is inside you. Yes, Lucilius, there resides within us a divine spirit, which guards us and watches us in the evil and the good we do. . . . He it is that prompts us to noble and exalted endeavours.

(1969: 86)

As Seneca presents it, the Stoic world view is integrated with the view of how to live well: moral integrity and a holistic account of physics and theology are not separable.

This interconnection sometimes leads Seneca to speak of the physical world and its beauty in far more life-affirming terms than he does in the passage quoted earlier where rivers, trees and precipices were seen as opportunities for suicide. In the same letter to Lucilius where he writes of the divine within him, Seneca goes on to speak of the divine in nature:

> If you have ever come on a dense wood of ancient trees that have risen to
> an exceptional height . . . your sense of wonderment at finding so deep and
> unbroken a gloom out of doors, will persuade you of the presence of a deity.
> Any cave in which the rocks have been eroded deep into the mountain resting
> on it . . . will strike into your soul some kind of inkling of the divine. We
> venerate the sources of important streams . . . the darkness or unfathomable
> depth of pools has made their waters sacred.
>
> (87)

Delight in the beauty of nature includes recognition of its divinity, which is at
one with the divinity within the person, the 'divine power' that has descended
into the body.

Seneca's description of that descent, at least as it is found in the life of a sage,
further connects the divinity of the universe with a life of wisdom. The soul of a
sage is in some sense still in the heaven from which it descends and to which it
longs to return.

> In the same way as the sun's rays touch the earth but are really situated at the
> point from which they emanate, a soul possessed of greatness and holiness,
> which has been sent down into this world in order that we may gain a nearer
> knowledge of the divine, associates with us, certainly, but never loses contact
> with its source. On that source it depends; that is the direction in which its
> eyes turn, and the direction it seeks to climb in; the manner in which it takes
> part in our affairs is that of a superior being.
>
> (88)

Seneca's views here are, arguably, not the same as those of the Old Stoics (Rist
1969: 206–18), and are inconsistent with his own statements elsewhere; they have,
in fact, much in common with the ideas of Plotinus as we shall see in the final
chapter. Their importance here is the way in which they indicate a life-affirming
position of integration which Seneca sometimes embraces, only to slip from it into
a perspective of violence, preoccupation with death and contempt for life. How
does this slippage take place?

The initial implication, drawn by Seneca in unity with Stoic teaching from its
earliest expression, is that God, or nature, is identical with reason. Reason or
rational law structures the universe; its activities are not random. The laws of the
universe can be investigated and understood; and this investigation is itself an
effort to understand the divine. Seneca expresses these interconnections, passing
easily between 'nature', 'god' and the activity of an enquiring mind:

> I myself am grateful to nature, both when I view it in the aspect which is open
> to everyone, and when I have entered into its mysteries: when I learn what
> is the material substance of the universe; who is its author or guardian; what
> god is; whether he is entirely wrapped up in himself or sometimes has regard

> for us as well; whether he creates something daily or has created it only once;
> whether he is part of the world or he is the world . . .
>
> (1997: 107)

This, says Seneca, is the highest value in life: if he had not been able to undertake these studies 'it would not have been worth while being born' (107). For a man of enormous wealth and even greater influence, at the centre of imperial power as chief advisor to Nero, this is a very strong statement indeed. Even allowing for the rhetorical license and dissimulation characteristic of Seneca's prose (Rudich 1997), Seneca's emphasis on the life of reason adopts the Stoic notion of divine permeation of the world and the human person. In the letter to Lucilius he is explicit: what is 'peculiarly a man's' is 'his spirit, and the perfection of his reason in that spirit'.

> For man is a rational animal. Man's ideal state is realized when he has fulfilled the purpose for which he was born. And what is it that reason demands of him? Something very easy – that he live in accordance with his own nature.
>
> (1969: 88–9)

This 'life in accordance with nature' will thus be both the fulfilment of his individual self and in harmony with nature in the wider sense of natural law. The rational person will not be in conflict with the universe.

It is the unity between universal nature and human nature that is the basis of the much prized ideal of tranquillity. Natural law cannot be altered. It is therefore the best part of wisdom to accept what happens with equanimity and refuse to allow oneself to be disturbed. Seneca explains that it is this determination to equanimity that is what the Greek Stoics meant by passionlessness (*apatheia*): it signifies 'the man who refuses to allow anything that goes badly for him to affect him', even such things as the loss of a friend or the loss of a hand or an eye (1969: 48).[4]

Seneca in many of his writings moves through the sorts of things which could be expected to cause distress or agitation of the passions, trying to show how tranquillity can be sustained. The ultimate test case is death. Indeed whereas in other Stoic writings death is just one of a list of things about which fear and distress must be overcome, in Seneca it often seems that it is death that weighs most heavily upon his mind: the other evils or difficulties are discussed as a way of leading up to death, which is what he really wants to write about. Thus, for example, in his essay 'On Tranquillity of Mind' Seneca sets out the ideal as 'supreme and nearly divine':

> seeking how the mind can follow a smooth and steady course, well disposed to itself, happily regarding its own condition and with no interruption to this pleasure, but remaining in a state of peace with no ups and downs: that will be tranquillity.
>
> (1997: 33)

Since life is full of vicissitudes, such peace must obviously be immune to changes of fortune; and to ensure this immunity an attitude of detachment must be cultivated. Wealth and private possessions are 'the greatest source of human misery' because of the greedy preoccupation money engenders: a sage recognizes that poverty is freedom. The same is true of prestige and high political office. These may be pursued for the sake of the public good; but no one should cling to them in such a way that their loss would disturb the tranquillity of their mind. The vices and human failings of others should be held as 'not hateful but ridiculous': it is better to laugh about the moral failures of others than to allow them to 'drive the mind into a darkness whose shadows overwhelm it' (54). Seneca was writing this during the time that he was Nero's tutor, and was having to confront increasing levels of selfishness, cruelty and vice in his young but all-powerful charge: in this context his words can be read as his counsel to himself not to fall into despair. 'So we should make light of all things and endure them with tolerance: it is more civilized to make fun of life than to bewail it' (54).[5]

What if the troubles that must be faced are not external ones like loss of wealth or the bad behaviour of others, but rather have a much nearer personal impact: illness, exile, torture, or death? In one of his letters to Lucilius Seneca gives advice on how to deal with such eventualities. Rather than dismiss thoughts and fears about what might never happen, Seneca's counsel is to face up to the worst possible scenario, 'then mentally calculate all the evil involved in it and appraise your own fear' (1997: 87). Each dreadful thing should be imagined: exile, imprisonment, burning, death: 'set up these horrors one by one', examine them in detail in the imagination. In each case, Seneca says, it is possible to think of people who have faced such a situation with courage.

> But this above all remember: to banish life's turbulence and see clearly the essence of everything. You will then realize that there is nothing fearful there except fear itself.
>
> (89)

Crucial to all of this is contempt for death: if once the fear of death is overcome, then all other fears can be seen in proportion to it: 'death is so far not to be feared that, thanks to it, nothing is to be feared' (89). Every kind of torment ceases with death; and every kind of torment can in fact be borne until death comes to release the sufferer. Seneca writes with rhetorical flourish:

> Why do you show me swords and flames and a crowd of executioners clamouring around you? Away with that parade behind which you lurk to terrify fools: you are death, whom lately my slave and my handmaid despised. Why display again all the equipment of whips and racks – the instruments specially designed to tear apart individual joints, and a thousand other tools for slaughtering a man bit by bit? Lay aside those means of paralyzing us with horror; silence the groans, the shrieks, the hoarse cries extorted under torture . . .
>
> (1997: 89–90)

and so Seneca continues, outlining in graphic detail various possibilities of pain from which death offers an attractive escape. Gradually the suspicion arises: does Seneca actually take pleasure in recounting such horrific possibilities?

The suspicion is increased when we observe the way in which Seneca sometimes slides from the contempt of death to a bitterness towards life. The former is of course standard Stoic teaching: to overcome the fear of death, death is to be frequently rehearsed.

> 'Rehearse death'. To say this is to tell a person to rehearse his freedom. A person who has learned how to die has unlearned how to be a slave. He is above, or at any rate beyond the reach of, all political powers. What are prisons, warders, bars to him? He has an open door. There is but one chain holding us in fetters, and that is our love of life.
>
> (1969: 72)

We are back with the availability of suicide as a means to end a situation if it is truly unbearable. But as Seneca continues, his words show not only contempt for death but contempt for life: his very denial betrays his preoccupation:

> There is no need to cast out this love [of life] altogether, but it does need to be lessened somewhat so that, in the event of circumstances ever demanding this, nothing may stand in the way of our being prepared to do at once what we must do at some time or other.
>
> (Ibid.)

The way in which Seneca tries to persuade his correspondent (and himself) that death is to be welcomed rather than feared is by disparaging the pleasures of life.

> Pleasures themselves lead to pain, banquets bring indigestion, excessive drinking brings muscular paralysis and fits of trembling, lust brings deformity in hands, feet and all the joints. I shall become poor . . . I shall be bound in fetters: so what? Am I free now? Nature has tied me to this grievous weight of my body. I shall die: what you mean is this – I shall cease to be liable to illness, I shall cease to be liable to bonds, I shall cease to be liable to death.
>
> (1997: 90)

Life is not something to be treasured or clung to. Rather, Seneca sees life as an effort which takes a great deal of courage: far more courage, in fact, than death. 'There are times when even to live is an act of bravery' (1969: 171).

Seneca thus moves from the standard Stoic teaching that death is not to be feared but rather to be accepted with tranquillity of mind, to a non-Stoic contempt for life itself. He struggles against what he calls 'a passion for dying' (1997: 92) in a way that shows he is gripped by it (see Rist 1969: 248–50; for an opposing view see Griffin 1976: 385). He rejects a death wish; but his very rejection trails off into a sense of the utter pointlessness of life. He says,

> there is an unthinking tendency towards death, which often gets hold of men of noble and most energetic character, and often men who are indolent and spiritless: the former despise life, the latter are flattened by it. . . . Theirs is not a contempt for life but boredom with it, a feeling we sink into when influenced by the sort of philosophy which makes us say, 'How long the same old things? I shall wake up and go to sleep, I shall eat and be hungry, I shall be cold and hot. There's no end to anything. . . . All things pass on only to return. Nothing I do or see is new: sometimes one gets sick even of this'. There are many who think that life is not harsh but superfluous.
>
> (1997: 92)

And with that his letter ends. If his aim was to refute such a view of the superfluity of life, he prosecutes the aim at best half-heartedly. There is a sense in this letter of utter world-weariness, a search for 'a tolerable pretext to die' (Rist 1969: 249).

The desire for death was not linked to any particular view of post-mortem existence. It is true that Seneca occasionally speculates about the possibility of the soul surviving the death of the body (1997: 94) but more often speaks of immortality in terms of glorious memory, reminiscent of Homer (1997: 56; 1969: 131). His love of death, however, is related firmly to the recurring sense that life is worthless; that there is no point to it. Although Seneca struggles against the death wish, *libido moriendi*, the very terms of his struggle show the extent to which he himself was gripped by it. When this contempt for life and for this world in which life is lived was linked with a belief in immortality in medieval christendom, it would have an incalculable influence on the genealogy of death, as we shall see in a later volume.

'All life is a servitude'

Seneca's world-weariness and preoccupation with death can be read in another way, however, when we look more closely at his own precarious position as tutor and advisor to Nero. It was a situation within which he wielded enormous power and from which he derived great wealth. On the face of it, it is not consistent with his stance as a Stoic philosopher. What was a Stoic sage doing in the top echelons of power? What sort of integrity is it that can pour scorn on money and possessions in his writings and yet use his position in Nero's court to amass and enjoy luxury available only to the very few? Such questions were asked even in his own time. Tacitus gives an account of the accusations of Publius Suillius Rufus who says that Seneca 'only understands academic activities and immature youths', that he seduced the imperial princess, and above all that he used his position to amass wealth.

What branch of learning, what philosophical school, won Seneca three hundred million sesterces during four years of imperial friendship? In Rome, he entices into his snares the childless and their legacies. His huge rates of interest suck Italy and the provinces dry.

(1996: 304–5)

Suillius' words came to Seneca's ears and the accusations were silenced. But the questions did not go away. Seneca is one of a long line of thinkers whose lives raise the issue of how their philosophical insights are affected or even contaminated by their political and moral position. Can his words carry the moral weight and respect which they are usually accorded, or are they compromised from the outset?

The questions become all the more insistent in the face of Nero's character and behaviour, in some of which, at least, Seneca was implicated. Seneca was recalled from exile in 49 CE by Agrippina, Nero's mother, to be his tutor.[6] Even if it is granted that Nero was not the monstrous tyrant of popular historical mythology, and that especially in the first years of his reign he had the good of Rome and the Empire much at heart (Holland 2000), there is no escaping the fact that he could be selfish, cruel and treacherous. When he became emperor in 54 CE he was only fourteen years old.

At first Nero heeded the advice of Seneca and his co-advisor Burrus. As Tacitus puts it, Seneca and Burrus 'collaborated in controlling the emperor's perilous adolescence; their policy was to direct his deviations from virtue into licensed channels of indulgence', thereby sidelining Agrippina and igniting her hostility (1996: 284–5). Nero was, however, susceptible to jealousy; and would stop at nothing to achieve his wishes. Seneca's position was soon compromised. In 55 CE, for example, Nero's mother Agrippina exerted her influence to show favour to Claudius' son Britannicus. He died very soon after. According to Tacitus, the death, which occurred in public while Britannicus was dining with Nero, was murder by poison in a plot initiated by Nero. What was Seneca to do? If he did not accept what had happened he risked forfeiting his friendship with Nero, his privileges, perhaps even his life. Yet surely for a Stoic philosopher these were small risks compared with the loss of truth and integrity? There was, moreover, another way to look at the matter. If Seneca distanced himself from Nero he would lose such considerable influence as he still had over him, and things would go even worse for the Empire.

One of the things Seneca did in response was to write a treatise, De Clementia (On Clemency), in which he praised Nero's virtues and eulogized his innocence. Seneca presents it as a mirror within which Nero can look at his own good qualities; and then exhorts the young Emperor to maintain those virtues and the responsibilities that go with his power. At best, De Clementia can be read as an admonition to Nero and reassurance to the Roman elite about the character of government (Griffin 1976: 138). But such a charitable reading stretches credulity.

The exuberant praise of Nero's innocence leaves a taste of calculated hypocrisy and inordinate *dissimulatio*. Whatever the degree of his opportunism or his attachment to Nero, the philosopher could not possibly in his own mind have condoned this crime without suffering moral bankruptcy.

(Rudich 1997: 48)

Rudich argues throughout his book for a strong version of *dissimulatio*, where writers as skilled as Seneca and Lucan write for equally skilled readers who will be able to discern that they mean something very different from what they actually say. In this way, he suggests, Seneca could have found emotional release and self-excuse in his unbearable moral predicament. Even if that is so, however, the problem is not only with what Seneca wrote but with what he did. He continued as Nero's adviser; and if he was compromised in the murder of Britannicus, much worse was soon to follow.

After the death of Britannicus, Agrippina was increasingly marginalized. She struggled to retain a hold on Nero and on power; he, aided and abetted by Seneca, pushed her ever farther away. There were struggles between Nero and his mother about his mistress; Tacitus goes so far as to repeat a story that Agrippina attempted to entice her son to incest (1996: 313). Whatever the truth of such allegations, Nero found her interference intolerable and 'decided to kill her. His only doubt was whether to employ poison, or the dagger, or violence of some other kind' (ibid.). The method he decided upon – a contrived shipwreck – misfired; and in the end Nero sent an assassin to kill his mother. If Seneca was not actively involved in planning Agrippina's murder (and he may well have been), he certainly colluded with it, and after the fact wrote a speech of feeble self-exoneration for Nero to deliver to the Senate. The most charitable construction of this episode is given by Rudich: 'The entire story of Seneca's career under Nero is a sorrowful lesson in the cost of engagement with evil for the sake – presumably – of the good' (1997: 72). But could the end justify the means? Can anything justify matricide?

Seneca's political involvement puts his writings on virtue and death into a new perspective. According to Stoic philosophy, moral integrity was of the highest value; yet while Seneca was entangled with the court of Nero he compromised that integrity repeatedly. The Jewish historian of his time, Josephus, commented upon the way in which a tyrannical political system made people slaves not only to the system but even to the worst in themselves. They are 'trained to live the life of slaves', and prefer 'rather to await their end in utmost degradation than to die with virtue' (Josephus *Antiquities of the Jews* 2.181, cited in MacMullen 1967: 31). Seneca, with all his learning, power, wealth and political influence is hardly one for whom the description of 'slave' would seem apt. And yet when we consider how he was involved in intrigue and murder in Nero's court, prostituting his Stoic principles which did not reckon death too high a price to pay for moral integrity, perhaps 'slave' is not too strong a term after all.

In spite of Seneca's support for Nero through these and other atrocities, his influence on the Emperor steadily declined; and it is clear that Seneca felt more and more uncomfortable in his position as advisor to Nero. According to Tacitus' account, the discomfort came to a head after the event for which Nero is most often remembered: the burning of Rome. It is probably not true that Nero was 'fiddling while Rome burned'; indeed a case can be made that he actually worked indefatigably to try to quench the flames and did everything he could to prevent them from spreading further and ploughed great resources into a rebuilding programme (Holland 2000: 171–2). Nevertheless, the suspicion was rife that Nero had started the fire. 'To suppress this rumour', says Tacitus, 'Nero fabricated scapegoats – and punished with every refinement the notoriously depraved Christians'. With Christians as victims, Nero appeased the populace by a huge spectacle of death.

> Dressed in wild animals' skins, they were torn to pieces by dogs, or crucified, or made into torches to be ignited after dark as substitutes for daylight. Nero provided his Gardens for the spectacle, and exhibited displays in the Circus . . .
>
> (1996: 365)

But Nero went too far. Although Christians might have been hated by many, 'the victims were pitied. For it was felt that they were being sacrificed to one man's brutality rather than to the national interest'.

(366)

I shall return to Christian martyrdom and the spectacles of death in the next chapter. The question here is: where was Seneca in all this? There is no evidence that he protested to Nero about his treatment of the Christians, though it is only fair to add that by this stage Nero might have been unlikely to heed Seneca's advice. Tacitus repeats as a 'rumour' that Seneca 'sought to avoid the odium of this sacrilege by asking leave to retire to a distant country retreat' (366). Permission was not granted. Seneca pretended he was ill, and stayed in his bedroom. Nero tried to poison him; but Seneca avoided the poison. Clearly, relations between the two were very low; but to what extent this was because Seneca was at last paying heed to his overburdened conscience can only be conjectured.

'Even his gait'

It was, however, probably during this year (64 CE) that Seneca composed the dialogue 'On Tranquillity of Mind', a large part of which sets out his attitude towards public political service. It was standard Stoic teaching that a sage should be an active citizen, serving the public good to the best of his ability. Each person must decide how best he can fulfil this role.

> Suppose he cannot be a soldier: let him seek public office. Suppose he has to live in a private capacity: let him be an advocate. . . . Even if a man's hands

are cut off, he finds he can yet serve his side by standing firm and cheering them on. You should do something like that: if Fortune has removed you from playing a leading role in public life you should still stand firm and cheer others on, and if someone grips your throat, still stand firm and help though silent. The service of a good citizen is never useless: being heard and seen, he helps by his expression, a nod of his head, a stubborn silence, even his gait.

(1997: 38)

How much autobiography is in this passage? Did Seneca feel that his hands had been cut off and his throat gripped? Was he being asked for approval which he refused to give, so that even his silence or his very presence became a rebuke?

The sense that Seneca is talking about himself increases when in the next paragraph he invokes Socrates (with whom as we have noted he was often identified): Socrates not so much as the intellectual interlocutor of Plato's dialogues but Socrates as the 'free spirit' in Athens during the grim period of the Thirty Tyrants. In spite of the fact that Socrates could do nothing, Seneca says, his presence was influential. He was powerless, and in the end he was executed; but his very fearlessness was an example. 'To those willing to imitate him he was a walking inspiration' (39). Is Seneca thinking about his own role in Rome under the tyranny of the young Emperor whom he could no longer influence?

Seneca considers alternatives. What if public life has become intolerable? There comes a point, he says, when

if you happen to live at a time when public life is hard to cope with, you will just have to claim more time for leisure and literary work, seek a safe harbour from time to time as if you were on a dangerous voyage, and not wait for public life to dismiss you but voluntarily release yourself from it first.

(40)

It was of course what Seneca himself had tried to do in his petition to be allowed to retire to the countryside. As Ramsey MacMullen has pointed out, in the tyrannical reign of despots like Nero, there were few available means of dissent, and retirement from action to philosophy was itself an action of protest (1967: 51). It was taken as such, too, by the emperors themselves, who felt so threatened by it that 'to Stoicize' or 'philosophize' became a crime, a rebuke to government, and philosophers were banished (57). It is no accident that both in *On the Tranquillity of Mind* and in his letters, Seneca regularly uses metaphors either of warfare or of the arena to describe the life and training of the philosopher. 'To read and reread, to "train", "exercise", "arm", and "drill" under ones teachers added great strength to inborn tendencies. It is here that one can begin to sense the overt, historic power of philosophy' (52). This is philosophy as dissent, philosophy up to its neck in power politics, with no pretence of clean hands but nonetheless working for the public good.

However, if this was Seneca's intention he had left it too late. He was mired in the affairs of the court; and although (or because?) Nero despised and probably feared him, he refused Seneca permission to retire. Seneca complains of captivity: the captivity of high office and wealth. 'All life is a servitude', he says (1997: 46). His privileged position has become a gilded cage, and a highly dangerous one. He exhorts his reader with feeling that surely reflects his own experience:

> Let us not envy those who stand higher than we do: what look like towering heights are precipices. . . . Indeed there are many who are forced to cling to their pinnacle because they cannot descend without falling; but they must bear witness that this in itself is their greatest burden, that they are forced to be a burden to others, and that they are not so much elevated as impaled.
>
> (47)

For Seneca the pinnacle of power and success had indeed become a precipice. He knew that his fall must be near. His meditations on death and preparation for suicide, his contempt of life, must all be read in relation to this. For him, these preparations had soon to be put into effect. He was eventually granted permission to retire; but his time was brief. The invitation by the Emperor to cut his veins was not long in arriving, as Seneca had known it must. Whatever the compromise of his principles during his privileged life, he died at last as a Stoic.

Seneca was at the very top of the hierarchy of power and wealth in the early years of Nero's reign, and his gradual distancing of himself from the court, and ultimate suicide, must be seen as a protest against it, even if ambiguous. But there is little in Seneca's writing or career that would allow that protest to be read as a rejection of the ideals of manliness and violence that were part of imperial ideology, let alone to read his dissent as celebration of life. For that it is necessary to turn to those on the opposite end of the spectrum of wealth and status: the victims of the amphitheatre. In the next chapter I shall turn to this phenomenon of violent death in Roman culture, and shall show how, for some of its victims, it offered a way, *in extremis*, of celebrating life.

Chapter 18

Spectacles of death

Topping the list of things to see for today's visitor to Rome is the Colosseum, the ruins of the huge circular amphitheatre in which gladiatorial spectacles took place. These spectacles, I suggest, are crucial for an understanding of Roman ideology and its investment in death and violence. I have already mentioned them in connection with the slave trade as well as in relation to Roman constructions of gender. In this chapter I shall take a closer look at the spectacles and argue that, contrary to the claims of some modern scholars, these spectacles of death are not a mystifying aberration to the otherwise humane and civilized values of the Roman Empire. Rather, they consolidate and even celebrate key aspects of the Roman ideology of gender, violence and empire.

I shall also argue that there is another side to the story. One of the most insightful lessons of the work of Michel Foucault is that power ignites counterpower. At just the place where dominance is exerted at its most forceful, we should look for resistance. In the second half of this chapter I shall consider the resistance offered by the Christian martyrs who lost their lives in Roman amphitheatres, and shall examine their martyrdom as a protest against the Empire and its violent values. Moreover, I shall argue that they did more than protest. They offered a life-affirming alternative in which resurrection, fertility and new life were central symbols. Ironically, it was in order to bring newness into the world that they had to die.

A 'satisfying spectacle'

The Colosseum in its present form was begun by Vespasian and inaugurated by Titus in 80 CE with games lasting a hundred days.

> . . . animals both tame and wild were slain to the number of nine thousand . . . several [men] fought in single combat and several groups contended together both in infantry and naval battles. For Titus suddenly filled this same theatre with water. . . . He also brought in people on ships, who engaged in a sea-fight there . . . and others gave a similar exhibition outside the city. . . . There, too, on the first day there was a gladiatorial exhibition and a wild beast

hunt. . . . On the second day there was a horse-race, and on the third day a naval battle between three thousand men, followed by an infantry battle.

(Dio 66.25.1–5, in Kyle 1998: 35)

Although not all these events took place in the Colosseum itself, they were staged to celebrate its opening.

For all its grandeur, however, the Colosseum was not a new concept. There were amphitheatres in many parts of the Roman Empire from the late Republic onwards, partly to meet the demands of the army and its veterans; and in Rome itself gladiatorial games had been held (often in the Roman Forum) from a very early date. Besides the gladiatorial games and spectacles, Romans also watched chariot races and other large displays, including mock land battles and *naumachiae*, mock naval battles complete with ships and sailors. The chariot races were held in the Circus Maximus, a huge structure with long parallel sides and a semi-circular end: it could accommodate up to 320,000 spectators at a time. The naval battles were held on an artificial lake dug for the purpose, or sometimes (as above) in the Colosseum, which could be flooded. Suetonius describes the public shows given by Julius Caesar:

They included a gladiatorial contest, stage-plays for every Roman ward performed in several languages, chariot races in the Circus, athletic competitions, and a mock naval battle. . . . Wild beast hunts took place five days running, and the entertainment ended with a battle between two armies, each consisting of 500 infantry, twenty elephants, and thirty cavalry.

(1979: 30–1)

The games and spectacles held in these vast buildings were grand events, celebrations central to the triumphant self-identity of Rome. They were also brutal. Although they were 'entertainments' and the battles on land and water were mock battles, they were not harmless displays. Rather, as Donald Kyle shows, 'these "mock battles" were spectacular mass executions of captives'; they involved 'large numbers of victims and mass killing' (1998: 51), staged for the enjoyment of the Roman populace. The massive cruelty, and the delight with which it was watched by Romans of all classes over many centuries has caused subsequent scholars disquiet. How could the very civilization from which the west has derived many of its values take such pleasure in blood-thirsty spectacles? How can the undeniable facts of the games be reconciled with the high-minded ideals associated with classical culture? What must be said of the ideals and cultural capital of any civilization, ancient or modern, which sees itself as the apex of humanity with the right to police the world and yet requires ever escalating spectacles of violence (often eroticized violence) as a staple of its entertainment industry?

In their efforts to answer these questions in relation to Rome, scholars have offered varying interpretations of the games, ranging 'without consensus from pagan piety to human sacrifice and from sadism to imperial politics' (Kyle 1998:

7; cf Hopkins 1983: 27–30). There are plenty of attempts to show either that the spectacles were an aberration, or that they were much less brutal and cruel than they appear to us: in short that modern revulsion is a failure of understanding. Thus, for example, Roland Auguet rejects the idea that the Roman games were sadistic or that they had anything to do with vengefulness. He asserts that 'no link necessarily existed between the Roman mind and the cruelty implicit in certain games' (1972: 15) and believes that the games were in fact a rational aspect of the empire and its civilization, not an aberration.

Now, I agree with Auguet that the games were not an aberration. They were far too popular with a wide cross section of society over too long a time scale for an aberration theory to be at all plausible. Rather, it seems to me that Gunderson is right in arguing that 'nearly every major theme of the Roman power structure was deployed in the spectacles: social stratification; political theatre; crime and punishment; representations of civilization and empire; repression of women and exaltation of bellicose masculinity' (Gunderson 1996: 149). All these strands were interwoven in the Roman preoccupation with violence. Moreover, although the games themselves ended with the collapse of the Empire, the eroticized violent and necrophilic values they represent were encoded in subsequent western culture, not least in what would count as entertainment.

Connections with death

The spectacles were from the first connected with death. Gladiatorial contests were initially put on by the family after the funeral of a prominent citizen. They were 'funeral games', looking back perhaps to the practice of early Greeks as described by Homer in the chariot races and athletic competitions Achilles staged in honour of his friend Patroclus. The games in Rome escalated in size and in the number of participants: from two or three pairs of gladiators in 264 BCE, there was a steady increase until Julius Caesar announced in 45 BCE that in the games he was planning in honour of his daughter there would be 320 pairs. The celebrations of Trajan in 117 CE were said to involve 10,000 gladiators; and even if this is taken as a symbolic rather than a literal number, it is obvious that very many men were involved.

Trajan's games were not funeral games but rather celebrations of military victory over the Dacians. They show, however, how politically important the staging of games had become.[1] The public loved them. Aspiring politicians and generals vied with one another to provide the populace with spectacles. They would find some appropriate relative to honour with funeral games: Julius Caesar staged games for his long deceased father, and on another occasion for his daughter Julia. She had died eight years before, and thus her death was obviously a pretext; but the link between the spectacle and individual mortality was (at least rhetorically) maintained.

Moreover, death was linked with death. I have already discussed the importance of the spectacles in relation to military training and acquiring the manly hardness necessary for the violence of warfare. And it was that warfare, at least during the centuries in which the Empire was expanding, that provided large numbers of victims for the spectacles. Victorious generals had the right, on their return, to stage a 'triumph'. In order to be granted that right, a general was required to have slaughtered at least 5,000 people on his campaign, besides those whom he took captive. The spectacle of the triumph, therefore, not only involved carnage itself but also 'functioned as visible "proof" of deaths' (Kyle 1998: 42; see also Harris 1979: 25–6).

A triumph involved a public procession in which the general was honoured, followed by a spectacle in the amphitheatre or circus which recreated for the viewers the achievements of his campaign. In the procession might be included large numbers of wild animals, and parades of captives brought back from the wars. The *Historia Augusta*, for example, lists the participants in the triumphal processions of Probus and Aurelius respectively:

> One hundred Libyan leopards were produced, and one hundred Syrian ones; one hundred lionesses, together with three hundred bears. . . . Three hundred pairs of gladiators were also produced. . . . Four tigers, spotted giraffes, elks and other such, eight hundred pairs of gladiators in addition to the prisoners taken from barbarian races . . . all captives with their hands bound . . .
>
> (Cited in Wiedemann 1992: 13)

The *Historia Augusta* cannot be taken literally; but even as propaganda it reveals the ideology of the power of Rome over the lives and deaths of people and animals to the ends of the earth. What would happen to all these captives after the procession? Some of the prisoners might be taken to the slave market. The animals and the rest of the prisoners would be taken to the circus or amphitheatre, made to fight with one another in mock wars or *naumachiae*. There was a difference between gladiators and ordinary captives. The former, even if most of them were forced to become gladiators against their will, nevertheless received training and had a chance of fame and profit if they won (Kyle 1998: 79). The captives had no such opportunity. They were hopeless victims subjected to mass butchery. In the mock battles they were made to fight to the last man.

The public investment in death went well beyond the entertainment value of the spectacles, in a whole economy of slaughter. The captive people were taken prisoner and transported to Rome by the army – a major logistical exercise in itself. But there was also the immense cost and effort of hunting the wild animals and bringing them to Rome. All this must have taken the labour of large numbers of people. Then there was the matter of taking care of all the captive people and animals after they arrived, marshalling them through the streets during the procession itself, and forcing them to do what was required in the spectacles. Their treatment would have been brutal, but even so it would have needed a considerable workforce to supply food for the animal and human captives, to guard them and prevent escape, and to keep them alive and fit enough so that they would provide entertainment at the spectacle: the public did not like to watch shows where the victims were passive. And then there was the question of disposal of the very large numbers of animal and human corpses. Some of the animals may have been used for food; and the human bodies were probably dumped in pits or in the Tiber (Kyle 1998: 193, 220). There is no question of individual funerals or burial rites, but even so, a large labour force would have been required to dispose of the dead. The point is that there was a whole economy built around the spectacles of death.

One of the consequences of the later empire and the relative stability of the *Pax Romana* from Trajan onwards was that the Empire was not continually expanding and bringing new captives for execution in Roman spectacles. More and more of the victims that fed the amphitheatres were therefore common citizens perceived by an abusive legal system or a tyrannical emperor as internal foes. The public demanded entertainment. Trained gladiators could provide some of it; but 'condemned men and slaves were far more available and convenient' and became the victims of spectacles of death (Kyle 1998: 101). The mock battles and *naumachiae* involved many participants; there were also spectacles in which men (and sometimes women) were made to fight with one another individually, possibly nude or dressed up like gods or wrapped in animal skins. Alternatively they might be forced to fight wild animals. All these games required vast numbers of victims, either from defeated enemies or from within the empire.

The spectacles of the Colosseum and similar amphitheatres throughout the Empire thus brought together many strands of the Empire's investment in death. Spectacles were staged (at least initially) to commemorate a death; they did so by enacting many more deaths. They were made possible only because of a huge, and hugely successful, army, where 'success' was defined in terms of conquest, killing and enslavement. Spectacles confirmed and heightened the lust for slaughter among the Roman populace: emperors knew that their own popularity required ever escalating displays of violence. They served to reinforce structures of gender and ideals of manliness. Far from being an aberration, the spectacles in all their cruelty can be seen as a symbol of some of the core values of the Empire, the violent underside of its civilization.

'A race ready for death'

From the time of Nero, when Christians were made scapegoats for the fire of Rome and crucified or made into human torches or torn by dogs in a spectacle of death, Christians faced sporadic persecution and martyrdom. They were among the victims of the spectacles, in the Colosseum in Rome and in amphitheatres across the Empire. Their status as potential martyrs became part of their own self-identity; and their attitude to death was notorious among their contemporaries. The Christian ideology of martyrdom had an enormous and complicated impact on the genealogy of death and violence in late antiquity and the Middle Ages, in some respects increasing the preoccupation with death and in other respects subverting it. Detailed consideration of that impact must be deferred to the next volume of this project. Here I propose to consider Christian martyrs only in terms of their protest against Rome and its cost. I shall argue that in the spectacles of death, at the very point when Christians were utterly helpless and in the power of the emperor or his representative, they claimed victory, not by escape *from* death but by triumph *within* death. In so doing they undermined the whole structure of power and the values of gendered violence of the Roman Empire, and transformed the meaning of death for western culture.[2]

In statistical terms, the number of Christians killed for their faith was relatively small. Until the middle of the third century, when there was a period of organized persecution, Christians were, with a few exceptions, not hunted down, and Christianity was often tolerated as one religion among many. Under Domitian (81–96 CE) Christians, like all citizens, were required to take an oath of loyalty to the emperor as god, and could be persecuted if they refused; but under Trajan (98–117) this requirement was relaxed, though officially to be a Christian was a capital offence. Provincial governors might or might not take action against Christians, perhaps depending upon the mood of the populace. In Rome Christianity was making converts among the upper classes, and persecutions were limited. Even after the 'Great Persecution' of the mid third century, Christianity continued to expand and to make many new converts, so that by the time of the conversion of the emperor Constantine in the early fourth century, Christians were ready to penetrate every part of society (Chadwick 1967: 25–31; Brown 1971: 82–9; Fox 1986: ch. 9).

Although the actual number of Christian martyrs in the early centuries was relatively small, their impact was out of all proportion to their number. This was partly because of the way they represented themselves, but also partly because of the shock they caused among pagan observers who were astonished at their courage and at the divergence of their values from imperial ideology. It is worth looking a little more closely at both the self-representation and at the perception of others for the light which they cast on the possibilities of dissent. Though it cost them their lives, the Christian martyrs resisted imperial power at the very place where it was most concentrated, in the arena, and by their stance showed that power to be ephemeral.

To begin with pagan perceptions of Christianity, one of the things that comes across most clearly from varied sources is their non-Roman attitudes (taken as anti-social) and above all their lack of fear of death. When Tacitus described Nero's scape-goating of Christians after the fire of Rome, for example, he called Christianity a 'deadly superstition' and said that they were condemned 'for their anti-social tendencies' (1996: 365). In his view they deserved 'ruthless punishment' as Christians, though not for any guilt in relation to the fire. Tacitus would be unlikely to express himself so strongly if all he was referring to was a few odd beliefs or practices: in his view the 'anti-social tendencies' must have been sufficiently threatening to the public good to warrant severe punishment.

From other sources it becomes clear what those threatening attitudes were. Crucially, Christians refused to sacrifice to the emperor or to take an oath which honoured him as divinity. The test which Pliny the Younger, governor of Bithynia and Pontus during the reign of Trajan, used to determine whether or not an accused person was a Christian (and therefore should be executed) was whether they were willing to make offerings of wine and incense in front of Trajan's statue 'none of which . . . any genuine Christian can be induced to do' (1963: 294). As far as Christians were concerned, the emperor was not divine. He was therefore not all powerful, nor was he always right. He, and the values he stood for, could be challenged. We have seen one such challenge from John, author of the book of Revelation, regarding the economic oppression of the Empire: its policies and practices, its values and its self-concept could be weighed up and found wanting. The same challenge to the Empire was implicit every time Christians refused to venerate the emperor, and sometimes was put into forthright words. The second-century Christian Justin, who suffered martyrdom under Marcus Aurelius, invited the emperor to be converted to Christianity; but added, 'for we forewarn you, that you shall not escape the coming judgement of God, if you continue in injustice' (1885: 186). Even emperors could be judged. Only God was all powerful; only God – not Rome – was eternal. Here was dissent that struck at the heart of imperial ideology.

Now, most other dissenters could be dealt with by exile or death: the power of the Empire and its hegemony was retained by violence. If someone dissented, they could be eliminated. Knowledge of this ruthless truth kept most people from stepping out of line: the threat of death and violence kept the Empire with its ideology of death and violence in place. But the astonishing – and to some, exasperating – thing about Christians was that they did not fear death. They were willing, and sometimes even eager, to suffer and die. In a typical trial account, the judge is represented as pleading with his prisoner to save himself, but the reply was simply, 'the death which is coming to me is more pleasant than the life which you would give' (cited in Fox 1986: 421). In case after case Christians show their 'contempt of death and of its sequel', as Galen puts it (Walzer 1949: 15). Lucian of Samosata, writing in the early second century, complained that

> the poor wretches have convinced themselves, first and foremost, that they are going to be immortal and live for all time, in consequence of which they despise death and even willingly give themselves into custody most of them.
> (Lucian 1936: 13)

This was overstated: many Christians did what they could to avoid trouble. Moreover, Christians did not use violence against the emperor, or attack pagans (Fox 1986: 421). Nevertheless those who did volunteer for trial as Christians, or who met their death bravely when it came, made a deep impression.

What was to be done with them? If they refused to sacrifice to the emperor or treat him – or the imperial values which he represented – as divine and unchallengeable, they could be persecuted; but they did not fear persecution. They could be made to face leopards or bears or other wild beasts in the amphitheatre; but they welcomed the opportunity, so that the watching crowds observed their witness. The power of the Empire was exerted in violence crystallized in spectacles of death. By despising death, the martyrs despised also that power and that violence, and by despising power they rendered it powerless. It could kill them, but it could not overcome them. On its own terms, the violent ideology of omnipotent empire was undone.

I am not suggesting that such undermining of imperial ideology was conscious or deliberate on the part of Christians, only that it was a consequence of their stance. Their own self-representation, as Judith Perkins (1995) has shown, was of their willingness to suffer and die; but they represented this more in terms of identification with Christ's suffering and death, and their hopes for eternal life, than in terms of rejection of imperial values. Thus, famously, Ignatius, Bishop of Antioch, who was arrested and transported to Rome for execution, wrote:

> I am the wheat of God, and let me be ground by the teeth of the wild beasts, that I may be found the pure bread of Christ. Rather entice the wild beasts, that they may become my tomb. . . . Then shall I truly be a disciple of Christ . . . when I suffer, I shall be the freedman of Jesus, and shall rise again emancipated in him.
>
> (1885: 75)

As they understood it, Jesus had been executed as a common prisoner, and so had several of the disciples: Peter and Paul, by tradition, had both been killed by Nero, the former by being crucified upside down, and in the Acts of the Apostles others including Stephen and James had been martyred. Polycarp, writing to the Christian community at Philippi shortly before his own execution, encouraged his readers to follow the example of these martyrs, 'in the assurance that all these have not [died] in vain, but in faith and righteousness, and that they are [now] in their due place in the presence of the Lord, with whom also they suffered' (1885: 35).

This same Polycarp was captured and brought to trial when he was in advanced old age. The proconsul tried repeatedly to get Polycarp to renounce Christ and venerate Caesar, but the old man replied, 'Eighty and six years have I served him, and he never did me any injury: how can I blaspheme my King and my Saviour?' (41). When threatened with wild beasts, he said 'Call them then'; and when the punishment was changed to being burnt alive, he replied to the proconsul,

> Thou threatened me with fire which burneth for an hour, and after a little is extinguished, but art ignorant of the fire of the coming judgement and of eternal punishment reserved for the ungodly. But why tarriest thou? Bring forth what thou wilt'.
>
> (Ibid.)

And so the old man was led to the stake, but when they were about to nail him to it he said, 'Leave me as I am, for he that giveth me strength to endure the fire, will also enable me, without your securing me by nails, to remain without moving in the pile.' When the fire was lit the flames formed an arch around him, 'And he appeared within not like flesh which is burnt, but as bread that is baked, or as gold and silver glowing in a furnace.'

The historical accuracy of this account is not the point. What matters is that this letter and many others like them circulated among Christian communities and in the wider world, and held up the martyrs for admiration and as patterns to imitate. They offered 'a narrative path for Christians, a path that without exception ended in premature and welcome death' (Perkins 1995: 25). As more and more Christians were willing to follow the example of the early martyrs, both their own self-representation and the perception of them by non-Christians was of people who preferred to die rather than renounce their faith in one whose *imperium*, they claimed, was not of this world. In the spectacles of death, at the very point where the imperial power crystallized against them, that power was rendered impotent and the ideology of empire subverted, precisely because death was constructed differently.

In the light of what we have already seen of the connections between constructions of death and gender, it is no surprise that the Christian martyrs also undermined Roman ideas of gender. The categories of 'penetrator' and 'penetrated' did not map on to the executioner and the martyr as they usually did in the spectacles of death. The martyrs were penetrated: gored, burnt, stabbed or hacked. Yet they were the ones who presented themselves not as feminized victims but as those who claimed active – divine – power, strength sufficient to withstand any torture. By contrast, the penetrator was impotent. Virile power or brute force could be brought to bear on the victims, but the manliness of that power was undermined.

The categories of gender are radically destabilized throughout the martyr literature,[3] perhaps nowhere more vividly than in the account of the deaths of Perpetua and Felicitas, mentioned in chapter 14. Perpetua was a young woman with a baby; Felicitas was pregnant when she came before the judge and gave birth prior to her execution. No one could forget that they were women. But while they were in prison prior to their appearance in the amphitheatre, Perpetua had a dream which she recorded. She dreamed that she was in the arena, 'condemned to the beasts', with 'a huge crowd watching eagerly'.

> And there came out an Egyptian, foul of look, with his attendants to fight against me. And to me also there came goodly young men to be my attendants and supporters. And I was stripped and was changed into a man.
>
> (Musarillo 1972: x)

From this point onwards, in her dream, Perpetua is victorious. She gives a vivid account of her fight with the Egyptian gladiator, fists and heels flying, until finally she trips him up 'and he fell on his face; and I trod on his head', victorious. All this time she is a man.

But then she wakes up, a woman. She takes the dream, however, as a sign that she will be as 'manly' and courageous in reality as she has been in the dream; she is the one who encourages her Christian companions. When the day of the spectacle comes, the Christian men in the arena with her were gored and mauled by wild animals: leopard, bear and boar; but for the women 'the Devil made ready a mad heifer, an unusual animal selected for this reason, that he wished to match their sex with that of the beast' (xx). Again gender is foregrounded. Perpetua and Felicitas were tossed and gored by the heifer as the men were by the wild beasts, but not killed, so they were 'flung on to the place allotted to the throat-cutting'. But when it came to it, the gladiator could not do it: Perpetua 'herself guided to her throat the wavering hand' that held the sword. And the recorder concludes, 'Perhaps so great a woman . . . could not otherwise be slain except she willed' (xxi).

Who was active and who was passive in this representation of death and gender? Perpetua and her companions were feminized in the sense of being multiply penetrated; yet they are the ones who in the account are in control while the gladiator is unmanned. As in Roman constructions of suicide, Perpetua's autonomy is emphasized, yet with a 'womanly' kindness to the trembling gladiator. In the earlier narrative there remains a troublesome sense in which gender stereotypes are reinforced: Perpetua can only think of herself as victorious when she thinks of herself as a man. But in the arena itself those stereotypes are overcome, and gender categories are destabilized along with constructions of death.

A new symbolic?

There can be little doubt that the Christian martyrs radically reconfigured constructions of death and gender in ways that would have a lasting impact on the genealogy of death in the Middle Ages and beyond. But to what extent did this reconfiguration signal a move *away* from preoccupation with death and to what extent did it merely shift the *nature* of that preoccupation? Did it remain necrophilic, or was there a move to a new symbolic in which life rather than death is central?

The answer, I think, must be ambiguous. Certainly Christians who took the martyrs as examples represented themselves as willing to suffer and die. Indeed in their eagerness to do so they could be seen as just as preoccupied with death – death configured differently – as was Lucretius or Seneca. Yet there are persistent metaphors in early Christian writing, metaphors of seeds and plants and flourishing, connected with metaphors of resurrection, which give a different impression. In these writings, I suggest, there are possibilities for a symbolic of natality. During subsequent centuries the ambiguity continues, with on the one hand the necrophilia of preoccupation with final judgement, heaven, hell and purgatory, and the violence of the crusades and the inquisition; yet on the other hand in such texts as those of some medieval women mystics a symbolic of natality forms part of a vision of hope. Examination of that enduring ambiguity must be left to a later volume; here I propose to consider briefly the metaphors of seed and resurrection as they arise out of the martyr literature and subvert the imperial ideology of death.

Ever since the writings of Paul, the metaphor of the seed that is sown in the earth and sprouts to bring forth new life had been used as an image of death and resurrection. Paul wrote, of the body,

> What you sow does not come to life unless it dies. And what you sow is not the body which is to be, but a bare kernel, perhaps of wheat or of some other grain. . . . What is sown is perishable, what is raised is imperishable. It is sown in weakness, it is raised in power. It is sown a physical body, it is raised a spiritual body.
>
> (1 Cor. 15: 36–44 RSV)

These words are patent of many interpretations, some of them mutually contradictory, as Caroline Walker Bynum has shown (1995: 1–42). But one of those interpretations was to connect the seed imagery with fertility and with the growth and flourishing of new life. The God who created life in the first place, it was held, could bring new life out of death. Just as Jesus had risen from the dead with a transformed but recognizable body, they held, so too would the martyrs be the first to live again and flourish in a world that had been transformed. Later, this transformed world was thought of either as heaven or as indefinitely deferred; but in the early centuries at least, some Christians expected an earthly paradise, brought about by God to replace the Roman Empire, and anticipated by their own actions (Shaw 1998: ch. 5).

The 'extraordinary fertility' (Bynum 1995: 23) of this earthly paradise is expressed, for example, by Papias, an early Christian writer, who says,

> A time is coming when vineyards spring up, each having ten-thousand vines . . . and every grape, when pressed, will yield twenty-five measures of wine. And when anyone of the saints takes hold of one of their clusters, another cluster will cry out: 'I am better. Take me. . . . ' In like manner, a grain of wheat will grow ten thousand heads . . . and every grain will yield ten pounds of clean, pure flour; but the other fruit trees, too, as well as seeds and herbs, will bear in proportions suited to each kind. . . .
>
> (Frag. I.2–3, quoted in Bynum 1995: 23)

Not only plants and trees but also people will flourish: Bynum cites the early text known as *The Shepherd of Hermas* which says that 'in the world to come the righteous will be like living trees that flower' (ibid.).

The earthly paradise which God would bring about was a restoration of the Garden of Eden, where plants, animals and people would live life to the full.

It was a place of great beauty, beauty not pressed into the service of imperial ideology but manifesting the wonder of life and divine creativity. Men and women would live together harmoniously; there would be no greed and no violence; and the focus and meaning of life would be found in the worship of God. Teresa Shaw (1998) has shown how this earthly paradise turned from the preoccupation with death to the love of life, and how Christian communities developed the ideal of living even now within that life, anticipating it and helping to bring it about by their actions.

According to such thinking, death was not to be dreaded, since God would raise up any who had died before the earthly paradise was established, to take their place alongside those Christians who lived to see the day. But the martyrs were a special case. They would be given great reward for the suffering they had endured through faithfulness to Christ. Christians who witnessed the martyrdom of members of their community often claimed that the life and extraordinary beauty of paradise was already upon them even while they suffered. As Perpetua saw in her dream, Christ would be with her in the amphitheatre; and those who recorded her death witnessed that this was the case. Alternatively, Christians were assured in a later vision that all was well with the one whose death they had watched. Thus the night after Ignatius had been thrown to the beasts he appeared to his grieving friends assuring them of his wellbeing and urging them also to be faithful until God's rule was established on earth (Ignatius 1885: 131). Polycarp, the old man burnt at the stake, was said to give off a sweet perfume like baking bread, not like charred flesh.

> the uncanny beauty that had superimposed itself over Polycarp's horrendous death was a glimpse of the future. The new body . . . would live in a fully material world that was as heavy with goodness as the intoxicating breath of a field in full flower.
>
> (Brown 1988: 73)

It was a foretaste of the paradise of God: newness entered the world.

Such talk of earthly paradise now sounds heavily tinged with compensatory romanticism. At the time, however, it carried major practical consequences. The most obvious of these was the requirement upon all Christians to be prepared for martyrdom, to see death not according to the ideology of the Empire but as an opportunity of faithfulness to Christ: the new Adam who would inaugurate paradise. But the life of the Christian community, even while the Roman Empire continued, was to be lived according to the values of that paradise. Christians were to renounce violence and live peaceably; they were not to give way to greed or selfishness but to practise love and kindness and generosity to all, celebrating the beauty of life in the Spirit. The earthly remains of the martyrs symbolized victorious entry into the fullness of that life, and were venerated by the Christian community: already in the case of Ignatius, when the wild beasts had finished their gruesome work 'the harder portions of his holy remains were left, which were conveyed to Antioch and wrapped in linen, as an inestimable treasure left to the holy Church by the grace that was in the martyr' (Ignatius 1885: 131).

Even at the time, the emphasis on life was not unambiguous; and as time went on more and more of that emphasis was recuperated to preoccupation with death. Alongside the writings about earthly paradise were texts insisting on another heavenly world and contempt for this one. Though there were those who exhorted Christians to be peaceable and to renounce violence and the bearing of arms, there were also those who looked for divine vengeance and violent overthrow of earthly powers, and, later, those who marched in the crusading armies of the Lord. The veneration of the remains of martyrs became an unedifying trade in relics. All of this is the material of another volume. The crucial point here is that at the very point of greatest imperial power and most intense necrophilia, in the spectacles of death, that power was undone by the courageous resistance of those who, by their reconfiguration of death, bore witness to the possibilities of an imaginary of life, flourishing and natality.

Chapter 19

Violence to eternity

Plotinus and the mystical way

At the same time as Christians were offering a reconfiguration of death through their willingness for martyrdom, another reconfiguration was taking place that would have an immense impact on the genealogy of death. Neopythagoreans and Neoplatonists were turning away from this world of change and chance and looking toward another world, eternal as Rome was not, unchanging and beautiful. In this final chapter I shall look briefly at Ovid's presentation of Pythagoras' teaching, and then focus on the writings of Plotinus, who, I shall argue, turned from the violence of the fragmenting empire to an eternal world, where beauty never decays, and where life is redefined as having nothing to do with gendered bodies or the material world of change.

Legless frogs and personal piety

> O mortals
> Dumb in cold fear of death, why do you tremble
> At Stygian rivers, shadows, empty names,
> The lying stock of poets, and the terrors
> Of a false world? I tell you that your bodies
> Can never suffer evil, whether fire
> Consumes them, or the waste of time. Our souls
> Are deathless; always, when they leave our bodies,
> They find new dwelling-places
>
> (Ovid 1955: 370)

Ovid puts these words into the mouth of Pythagoras, the Presocratic philosopher of the sixth century BCE whose work influenced Plato in his theories of the separation of body and soul. As we have seen, Ovid's works are full of jokes at the expense of writers who were taken – and took themselves – very seriously. As Ovid represents Pythagoras, he looks ridiculous, spouting 'a comic grab bag of soapbox philosophy' (Mack 1988: 142) in the examples he gives of the reincarnation of birds and serpents and legless green frogs emerging out of mud.

Yet Ovid's jokes often carry a serious message: we have already seen how this is true of his representation of Pythagoras' teaching that nothing – not even 'eternal Rome' – lasts forever. How literally are his readers meant to take Pythagoras' teaching that death is not to be feared because when the soul is separated from the body it takes up residence in some other body, going from form to form in the great pattern of Nature?

> Nothing remains the same: the great renewer,
> Nature, makes form from form, and, oh, believe me
> That nothing ever dies. What we call birth
> Is the beginning of a difference,
> No more than that, and death is only ceasing
> Of what had been before. The parts may vary,
> Shifting from here to there, hither and yon,
> And back again, but the great sum is constant.
> (Ovid 1955: 373)

Ovid might well have been laughing when he wrote that; his picture of Pythagoras' concern that we not eat meat lest we be eating our deceased relatives is comical.

Whether or not Ovid himself found them funny, his readers began to take Pythagoras' theories very seriously indeed. Neopythagorian beliefs in a soul that was separable from the body, that could survive bodily death and could be reincarnated in another body became popular in the second to fourth centuries. The believer could conquer death. Especially among the masses the belief in reincarnation was often coupled with magical practices and attempts to invoke the spirit world. Ascetic exercises, intended to loosen the bond between body and soul and to liberate the spirit for the realm of truth, gained popularity. Wonder workers and theurges found a ready reception among those who turned to an inner world, associated with the world beyond death and differentiated from the material and political world. Various teachers claimed to be reincarnations of figures from the past: Alexander of Abonoteichus alleged that he was the reincarnation of Pythagoras himself (MacMullen 1967: 97–108).

As the Roman Empire increasingly distanced itself from the politics of its republican era and became in fact, if not in name, a military dictatorship, ordinary people had less and less effect on the policies of the Empire. Philosophers, too, had little scope for intervention. A despotic ruler will not care for the interventions of intellectuals, especially if they criticize absolute power and its abuses. In such circumstances intellectuals face a choice. Either they can continue their efforts to speak truth to power and accept the consequences, as Seneca ultimately did. Or they can redefine intellectual endeavour in such a way that it is no longer a threat, no longer in active engagement with public life.

The Neopythagoreans of the second to the fourth century increasingly fall into this latter category. Their concerns shifted to immortality, freedom of the soul from the fetters of this material existence. Ethics was seen not as a question of public virtue but of personal piety, purification that would enable the soul to live in a manner least encumbered by bodily concerns and ultimately to escape them altogether. The genealogy of death therefore shifted dramatically once again as the central concern became, not violence but eternity.

The politics of purity

As we have seen, questions of escape from the body to an eternal world had already figured prominently among some of the Presocratic figures and in Platonic dialogues like the *Phaedo*. Therefore it was possible for Porphyry, in his biography of Plotinus, to claim that Plotinus was the philosopher who best combined the first principles of Pythagoras and Plato (1966: cxix). Plotinus is usually labelled a Neoplatonist, but the term is a modern invention: in his own time he would have considered himself simply a Platonist (Gatti 1996). But unlike Plato, politics has no place in Plotinus' philosophy; his is a spiritualized system in which ontology is understood above all in terms which allow for the transcendence of mortality.

According to tradition, Plotinus was born in Egypt, possibly Lycopolis, about 205 CE. His early study of philosophy culminated in a period of eleven years in Alexandria, taught by Ammonius (who was probably also the teacher of Origen the Christian theologian). The scene appears peaceful; but although in Rome, as in Alexandria, life went on as usual, the frontiers of the empire were crumbling. During Plotinus's lifetime, the Persians rose to power, the Goths formed a confederacy in the Danube basin, and war bands surged across the Rhine: 'the empire had to face war on every front' and failed even though the army doubled in size and became a huge drain on resources (Brown 1971: 22). Frontiers collapsed. Meanwhile, the combination of the new military aristocracy and the inadequacy of the army to secure the boundaries of the Empire led to political instability at home, exacerbated by spectacular inflation (Fox 1986: 573), increasing social inequality, and an outbreak of plague in the 250s. In 47 years there were 25 emperors, all but one of whom died by violence (Brown 1978: 28). From about 235 onwards, the southern movement of Goths and Vandals had a direct impact on imperial territory; and in 243 the young emperor, Gordian III, went on an expedition against the Persians. Plotinus joined this expedition. According to Porphyry his reason for doing so was to learn something of the thought of the East; but it all came to nothing. Gordian was murdered by his own soldiers, and Plotinus barely escaped with his life.

He settled in Rome; and spent the rest of his life there teaching and writing. The society in which he moved included prominent Romans, among them senators and even the Emperor Gallienus, who with his wife Salonina had considerable admiration for Plotinus. Yet when Plotinus asked them to allow him to rebuild a city in Campania, to be called Platonopolis and to be run on philosophical principles, the scheme was rejected. There is no indication in his writings that give any clue as to how it could have succeeded, since it insists that the true philosopher is to rise above all such earthly affairs: how such a philosophy could be consistent with effective governance of a city is not obvious.

In any case, while the Empire was under increasing external pressure and internal instability, Plotinus' writings turned away from the public political world to the realm of the spirit (Rist 1967: 2–20). A.H. Armstrong has remarked that 'there is practically nothing in the whole extent of Plotinus's writings which can be construed as even the remotest allusion to contemporary affairs' (1979: I.23). This is true in the sense that Plotinus offers no positive political philosophy; nor does he comment on social affairs. Nevertheless I suggest that the crisis of empire that obtained during Plotinus' life, the internal insecurity and external threat, had a profound impact on his thought. To what extent his writings were consciously addressed to the perilous times in which he lived is open to debate; but I shall show that reading his work with the events of empire in mind casts a whole new light on Plotinus' place in a genealogy of death. Whether or not he himself was apolitical, his readers were directed to leave their preoccupation with the bodily, material world and to focus instead on the One, far beyond the military defeats and disasters that signalled the decline of the Roman Empire.

The One beyond mortality

Plotinus' main concern is for union with the One. This One, identical with the Good, is similar in conception to that of Plato, though it also arguably owes something to Aristotle's Unmoved Mover and the World Soul of the Stoics. It is simple – non-composite – and distinct from everything else, though all things derive from it. In Plotinus' words,

> There must be something simple before all things, and this must be other than all the things that come after it, existing by itself, not mixed with the things that derive from it, and all the same to be present in a different way to these other things, being really one . . . it is also said to be 'beyond being'. For if it is not to be simple, outside all coincidence and composition, it could not be a first principle. . . . A reality of this kind must be one alone.
>
> (V.4.1)[1]

Plato in the *Republic* described the person who emerged from the cave into sunlight as finally recognizing that the sun is the light by which everything is illuminated but also ultimately the source of all life. The sun therefore is for Plato an allegory of the One. Plotinus follows Plato in this. He speaks of the One as a sun whose inexhaustible light eternally produces everything else, without being diminished by its emanation. The first production of this procession from the One Plotinus calls Intellect.

> The activity, which, so to speak, flows from [the One] like a light from the sun, is Intellect and the whole intelligible nature, but [the One] himself,

> staying still at the summit of the intelligible, rules over it; he does not thrust the outshining away from himself . . . but he irradiates it forever, abiding unchanged over the intelligible. For what comes from him has not been cut off from him, nor is it the same as him.
>
> (V.3.12)

Just as the rays of the sun are not the sun and yet are inseparable from it, and change everything without changing the sun itself, so also with the 'rays' of being that emanate (or, better, 'proceed': see Bussanich 1996: 46) from the One.

There are obvious paradoxes here, which I leave to specialist discussions of Plotinus' metaphysics (Rist 1967; O'Meara 1993; Bussanich 1996; Emilsson 1999). We will encounter some of them again in the next volume when we consider Neoplatonist influences on a Christian understanding of God (see Rist 1996). The important point for the present is that the One is not only the source of all things; it is also their end. Everything longs for the Good: it is 'the most longed for and most lovable, and love for it would be immeasurable' (VI.7.32).

> The One is the source (*archê*) of all beings and, as the Good, the goal (*telos*) of all aspirations, human and non-human. As the indemonstrable first principle of everything, as transcendent infinite being, and as the supreme object of love, the One is the centre of a vibrant conception of reality many of whose facets resist philosophical analysis.
>
> (Bussanich 1996: 38)

It is not for nothing that Plotinus' system underlies much medieval Christian mysticism (McGinn 1991: 44–55). For Plotinus, the whole point of philosophy is to enable reunification with the eternal One.

According to Plotinus, the procession of all reality from the One is best understood in terms of a hierarchy. There are various levels of being, which we can think of as arranged according to their proximity to the One. Nearest the One is the Intellect. This is not the human intellect; rather it has been described as 'the unification of Aristotle's God . . . and the realm of Platonic Ideas' (Emilsson 1999: 366): it is sometimes thought of as the Divine Mind (Rist 1967: 42). Next is the level of Soul, which unifies the world: there are links here to the world soul of Stoic philosophy (Clark 1996: 286). The complexities of this hierarchy need not detain us here. What is important is that these three first principles, the One, Intellect and Soul, together form the intelligible world; and from this in turn proceeds the world of the senses, which derives the reality it has from its participation in the higher reality of the intelligible world. The One, and the intelligible world that derives from it, is living; indeed it is the source of life. Mortality has no purchase on it. It is only the material world that is the realm of death.

Reunification

Now, human beings are in some sense a 'mixture' or interweaving of body and soul (I.1.4), connected with the material world through the body but with the intelligible world through the soul, whose main desire is intellectual. Plotinus speaks of 'the descent of the soul' (I.1.12). It gives life to the body and is connected with it; yet it retains a higher life of intellectual activity which yearns ever upward, retracing in reverse the path of the descent in its longing to be reunited with the One. Insofar as this union is achieved, the world of death and mortality is left behind.

There is one sense in which it is obviously true to say that Plotinus is a dualist, seeing the human being as a union of body and soul (Blumenthal 1996). Yet in another sense Plotinus says that 'Man, and especially the good man, is not the composite of soul and body' but is rather identified entirely with the soul, and seeks separation from the body (I.4.14). Like Socrates in the *Phaedo*, Plotinus teaches that it is the path of wisdom and philosophy to try as much as possible to curtail the demands of the body. He says for example,

> Since the soul is evil when it is thoroughly mixed with the body and shares its experiences and has all the same opinions, it will be good and possess virtue when it no longer has the same opinions but acts alone – this is intelligence and wisdom – and does not share the body's experiences – this is self-control – and is not afraid of departing from the body – this is courage – and is ruled by reason and intellect, without opposition – and this is justice. One would not be wrong in calling this state of the soul likeness to God, in which its activity is intellectual, and it is free in this way from bodily affections.
>
> (I.2.3)

Now, wisdom, self-control, courage and justice are of course chief among the virtues in ethical philosophy from Plato and Aristotle onwards. In their writings, however, these virtues had to do with public life, with the duties one had as a citizen. Plotinus reinterprets them, so that virtues are not what he calls 'civic virtues' but rather are purifications of the soul for likeness to God.

There is no reason to suppose that Plotinus was advocating antinomian or even antisocial behaviour, or to think that he was anything but a model citizen. But as he said, 'Our concern . . . is not to be out of sin, but to be God' – to be divine by unity with the One (I.2.6). The person who has these 'greater virtues' is beyond civic or political concerns.

> He will altogether separate himself, as far as possible, from his lower nature and will not live the life of a good man which civic virtue requires. He will leave that behind, and choose another, the life of the gods: for it is to them, not to good men, that we are to be made like.
>
> (I.2.7)

Moreover it is clear that Plotinus believed that he himself had achieved such a likeness, at least some of the time:

> Often I have woken up out of the body to myself and have entered into myself, going out from all other things; I have seen a beauty wonderfully great and felt most assurance that then most of all I belonged to the better part; I have actually lived the best life and come to identify with the divine . . . setting myself above all the rest of that which is, in the intelligible.
>
> (IV.8.1)

Plotinus takes it as a matter of course that decent standards of 'vulgar virtues' will be observed; but all this is left behind in the quest for unity with the divine. Later Christian mystical writers who drew on Plotinus were to treat these mundane virtues as crucial: it was through observing them that the moral purification began which would be the first step in the ascent to higher things. This is not Plotinus' position. For him, the civic virtues and vulgar morality are quite distinct concerns from the life of the gods. As John Dillon has remarked, 'One feels of Plotinus that he would have very gladly helped an old lady across the road – but he might very well fail to notice her at all. And if she were squashed by a passing wagon, he would remain quite unmoved' (1996: 324).

Personal rectitude and political withdrawal

This sounds – and is – harsh; but it is consistent with what Plotinus says about things that are normally considered evils or even tragedies. Suppose there is war, and the city is destroyed, and the philosopher is in danger of death.

> If he thought that they were great evils, or evils at all, he would deserve to be laughed at for his opinion; there would be no virtue left in him if he thought that wood and stones, and (God help us!) the death of mortals were important, this man who, we say, ought to think about death that it is better than life with the body!
>
> (I.4.7)

As to concern about what might happen to the body – whether it is properly buried according to Roman funeral rites – such concern is beneath contempt. So too is the desire for a monument or any other commemoration such as had been coveted since Homeric times as a preservation of the glorious name of the deceased.

> If he is not buried, his body will rot anyhow, on the earth or under it.[2] If he is distressed because he does not have an expensive funeral but is buried without a name and not thought worth a lofty monument – the pettiness of it!
>
> (Ibid.)

Plotinus dismisses at a stroke the whole idea of immortality based on memory of glorious deeds, whether that memory is preserved in a poet's song or a gravestone. That is not the sort of immortality he desires; it has nothing to do with becoming divine.

But of course worse things than death can happen. The empire was crumbling: what if it was defeated, and the victors did to the Romans the sorts of things that the Romans had done when they were the conquerors? What if the philosopher is dragged away as a war slave? And even if he can bear it for himself, what if his daughters are taken? Any Roman acquainted with the spectacles of death in the Colosseum and with the market of captured slaves would have only too vivid an imagination of what might be entailed. But these possibilities too Plotinus waves away. Everyone knows that such things happen: the philosopher would be a fool if he thought that he or his relatives were immune: and anyway, he says, 'many people will do better by becoming war-slaves'.

> For he [the philosopher] will think that the nature of this universe is of a kind to bring these sorts of misfortunes, and we must follow it obediently. . . . The good man will not be involved in evil because of the stupidity of others, even if they are his relatives; he will not be dependent on the good or bad fortune of other people.
>
> (Ibid.)

None of these things 'penetrate to the inner self'. And in any case, suicide is always a possibility if things become really intolerable.

There is much here that echoes Stoic themes of passionlessness; indeed Plotinus takes the idea of detachment further than many Stoics would have been willing to do. The themes would be taken up again in medieval christendom's ascetical strands. But whereas these connections have been often noted, scholars have paid less attention to the significance of the political context within which Plotinus was situated. Implicit in his insistence on the life of wisdom far above earthly concerns is a rejection bordering on contempt for the political and social reality of the late Roman imperial system, in which the upper echelons of society in cities like Rome and Alexandria carried on in their accustomed luxury while the forces that would destroy the empire and change their way of life forever were steadily advancing. Plotinus had marched with Gordian III; he must have known that the empire was in trouble.

Sometimes, indeed, Plotinus' rejection of politics and of every kingdom of this world is more than implicit. He says, for instance, of the vision of the One:

> A man has not failed if he fails to win beauty of colours or bodies, or power or office or kingship even, but if he fails to win this and only this. For this he should give up the attainment of kingship and of rule over all earth and sea and sky, if only by leaving and overlooking them he can turn to That and see.
>
> (I.6.7)

Similarly, he writes,

> What human circumstance is so great that a man will not think little of it
> who has climbed higher than all this and depends on nothing below? He does
> not think any piece of good fortune great, however important it may be,
> kingship, for instance, and rule over cities and peoples, or founding of colonies
> and states (even if he founds them himself). Why then should he think that
> falling from power and the ruin of his city are great matters?
>
> (I.4.7)

There is an important sense, of course, in which Plato and even Aristotle could
agree: the life of wisdom in union with true Reality, or for Aristotle the life of
contemplation, is the highest good, the best of human flourishing. Yet Plato's hero
who emerges from the cave and sees things as they are and sees the sun in all its
glory turns back to the cave to try to bring his wisdom to his deluded fellows; Plato
writes the *Republic* as an effort to clarify what an enlightened political system would
be. Plotinus, in the decline of empire, shrugs off the loss of colonies and the possibility of loss of power: they are of no consequence for the life of wisdom.

As Plotinus conceives it, this is in fact a highly self-centred life. There is no
indication of a sense of responsibility for the welfare of others, or even concern
about them. If daughters are sold into slavery, if a colony is lost, if a city is ruined,
well, these things happen in this universe and there is no point worrying about
them. Plotinus never suggests that the king has a duty to try to avoid disaster, even
though such disaster would be not for himself alone but for all the people whose
lives would be ruined if his kingdom crumbles. The path of wisdom is not a political
path, a path of the kingdoms of this world.

> The man who belongs to this world may be handsome and tall and rich and
> the ruler of all mankind . . . and we ought not to envy him for things like
> these, by which he is beguiled. The wise man will perhaps not have them at
> all, and if he has them will himself reduce them, if he cares for his true self.
> He will reduce and gradually extinguish his bodily advantages by neglect, and
> will put away authority and office.
>
> (I.4.14)

The man of wisdom who devotes himself to contemplation will pass beyond all
such concerns; indeed he will pass even beyond virtue in his ascent to the One.
This of course need not mean that ordinary standards of good behaviour are
repudiated: indeed A.H. Armstrong has argued that the sage who has reached the
Good, the source of virtue, 'must be morally better, not worse, than before' in this
world of virtue and vice (Armstrong 1970: 259). While this may be true, however,
it would be true only at an individual level of personal rectitude. Plotinus' account
of virtue involves a withdrawal from the political sphere, and from any struggle
for social justice.

Laying down the lyre

Plotinus agrees with Plato in the *Phaedo* that true life is other than bodily life, and has nothing to do with material success or even physical health. These things are fine if they are available and as long as they are not a distraction; but sooner or later they will fail in any case. Death will come. A wise person will therefore treat his body with care, 'like a musician with his lyre'; but when the lyre is no longer of use, the musician lays it down and takes up another instrument or abandons those activities altogether. 'Yet the instrument was not given him at the beginning without good reason. He has used it often up till now' (I.4.16). From this comment and others like it one might draw the impression that Plotinus' attitude to the body was not wholly negative. Rather, it was to be treated with appropriate care, always recognizing however that in the scale of things it has a lower place than the life of the mind or the music of the soul; and above all remembering that it will die. Plotinus' recognition of the appropriate needs of the body, together with the important role of bodies in his account of beauty which I shall discuss below has led Margaret Miles (1999) and Pierre Hadot (1993) to argue that Plotinus had a much more positive attitude to the body than is sometimes attributed to him.

This relatively benign attitude to the body is belied, however, by Plotinus' own practice, at least as it was perceived by Porphyry. In the very first sentence of his 'Life of Plotinus' Porphyry writes that 'Plotinus, the philosopher of our times, seemed ashamed of being in the body' (1966: 3). Porphyry also describes Plotinus as a strict vegetarian, and as refusing to use the public baths. He was intent on preserving his inner thought, even when involved in the care of others or in teaching and conversation.

> In this way he was present at once to himself and to others, and he never relaxed his self-turned attention except in sleep: even sleep he reduced by taking very little food, often not even a piece of bread, and by his continuous turning in contemplation to his intellect.
>
> (31)

Porphyry is writing hagiography, of course: nevertheless it is instructive that someone who was a disciple of Plotinus should put such a strong emphasis on asceticism. Moreover Porphyry fully accepts the Platonic idea that death is the release of the soul from the body. He tells of an 'oracle' which announced that 'after his [Plotinus'] deliverance from the body the god says that he came to "the company of heaven", and that there affection rules and desire and joy and love are kindled by God': Plotinus, he says, went not to have his own soul judged but to join the panel of judges, among whom also are, significantly, Plato and Pythagoras (71). 'There, he [the oracle] says, the most blessed spirits have their birth and live a life filled full of festivity and joy; and this life lasts forever, made blessed by the gods' (73).

To what extent Porphyry's portrait of Plotinus is accurate is open to debate. In broad terms, however, it is consistent with Plotinus' emphatic teaching that real life is the life of the inner self, the self turned towards the intellect and union with the One, not the life of the body or of public, political activity.

> We have often said that the perfect life, the true, real life, is in that tran-scendent intelligible reality, and that other lives are incomplete, traces of life, not perfect or pure and no more life than its opposite.
>
> (I.4.3)

The 'outer life' is not a life which should be dignified with attention; and 'when we leave our bodily existence behind, we shall be altogether free of bodily disturbances, and, like the Gods, we shall live a life of pure contemplation' (Rist 1967: 154).

The emphasis on the life of contemplation and the pathway to it through beauty which I shall discuss below has led some scholars of Plotinus to argue that 'unlike Plato, he was not primarily concerned with death. He sought, rather, to understand life' (Miles 1999: 56). A.H. Armstrong similarly states that of all the major pagan and Christian thinkers of late antiquity, Plotinus 'is the least interested in life after death and escape from the body' (1979 xxi.115). I am suggesting quite the opposite. It is true that Plotinus is focused upon life; but the life he points to is not the 'outer life' of bodily existence but rather the life of contemplation which has nothing to do with mortality. The awareness of our actual fragile existence can thereby be repressed. In this sense Plotinus' philosophy is entirely geared to concern with death and with the life beyond death. Indeed he brings eternity forward, so to speak: he holds that the person who is focused on the true life, the life of contemplation, participates in the eternal realm even now. It is precisely because of this that death is of no concern, or even welcomed. In the late Roman Empire Plotinus takes up Platonic themes in a way that turns away not only from personal bodily pleasures and pains but even from the sufferings of others and from the most momentous political and public events: all these things are but shadows in the light of eternity.

> For really here in the events of our life it is not the soul within but the outside shadow of man which cries and moans and carries on in every sort of way on a stage which is the whole earth.
>
> (III.2.15)

This world is a game, a complex theatre production. Our individual bodily lives are parts of the drama; and 'death is a changing of body, like changing of clothes on the stage, or, for some of us, a putting off of body, like in the theatre the final exit'. It would be silly to take this too seriously, like children who take toys or plays as though they were the real thing, and get upset about them.

And when men, mortal as they are, direct their weapons against each other, fighting in orderly ranks, doing what they do in sport in their war-dances, their battles show that all human concerns are children's games, and tell us that deaths are nothing terrible, and that those who die in wars and battles anticipate only a little the death which comes in old age . . . We should be spectators of murders, and all deaths, and takings and sackings of cities, as if they were on the stages of theatres, all changes of scenery and costume and acted wailings and weepings.

(III.2.15)

When we see tragedy we weep, of course; but it should be the sort of crying that we do in the theatre when vivid acting moves our tears. Even when we ourselves or those we love are involved, at another, truer level we are detached, watching from the outside the spectacle of death. Plotinus turns his back on political engagement. Let the barbarians come; let the cities be sacked; let daughters be taken captive and sold into slavery. We are only spectators.

And who exactly are 'we' who can remain thus aloof? Obviously 'we' are the wise men, the few who have learned contempt for death and detachment from life in contemplation of the eternal world. Plotinus has nothing to say about gender; but implicit in all his writing is the Platonic assumption of the male philosopher. This is, to be sure, a long way from the 'manly man', the *vir* of Roman military valour. Plotinus' idea of masculinity is not that of Cicero or Vergil. Nevertheless the one who is capable of philosophical detachment and of rising to union with the One is unquestionably and unthinkingly male.

Beauty's ladder

This becomes very clear in Plotinus' discussion of beauty. Plotinus goes through the theme several times in his writings, with slightly different emphases. In *Ennead* I.3 he speaks of the stages of response to beauty by referring to three sorts of people (referring back to Plato's *Phaedrus* 248d): the musician, the lover and the philosopher. The musician, Plotinus says, is 'easily moved and excited by beauty' and avoids the inharmonious or unrhythmical. From this starting point the musician must learn to abstract from the material element and discover 'the intelligible harmony and the beauty in it, and beauty universal, not just some particular beauty' (I.3.1). The musician may turn into a lover, excited and amazed by the visible beauty of a body: but like the lover in Plato's *Symposium*

he must be taught not to cling round one body and be excited by that, but must be led by the course of reasoning to consider all bodies and shown the beauty that is the same in all of them and that it is something other than the bodies and must be said to come from elsewhere.

(I.3.2)

Just as the musician must not be trapped by individual pieces of music or their sensuous qualities, so a lover must go beyond the individual body and even bodiliness itself. In that process of climbing to the immaterial and contemplating the beauty of the intelligible rather than the sensory world, the musician/lover turns into the philosopher, the one who moves already in the higher world (I.3.3). Bodies can serve as a stepping stone to contemplation; but if one does not move beyond the individual body (of a person or a piece of music) then they are a hindrance. Nothing is said to encourage the lover to care for the beloved, who, it would seem, exists in Plotinus' system only to help the lover on his contemplative way. Plato had presented the lovers as progressing together as the wings of their souls grow through their mutual care for each other (*Phaedrus* 246); but in Plotinus the ascent to beauty is quickly assimilated to that of the *Symposium* in which the individual beloved and especially any concern for bodily reproduction is rapidly left behind as the soul yearns forward to the beauty that is beyond mortality.

In the *Symposium* the (male) philosopher rejects women entirely in his choice of reproduction of the spirit rather than of the mind. The body he falls in love with is explicitly the body of a boy. In the later Roman Empire male homosexuality was less acceptable than it had been in Plato's Athens, and Plotinus hurries over this aspect of the ascent. It is clear, however, that women's bodies and female sexuality are at best of instrumental value to the man in pursuit of beauty. Elsewhere, Plotinus invokes Pythagoras' table of opposites, placing 'beauty' in the column which also includes 'male' and 'good', and 'ugly' in the column which includes 'female' and 'evil' (III.5.1). In this passage Plotinus struggles again with questions of sexual attraction, recognizing that some men 'love women in order to perpetuate themselves, but if the women are not beautiful they fail in their purpose'. Although Plotinus recognizes the strength of sexual desire he sees it as much inferior to the desire for beauty as a path of union with the One: 'if they remain chaste there is no error in their intimacy with the beauty here below, but it is error to fall away into sexual intercourse. And the man whose love of the beautiful is pure will be satisfied with beauty alone.'

Nevertheless bodies, human and non-human, are beautiful; moreover Plotinus places great emphasis on the beauty of the universe. Indeed it is only by way of that beauty that the soul is able to return to union with the One. Beauty, therefore, can hardly be emphasized too strongly. As discussed above, the One is the source of the whole hierarchy of reality, which proceeds from it like rays of the sun. The beauty and harmony of the material world is a consequence of the unity and perfection that flows down to it through Intellect and Soul: 'physical beauty is thus a sign of spiritual beauty and a participation by the physical in the spiritual' (Bredin and Santoro-Brienza 2000: 48). A shapeless thing is ugly because it is 'outside the divine formative power'; it is sharing in the divine that forms a material body into beauty (I.6.2).

Plotinus gives an illustration which makes his meaning clearer.

Let us suppose a couple of great lumps of stone lying side by side, one shapeless and untouched by art, the other which has been already mastered by art and turned into a statue of a god or of a man . . . and if of a man not just of any man but of one whom art has made up out of every sort of human beauty. The stone which has been brought to beauty of form by art will appear beautiful not because it is a stone . . . but as a result of the form which art has put into it. Now the material did not have this form, but it was in the man who had it in his mind even before it came into the stone; but it was in the craftsman, not in so far as he had hands or eyes, but because he had some share of art. So this beauty was in the art.

(V.8.1)

The material in itself is not beautiful. It is made beautiful by being shaped into a beautiful form which is in the mind of the craftsman. The other stone, left untouched, remains without beauty. So we can see, Plotinus argues, that physical beauty results from beauty in the mind, spiritual beauty. 'Soul makes beautiful the bodies which are spoken of as beautiful; for since it is a divine thing and a kind of part of beauty, it makes everything it grasps and masters beautiful' (I.6.6).

Just the same principle applies to the universe. The world and the things in it are beautiful because they are shaped by the Intellect and thus participate in the beauty of the One, the 'great beauty' (I.6.9). The One or Good is a 'productive power', 'a beauty which makes beauty. For it generates beauty and makes it more beautiful by the excess of beauty which comes from it, so that it is the principle of beauty and the term of beauty' (VI.7.32). This goes down to the smallest detail; even to those things which might have been 'despised for their smallness'. Plotinus writes of

the workmanship which produces wonders in rich variety in ordinary animals, and the beauty of appearance which extends to the fruits and even the leaves of plants, and their beauty of flower which comes so effortlessly, and their delicacy and variety.

(III.2.13)

Throughout his writings Plotinus is acutely appreciative of the beauties of the natural world as well as of artistic creation.

All these are embodied beauties. Without matter they would be impossible. Yet as we have seen, according to Plotinus the beauty of bodies ultimately derives from that which is not body; the source of beauty of the material world is other-worldly. It is because of this that beauty is the path by which the soul can be reunited with the One. Just as the physical bodies have been made beautiful by being formed by the rays emanating through the hierarchy of being from the One, so also we can ascend that hierarchy by response to the beauty of each stage. 'So we must ascend again to the good, which every soul desires' (I.6.7). This (not the Roman Empire) is our fatherland, the country from which we came.

> Let him who can, follow, and come within, and leave outside the sight of his eyes and not turn back to the bodily splendours which he saw before. When he sees the beauty in bodies he must not run after them; we know that they are images, traces, shadows, and hurry away to that which they image.
>
> (I.6.8)

These shadows or images of beauty are in fact no better than mud if the soul wallows in the body: such a soul is 'impure . . . with a great deal of bodily stuff mixed into it . . . mud and filth; his ugliness has come from an addition of alien matter. . . . So we shall be right in saying that the soul becomes ugly by mixture and dilution and inclination towards the body and matter' (I.6.5). Plotinus explicitly links this with death. The soul that is taken up with the body is 'no longer pure, but by the admixture of evil living a dim life and diluted with a great deal of death'.

True life comes only by stripping away this mortality and the whole bodily nature. 'No eye ever saw the sun without becoming sun-like, nor can a soul see beauty without becoming beautiful. You must become first all godlike and all beautiful if you intend to see God and beauty' (I.6.9). This requires purging from the ugliness of body and matter and all its deathly ways. Just as gold is beautiful only when the dross is purged from it,

> in the same way the soul too, when it is separated from the lusts which it has through the body with which it consorted too much, and freed from its other affections, purged of what it gets from being embodied, when it abides alone has put away all the ugliness which came from the other [material] nature.
>
> (I.6.5)

Once again Plotinus reverts to the metaphor of the statue, but this time the statue is not a material artefact but the soul itself.

> Go back into yourself and look; and if you do not yet see yourself beautiful, then, just as someone making a statue which has to be beautiful cuts away here and polishes there and makes one part smooth and clears another till he has given his statue a beautiful face, so you too must cut away excess and straighten the crooked and clear the dark and make it bright, and never stop 'working on your statue' till the divine glory of virtue shines out on you.
>
> (I.6.9)

When the body and all that is mortal is purged away, 'you can trust yourself then . . . concentrate your gaze and see'. The unifying vision of the One is the vision of eternal life.

Beauty is therefore for Plotinus not a means of bringing newness into this world but a means of ascent out of it, to eternity. It provides the way out of the material world of crumbling empire, strife, plague and gendered bodies that suffer and die. Political and social upheaval is part of the material world from which the true self takes its distance; violence can be displaced by climbing beauty's ladder to eternity.

Plotinus' reconfiguration of death can thus be interpreted as completely opposite to that offered by the Christian martyrs. Whereas they offered at least the possibility of a symbolic of natality, even if ambiguously, Plotinus looked to another world. Whereas they resisted imperial violence and hoped for a paradise of peace, Plotinus distanced himself from politics and material concerns, and longed for the unchanging beauty of eternity. Yet opposed as these two perspectives are, in the centuries of the collapse of empire and the emergence of medieval christendom, Plotinus' teachings of reunification with the One through beauty and his immortal longings were taken up into Christian mysticism and blended with ideas of natality drawn from the literature of the martyrs. The implications for the genealogy of death and its legacy of violence for modernity are profound. So also are the voices of resistance and hope. All of that is the story of the second volume.

Notes

PART I: BEAUTY, GENDER AND DEATH

1 Redeeming the present: the therapy of philosophy

1 I believe the story to be true, but I have been unable to verify it.
2 I use 'west' and 'western' in this project as shorthand to indicate the cultural trajectory from Homer through christendom and the enlightenment to secular modernity and 'postmodern' thought. I do not propose to investigate 'nonwestern' cultures, and intend no comparison or claims about how death, violence, and beauty are configured in them.

4 Towards a poetics of natality

1 This is to a large extent also true of Catholic theology in modernity, with however the monumental exception of Hans Urs von Balthasar's seven volume *The Glory of the Lord* (1983).

PART II: OUT OF THE CAVE

5 The rage of Achilles

1 For the reasons given in the Introduction, I have chosen to use the readable Fagles translation rather than the more scholarly Lattimore text. All references to the *Iliad* are therefore page (not line) numbers in Homer (1990a) unless otherwise indicated.
2 I use the term 'Homer' as shorthand for the author(s) of the *Iliad* and the *Odyssey*, without implying a judgement about who the author(s) might have been. For a discussion of authorship see Finley 2002: ch. 2; Knox 1990.
3 Unless otherwise indicated, all references to Aristotle are to the McKeon (1941) edition, and follow standard book and line references.
4 All references to Plato are from the Huntington-Cairns edition and follow standard book and line references.

6 Odysseus on the barren sea

1 Unless otherwise indicated, all references to the *Odyssey* are to page (not line) numbers of the Fagles (1990) translation of Homer.

7 'The murderous misery of war'

1 I have used easily available Penguin editions in English translations for my citations of the tragedians in the hope that readers will turn to the dramas themselves. The numbers in my text are page (not line) references to these Penguin editions, which are listed in the bibliography.

2 Or possibly plays: only *Electra* survives, but it was probably part of a trilogy like that of Aeschylus', the other parts of which have been lost.

3 Unlike Aeshyclus' *Oresteia*, Euripides' *Electra* and *Orestes* were not parts of a trilogy, or at all events not part of the same trilogy. Vellacott places *Electra* in 415 or 418, and *Orestes* in 408 BCE.

4 Thucydides is of course presenting his interpretation of events: the speeches, in particular, must be his own words, not those of the original speakers. Nevertheless, modern historians accept his treatment as substantially correct (Meier 2000: 523–4).

5 Alternatively, if it was performed in 418, then its questions would already have been posed to those who went to war.

8 Whose tragedy?

1 See also the cases of Philoctetus (Sophocles 1953: 190); and Deianeira (Sophocles 1953: 143).

9 Parmenides meets the goddess

1 Unless otherwise stated, passages from Parmenides and presocratic philosophers will be cited by their Diels and Kranz (1951) reference number followed by their page reference in the easily available Waterfield (2000). For critical alternatives to the same fragments see Coxon 1986.

2 This is all the more surprising because in his other writings Plato often mentions goddesses, if only in passing: see *Republic* i.327a–328a; *Theaetetus* 149b; *Laws* 796c.

3 Which he then likens to the shamans of Siberia!

4 Whether this is historically accurate to an individual named Pythagoras rather than to his followers is disputed.

10 How to give birth like a man

1 References to Plato follow standard book and line references. All translations are from Plato (1961).

2 For purposes of this chapter I shall avoid protracted scholarly controversies about the order in which Plato's dialogues were actually written, accepting the main lines of the arguments of Kraut (1992a). Similarly I shall not enter into a discussion of the relation between the teaching of Socrates and that of Plato. I am drawing entirely on Plato's dialogues for Socrates' teaching, and shall treat the latter as a mouthpiece for Plato unless otherwise indicated, even though that could hardly have been true of the historical Socrates (see Annas 1991: 3–5).

3 Plato's dialogues should not be taken as accurate reporting; but the trial and death of Socrates are actual historical events which occurred in 399 BCE.

4 Some commentators (e.g. Annas 1991; Nussbaum 1986) use gender inclusive language in describing Plato's philosophers. However, for Plato philosophy is a male activity, as we shall see; indeed its masculinity remains firmly in place even in the unlikely event that women could participate in it as he speculates in *Republic* v. I shall therefore retain Plato's masculine language so that this point is not glossed over.

5 For an excellent extended discussion of this with particular reference to music, see Underwood 2001.

6 The banishment of poets from the Republic has of course often attracted scholarly attention (Nussbaum 1986; Bloom 1968; Murdoch 1977), but the issue of gender and control in the face of death has been largely overlooked.

7 Many analytic philosophers who comment on Plato ignore the frameworks of his dialogues as though they have nothing to do with the arguments. I suggest that the contrary is the case.

8 In fact, the *Parmenides* and the *Theaetetus*, significantly, are usually taken to derive from the same period of his career as the *Symposium* (Kraut 1992a: 9).

9 Andrea Nye says that Diotima emphasizes the importance of bodily love, overcomes dualism, and 'does not argue that heterosexual love is inferior' (1994: 199). On the contrary, the text clearly indicates that women and heterosexual encounter are left far behind in the ascent to immortality.

10 Susan Hawthorne (1994) has helpfully discussed 'Diotima's' metaphors of pregnancy, birth, becoming, death and transformation. In her view as in Nye's, they indicate the historicity of a woman, Diotima, actually making this speech. I believe, however, that these metaphors are better explained as male appropriation of reproduction, as already found in the *Theaetetus*.

11 It should not be forgotten that in the *Republic*, this whole discussion of mathematics occurs immediately after the myth of the cave.

12 In the *Phaedo* the philosopher who wants knowledge of the good will only get it by severe discipline of the pursuit of ordinary pleasures.

13 Philosophers discussing Plato's work typically take scant notice of his rhetorical strategies, concerning themselves with argument rather than literature – as if the two could be clearly distinguished. But in this case at least (and I suspect in many others) failure to pay attention to the 'literary' devices means that important clues are lost regarding the philosophical messages of the dialogue (cf Rosen 1987).

14 Scholars continue to discuss the dramatic date of the *Republic*, some arguing for the later date of 411, while others argue for two dates cobbled together as the books of the *Republic* were composed at different times. Although significant for other reasons, both these solutions still place the dramatic date to fall within the Peloponnesian War.

11 The open sea of beauty

1 Plato specifically appeals to the Pythagorean expertise in music in his discussion of music in the *Republic* 503d–531e.

2 For a careful reading of Plato on the mimesis of painting see Halliwell 2002. Halliwell interprets Plato's comments on the representational nature of art in *Republic* x differently from my reading of it; but emphasizes as I do Plato's concern for the psychological impact of art, especially tragedy.

3 The identification of the white and aquiline with the good and noble, and the black and snub nosed with the bad and uncontrollable, cannot be read today without massive racist overtones, whether or not these were already understood in fifth-century Athens.

4 Whether such destabilizations were Plato's intention I leave to others to ponder (see Halperin 1994; Berger 1994).

5 The close affinities between the *Phaedrus* and the *Symposium* are discussed by Burger (1980), and Rosen (1988) among many others.

6 For full discussion see Burkert 1979: 64–72; 1985: 82–4; Girard 1972: 93–9; 1986: 121–4.

12   The fault lines of flourishing

1   Or possibly his brother-in-law: sources do not agree. See Barnes 1995: 5; Gould 1990: 14.
2   The exception is the work of feminist scholars such as those in Bar On 1994 and Freeland 1998.
3   For a detailed account of Aristotle on sex and biology, see Deslauriers 1998.
4   Unless otherwise indicated, all quotations of Aristotle are from the 1941 McKeon edition and are cited by standard line reference.
5   For readings of these areas of his thought which argue about whether they, too, are infected with his misogyny, see Nye 1990 and Freeland 1998.
6   It is often accepted that Aristotle's *Poetics* is intended as a rebuttal of Plato's banishment of poets from the Republic (Halliwell 1986: 20; Curran 1998: 300). Paul Woodruff argues that this is misguided and that 'there is no good internal evidence that Aristotle was driven in the *Poetics* by the need to answer Plato' (Woodruff 1992: 73–4).
7   Each aspect of Aristotle's definition of tragedy, especially his accounts of mimesis and catharsis, repay more detailed study than is appropriate here. See especially Halliwell 1986, 2002; Rorty 1992; Nussbaum 1986; Davis 1999.
8   Or at least, none that has survived. An early work, written after his friend Eudemus of Cyprus died, seems to have echoed the radical dualism of soul and body of Plato's *Phaedo*, and the anticipation of personal survival; but this work is lost (Rist 1989: 10).
9   For the parallels of this to feminist epistemological methods, see Hirshman 1998. Hirshman does not, however, ponder the Aristotelian assumptions of privilege in relation to who can count as a knower.
10 John Rist has shown how Aristotle here, and in parts of *De Caelo*, replaces an earlier notion of a *self*-moved mover with that of an *un*moved mover, leaving inconsistencies unresolved (Rist 1989. 24).

PART III: ETERNAL ROME?

1   For comparison, Bradley points out that the peak average of Africans transported to the Americas at the height of the early modern slave trade was about 60,000 per year (Bradley 1994: 32).
2   The relationship between land ownership, taxation and military service was complex and went through many changes during the centuries of the Roman Empire, but the three were always implicated in one another. See Jones 1974; Duncan-Jones 1974; Grant 1979.

13   Anxiety about nothing(ness): Lucretius and the fear of death

1   To be distinguished from fear of prolonged intense suffering in the process of dying. Suicide was accepted or at least condoned as an escape from intolerable pain or distress.

14   'If we wish to be men': Roman constructions of gender

1   Women of exceptional courage or *virtus* were sometimes called 'honorary' men: it was a matter for awe and wonder (Jantzen 1995: 51–8).
2   Before we dismiss the Roman enthusiasm for entertainments featuring such displays of sex and violence as incomprehensible among civilized people, we might note that parallel questions can be asked of the present day entertainment industry in the west.

3 This assumes that the written account is accurate; but as Margaret Miles has pointed out, it is a voyeuristic account which could be taken as Christian propaganda (Miles 1989: 61; cf Jantzen 1995: 49–51).

15 Valour and gender in the *Pax Augusta*

1 Lavish as Horace was in his compliments, however, it is worth noting that he kept a certain distance: for example he declined the offer of becoming a private secretary to Augustus. The motives for his choice to retain independence are not available for scrutiny, but one possibility is that he was more aware than his writings express that the *Pax Augusta* in fact rested on violence and brutality, as we shall see. In his writings Horace seems so full of praise for Augustus that he does not recognize the deadly harshness lurking just below the gilded surface of the peace. But perhaps he was more aware than meets the eye?

2 For an entry into the extensive literature see the bibliographies of Huskinson 2000b; Garnsey and Whittaker 1978; Mattingly 1997.

3 For extensive discussion of the question of defensive war see Hardwick 2000; Garnsey and Whittaker 1978; Mattingly 1997.

4 Even those who were deeply disillusioned with empire and its values might use Latin imperial literature to make their point. Thus for example Wilfred Owen, writing from the trenches of the First World War, meditated on Horace's lines:

> If you could hear, at every jolt, the blood . . .
> Come gargling from the froth-corrupted lungs,
> Obscene as cancer, bitter as the cud
> Of vile, incurable sores on innocent tongues,
> My friend, you would not tell with such high zest
> To children ardent for some desperate glory,
> The old Lie: Dulce et decorum est
> Pro patria mori.
>
> (Owen 1963)

16 Dissent in Rome

1 In this I am following commentators like Mack 1988, Galinsky 1996, 1999; Newlands 2002. For an alternative reading, which argues that Ovid's writings were implicated in the Augustan imperialist agenda, see Habinek 2002.

17 Stoical death: Seneca's conscience

1 Scholars are divided about whether there may have been some truth in the accusation: see Holland 2000: 204–6; Griffin 1976: 367.

2 Shakespeare, for example, was heavily influenced by him, as were Marlowe, Jonson and other Elizabethan writers (Watling 1966); so also were philosophers from Descartes to Kant, the politicians of nineteenth-century Britain and the Founding Fathers of the USA (Nussbaum 1994: 4–5).

3 It is of course impossible in this context to discuss either of these exhaustively: I shall restrict myself to those aspects directly related to a genealogy of death. For fuller accounts of Stoicism see Rist 1969; Inwood 1999; Griffin 1976; and of Nero and his court see Holland 2000; Barrett 1996; Grant 1979; and their respective bibliographies.

4 But to his credit, Seneca cannot bring himself to say this without qualification. He keeps trying to affirm a Stoic ideal of being unaffected, or 'bearing the loss of a friend

with equanimity'; yet the passage as a whole shows that he actually places the highest value on friendship and recognizes that losing a friend is disastrous: he likens it to 'when the universe is dissolved' (51).

5 Martha Nussbaum (1994: chs 10–11) makes a similar point; but although in the first chapter of her book she makes much of the importance of social and political location for understanding Stoic ethics, she does not in fact examine Seneca's position in the court of Nero or the bearing it would have on his account of the passions and of death.

6 Seneca's exile to Corsica had been imposed by the Emperor Claudius in 41 CE for alleged adultery with Julia Livilla, sister of Gaius (who preceded Claudius as Emperor). Julia died on a separate island to which she was exiled: she was probably starved to death. The charge had been brought by Messalina, wife of Claudius, and may have had more to do with court intrigue and jealousy than with any actual relationship between Seneca and Julia Livilla.

18 Spectacles of death

1 Thomas Wiedemann (1992) draws a distinction between privately funded *munera* (funeral games) and publicly funded *ludi*, which might involve chariot races and theatrical displays and were not connected to the deaths of prominent individuals. As spectacles, however, and in terms of their social and ideological functions, the line between them becomes increasingly ambiguous from the late Republic onwards (Welch 1994: 61–2).

2 Christians were not the only group to die for their faith. Jews also were martyred; and Daniel Boyarin (1999) has shown how the self-representation of Jewish and Christian martyrs nourished one another.

3 The emphasis on virginity is an added crucial ingredient, but I will defer discussion of it to the next volume.

19 Violence to eternity: Plotinus and the mystical way

1 References to Plotinus are to the Loeb (1966f) edition, and follow standard book and line numbering.

2 The dark humour here echoes that of the Cynics, especially Diogenes, who when asked about instructions for his burial replied that there was no need to fuss; 'the stink will get me buried' (Lucian 1936: *Demonix* 66; see also Downing 1988: 44).

Bibliography

Addleston, Kathryn Pine (1983) 'The Man of Professional Wisdom' in Sandra Harding and Merrill B. Hintikka (eds) *Discovering Reality: Feminist Perspectives on Epistemology, Metaphysics, Methodology, and Philosophy of Science*, Dordrecht and London: D. Reidel.

Adorno,Theodor and Horkheimer, Max (1989) *Dialectic of Enlightenment*, trans. John Cumming, New York: Continuum.

Aeschylus (1961) *Prometheus Bound, The Suppliants, Seven Against Thebes, The Persians*, trans. Philip Vellacott, Harmondsworth and New York: Penguin.

Aeschylus (1976) *The Oresteia*, trans. Robert Fagles, Harmondsworth and New York: Penguin.

Alston, Richard (1998) 'Arms and the Man: Soldiers, Masculinity and Power in Republican and Imperial Roman Law' in Lin Foxhall and John Salmon (eds) *When Men were Men: Masculinity, Power and Identity in Classical Antiquity*, London and New York: Routledge.

Anderson, Alistair Scott (1987) 'The Imperial Army' in John Wacher (ed.) *The Roman World* Vol. I, London and New York: Routledge.

Andreadis, Harriette (1996) 'Sappho in Early Modern England: A Study in Sexual Reputation' in Ellen Greene (ed.) *Reading Sappho: Contemporary Approaches*, Berkeley and London: University of California Press.

Annas, Julia A. (1991) *An Introduction to Plato's Republic*, Oxford: Clarendon Press.

Arendt, Hannah (1977) *Between Past and Future*, Harmondsworth: Penguin.

Arendt, Hannah (1996) *Love and Saint Augustine*, eds Joanna Vecchiarelli Scott and Judith Chelius Stark, Chicago: University of Chicago Press.

Ariès, Philippe (1987) *The Hour of our Death*, trans. Helen Weaver, London: Penguin.

Aristotle (1912) *De Generatione Animalium*, trans. Arthur Platt in *The Works of Aristotle* Vol.V, eds J.A. Smith and W.D. Ross, Oxford: Clarendon Press.

Aristotle (1941) *The Basic Works of Aristotle*, ed. Richard McKeon, New York: Random House.

Aristotle (1982) *Eudemian Ethics*, trans. Michael Woods, Oxford: Clarendon Press.

Armstrong, A.H. (1970) 'Plotinus' in his (ed.) *The Cambridge History of Later Greek and Early Medieval Philosophy*, Cambridge: Cambridge University Press.

Armstrong, A.H. (1979) *Plotinus and Christian Studies*, London: Variorum.

Arthur, Marylin (1987) 'From Medusa to Cleopatra: Women in the Ancient World' in Renate Bridenthal, Cluadia Koonz and Susan Stuard (eds) *Becoming Visible: Women in European Tradition*, second edition, Boston: Houghton Mifflin.

Atwood, Margaret (1987) *The Handmaid's Tale*, London: Virago.

Auguet, Roland (1972) *Cruelty and Civilization: The Roman Games*, London: George Allen & Unwin.

Augustine (1972) *The City of God*, trans. Henry Bettenson, Harmondsworth: Penguin.

Augustine (1984) *Augustine of Hippo: Selected Writings*, trans. Mary T. Clark, Classics of Western Spirituality, London: SPCK.

Aurelius, Marcus (1945) 'Meditations' in *Marcus Aurelius and his Times: The Transition from Paganism to Christianity*, ed. Irwin Edman, Roslyn, NY: Walter J. Black Inc.

Austin, Scott (1986) *Parmenides: Being, Bounds, and Logic*, New Haven and London: Yale University Press.

Bacon, Francis (1973) *The Advancement of Learning*, ed. G.W. Kitchin, London: J.M. Dent.

Bar On, Bat-Ami (ed.) (1994) *Engendering Origins: Critical Feminist Readings in Plato and Aristotle*, Albany, NY: State University of New York Press.

Baring, Anne and Cashford, Jules (1991) *The Myth of the Goddess: Evolution of an Image*, London: Penguin.

Barnes, Jonathan (1979) *The Presocratic Philosophers. Vol. I: Thales to Zeno; Vol. II: Empedocles to Democritus*, London: Routledge & Kegan Paul.

Barnes, Jonathan (1995) 'Life and Work' in his (ed.) *The Cambridge Companion to Aristotle*, Cambridge: Cambridge University Press.

Barrett, Anthony A. (1996) *Agrippina: Sex, Power and Politics in the Early Empire*, New Haven and London: Yale University Press.

Barrett, J.C. (1997) 'Romanization: a Critical Comment' in D.J. Mattingly (ed.) *Dialogues in Roman Imperialism: Power, Discourse, and Discrepant Experience in the Roman Empire*, Journal of Roman Archaeology Supplement Series No.23, Portsmouth, RI: Cushing-Malloy Inc.

Bauckham, Richard (1991) 'The Economic Critique of Rome in Revelation 18' in Loveday Alexander (ed.) *Images of Empire*, Journal for the Study of the Old Testament Supplement Series 122, Sheffield: Sheffield Academic Press.

Beardsley, Monroe C. (1966) *Aesthetics from Classical Greece to the Present: A Short History*, New York: Macmillan.

Benjamin, Walter (1969) *Illuminations*, trans. H. Zohn, ed. Hannah Arendt, New York: Schoken Books.

Berger, Harry, Jr (1994) '*Phaedrus* and the Politics of Inscription' in Steven Shankman (ed.) *Plato and Postmodernism*, Glenside, PA: The Aldane Press.

Betts, R.F. (1971) 'The allusion to Rome in British Imperialist Thought of the Late Nineteenth and Early Twentieth Centuries' in *Victorian Studies* 15: 149–59.

Binyon, Laurence (1972) 'For the Fallen' in Helen Gardiner (ed.) *The New Oxford Book of English Verse 1250–1950*, Oxford: Oxford University Press.

Black, Jeremy (1997) *The British Abroad: The Grand Tour in the Eighteenth Century*, Stroud: Alan Sutton.

Blagg, T.F.C. (1990) 'Society and the Artist' in John Wacher (ed.) *The Roman World*, 2 vols, London and New York: Routledge.

Bloom, Allan (1968) *The Republic of Plato*, New York and London: Basic Books.

Blumenthal, Henry J. (1996) 'On Soul and Intellect' in Lloyd P. Gerson (ed.) *The Cambridge Companion to Plotinus*, Cambridge: Cambridge University Press.

Boardman, John (1996) *Greek Art*, fourth edition, London: Thames & Hudson.

Bodéüs, Richard (2000) *Aristotle and the Theology of the Living Immortals*, trans. Jan Garrett, Albany, NY: State University of New York Press.

Bourdieu, Pierre (1990) *The Logic of Practice*, trans. Richard Nice, Cambridge: Polity.

Bourdieu, Pierre (1998) *Practical Reason: On the Theory of Action*, Cambridge: Polity.

Boyarin, Daniel (1999) *Dying for God: Martyrdom and the Making of Christianity and Judaism*, Stanford, CA: Stanford University Press.

Bradley, Keith (1994) *Slavery and Society at Rome*, Cambridge: Cambridge University Press.

Bradley, Keith (1998) *Slavery and Rebellion in the Roman World, 140 BC–70 BC*, Bloomington: Indiana University Press.

Branigan, Keith (1991) 'Images – or Mirages – of Empire? An Archaeological Approach to the Problem' in Loveday Alexander (ed.) *Images of Empire*, Journal for the Study of the Old Testament Supplement Series 122, Sheffield: Sheffield Academic Press.

Braund, Susanna Morton (2002) *Latin Literature*, New York and London: Routledge.

Bredin, Hugh and Santoro-Brienza, Liberato (2000) *Philosophies of Art and Beauty: Introducing Aesthetics*, Edinburgh: Edinburgh University Press.

Bréhier, Émile (1963) *The Hellenic Age*, trans. Joseph Thomas, Chicago and London: University of Chicago Press.

Bréhier, Émile (1965) *The Hellenistic and Roman Age*, trans. Wade Baskin, Chicago: University of Chicago Press.

Brennan, Teresa (1993) *History after Lacan*, London: Routledge.

Brown, Peter (1971) *The World of Late Antiquity*, London: Thames & Hudson.

Brown, Peter (1978) *The Making of Late Antiquity*, Cambridge, MA: Harvard University Press.

Brown, Peter (1987) 'Late Antiquity' in Paul Veyne (ed.) *A History of Private Life I: From Pagan Rome to Byzantium*, trans. Arthur Goldhammer, Cambridge, MA and London: Belknap Press of Harvard University Press.

Brown, Peter (1988) *The Body and Society: Men, Women and Sexual Renunciation in Early Christianity*, Boston and London: Faber & Faber.

Bryce, James (1914) *The Ancient Roman Empire and the British Empire in India. The Diffusion of Roman and English Law Throughout the World. Two Historical Studies*, Oxford: Oxford University Press.

Burger, Ronna (1980) *Plato's Phaedrus: A Defence of a Philosophic Art of Writing*, University, Alabama: University of Alabama Press.

Burkert, Walter (1979) *Structure and History in Greek Mythology and Ritual*, Berkeley and London: University of California Press.

Burkert, Walter (1985) *Greek Religion*, trans. John Raffan, Cambridge, MA: Harvard University Press.

Bussanich, John (1996) 'Plotinus' Metaphysics of the One' in Lloyd P. Gerson (ed.) *The Cambridge Companion to Plotinus*, Cambridge: Cambridge University Press.

Bynum, Caroline Walker (1995) *The Resurrection of the Body in Western Christianity, 200–1336*, New York: Columbia University Press.

Cavarero, Adriana (1995) *In Spite of Plato: A Feminist Rewriting of Ancient Philosophy*, trans. Serena Anderlini-D'Onofrioi and Áine O'Healey, Cambridge: Polity Press.

Chadwick, Henry (1967) *The Early Church*, Harmondsworth: Penguin.

Chandos, John (1984) *Boys Together: English Public Schools 1800–1864*, London: Hutchinson.

Charlier, Catherine (1991) 'Ethics and the Feminine' in Robert Bernasconi and Simon Critchley (eds), *Re-Reading Levinas*, Bloomington, IN: Indiana University Press.

Chaucer, Geoffrey (1998) *The Canterbury Tales*, trans. David Wright, London: Folio Society.

Christ, Carol P. (1997) *The Return of the Goddess: Finding Meaning in Feminist Spirituality*, New York: Addison-Wesley.

Cicero (1971) *On the Good Life*, trans. Michael Grant, London and New York: Penguin.

Cicero (1972) *The Nature of the Gods*, trans. Horace C.P. McGregor, Harmondsworth: Penguin.

Cicero (1985) *Tusculan Disputations* I, trans. A.E. Douglas, Warminster: Aris & Phillips, and Chicago: Bolchazy-Carducci.

Clark, Gillian (1991) 'Let Every Soul be Subject: The Fathers and the Empire in Loveday Alexander (ed.) *Images of Empire*, Journal for the Study of the Old Testament Supplement Series 122, Sheffield: Sheffield Academic Press.

Clark, Isabelle (1998) 'The Games of Hera: Myth and Ritual' in Sue Blundell and Margaret Williamson (eds) *The Sacred and the Feminine in Ancient Greece*, London and New York: Routledge.

Clark, Stephen R.L. (1996) 'Plotinus: Body and Soul' in Lloyd P. Gerson (ed.) *The Cambridge Companion to Plotinus*, Cambridge: Cambridge University Press.

Clay, Diskin (1983) *Lucretius and Epicurus*, Ithaca and London: Cornell University Press.

Cole, Susan Guettel (1998) 'Domesticating Artemis' in Sue Blundell and Margaret Williamson (eds) *The Sacred and the Feminine in Ancient Greece*, London and New York: Routledge.

Cooper, David E. (ed.) (1997) *Aesthetics: the Classical Readings*, Oxford: Blackwell.

Copleston, Frederick (1962) *A History of Philosophy*, 9 vols. New York: Image, Doubleday.

Cornford, Francis Macdonald (1939) *Plato and Parmenides*, New York: Humanities Press, and London: Routledge & Kegan Paul.

Coxon, A.H. (1986) *The Fragments of Parmenides: A Critical Text and Introduction, Translation, the Ancient* Testimonia *and a Commentary*, Assen, NL: Van Gorcum.

Critchley, Simon (1998) 'Introduction' in Simon Critchley and William R. Schroeder (eds) *A Companion to Continental Philosophy*, Oxford: Blackwell.

Crombie, I.M. (1963) *An Examination of Plato's Doctrines. Vol.II: Plato on Knowledge and Reality*, London: Routledge and Kegan Paul; New York: The Humanities Press.

Cronin, Vincent (1967) *The Florentine Renaissance*, London: Collins.

Curran, Angela (1998) 'Feminisim and the Narrative Structure of the *Poetics*' in Cynthia A. Freeland (ed.) *Feminist Interpretations of Aristotle*, University Park, PA: Pennsylvania State University Press.

Dahlberg, Francis (1981) *Woman the Gatherer*, New Haven, CT: Yale University Press.

Daniélou, Jean (1973) *Gospel Message and Hellenistic Culture: A History of Early Christian Doctrine Before the Council of Nicaea*, Vol. II, trans. John Austin Baker, London: Darton, Longman & Todd, and Philadelphia: The Westminster Press.

Darwin, Charles (1868) *The Variation of Animals and Plants Under Domestication*, London: John Murray.

Darwin, Charles (1968) *The Origin of Species*, London: Penguin.

Davies, Jan (1999) *Death, Birth and Rebirth in the Religions of Antiquity*, London and New York: Routledge.

Davis, Michael (1999) *The Poetry of Philosophy: On Aristotles Poetics*, South Bend, IN: St Augustine's Press.

De Bella, Peter (1989) *The Discourse of the Sublime: History, Aesthetics and the Subject*, Oxford: Blackwell.

DeJean, Joan (1996) 'Sex and Philology: Sappho and the Rise of German Nationalism', in

Ellen Greene (ed.) *Reading Sappho: Contemporary Approaches*, Berkeley and London: University of California Press.

Derrida, Jacques (1978) *Writing and Difference*, trans. Alan Bass, London and New York: Routledge.

Derrida, Jacques (1987) *The Truth in Painting*, trans. Geoff Bennington and Ian McLeod, Chicago and London: University of Chicago Press.

Derrida, Jacques (1993) *Dissemination*, trans. Barbara Johnson, London: Athlone.

Deslauriers, Marguerite (1998) 'Sex and Essence in Aristotle's Metaphysics and Biology' in Cynthia A. Freeland (ed.) *Feminist Interpretations of Aristotle*, University Park, PA: Pennsylvania State University Press.

Detienne, Marcel (1977) *The Gardens of Adonis: Spices in Greek Mythology*, trans. Janet Lloyd, London: Harvester Press.

Dickson, Olive P. (1984) *The Myth of the Savage and the Beginnings of French Colonialism in the Americas*, Edmonton: University of Alberta Press.

Diels, H. and Kranz, W. (1951) *Die Fragmente der Vorsokratiker*, sixth edition, 3 vols, Zurich: Weidmann.

Dillon, John M. (1996) 'An Ethic for the Late Antique Sage' in Lloyd P. Gerson (ed.) *The Cambridge Companion to Plotinus*, Cambridge: Cambridge University Press.

Dio, Cassius (1987) *The Roman History: The Reign of Augustus*, trans. Ian Scott-Kilvert, London: Penguin.

Dixon, Suzanne (2001) *Reading Roman Women: Sources, Genres and Real Life*, London: Duckworth.

Dollimore, Jonathan (1998) *Death, Desire and Loss in Western Culture*, New York: Routledge.

Doniger, Wendy (1999) *Splitting the Difference: Gender and Myth in Ancient Greece and India*, Chicago and London: University of Chicago Press.

Downing, F. Gerald (1988) *The Christ and the Cynics*, Sheffield: *Journal of the Society of Old Testament Studies*.

du Bois, Page (1988) *Sowing the Body: Psychoanalysis and Ancient Representations of Women*, Chicago and London: University of Chicago Press.

du Bois, Page (1991) *Torture and Truth*, New York and London: Routledge.

du Bois, Page (1995) *Sappho is Burning*, Chicago and London: University of Chicago Press.

du Bois, Page (1996) 'Sappho and Helen', in Ellen Greene (ed.) *Reading Sappho: Contemporary Approaches*, Berkeley and London: University of California Press.

Duncan-Jones, Richard (1974) *The Economy of the Roman Empire: Quantitative Studies*, Cambridge: Cambridge University Press.

Dyer, Richard (1997) *White*, London and New York: Routledge.

Edwards, Catharine (1993) *The Politics of Immorality in Ancient Rome*, Cambridge: Cambridge University Press.

Edwards, Catharine (1999a) 'Introduction: Shadows and Fragments' in her (ed.) *Roman Presences: Receptions of Rome in European Culture, 1789–1945*, Cambridge: Cambridge University Press.

Edwards, Catharine (ed.) (1999b) *Roman Presences: Receptions of Rome in European Culture, 1789–1945*, Cambridge: Cambridge University Press.

Ehrenberg, Margaret (1989) *Women in Prehistory*, London: British Museum Publications.

Elias, Norbert (1994) *The Civilizing Process*, Oxford: Blackwell.

Emilsson, Eyjólfur K. (1999) 'Neo-Platonism' in David Furley (ed.) *From Aristotle to Augustine*, Routledge History of Philosophy Vol. II, London and New York: Routledge.

Erasmus (1964) *The Essential Erasmus*, ed. John P. Dolan, New York: New American Library.

Euripides (1953) *Ancestis, Hippolytus, Iphigenia in Tauris*, trans. Philip Vellacott, Harmondsworth and New York: Penguin.

Euripides (1963) *Medea and Other Plays*, trans. Philip Vellacott, London and New York: Penguin.

Euripides (1972) *Orestes and Other Plays*, trans. Philip Vellacott, London and New York: Penguin.

Euripides (1973) *The Bacchae and Other Plays*, revised edition, trans. Philip Vellacott, London and New York: Penguin.

Everitt, Anthony (2001) *Cicero: A Turbulent Life*, London: John Murray.

Fagles, Robert and Standford, W.B. (1966) 'A Reading of "The Oresteia": The Serpent and the Eagle' in Aeschylus *The Orseteia*, trans. Robert Fagles, Harmondsworth and New York: Penguin.

Feinberg, Joel (1993) 'Harm to Others' in John Martin Fischer (ed.) *The Metaphysics of Death*, Stanford, CA: Stanford University Press.

Feldherr, Andrew (2002) 'Metamorphoses in the *Metamorphoses*' in Philip Hardie (ed.) *The Cambridge Companion to Ovid*, Cambridge: Cambridge University Press.

Ferguson, John (1990) 'Ruler Worship' in John Wacher (ed.) *The Roman World*, 2 vols, London and New York: Routledge.

Ferrari, G.R.F. (1992) 'Platonic Love' in Richard Kraut (ed.) *The Cambridge Companion to Plato*, Cambridge: Cambridge University Press.

Ferrill, Arther (1985) *The Origins of War: From the Stone Age to Alexander the Great*, London: Thames & Hudson.

Finley, M.I. (1973) *The Ancient Economy*, London: Chatto & Windus.

Finley, M.I. (1980) *Ancient Slavery and Modern Ideology*, Harmondsworth: Penguin.

Finley, Moses (2002) *The World of Odysseus*, second revised edition, London: Folio Society.

Foucault, Michel (1984) 'What is Enlightenment?' in Paul Rabinow (ed.) *Foucault Reader*, New York: Pantheon.

Foucault, Michel (1986) 'Kant on Enlightenment and Revolution', trans. C. Gordon, in *Economy and Society* 15.1.

Foucault, Michel (1994) "Maurice Florence" 'Foucault, Michel, 1926–' in Gary Gutting (ed.) *The Cambridge Companion to Foucault*, Cambridge: Cambridge University Press.

Fox, Robin Lane (1986) *Pagans and Christians*, London: Penguin.

Fox, Robin Lane (1997) *Alexander the Great*, London: Folio Society.

Foxhall, Lin and Salmon, John (eds) (1998) *When Men were Men: Masculinity, Power and Identity in Classical Antiquity*, London and New York: Routledge.

Freeland, Cynthia A. (1992) 'Plot Imitates Action: Aesthetic Evaluation and Moral Realism in Aristotle's *Poetics*' in Amélie Oksenberg Rorty (ed.) *Essays on Aristotle's Poetics*, Princeton: Princeton University Press.

Freeland, Cynthia A. (ed.) (1998) *Feminist Interpretations of Aristotle*, University Park, PA: Pennsylvania State University Press.

Freeman, P.W.M. (1997) 'Mommsen through to Haverfield: the Origins of Romanization Studies in late 19th century Britain' in D.J. Mattingly (ed.) *Dialogues in Roman Imperialism: Power, Discourse, and Discrepant Experience in the Roman Empire*, Journal of Roman Archaeology Supplement Series No.23, Portsmouth, RI: Cushing-Malloy Inc.

Freud, Sigmund (1984) *Beyond the Pleasure Principle* in The Pelican Freud Library Vol. 11, trans. James Strachey, London: Penguin.

Freud, Sigmund (1985) 'Civilization and its Discontents' in his *Civilization, Society and Religion*, The Pelican Freud Library Vol. 12, trans. James Strachey, London: Penguin.

Freud, Sigmund (1991) *Why War?* in The Pelican Freud Library Vol. 12 trans. James Strachey, London: Penguin.

Fromm, Erich (1977) *The Anatomy of Human Destructiveness*, London: Penguin.

Gale, Monica (1994) *Myth and Poetry in Lucretius*, Cambridge: Cambridge University Press.

Galinsky, K. (1996) *Augustan Culture: an Interpretative Introduction*, Princeton: Princeton University Press.

Galinsky, K. (1999) 'Ovid's *Metamorphoses* and Augustan Cultural Thematics' in P.R. Hardie, A. Barchiesi and S.E. Hinds (eds) *Ovidian Transformations: Essays on Ovid's Metamorphoses and its Reception*, Cambridge Philological Society Supplement 23, Cambridge: Cambridge University Press.

Gardner, Jane F. (1998) 'Sexing a Roman: Imperfect Men in Roman Law' in Lin Foxhall and John Salmon (eds) *When Men were Men: Masculinity, Power and Identity in Classical Antiquity*, London and New York: Routledge.

Garnsey, P.D.A. (1978) 'Rome's African Empire under the Principate' in P.D.A. Garnsey and C.R. Whittaker (eds) *Imperialism in the Ancient World*, Cambridge: Cambridge University Press.

Garnsey, P.D.A. and Whittaker, C.R. (eds) (1978) *Imperialism in the Ancient World*, Cambridge: Cambridge University Press.

Gatti, Maria Luisa (1996) 'Plotinus: The Platonic Tradition and the Foundation of Neoplatonism' in Lloyd P. Gerson (ed.) *The Cambridge Companion to Plotinus*, Cambridge: Cambridge University Press.

Gay, Peter (1977) *The Enlightenment: An Interpretation. Vol. I: The Rise of Modern Paganism. Vol. II: The Science of Freedom*, New York and London: W.W. Norton.

Gerson, Lloyd P. (ed.) (1996) *The Cambridge Companion to Plotinus*, Cambridge: Cambridge University Press.

Gibbon, Edward (1960) *The Decline and Fall of the Roman Empire*, abridged by D.M. Low, London: Chatto & Windus.

Gimbutas, Maria (1982) *The Goddesses and Gods of Old Europe*, London: Thames & Hudson.

Gimbutas, Maria (1991) *The Civilization of the Goddess*, San Fransicso: Harper & Row.

Girard, René (1972) *Violence and the Sacred*, trans. Patrick Gregory, Baltimore: Johns Hopkins University Press.

Girard, René (1986) *The Scapegoat*, trans. Yvonne Freccero, Baltimore: Johns Hopkins University Press.

Glover, Jonathan (2001) *Humanity: A Moral History of the Twentieth Century*, London: Pimlico.

Godwin, Joscelyn (1981) *Mystery Religions in the Ancient World*, London: Thames & Hudson.

Goodman, Martin (1991) 'Opponents of Rome: Jews and Others' in Loveday Alexander (ed.) *Images of Empire*, Journal for the Study of the Old Testament Supplement Series 122, Sheffield: Sheffield Academic Press.

Gould, Thomas (1990) *The Ancient Quarrel Between Poetry and Philosophy*, Princeton: Princeton University Press.

Gramsci, Antonio (1971) *Prison Notebooks: A Selection*, trans. and eds Quinton Hoare and Geoffrey Nowell Smith, New York: International Publishers.

Grant, Michael (1979) *The History of Rome*, revised edition, London: Faber & Faber.

Graves, Robert (1953) *I, Claudius*, Harmondsworth: Penguin.

Green, Erich S. (1984) *The Hellenistic World and the Coming of Rome*, 2 vols, Berkeley and London: University of California Press.

Green, Peter (1991) *Alexander of Macedon 356–323 BC: A Historical Biography*, Berkeley and London: University of California Press.

Greene, Ellen (ed.) (1996a) *Reading Sappho: Contemporary Approaches*, Berkeley and London: University of California Press.

Greene, Ellen (ed.) (1996b) *Re-Reading Sappho: Reception and Transmission*, Berkeley and London: University of California Press.

Griffin, Jasper (1980) *Homer on Life and Death*, Oxford: Clarendon Press.

Griffin, Miriam T. (1976) *Seneca: A Philosopher in Politics*, Oxford: Clarendon Press.

Griffin, Miriam (1991) '*Urbs Roma, Plebs* and *Princeps*' in Loveday Alexander (ed.) *Images of Empire*, Journal for the Study of the Old Testament Supplement Series 122, Sheffield: Sheffield Academic Press.

Gunderson, E. (1996) 'The Ideology of the Arena' in *Classical Antiquity* 15.

Güntert, H. (1919) *Bedeutungsgeschichtliche Untersuchen auf dem Gebeit der Indogermanischen Sprachen*, Halle.

Guthrie, W.K.C. (1965) *A History of Greek Philosophy. Vol. II The Presocratic Tradition from Parmenides to Democritus*, Cambridge: Cambridge University Press.

Habinek, Thomas (2002) 'Ovid and Empire' in Philip Hardie (ed.) *The Cambridge Companion to Ovid*, Cambridge: Cambridge University Press.

Hackforth, R. (1952) *Plato's Phaedrus*, Cambridge: Cambridge University Press.

Hadot, Pierre (1993) *Plotinus or The Simplicity of Vision*, trans. Michael Chase, Chicago and London: University of Chicago Press.

Hale, John R. (2000) *The Renaissance in Europe*, second edition, Oxford: Blackwell.

Hall, Donald F. (ed.) (1994) *Muscular Christianity: Embodying the Victorian Age*, Cambridge: Cambridge University Press.

Hallett, Judith P. (1996) 'Sappho and her Social Context: Sense and Sensuality' in Ellen Greene (ed.) *Reading Sappho: Contemporary Approaches*, Berkeley and London: University of California Press.

Halliwell, Stephen (1986) *Aristotle's Poetics*, London: Duckworth.

Halliwell, Stephen (1992) 'Pleasure, Understanding, and Emotions' in Amélie Oksenberg Rorty (ed.) *Essays on Aristotle's Poetics*, Princeton: Princeton University Press.

Halliwell, Stephen (2002) *The Aesthetics of Mimesis: Ancient Texts and Modern Problems*, Princeton and Oxford: Princeton University Press.

Halperin, David (1994) 'Plato and the Erotics of Narrativity' in Steven Shankman (ed.) *Plato and Postmodernism*, Glenside, PA: The Aldane Press.

Halperin, David (1995) *Saint Foucault: Towards a Gay Hagiography*, New York and Oxford: Oxford University Press.

Hardwick, Lorna (2000) 'Concepts of Peace' in Janet Huskinson (ed.) *Experiencing Rome: Culture, Identity and Power in the Roman Empire*, London and New York: Routledge.

Harris, Roy (1988) *Language, Saussure and Wittgenstein: How to Play Games with Words*, London: Routledge.

Harris, W.V. (1979) *War and Imperialism in Republican Rome 327–30 BC*, Oxford: Clarendon Press.

Hartog, François (2001) *Memories of Odysseus: Frontier Tales from Ancient Greece*, trans. Janet Lloyd, Chicago: University of Chicago Press.

Hassall, Mark (1987) 'Romans and Non-Romans' in John Wacher (ed.) *The Roman World* Vol. II, London and New York: Routledge.

Haverfield, F.J. (1923) *The Romanization of Roman Britain*, fourth edition, Oxford: Clarendon Press.

Hawthorne, Susan (1994) 'Diotima Speaks Through the Body' in Bat-Ami Bar On (ed.) *Engendering Origins: Critical Feminist Readings of Plato and Aristotle*, Albany, NY: State University of New York Press.

Hegel, G.W.F. (1977) *Phenomenology of Spirit*, trans. A.V. Miller, Oxford: Clarendon Press.

Hegel, G.W.F. (1995) *Lectures on the History of Philosophy*, 3 vols, trans. E.S. Haldane, Lincoln, NB and London: University of Nebraska Press.

Heidegger, Martin (1971) *Poetry, Language, Thought*, trans. Albert Hofstadter, New York and London: Harper & Row.

Heidegger, Martin (1992) *Parmenides*, trans. André Schuwer and Richard Rojcewicz, Bloomington, IN: Indiana University Press.

Heineman, Robert (1997) 'Plato: Metaphysics and Epistemology' in C.C. W. Taylor (ed.) *Routledge History of Philosophy. Vol. I: From the Beginning to Plato*, London and New York: Routledge.

Hesiod and Theognis (1973) *Theogony; Works and Days; Elegies*, trans. Dorothea Wender, London: Penguin.

Hirshman, Linda Redlick (1998) 'The Book of "A"' in Cynthia A. Freeland (ed.) *Feminist Interpretations of Aristotle*, University Park, PA: Pennsylvania State University Press.

Holland, Richard (2000) *Nero: The Man Behind the Myth*, Stroud: Sutton Publishing.

Hollander, John and Kermode, Frank (eds) (1973) *The Literature of Renaissance England*, New York and London: Oxford University Press.

Homer (1960) *The Iliad*, trans. Richmond Lattimore, London and Chicago: University of Chicago Press.

Homer (1990a) *The Iliad*, trans. Robert Fagles, London: Penguin.

Homer (1990b) *The Odyssey*, trans. Robert Fagles, London: Penguin.

Hope, Valerie (2000) 'The City of Rome: Capital and Symbol' in Janet Huskinson (ed.) *Experiencing Rome: Culture, Identity and Power in the Roman Empire*, London and New York: Routledge.

Hopkins, K. (1978) *Conquerors and Slaves*, Cambridge: Cambridge University Press.

Hopkins, K. (1983) *Death and Renewal*, Sociological Studies in Roman History Vol. 2, Cambridge: Cambridge University Press.

Horace (1997) *The Complete Odes and Epodes*, trans. David West, Oxford and New York: Oxford University Press.

Hornblower, Simon (1991) *The Greek World 479–323 BC*, revised edition, London and New York: Routledge.

Hornblower, S. and Spawforth, A. (1996) *The Oxford Classical Dictionary*, Oxford: Oxford University Press.

Hornblower, Simon and Spawforth, Antony (eds) (1998) *The Oxford Companion to Classical Civilization*, Oxford and New York: Oxford University Press.

Huet, Valérie (1999) 'Napoleon I: A New Augustus?' in Catherine Edwards (ed.) *Roman*

Presences: Receptions of Rome in European Culture, 1789–1945, Cambridge: Cambridge University Press.

Huskinson, Janet (2000a) 'Elite Culture and the Identity of Empire' in her *Experiencing Rome: Culture, Identity and Power in the Roman Empire*, London and New York: Routledge.

Huskinson, Janet (ed.) (2000b) *Experiencing Rome: Culture, Identity and Power in the Roman Empire*, London and New York: Routledge.

Ignatius (1885) 'Epistle of Ignatius to the Romans' in *The Ante-Nicene Fathers*, Vol. 1, trans. Alexander Roberts and James Donaldson, Grand Rapids, MI: Eerdmans.

Inwood, Brad (1999) 'Stoicism' in David Furley (ed.) *From Aristotle to Augustine: Routledge History of Philosophy, Vol. II*, London and New York: Routledge.

Irigaray, Luce (1985) *Speculum of the Other Woman*, trans. Gillian C. Gill, Ithaca, NY: Cornell University Press.

Irigaray, Luce (1991) 'Questions to Emmanuel Levinas: On the Divinity of Love' in Robert Bernasconi and Simon Critchley (eds) *Re-Reading Levinas*, Bloomington, IN: Indiana University Press.

Irigaray, Luce (1993) *An Ethics of Sexual Difference*, trans. Carolyn Burke and Gillian C. Gill, London: Athlone.

Irwin, Terence (1977) *Plato's Moral Theory*, Oxford: Clarendon Press.

James, Lawrence (1994) *The Rise and Fall of the British Empire*, London: Abacus.

James, Lawrence (1997) *Raj: The Making of British India*, London: Abacus.

James, P.D. (1992) *The Children of Men*, London: Penguin.

James, Paula (2000) 'The Language of Dissent' in Janet Huskinson (ed.) *Experiencing Rome: Culture, Identity and Power in the Roman Empire*, London and New York: Routledge.

Janson, H.W. (1969) *History of Art: A Survey of the Major Visual Arts from the Dawn of History to the Present Age*, revised edition, Englewood Cliffs, NJ: Prentice Hall, and New York: Harry N. Abrams.

Jantzen, Grace M. (1995) *Power, Gender and Christian Mysticism*, Cambridge: Cambridge University Press.

Jantzen, Grace M. (1998) *Becoming Divine: Towards a Feminist Philosophy of Religion*, Manchester: Manchester University Press, and Bloomington, IN: Indiana University Press.

Jantzen, Grace M. (2001) 'Before the Rooster Crows: John Locke, Margaret Fell, and the Betrayal of Knowledge in Modernity' in *Literature and Theology* 15.1.

Jay, Martin (1994) *Downcast Eyes: The Denigration of Vision in Twentieth-Century French Thought*, Berkeley: University of California Press.

Jenkyns, Richard (1980) *The Victorians and Ancient Greece*, Cambridge, MA: Harvard University Press.

Jenkyns, Richard (ed.) (1992) *The Legacy of Rome: A New Appraisal*, Oxford: Oxford University Press.

Jones, A.H.M. (1974) *The Roman Economy: Studies in Ancient Economy and Administrative History*, Oxford: Blackwell.

Justin (1885) 'The First Apology of Justin' in *The Ante-Nicene Fathers*, Vol. 1, trans. Alexander Roberts and James Donaldson, Grand Rapids, MI: Eerdmans.

Justin (1977) 'The First Apology' in Alexander Roberts and James Donaldson (eds) *The Ante-Nicene Fathers: The Writings of the Fathers down to A.D. 325*, Vol. I, Grand Rapids, MI: Eerdmans.

Juvenal (1998) *The Sixteen Satires*, third edition, trans. Peter Green, London: Penguin.

Kampen, Natalie Boymel (1991) 'Between Public and Private: Women as Historical Subjects in Roman Art' in Sarah B. Pomeroy (ed.) *Women's History and Ancient History*, Chapel Hill and London: University of North Carolina Press.

Kappeler, Susanne (1995) *The Will to Violence: The Politics of Personal Behaviour*, Cambridge: Polity.

Keeley, Lawrence H. (1996) *War Before Civilization*, Oxford and New York: Oxford University Press.

Kellner, Douglas (1989) *Critical Theory, Marxism and Modernity*, Baltimore: Johns Hopkins University Press.

King, R.A.H. (2001) *Aristotle on Life and Death*, London: Duckworth.

Klein, Melanie (1988) *Love, Guilt and Reparation and Other Works 1921–1945*, London: Virago.

Knox, Bernard (1990) 'Introduction', in Homer *The Iliad*, trans. Robert Fagles, London: Penguin.

Koch, Adrienne (1961) *Power, Morals, and the Founding Fathers: Essays in the Interpretation of the American Enlightenment*, Ithaca, NY and London: Cornell University Press.

Kraut, Richard (1992a) 'Introduction to the Study of Plato' in his (ed.) *The Cambridge Companion to Plato*, Cambridge: Cambridge University Press.

Kraut, Richard (ed.) (1992b) *The Cambridge Companion to Plato*, Cambridge: Cambridge University Press.

Kristeva, Julia (1989) *Black Sun: Depression and Melancholia*, trans. Leon S. Roudiez, New York: Columbia University Press.

Kyle, Donald G. (1998) *Spectacles of Death in Ancient Rome*, London and New York: Routledge.

Lacan, Jacques (1977) *Écrits: A Selection*, trans. Alan Sheridan, London: Tavistock/Routledge.

Le Doeuff, Michelle (1989) *The Philosophical Imaginary*, trans. Colin Gordon, London: Athlone.

Lee, A.D. (ed.) (2000) *Pagans and Christians in Late Antiquity: A Sourcebook*, London: Routledge.

Lefkowitz, Mary R. and Fant, Maureen B. (eds) (1992) *Women's Life in Greece and Rome: A Sourcebook in Translation*, second edition, Baltimore and London: Johns Hopkins University Press.

Lepper, F. and Frere, S. (1988) *Trajan's Column*, Stroud: Alan Sutton.

Levinas, Emmanuel (1969a) *Totality and Infinity: An Essay in Exteriority*, trans. Alphonso Lingis, Pittsburgh: Duquesne University Press.

Levinas, Emmanuel (1969b) 'Judaism and the Feminine Element', trans. E. Wyschogrod in *Judaism* 181, no.1.

Levinas, Emmanuel (1986) 'The Trace of the Other', trans. Alphonso Lingis in Mark Taylor (ed.) *Deconstruction in Context*, Chicago: University of Chicago Press.

Levinas, Emmanuel (1987) *Time and the Other*, trans. Richard A. Cohen, Pittsburgh: Duquesne University Press.

Lévi-Strauss, Claude (1963, 1978) *Structural Anthropology*, Vols. I and II, trans. Claire Jacobson, Brooke Grundfest Schoepf and Monique Layton, London: Penguin.

Livy (2002) *The Early History of Rome*, trans. Aubrey de Sélincourt, London: Penguin.

Loraux, Nicole (1987) *Tragic Ways of Killing a Woman*, trans. Anthony Forster, Cambridge, MA and London: Harvard University Press.

Loraux, Nicole (1992) 'What is a Goddess?' in Pauline Schmitt Pantel (ed.) A History of Women: From Ancient Goddesses to Christian Saints, trans. Arthur Goldhammer, Cambridge, MA and London: Harvard University Press.

Lord, Carnes (1982) Education and Culture in the Political Thought of Aristotle, Ithaca, NY and London: Cornell University Press.

Lubac, Henri de (1998 and 2000) Medieval Exegesis: The Four Senses of Scripture, Vol. I, trans. Mark Sebanc; Vol. II, trans. E.M. Macierowski, Grand Rapids, MI: Eerdmans, and Edinburgh: T&T Clark Ltd.

Lucas, C.P. (1912) Greater Rome and Greater Britain, Oxford: Oxford University Press.

Lucian (1936) Lucian with an English Translation, trans. A.M. Harmon, Loeb Classical Library, Cambridge, MA: Harvard University Press.

Lucretius (1951) On the Nature of the Universe, trans. Ronald Latham, Harmondsworth: Penguin.

Lyons, Deborah (1997) Gender and Immortality: Heroines in Ancient Greek Myth and Cult, Princeton: Princeton University Press.

Lyotard, Jean-François (1984) The Postmodern Condition: A Report on Knowledge, trans. Geoff Bennington and Brian Massumi, Manchester: Manchester University Press.

Lyotard, Jean-François (1989) 'The Sublime and the Avant-Garde' in The Lyotard Reader, ed. Andrew Benjamin, Oxford: Blackwell.

Machlis, Joseph (1977) The Enjoyment of Music, fourth edition, New York and London: W.W. Norton.

MacIntyre, Alistair (1988) Whose Justice? Which Rationality?, London: Duckworth.

Mack, Sara (1988) Ovid, New Haven and London: Yale University Press.

MacMullen, Ramsey (1967) Enemies of the Roman Order: Treason, Unrest, and Alienation in the Empire, Cambridge, MA: Harvard University Press, and London: Oxford University Press.

Majeed, Javed (1999) 'Comparativism and References to Rome in British Imperial Attitudes to India' in Catherine Edwards (ed.) Roman Presences: Receptions of Rome in European Culture, 1789–1945, Cambridge: Cambridge University Press.

Marchand, Suzanne L. (1996) Down from Olympus: Archaeology and Philhellinism in Germany 1750–1970, Princeton: Princeton University Press.

Mattingly, D.J. (1997) Dialogues in Roman Imperialism: Power, Discourse, and Discrepant Experience in the Roman Empire, Journal of Roman Archaeology Supplement Series No.23, Portsmouth, RI: Cushing-Malloy Inc.

McGinn, Bernard (1991) The Presence of God: A History of Western Christian Mysticism. Vol. I: The Foundations of Mysticism, London: SCM Press.

McKeon, Richard (1941) 'Introduction' in his (ed.) The Basic Works of Aristotle, New York: Random House.

McNamara, JoAnn (1987) 'Matres Patriae, Matres Ecclesiae: Women of the Roman Empire' in Renate Bridenthal, Claudia Koonz and Susan Stuard (eds) Becoming Visible: Women in European Tradition, second edition, Boston: Houghton Mifflin.

Meier, Christian (1993) The Political Art of Greek Tragedy, trans. Andrew Webber, Cambridge: Polity.

Meier, Christian (2000) Athens: A Portrait of the City in its Golden Age, trans. Robert and Rita Kimber, London: Pimlico.

Meijer, P.A. (1997) Parmenides Beyond the Gates: The Divine Revelation on Being, Thinking and the Doxa, Amsterdam: J.C. Gieben.

Mennell, Stephen (1992) Norbert Elias: An Introduction, Oxford: Blackwell.

Metcalf, Thomas (1994) *Ideologies of the Raj*, Cambridge: Cambridge University Press.

Meyers, Diana Tietjens (1994) *Subjection and Subjectivity: Psychoanalytic Feminism and Moral Philosophy*, New York and London: Routledge.

Miles, Margaret (1985) *Image as Insight: Visual Understanding in Western Christianity and Secular Culture*, Boston: Beacon Press.

Miles, Margaret R. (1989) *Carnal Knowing: Female Nakedness and Religious Meaning in the Christian West*, Boston: Beacon Press.

Miles, Margaret R. (1999) *Plotinus on Body and Beauty: Society, Philosophy and Religion in Third-Century Rome*, Oxford: Blackwell.

Mills, Patricia Jagentowicz (1996) 'Hegel's Antigone' in her (ed.) *Feminist Interpretations of G.W.F. Hegel*, University Park, PA: Pennsylvania State University Press.

Mommsen, T. (1996) *A History of Rome under the Emperors*, trans. C Krojzl, London: Routledge.

Montaigne, Michel de (1991) *The Complete Essays*, trans. M.A. Screech, London: Penguin.

Montesserat, Dominic (1998) 'Experiencing the Male Body in Roman Egypt' in Lin Foxhall and John Salmon (eds) *When Men were Men: Masculinity, Power and Identity in Classical Antiquity*, London and New York: Routledge.

Morgan, Michael L. (1992) 'Plato and Greek Religion' in Richard Kraut (ed.) *The Cambridge Companion to Plato*, Cambridge: Cambridge University Press.

Moulton, Janice (1983) 'A Paradigm of Philosophy: The Adversary Method' in Sandra Harding and Merrill B. Hintikka (eds) *Discovering Reality: Feminist Perspectives on Epistemology, Metaphysics, Methodology, and Philosophy of Science*, Dordrecht: D. Reidel.

Mourelatos, Alexander P.D. (1970) *The Route of Parmenides: A Study of Word, Image and Argument in the Fragments*, New Haven and London: Yale University Press.

Mueller, Ian (1992) 'Mathematical Method and Philosophical Truth' in Richard Kraut (ed.) *The Cambridge Companion to Plato*, Cambridge: Cambridge University Press.

Murdoch, Iris (1977) *The Fire and the Sun: Why Plato Banished the Artists*, Oxford: Clarendon Press.

Murnaghan, Sheila (1995) 'The Plan of Athena' in Beth Cohen (ed.) *The Distaff Side: Representing the Female in Homer's Odyssey*, Oxford: Oxford University Press.

Murray, Penelope (1992) 'Inspiration and Mimēsis in Plato' in Andrew Barker and Martin Warner (eds) *The Language of the Cave*, Edmonton, Canada: Academic Printing and Publishing.

Musarillo, H.R. (ed.) (1972) *The Acts of the Christian Martyrs*, Oxford: Clarendon Press.

Nagel, Thomas (1979) 'Moral Luck' in his (ed.) *Mortal Questions*, Cambridge: Cambridge University Press.

Nagler, Michael N. (1993) 'Penelope's Male Hand: Gender and Violence in the *Odyssey*' in *Colley Quarterly* 29.

Newlands, Carole (2002) '*Mandati memores*: Political and Poetic Authority' in Philip Hardie (ed.) *The Cambridge Companion to Ovid*, Cambridge: Cambridge University Press.

Newsome, David (1961) *Godliness and Good Learning: Four Studies on a Victorian Ideal*, London: John Murray.

Nussbaum, Martha C. (1986) *The Fragility of Goodness: Luck and Ethics in Greek Tragedy and Philosophy*, Cambridge: Cambridge University Press.

Nussbaum, Martha C. (1992) 'Tragedy and Self-Sufficiency: Plato and Aristotle on Fear and Pity' in Amélie Oksenberg Rorty (ed.) *Essays on Aristotle's Poetics*, Princeton: Princeton University Press.

Nussbaum, Martha C. (1994) *The Therapy of Desire: Theory and Practice in Hellenistic Ethics*, Princeton: Princeton University Press.

Nussbaum, Martha C. (1998) 'Aristotle, Feminism, and Needs for Functioning' in Cynthia A. Freeland (ed.) *Feminist Interpretations of Aristotle*, University Park, PA: Pennsylvania State University Press.

Nutton, V. (1978) 'The Beneficial Ideology' in P.D.A. Garnsey and C.R. Whittaker (eds) *Imperialism in the Ancient World*, Cambridge: Cambridge University Press.

Nye, Andrea (1990) *Words of Power: A Feminist Reading of the History of Logic*, New York: Routledge.

Nye, Andrea (1994) 'Irigaray and Diotima at Plato's Symposium' in Nancy Tuana (ed.) *Feminist Interpretations of Plato*, University Park, PA: Pennsylvania State University Press.

O'Brien, John Maxwell (1992) *Alexander the Great: The Invisible Enemy*, London and New York: Routledge.

O'Meara, Dominic J. (1993) *Plotinus: An Introduction to the Enneads*, Oxford: Clarendon Press.

Ogilvie, R.M. and Richmond, I.A. (1967) *Tacitus: De Vita Agricolae*, Oxford: Clarendon Press.

Okin, Susan Moller (1979) *Women in Western Political Thought*, Princeton: Princeton University Press.

Origen (1965) *Contra Celsum*, trans. Henry Chadwick, Cambridge: Cambridge University Press.

Overall, Christine (2003) *Aging, Death, and Human Longevity: A Philosophical Inquiry*, Berkeley and London: University of California Press.

Ovid (1955) *Metamorphoses*, trans. Rolfe Humphries, Bloomington, IN, and London: Indiana University Press.

Ovid (1958) *Ars Amatoria*, trans. Rolfe Humphries, London: Calder.

Ovid (1968) *Amores*, trans. G. Lee, London: John Murray.

Ovid (1990) *Heroides*, trans. Harold Isbell, London: Penguin.

Owen, Wilfred (1963) *The Collected Poems of Wilfred Owen*, ed. C.D. Lewis, London: Chatto & Windus.

Patrides, C.A. (ed.) (1985) *The Complete English Poems of John Donne*, London: Everyman, J.M. Dent.

Patterson, Cynthia B. (1991) 'Marriage and the Married Woman in Athenian Law' in Sarah B. Pomeray (ed.) *Women's History and Ancient History*, Chapel Hill and London: University of North Carolina Press.

Pelikan, Jaroslav (1971) *The Christian Tradition: A History of the Development of Doctrine. Vol. I: The Emergence of the Catholic Tradition (100–600)*, Chicago: University of Chicago Press.

Penner, Terry (1992) 'Socrates and the Early Dialogues' in Richard Kraut (ed.) *The Cambridge Companion to Plato*, Cambridge: Cambridge University Press.

Peperzak, Adriaan T. (ed.) (1995) *Ethics as First Philosophy: The Significance of Emmanuel Levinas for Philosophy, Literature and Religion*, New York and London: Routledge.

Perkins, Judith (1995) *The Suffering Self: Pain and Narrative Representation in the Early Christian Era*, London and New York: Routledge.

Peters, F.E. (1968) *Aristotle and the Arabs: The Aristotelian Tradition in Islam*, New York: New York University Press, and London: University of London Press.

Pindar (1976) *The Odes of Pindar*, second edition, trans. Richmond Lattimore, Chicago and London: University of Chicago Press.

Pitcher, George (1993) 'The Misfortunes of the Dead' in John Martin Fischer (ed.) *The Metaphysics of Death*, Stanford, CA: Stanford University Press.

Plato (1961) *The Collected Dialogues of Plato*, ed. Edith Hamilton and Huntington Cairns, Princeton: Princeton University Press.

Pliny the Elder (1991) *Natural History: A Selection*, trans. John F. Healy, London: Penguin.

Pliny the Younger (1963) *The Letters of the Younger Pliny*, trans. Betty Radice, London: Penguin.

Plotinus (1966f) *The Enneads*, 7 vols, trans. A.H. Armstrong, Loeb Classical Library, Cambridge MA: Harvard University Press, and London: William Heinemann Ltd.

Plotinus (1991) *The Enneads*, trans. Stephen MacKenna, London: Penguin.

Plutarch (1927) 'Advice on Marriage' in his *Moralia* II. 12, trans. Frank Lloyd Babbitt, Loeb Classical Library, London: William Heinemann Ltd.

Plutarch (1972) *Fall of the Roman Republic*, trans. Rex Warner, second edition, London: Penguin.

Plutarch (1998) *Greek Lives*, trans. Robin Waterfield, Oxford: Oxford University Press.

Podlecki, Anthony J. (1966) *The Political Background of Aeschylean Tragedy*, Ann Arbor: University of Michigan Press.

Polybius (1979) *The Rise of the Roman Empire*, trans. Ian Scott-Kilvert, London: Penguin.

Polycarp (1885) 'The Epistle of Polycarp to the Philippians' and 'The Martyrdom of Polycarp' in *The Ante-Nicene Fathers*, Vol. 1, trans. Alexander Roberts and James Donaldson, Grand Rapids, MI: Eerdmans.

Poole, Adrian (1987) *Tragedy: Shakespeare and the Greek Example*, Oxford: Oxford University Press.

Popper, Karl (1998) *The World of Parmenides: Essays on Presocratic Enlightenment*, Arne F. Petersen and Jørgen Mejer (eds) London and New York: Routledge.

Porete, Marguerite (1993) *The Mirror of Simple Souls*, trans. Ellen L. Babinsky, The Classics of Western Spirituality, New York: Paulist Press.

Porphyry (1966) 'On the Life of Plotinus and the Order of his Books' in Plotinus *The Enneads*, 7 vols, trans. A.H. Armstrong, Loeb Classical Library, Cambridge, MA: Harvard University Press, and London: William Heinemann Ltd.

Porter, H.N. (1962) 'Introduction' to *The Odyssey of Homer*, trans. G.H. Palmer, New York.

Price, Simon (1999) *Religions of the Ancient Greeks*, Cambridge: Cambridge University Press.

Rabinow, Paul (1996) *Essays on the Anthropology of Reason*, Princeton: Princeton University Press.

Rabinowitz, Nancy Sorkin (1993) *Anxiety Veiled: Euripides and the Traffic in Women*, Ithaca, NY and London: Cornell University Press.

Ragland, Ellie (1995) *Essays on the Pleasures of Death: From Freud to Lacan*, New York and London: Routledge.

Rayor, Diane (1991) *Sappho's Lyre: Archaic Lyric and Women Poets of Ancient Greece*, Berkeley and Oxford: University of California Press.

Rehm, Rush (1994) *Marriage to Death: The Conflation of Wedding and Funeral Rituals in Greek Tragedy*, Princeton: Princeton University Press.

Richard, C.J. (1994) *The Founders and the Classics: Greece, Rome and the American Enlightenment*, Cambridge, MA: Harvard University Press.

Rist, John M. (1967) *Plotinus: The Road to Reality*, Cambridge: Cambridge University Press.

Rist, J.M. (1969) *Stoic Philosophy*, Cambridge: Cambridge University Press.

Rist, J.M. (1972) *Epicurus: An Introduction*, Cambridge: Cambridge University Press.

Rist, John M. (1989) *The Mind of Aristotle: A Study in Philosophical Growth*, Toronto and London: University of Toronto Press.

Rist, John M. (1996) 'Plotinus and Christian Philosophy' in Lloyd P. Gerson (ed.) *The Cambridge Companion to Plotinus*, Cambridge: Cambridge University Press.

Ritvo, Lucille B. (1990) *Darwin's Influence on Freud: A Tale of Two Sciences*, New Haven and London: Yale University Press.

Robinson, John Mansley (1968) *An Introduction to Early Greek Philosophy*, Boston: Houghton Mifflin Co.

Rocco, Christopher (1997) *Tragedy and Enlightenment: Athenian Political Thought and the Dilemmas of Modernity*, Berkeley and London: University of California Press.

Rorty, Amélie Oksenberg (ed.) (1992) *Essays on Aristotle's Poetics*, Princeton: Princeton University Press.

Rose, Jacqueline (1993) *Why War?*, Oxford: Blackwell.

Rosen, Stanley (1987) *Plato's Symposium*, second edition. New Haven and London: Yale University Press.

Rosen, Stanley (1988) *The Quarrel Between Philosophy and Poetry*, London and New York: Routledge.

Ross, D.J.A. (ed.) (1956) *The Medieval Alexander*, Cambridge: Cambridge University Press.

Ross, W.D. (1930) *Aristotle*, second edition, London: Methuen.

Rossi, L. (1971) *Trajan's Column and the Dacian Wars*, trans. J.M.C. Toynbee, London: Thames & Hudson.

Rousselle, Aline (1992) 'Body Politics in Ancient Rome' in Pauline Schmitt Pantel (ed.) *A History of Women in the West. Vol. I: From Ancient Goddesses to Christian Saints*, trans. Arthur Goldhammer, Cambridge, MA and London: Harvard University Press.

Rudich, Vasily (1997) *Dissidence and Literature under Nero: The Price of Rhetoricization*, London and New York: Routledge.

Sagan, Eli (1979) *The Lust to Annihilate: A Psychoanalytic Study of Violence in Ancient Greek Culture*, New York: The Psychohistory Press.

Samons, Loren J. II (ed.) (1998) *Athenian Democracy and Imperialism*, Boston: Houghton Mifflin.

Saussure, Ferdinand de (1983) *Course in General Linguistics*, trans. Roy Harris, London: Duckworth.

Saxonhouse, Arlene W. (1994) 'The Philosopher and the Female in the Political Thought of Plato' in Nancy Tuana (ed.) *Feminist Interpretations of Plato*, University Park, PA: Pennsylvania State University Press.

Scarry, Elaine (1999) *On Beauty and Being Just*, Princeton: Princeton University Press.

Schein, Seth (1995) 'Female Representation and Interpreting the *Odyssey*' in Beth Cohen (ed.) *The Distaff Side: Representing the Female in Homer's* Odyssey, Oxford and New York: Oxford University Press.

Schmidt, Dennis J. (2001) *On Germans and Other Greeks: Tragedy and Ethical Life*, Bloomington: Indiana University Press.

Schmitt, Charles B. (1983) *Aristotle and the Renaissance*, Cambridge, MA and London: Harvard University Press.

Segal, Charles (1981) *Tragedy and Civilization: An Interpretation of Sophocles*, Cambridge, MA and London: Harvard University Press.

Segal, Charles (1990) *Lucretius on Death and Anxiety: Poetry and Philosophy in De Rerum Natura*, Princeton: Princeton University Press.

Segal, Charles (1993) *Euripides and the Poetics of Sorrow: Art, Gender, and Commemoration in* Alcestis, Hippolytus, *and* Hecuba, Durham, NC and London: Duke University Press.

Segal, Charles (1995) *Sophocles' Tragic World: Divinity, Nature, Society*, Cambridge, MA and London: Harvard University Press.

Seneca (1966) *Four Tragedies and Octavia*, trans. E.F. Watling, London: Penguin.

Seneca (1969) *Letters from a Stoic*, trans. Robin Campbell, London: Penguin.

Seneca (1997) *Dialogues and Letters*, trans. C.D.N. Costa, London: Penguin.

Sextus Empiricus (1939–61) *Against the Logicians (Adversus Mathematicos)*, trans. R.G. Berry, 4 vols, London: Heinemann, and Cambridge, MA: Harvard University Press.

Shakespeare, William (1980) *The Complete Works of William Shakespeare*, ed. John Dover Wilson, London: Octopus Books.

Shapiro, H.A. (1991) 'The Iconography of Mourning in Athenian Art' in *American Journal of Archaeology* 95.

Sharrock, Alison (2002) 'Gender and Sexuality' in Philip Hardie (ed.) *The Cambridge Companion to Ovid*, Cambridge: Cambridge University Press.

Shaw, Teresa M. (1998) *The Burden of the Flesh: Fasting and Sexuality in Early Christianity*, Minneapolis, MN: Fortress Press.

Shelton, J. (ed.) (1988) *As the Romans Did: A Sourcebook in Roman Social History*, Oxford: Oxford University Press.

Skinner, Quentin (1978) *The Foundation of Modern Political Thought. Vol. I: The Renaissance; Vol. II: The Age of Reformation*, Cambridge: Cambridge University Press.

Smith, Janet Farrell (1994) 'Plato, Irony, and Equality' in Nancy Tuana (ed.) *Feminist Interpretations of Plato*, University Park, PA: Pennsylvania State University Press.

Sommerstein, Alan H. (1996) *Aeschylean Tragedy*, Bari, Italy: Levante Editori.

Soper, Kate (1995) *What Is Nature? Culture, Politics and the non-Human*, Oxford: Blackwell.

Sophocles (1953) *Electra and Other Plays*, trans. E.F. Watling, Harmondsworth: Penguin.

Sophocles (1982) *The Three Theban Plays: Antigone, Oedipus the King, Oedipus at Colonus*, trans. Robert Fagles, New York and London: Penguin.

Sorabji, Richard (2000) *Emotion and Peace of Mind: From Stoic Agitation to Christian Temptation*, Oxford: Oxford University Press.

Sourivinou-Inwood, Christiane (1995) *'Reading' Greek Death: To the End of the Classical Period*, Oxford: Clarendon Press.

Spelman, Elizabeth V. (1988) *Inessential Woman: Problems of Exclusion in Feminist Thought*, Boston: Beacon Press.

Spelman, Elizabeth V. (1997) *Fruits of Sorrow: Framing our Attention to Suffering*, Boston: Beacon Press.

Spence, Sarah (1998) *Rhetorics of Reason and Desire: Vergil, Augustine, and the Troubadours*, Ithaca, NY and London: Cornell University Press.

Stears, Karen (1998) 'Death Becomes Her: Gender and Death in Athenian Death Ritual' in Sue Blundell and Margaret Williamson (eds) *The Sacred and the Feminine in Ancient Greece*, London and New York: Routledge.

Stewart, Andrew (2000) 'Greek Sculpture' in *The Oxford Dictionary of Western Art*, ed. Martin Kemp, Oxford: Oxford University Press, pp. 12–23.

Strauss, Leo (1952) *Persecution and the Art of Writing*, Glencoe, IL: Free Press.

Strauss, Leo (1964) *The City and the Man*, Chicago: Rand McNally.

Strauss, Leo (1983) *Studies in Platonic Political Philosophy*, Chicago: University of Chicago Press.

Stray, Christopher (1992) *Classics Transformed: Schools, Universities and Society in England 1830–1960*, Oxford: Oxford University Press.

Suetonius. (1979) *The Twelve Caesars*, trans. Robert Graves, London: Penguin.

Tacitus (1970) *The Agricola and the Germania*, trans. H. Mattingly, London: Penguin.

Tacitus (1996) *The Annals of Imperial Rome*, trans. Michael Grant, revised edition, London: Penguin.

Tatarkiewicz, Wladyslaw (1970) *History of Aesthetics. Vol. I: Ancient Aesthetics; Vol. II: Medieval Aesthetics*, The Hague and Paris: Mouton.

Tatarkiewicz, Wladyslaw (1972) 'The Great Theory of Beauty and its Decline' in *Journal of Aesthetics and Art Criticism* XXXI.

Tatum, James (2003) *The Mourner's Song: War and Remembrance from the Iliad to Vietnam*, Chicago: University of Chicago Press.

Taylor, C.C.W. (1997) 'Anaxagoras and the Atomists' in his (ed.) *From the Beginning to Plato: Routledge History of Philosophy*, Vol. I, London and New York: Routledge.

Teubal, Sabina J. (1997) 'The Rise and Fall of Female Reproductive Control as Seen through Images of Women' in Karen King (ed.) *Women and Goddess Traditions in Antiquity and Today*, Minneapolis, MN: Augsburg Fortress.

Thucydides (1954) *History of the Peloponnesian War*, trans. Rex Warner, London: Penguin.

Underwood, Barbara (2001) *Plato's Gender Configurations of Music*, unpublished PhD thesis, University of Manchester.

Vance, Norman (1997) *The Victorians and Ancient Rome*, Oxford: Oxford University Press.

Vance, William L. (1989) *America's Rome*, 2 vols. New Haven and London: Yale University Press.

Vellacott, Philip (1963) 'Introduction' to Euripides *Medea and Other Plays*, trans. Philip Vellacott, London: Penguin.

Vellacott, Philip (1972) 'Introduction' to Euripides *Orestes and Other Plays*, trans. Philip Vellacott, London: Penguin.

Vellacott, Philip (1975) *Ironic Drama: A Study of Euripides' Method and Meaning*, Cambridge: Cambridge University Press.

Vergil/Virgil (1990) *The Aeneid*, trans. David West, London: Penguin.

Vernant, Jean-Pierre (1991) *Mortals and Immortals: Collected Essays*, trans. Froma I. Zeitlin, Princeton: Princeton University Press.

Veyne, Paul (1987) 'The Roman Empire' in Paul Veyne (ed.) *A History of Private Life. Vol. I: From Pagan Rome to Byzantium*, trans. Arthur Goldhammer, Cambridge, MA and London: Harvard University Press.

Vincent, Gérard (1991) 'A History of Secrets?' in Antoine Prost and Gérard Vincent (eds) *A History of Private Life. Vol. 5: Riddles of Identity in Modern Times*, trans. Arthur Goldhammer, Cambridge, MA and London: Harvard University Press.

Vlastos, Gregory (ed.) (1970) *Plato: A Collection of Critical Essays. Vol. 1: Metaphysics and Epistemology*, Garden City, NY: Doubleday.

Vlastos, Gregory (1994) 'Was Plato a Feminist?' in Nancy Tuana (ed.) *Feminist Interpretations of Plato*, University Park, PA: Pennsylvania State University Press.

Von Balthasar, Hans Urs (1983f) *The Glory of the Lord: A Theological Aesthetics*, 7 vols, trans. Erasmo Leiva-Merikakis *et al.*, Edinburgh: T&T Clark.

Von Balthasar, Hans Urs (1989) *The Glory of the Lord: A Theological Aesthetics. Vol. IV: The Realm of Metaphysics in Antiquity*, trans. Brian McNeil *et al.*, Edinburgh: T&T Clark.

Walker, Michelle (1998) *Philosophy and the Maternal Body: Reading Silence*, London and New York: Routledge.

Walker, S. (1985) *Memorials to the Roman Dead*, London: British Museum Publications.

Wallach, Barbara Price (1976) *Lucretius and the Diatribe Against the Fear of Death; De Rerum Natura III 830–1094*, Leiden: E.J. Brill.

Walters, Jonathan (1997) 'Invading the Roman Body: Manliness and Impenetrability in Roman Thought' in Judith P. Hallett and Marilyn B. Skinner (eds) *Roman Sexualities*, Princeton: Princeton University Press.

Walzer, R. (1949) *Galen on Christians and Jews*, London: Oxford University Press.

Waterfield, Robin (2000) *The First Philosophers: The Presocratics and the Sophists*, Oxford: Oxford University Press.

Watling, E.F. (1966) 'Introduction' and 'Appendix I' in Seneca *Four Tragedies and Octavia*, London: Penguin.

Watson, G.R. (1987) 'The Army of the Republic' in John Wacher (ed.) *The Roman World*, Vol. I, London and New York: Routledge.

Webster, Graham (1998) *The Roman Imperial Army of the First and Second Centuries AD*, third edition, London: A&C Black.

Wee, C.J.W.-L. (1994) 'Christian Manliness and National Identity: The Problematic Construction of a Racially "Pure" Nation' in Donald F. Hall (ed.) *Muscular Christianity: Embodying the Victorian Age*, Cambridge: Cambridge University Press.

Weil, Simone (1951) *Waiting on God*, trans. Emma Craufurd, London: Routledge and Kegan Paul.

Welch, K. (1994) 'The Roman Arena in Late-Republican Italy: a New Interpretation' in *Journal of Roman Archaeology* 7.

Wheeler, Mortimer (1964) *Roman Art and Architecture*, London and New York: Thames & Hudson.

Wiedemann, Thomas (1992) *Emperors and Gladiators*, London and New York: Routledge.

Williams, Bernard (1976) 'Moral Luck' in *Proceedings of Aristotelian Society*, Vol. L.

Williams, Bernard (1993) *Shame and Necessity*, Berkeley and London: University of California Press.

Williams, Margaret (2000) 'Jews and Jewish Communities in the Roman empire' in Janet Huskinson (ed.) *Experiencing Rome: Culture, Identity and Power in the Roman Empire*, London and New York: Routledge.

Williams, R.D. (1987) *The Aeneid*, London: Allen & Unwin.

Williamson, Margaret (1995) *Sappho's Immortal Daughters*, Cambridge, MA and London: Harvard University Press.

Wilson, Lyn Hatherby (1996) *Sappho's Sweetbitter Songs: Configurations of Female and Male in Ancient Greek Lyric*, London and New York: Routledge.

Wohl, Victoria Josselyn (1993) 'Standing by the Stathmos: The Creation of Sexual Ideology in the *Odyssey*' in *Arethusa* 26.

Wolin, Richard (1994) *Walter Benjamin: An Aesthetic of Redemption*, Berkeley and London: University of California Press.

Woodruff, Paul (1992) 'Aristotle on Mimēsis' in Amélie Oksenberg Rorty (ed.) *Essays on Aristotle's Poetics*, Princeton: Princeton University Press.

Wright, M.R. (1997) 'Empedocles' in C.C.W. Taylor (ed.) *From the Beginning to Plato: Routledge History of Philosophy*, Vol. I, London and New York: Routledge.

Wright, Ronald (1993) *Stolen Continents: The 'New World' Through Indian Eyes*, London: Penguin.

Zuckert, Catherine H. (1996) *Postmodern Platos*, Chicago and London: University of Chicago Press.

Index